PARTNERS
IN THE KITCHEN
·
FROM OUR HOUSE
TO YOURS

Building houses in partnership with God's people in need

This cookbook is a collection of our favorite recipes, but are not necessarily original recipes.

All Biblical quotations are from the New International Verson published by Zondervan Publishing Company.

Published by: Favorite Recipes® Press
P.O. Box 305142
Nashville, Tennessee 37230
1-800-358-0560

Library of Congress Number: 93-072357
ISBN: 0-87197-384-7

Manufactured in the United States of America
First Printing: 1993   50,000 copies

All photographs from
Habitat for Humanity International

Contents

Foreword

I have visited many Habitat projects over the years, enjoying meals at large gatherings and in private homes. Sometimes, I was fortunate enough to acquire recipes of particularly tasty dishes. I began to realize that many Habitat folks are as good at preparing food as they are at building and renovating houses!

It has been interesting and fun working on *Partners in the Kitchen*. Interesting, as the hundreds of recipes came pouring in from all over North America. And fun, because I received recipes like "Baked Salmon in the Dishwasher" and "Lenora's Bullfrog Cheesecake." Some sounded so delicious I wanted to try them right away. I did, and were they ever good!

Linda Fuller

This book of great recipes proves once again that Habitat for Humanity is a wonderful family of friends and partners. Already sharing ideas, tools, construction know-how, joys and disappointments in the work of building houses and building families, this cookbook is one more way to share—"from our house to yours"—and, at the same time, generate funds to build more houses.

To all our Habitat Partners who contributed recipes, I want to express deep appreciation. As you and so many others enjoy these special dishes, take satisfaction in knowing that you are helping make it possible for others to have decent homes in which to prepare and share meals, too.

I want to give special recognition and thanks to Doug Bright, Director of Communication Services at Habitat for Humanity International, who worked so diligently with me. I also want to express my deep appreciation for the talented people at Favorite Recipes® Press, particularly Dave Kempf and Mary Cummings, who helped "hammer" out every detail of this publication. Other Habitat staff persons who contributed helpful ideas and suggestions as the project progressed are Nancy Cardwell, Allan Donaldson and Carol Gregory, and I want to express thanks and appreciation to them, too.

Bon appétit!

Linda Fuller, Editor

Introduction

Proceeds from the sale of this cookbook are used to further the work of Habitat for Humanity. Thank you for supporting the work of Habitat through your purchase. We hope this book will prove to be a blessing to all who use it—and to all who are fortunate enough to sample its recipes!

The recipes in the book were submitted to the Editor in response to a call-for-recipes sent to all Habitat for Humanity affiliates and campus chapters, as well as some special friends of this ministry. As you might expect of Habitat, we received a gratifying number of responses from widely diverse people throughout the U.S.

This collection of recipes from our partners is a natural outgrowth of our work. Meals at Habitat work sites are special times. The goodwill and cameraderie developed by volunteer workers, homeowners and other partners as they labor together for a common good is sealed by a time of rest, conversation and good food.

A special Make and Take section is devoted to recipes that are particularly suitable for preparing ahead of time and serving later. They are ideal for special Habitat occasions, such as lunch at a work site, covered dish dinners, or a house dedication.

The publisher of this cookbook, Favorite Recipes® Press, and Habitat for Humanity have an interesting connection. In the early sixties, the president of Favorite Recipes® Press was a young man named Millard Fuller. Millard sold all of his interest in the company in 1966, ten years later becoming the founder and president of Habitat for Humanity International. In 1993, Favorite Recipes® Press expressed an interest in doing what they could to help the work of Habitat for Humanity. This cookbook is the result of their interest.

As you join with others to enjoy meals prepared from these recipes, we hope your conversation will be rewarding—and will include, of course, Habitat for Humanity.

Douglas Bright

Douglas Bright, Director
Communication Services
Habitat for Humanity International

Nutritional Guidelines

The editors have attempted to present these family recipes in a form that allows approximate nutritional values to be computed. Persons with dietary or health problems or whose diets require close monitoring should not rely solely on the nutritional information provided. They should consult their physicians or a registered dietitian for specific information.

Abbreviations for Nutritional Profile

Cal — Calories	Fiber — Dietary Fiber	Sod — Sodium
Prot — Protein	T Fat — Total Fat	g — gram
Carbo — Carbohydrates	Chol — Cholesterol	mg — milligrams

Nutritional information for these recipes is computed from information derived from many sources, including materials supplied by the United States Department of Agriculture, computer databanks and journals in which the information is assumed to be in the public domain. However, many specialty items, new products and processed foods may not be available from these sources or may vary from the average values used in these profiles. More information on new and/or specific products may be obtained by reading the nutrient labels. Unless otherwise specified, the nutritional profile of these recipes is based on all measurements being level.

- **Artificial sweeteners** vary in use and strength so should be used "to taste," using the recipe ingredients as a guideline. Sweeteners using aspartame (NutraSweet and Equal) should not be used as a sweetener in recipes involving prolonged heating which reduces the sweet taste. For further information on the use of these sweeteners, refer to package information.
- **All recipes** have been analyzed to ensure uniformity of measurements and to determine the nutritional content as noted for each.
- **Buttermilk, sour cream** and **yogurt** are the types available commercially.
- **Cake mixes** which are prepared using package directions include 3 eggs and ½ cup oil.
- **Chicken**, cooked for boning and chopping, has been roasted; this method yields the lowest caloric values.
- **Cottage cheese** is cream-style with 4.2% creaming mixture. Dry curd cottage cheese has no creaming mixture.
- **Eggs** are all large. To avoid raw eggs that may carry salmonella as in eggnog or 6-week muffin batter, use an equivalent amount of commercial egg substitute.
- **Flour** is unsifted all-purpose flour.
- **Garnishes**, serving suggestions and other optional additions and variations are not included in the profile.
- **Margarine** and **butter** are regular, not whipped or presoftened.
- **Milk** is whole milk, 3.5% butterfat. Lowfat milk is 1% butterfat. Evaporated milk is whole milk with 60% of the water removed.
- **Oil** is any type of vegetable cooking oil. Shortening is hydrogenated vegetable shortening.
- **Salt** and other ingredients to taste as noted in the ingredients have not been included in the nutritional profile.
- If a choice of ingredients has been given, the nutritional profile information reflects the first option. If a choice of amounts has been given, the nutritional profile reflects the greater amount.

FEEDING HUNGRY WORKERS

MAKE AND TAKE

"He's taken me to his banqueting hall, and his banner over me is love."

Song of Songs 2:4

Barbecued Beef

Yield: 20 servings

1 4-pound pot roast
1 10-ounce can
  tomato soup
1 14-ounce bottle of
  catsup
1 cup water
2 tablespoons brown
  sugar
1/2 cup chopped celery

1 medium onion,
  chopped
2 tablespoons
  Worcestershire sauce
2 tablespoons lemon
  juice
1/2 teaspoon dry mustard
3 or 4 bay leaves
Salt and pepper to taste

■ Cook pot roast as desired until very tender. Shred beef, discarding fat and bones. Skim grease from pan juices. Combine shredded beef and pan juices in large saucepan; set aside. Combine soup, catsup, water, brown sugar, celery, onion, Worcestershire sauce, lemon juice, dry mustard, bay leaves, salt and pepper in medium saucepan. Simmer for 30 minutes. Add to beef. Simmer for 1 hour longer; discard bay leaves. Serve on sandwich buns.
Approx Per Serving: Cal 160; Prot 18 g; Carbo 9 g; Fiber 1 g; T Fat 6 g; 31% Calories from Fat; Chol 51 mg; Sod 351 mg.

Karla Rozeboom, HFH of South Central Minnesota
Mankato, MN

Barbecued Brisket of Beef

Yield: 12 servings

1 6-pound beef
  brisket
1 large onion, sliced 1/2
  inch thick
1 clove of garlic, cut
  into halves
16 whole cloves
1 bay leaf

2 cups catsup
1/4 cup Worcestershire
  sauce
2 tablespoons brown
  sugar
2 tablespoons dry
  mustard

■ Combine beef with water to cover in large saucepan. Add onion slices, garlic halves, whole cloves and bay leaf. Simmer, covered, for 4 hours. Cool in cooking juices; drain, discarding bay leaf and cloves. Trim fat from beef. Chill, wrapped in foil, overnight. Slice beef very thin cross grain, keeping slices together; stand on edge in large shallow baking pan. Combine catsup, Worcestershire sauce, brown sugar and dry mustard in bowl; mix well. Pour over beef. Bake at 350 degrees for 40 minutes.
Approx Per Serving: Cal 371; Prot 44 g; Carbo 16 g; Fiber 1 g; T Fat 14 g; 34% Calories from Fat; Chol 128 mg; Sod 594 mg.

Maureen Platt, HFH of Rabun County, Sky Valley, GA

Yield: 20 servings

Fuller's Barbecue

Great when expecting a crowd. Millard's Aunt Irene gave me this recipe years ago. It's been one we've enjoyed many times.

2 onions, chopped
4 tablespoons
  margarine
4 tablespoons brown
  sugar
4 tablespoons vinegar
4 tablespoons lemon
  juice

2 cups catsup
1 tablespoon prepared
  mustard
6 tablespoons
  Worcestershire sauce
1 cup water
4 pounds fresh pork,
  roasted, chopped

■ Brown onions in margarine in skillet. Add next 7 ingredients. Cook until heated through. Add pork; simmer for 15 to 20 minutes or until the flavors have been absorbed into pork.
Approx Per Serving: Cal 0; Prot 0 g; Carbo 0 g; Fiber 0 g; T Fat 0 g; 0% Calories from Fat; Chol 0 mg; Sod 0 mg.

Linda Fuller, HFH International, Americus, GA

Linda Fuller
Co-founder of Habitat for Humanity

Jamaican Beef Patties

Yield: 20 servings

4 cups flour
1 tablespoon curry powder
1 teaspoon salt
1 cup shortening
2 pounds boneless beef, minced
2 onions, minced
1   2-ounce scallion, minced

2 hot peppers, minced
1/4 cup oil
2 cups bread crumbs
3 sprigs of thyme, minced
2 tablespoons curry powder
1 tablespoon salt
1 cup water

■ Sift flour, 1 tablespoon curry powder and 1 teaspoon salt in bowl. Cut in shortening until crumbly. Add enough water to hold mixture together. Chill, wrapped in foil, for 12 hours. Let stand at room temperature for 15 minutes before using. Combine beef, onions, scallion and peppers in bowl; mix well. Heat oil in skillet. Add beef mixture. Cook for 10 minutes, stirring constantly. Add bread crumbs, thyme, 2 tablespoons curry powder, 1 tablespoon salt and water; mix well. Simmer for 30 minutes. Cool slightly. Roll dough on floured surface. Cut into 6-inch circles. Coat each with flour. Fill each circle with beef mixture. Fold over; crimp edge. Place on greased baking sheet. Bake at 400 degrees for 25 to 35 minutes or until golden brown.
Approx Per Serving: Cal 315; Prot 13 g; Carbo 29 g; Fiber 2 g; T Fat 17 g; 47% Calories from Fat; Chol 26 mg; Sod 516 mg.

Wiley M. Jackson, Mid-Hudson Valley HFH
Poughkeepsie, NY

Beef and Bean Barbecue

Yield: 10 servings

1.pound ground beef
1/4 cup chopped green bell pepper
1/2 cup minced onion
1/2 cup chopped celery
1   8-ounce can tomato sauce
1/2 cup water

1 clove of garlic, minced
2 tablespoons vinegar
1 tablespoon brown sugar
1 teaspoon dry mustard
1/2 teaspoon thyme
1   20-ounce can pork and beans

■ Brown ground beef with green pepper, onion and celery in skillet, stirring until ground beef is crumbly and vegetables are tender; drain. Add tomato sauce, water, garlic, vinegar, brown sugar, dry mustard and thyme; mix well. Simmer for 5 minutes. Stir in pork and beans. Spoon into baking dish. Bake at 375 degrees for 45 minutes. May continue to simmer on stove-top if preferred.
Approx Per Serving: Cal 186; Prot 13 g; Carbo 19 g; Fiber 4 g; T Fat 8 g; 35% Calories from Fat; Chol 33 mg; Sod 237 mg.

Lupe Maginnis, Benton HFH, Philomath, OR

Midwest Chili

Yield: 12 servings

Serve this on a cold day for lunch with crackers or over rice with a salad for dinner.

4 pounds lean ground beef
2 tablespoons butter
4 medium onions, chopped
4 green bell peppers, chopped
2 teaspoons salt
1/2 teaspoon pepper

2 tablespoons (heaping) chili powder
2   28-ounce cans tomatoes
4   10-ounce cans tomato soup
4   15-ounce cans dark red kidney beans

■ Brown ground beef in butter, stirring until crumbly; drain. Add onions, green peppers, salt, pepper and chili powder; mix well. Cook for several minutes. Stir in tomatoes, soup and beans. Simmer, covered, for 1 to 2 hours or until done to taste, stirring occasionally.
Approx Per Serving: Cal 557; Prot 39 g; Carbo 45 g; Fiber 14 g; T Fat 26 g; 41% Calories from Fat; Chol 104 mg; Sod 1836 mg.

Carl W. Umland, Houston HFH, Houston, TX

*I*t *[a Habitat for Humanity house] can make all the difference in the world. And the thing that we hear the most from the homeowners, and so many times it's said with tears in their eyes, is that it's the answer to prayer, a dream come true. Otherwise, these families just do not have any way to better their living conditions. They cannot get a loan at the bank or any other conventional financing, and it can really touch their heart and change their lives.*

Linda Fuller, co-founder, Habitat for Humanity

Famous Chili
Yield: 16 servings

3¹/₂ to 4 pounds
   ground beef
8 ounces bacon
3 medium onions,
   chopped
1 green bell pepper,
   chopped
2 stalks celery, chopped
1 43-ounce can baked
   beans

4 26-ounce cans
   tomato soup
1 15-ounce can
   tomato sauce
3 tablespoons mild
   chili powder
¹/₄ teaspoon (or more)
   red pepper
¹/₂ teaspoon salt

■ Brown ground beef in large saucepan, stirring until crumbly; drain. Chop bacon into ¹/₄-inch pieces. Brown in skillet, stirring constantly. Add onions, green pepper and celery to skillet. Sauté for 5 minutes. Add to ground beef with remaining ingredients; mix well. Simmer for 1 to 3 hours or until of desired consistency, stirring occasionally. May substitute Mrs. Dash seasoning for salt.
Approx Per Serving: Cal 475; Prot 30 g; Carbo 45 g; Fiber 4 g; T Fat 22 g; 39% Calories from Fat; Chol 78 mg; Sod 1962 mg.

Eileen Evers, Northern Straits HFH, St. Ignace, MI

Lasagna
Yield: 8 servings

This recipe has always been a hit with family and friends. It can be prepared in advance so there is minimal kitchen time when guests arrive.

2 pounds ground chuck
¹/₄ cup chopped onion
1 clove of garlic,
   crushed
2 6-ounce cans tomato
   paste
1 20-ounce can
   tomatoes
1 teaspoon Italian
   seasoning

1¹/₂ teaspoons oregano
1¹/₂ teaspoons salt
¹/₄ teaspoon pepper
6 ounces lasagna
   noodles, cooked
8 ounces mozzarella
   cheese, shredded
¹/₂ cup grated
   Parmesan cheese

■ Brown ground chuck with onion and garlic in saucepan. Stir in tomato paste. Simmer for 5 minutes. Add tomatoes, Italian seasoning, oregano, salt and pepper. Simmer for 1 hour, stirring occasionally. Alternate layers of noodles, meat sauce and mozzarella cheese in 9x13-inch baking dish until all ingredients are used; top with Parmesan cheese. Bake at 375 degrees for 30 to 40 minutes or until heated through.
Approx Per Serving: Cal 465; Prot 34 g; Carbo 28 g; Fiber 3 g; T Fat 24 g; 47% Calories from Fat; Chol 100 mg; Sod 809 mg.

Cheryl Hammond, Sheboygan County HFH, Sheboygan, WI

Piquant Meatballs
Yield: 10 servings

These are delicious to serve from a chafing dish or to fondue at a picnic.

2 pounds lean ground
   beef
2 eggs
¹/₄ cup water
1 cup bread crumbs
1 small onion, grated
1¹/₂ teaspoons salt
¹/₈ teaspoon pepper

1 16-ounce can
   cranberry sauce
1 12-ounce bottle of
   chili sauce
1 tablespoon lemon
   juice
2 tablespoons brown
   sugar

■ Combine ground beef, eggs, water, bread crumbs, onion, salt and pepper in large bowl; mix well by hand. Shape into small meatballs. Chill overnight. Fry meatballs in large nonstick skillet; drain. Combine cranberry sauce, chili sauce, lemon juice and brown sugar in saucepan; mix well. Add meatballs. Simmer for 1 hour.
Approx Per Serving: Cal 360; Prot 18 g; Carbo 36 g; Fiber <1 g; T Fat 18 g; 45% Calories from Fat; Chol 99 mg; Sod 927 mg.

Dorothy M. Boyd, Culpeper, VA

Mexican Casserole
Yield: 8 servings

2 pounds ground beef
1 10-ounce can cream
   of chicken soup
1 10-ounce can cream
   of mushroom soup
1 16-ounce can
   tomato sauce
1 4-ounce can chopped
   green chilies

1 16-ounce can ranch-
   style chili beans
1 10-ounce can
   enchilada sauce
1 8-ounce package
   taco-flavored tortilla
   chips
8 ounces Cheddar
   cheese, shredded

■ Brown ground beef in skillet, stirring until crumbly; drain. Add soups, tomato sauce, green chilies, beans and enchilada sauce; mix well. Layer chips, beef mixture and cheese in 9x13-inch baking dish. Bake at 350 degrees for 30 minutes.
Approx Per Serving: Cal 675; Prot 36 g; Carbo 45 g; Fiber 2 g; T Fat 40 g; 53% Calories from Fat; Chol 107 mg; Sod 1979 mg.

Elva M. Steffer, Morgan County HFH, Fort Morgan, CO

Mexican Party Meal

Yield: 8 servings

2 pounds ground beef
1 teaspoon cumin
1 envelope onion soup mix
1/2 teaspoon garlic powder
1/4 teaspoon each chili powder, salt and pepper
2 cups stewed tomatoes
1 20-ounce can medium chili beans
1 24-ounce bottle of catsup

1/2 16-ounce jar mild chunk salsa
1/2 cup packed brown sugar
1/2 teaspoon cumin
1 8-ounce package corn chips
4 cups shredded lettuce
2 tomatoes, chopped
2 cups shredded Cheddar cheese
1 onion, chopped
1 cup sour cream

■ Brown ground beef with 1 teaspoon cumin in skillet, stirring until crumbly; drain. Combine with soup mix, garlic powder, chili powder, salt, pepper, tomatoes and beans in slow cooker. Combine catsup, salsa, brown sugar and 1/2 teaspoon cumin in saucepan; mix well. Bring to a boil, stirring frequently. Stir half the catsup mixture into slow cooker; chill remaining mixture. Cook beef mixture, loosely covered, in slow cooker on High for 4 hours. Spoon into serving bowl. Serve with bowls of corn chips, lettuce, tomatoes, cheese, onion, sour cream and chilled sauce. May also serve with Party White Flour Tortillas (see below).
Approx Per Serving: Cal 821; Prot 37 g; Carbo 77 g; Fiber 4 g; T Fat 41 g; 45% Calories from Fat; Chol 117 mg; Sod 2181 mg.

Tammy Cadwell, HFH Greater Steubenville Area
Stratton, OH

Party White Flour Tortillas

Yield: 12 servings

5 cups flour
1 teaspoon baking powder
1/2 teaspoon salt

1/2 cup lard
1 1/2 cups lukewarm water

■ Mix first 3 ingredients in bowl. Cut in lard until crumbly. Stir in water gradually until soft dough forms. Knead; let stand for 5 minutes. Roll into 12 thin circles on floured surface. Bake on both sides in ungreased hot cast-iron skillet until brown.
Approx Per Serving: Cal 267; Prot 5 g; Carbo 40 g; Fiber 1 g; T Fat 9 g; 31% Calories from Fat; Chol 8 mg; Sod 117 mg.

Olga Granado, Mesilla Valley HFH, Las Cruces, NM

Spaghetti Bake

Yield: 8 servings

1 pound ground beef
8 ounces sausage
1 cup chopped onion
1 clove of garlic, minced
1 28-ounce can tomatoes, chopped
1 15-ounce can tomato sauce
1 4-ounce can chopped mushrooms, drained

2 teaspoons sugar
1 1/2 teaspoons oregano
1 teaspoon each basil and salt
8 ounces spaghetti, broken, cooked, drained
8 ounces mozzarella cheese, shredded
1/3 cup grated Parmesan cheese

■ Brown ground beef and sausage with onion and garlic in heavy saucepan, stirring until meat is crumbly; drain. Stir in next 7 ingredients; mix well. Simmer for 20 to 25 minutes, stirring occasionally; remove from heat. Add spaghetti; mix gently. Layer half the spaghetti mixture, mozzarella cheese, remaining spaghetti mixture and Parmesan cheese in 9x13-inch baking dish. Bake at 375 degrees for 30 minutes.
Approx Per Serving: Cal 414; Prot 26 g; Carbo 34 g; Fiber 4 g; T Fat 20 g; 43% Calories from Fat; Chol 73 mg; Sod 1184 mg.

Elsie C. Oliver, North Country HFH, Malone, NY

Taco Salad

Yield: 8 servings

8 ounces chopped or shredded cooked beef
2 cups sliced lettuce
1 16-ounce can pinto beans
2 tomatoes, chopped
1 4-ounce can chopped green chilies
1 8-ounce can pitted black olives

1 large avocado, sliced
1 cup sour cream
2 tablespoons vinegar and oil salad dressing
1/2 onion, minced
1/2 cup salsa
1 cup shredded Cheddar cheese
1 cup crushed corn chips

■ Layer beef, lettuce, beans, tomatoes, green chilies, olives, avocado, sour cream, salad dressing, onion, salsa, cheese and corn chips in order listed in large serving bowl.
Approx Per Serving: Cal 432; Prot 19 g; Carbo 25 g; Fiber 5 g; T Fat 31 g; 61% Calories from Fat; Chol 55 mg; Sod 887 mg.

Carol Verploegh, Mesilla Valley HFH, Mesilla Park, NM

Tagliarini

Yield: 12 servings

1 16-ounce package
   fine noodles
Salt to taste
2 pounds ground round
Pepper to taste
2 tablespoons
   shortening
2 medium onions,
   chopped

2 10-ounce cans
   tomato soup
1 16-ounce Mexicorn
8 ounces Cheddar
   cheese, sliced
1 pound New York
   cheese

■ Cook noodles in boiling salted water in saucepan for 7 minutes; drain. Sprinkle ground round with salt and pepper. Brown in shortening in large skillet until partially cooked. Add onions. Cook until ground round is brown, stirring until crumbly; drain. Add soup, corn and noodles; mix gently. Spoon into round 3-quart baking dish lined with Cheddar cheese. Cut New York cheese into strips; push into casserole. Bake at 300 degrees for 45 minutes.

Approx Per Serving: Cal 617; Prot 35 g; Carbo 42 g; Fiber 1 g; T Fat 34 g; 50% Calories from Fat; Chol 175 mg; Sod 851 mg.

Florine Rena Arnold, Peach Area HFH, Fort Valley, GA

Reuben Jack Casserole

Yield: 12 servings

1 16-ounce loaf
   pumpernickel bread,
   cut into halves
   lengthwise
1 16-ounce can
   sauerkraut, drained
1 12-ounce can corned
   beef

1/2 cup shredded
   Monterey Jack
   cheese
1/2 cup shredded
   mozzarella cheese
2 cups sour cream
1/4 cup melted
   margarine

■ Cut half the bread into cubes; set aside. Place remaining half in 9x13-inch baking dish. Layer with sauerkraut, corned beef, cheeses and sour cream. Top with cubed bread; drizzle with margarine. Bake at 350 degrees for 45 minutes. Slice into serving portions

Approx Per Serving: Cal 320; Prot 15 g; Carbo 22 g; Fiber 3 g; T Fat 20 g; 55% Calories from Fat; Chol 49 mg; Sod 852 mg.

Bill Dixon, Northwest Nebraska HFH, Chadron, NE

Glazed Ham Loaves

Yield: 16 servings

2 pounds ground lean
   smoked ham
2 pounds ground lean
   pork
1 1/2 cups cracker crumbs
4 eggs, beaten
2 cups milk
1/3 cup chopped onion
1 1/4 teaspoons salt
2 tablespoons chopped
   parsley
1 cup packed brown
   sugar

1 1/2 tablespoons dry
   mustard
1/2 cup cider vinegar
1/2 cup mayonnaise
1/4 cup prepared sharp
   mustard
2 tablespoons
   prepared horseradish
1/2 cup sour cream
1 tablespoon minced
   chives
Lemon juice and salt
   to taste

■ Combine first 8 ingredients in large bowl; mix well. Pack into two 5x9-inch loaf pans. Bake at 350 degrees for 30 minutes. Combine brown sugar, mustard and vinegar in saucepan. Bring to a boil. Boil for 1 minute, stirring constantly; remove from heat. Brush glaze mixture evenly over loaves. Bake for 1 hour longer. Mix remaining ingredients in small bowl. Serve sauce with ham loaves.

Approx Per Serving: Cal 397; Prot 31 g; Carbo 26 g; Fiber <1 g; T Fat 18 g; 42% Calories from Fat; Chol 140 mg; Sod 1185 mg.

Catherine Ranger, HFH-Anchorage, Anchorage, AK

Ham and Cheese Fondue Casserole

Yield: 12 servings

2 teaspoons butter,
   softened
12 slices white bread,
   crusts removed
12 thin slices cooked
   ham
4 ounces sharp
   Cheddar cheese,
   shredded

8 ounces Swiss cheese,
   shredded
3 eggs, beaten
1 1/2 cups milk
1/2 cup chicken broth
1/2 cup white wine
Salt, pepper and
   paprika to taste

■ Spread butter lightly on one side of bread slices. Place buttered side up in greased 9x13-inch baking dish. Place ham on bread slices; sprinkle with mixture of half the cheeses. Beat eggs, milk, chicken broth, wine, salt and pepper in bowl. Pour half the mixture over layers. Sprinkle with remaining cheese. Pour remaining egg mixture over top. Sprinkle with paprika. Chill, covered, for 12 hours. Bake, uncovered, at 350 degrees for 1 hour or until puffed and browned.

Approx Per Serving: Cal 259; Prot 19 g; Carbo 12 g; Fiber <1 g; T Fat 14 g; 50% Calories from Fat; Chol 102 mg; Sod 653 mg.

Judy Caner, AuSable HFH, Keene, NY

Yield: 20 servings

Country Store Brunswick Stew

This is the official Brunswick Stew recipe for the Oktoc Country Store, developed by Allison (Preacher) White and his hunting buddies. The original recipe made about 220 gallons; this one has been reduced to prepare in your kitchen.

1 pound beef
²/₃ pound pork shoulder
1 pound venison
²/₃ pound chicken
1 quart chopped tomatoes
1 quart butter beans
1 quart cream-style corn
1 quart tomato catsup

1 quart sliced okra
8 ounces uncooked rice
²/₃ pound potatoes, chopped
8 ounces onions, chopped
¹/₂ cup cider vinegar
1 ounce Tabasco sauce
2 ounces Worcestershire sauce
Salt and pepper to taste

■ Cut beef, pork and venison into 1-inch cubes. Rinse chicken and pat dry. Combine meats and chicken with water to cover in large stockpot. Cook until very tender. Remove and chop chicken, discarding skin and bones; return to stockpot. Add tomatoes with juice, butter beans, corn, catsup, okra, rice, potatoes, onions, vinegar, Tabasco sauce, Worcestershire sauce, salt and pepper. Cook for 10 hours or longer, stirring occasionally and adding water as needed for desired consistency. May add 1 tablespoon butter if meat is very lean.
Approx Per Serving: Cal 296; Prot 20 g; Carbo 47 g; Fiber 4 g; T Fat 4 g; 12% Calories from Fat; Chol 39 mg; Sod 938 mg.

Contributed by the Starkville HFH, Starkville, MS

Yield: 6 servings

Chicken Casserole

1 8-ounce package macaroni
1 10-ounce can cream of celery soup
1 10-ounce can cream of mushroom soup
8 ounces Velveeta cheese, cubed

2¹/₂ cups milk
2 cups chopped cooked chicken
1 10-ounce package frozen peas

■ Combine uncooked macaroni, soups, Velveeta cheese, milk, chicken and peas in bowl; mix well. Spoon into 2-quart baking dish. Chill overnight. Bake, covered, at 350 degrees for 45 minutes. Bake, uncovered, for 15 minutes longer. May top with Parmesan cheese or buttered bread crumbs before baking or substitute turkey for chicken.
Approx Per Serving: Cal 550; Prot 34 g; Carbo 47 g; Fiber 4 g; T Fat 25 g; 41% Calories from Fat; Chol 97 mg; Sod 1417 mg.

Mary Lee Reiff, HFH of Greater Bucks, Doylestown, PA

Yield: 12 servings.

Chicken-Noodle Casserole

3 cups chopped cooked chicken
1 8-ounce package noodles, cooked
2 10-ounce cans cream of chicken soup

1 12-ounce can evaporated milk
8 ounces process cheese, cubed
1 cup crushed cornflakes

■ Combine first 5 ingredients in bowl; mix well. Spoon into buttered 4-quart baking dish. Top with cornflakes. Bake at 350 degrees for 1 hour.
Approx Per Serving: Cal 314; Prot 21 g; Carbo 25 g; Fiber <1 g; T Fat 14 g; 42% Calories from Fat; Chol 95 mg; Sod 775 mg.

Georgia L. Foster, Midland County HFH, Sanford, MI

Yield: 8 servings

Liz's Mom's Chicken Casserole

4 cups chopped cooked chicken
2 10-ounce cans cream of mushroom soup
1 cup mayonnaise
2 cups chopped celery
2 cups cooked rice
2 teaspoons (or more) grated onion
2 4-ounce cans mushrooms

2 tablespoons lemon juice
¹/₄ teaspoon saffron
6 tablespoons melted butter
2 cups crushed cornflakes
¹/₄ cup slivered almonds, toasted

■ Combine chicken, soup, mayonnaise, celery, rice, onion, mushrooms, lemon juice and saffron in large bowl; mix well. Spoon into 9x13-inch baking dish. Top with mixture of butter and cornflakes; sprinkle with almonds. Bake at 350 degrees for 40 minutes.
Approx Per Serving: Cal 638; Prot 26 g; Carbo 37 g; Fiber 2 g; T Fat 44 g; 61% Calories from Fat; Chol 103 mg; Sod 1221 mg.

Maranell Fleming, Rabun County HFH, Sky Valley, GA

Chicken and Rice Casserole

Yield: 8 servings

1 small chicken
4 chicken bouillon
   cubes
1 teaspoon each sweet
   basil and salt
1/2 teaspoon pepper
1 16-ounce package
   frozen broccoli,
   thawed
1/2 onion, finely
   chopped

1 4-ounce can
   mushrooms, drained
3 tablespoons
   cornstarch
1/2 cup water
4 cups cooked rice
8 ounces mozzarella
   cheese, shredded
8 ounces Cheddar
   cheese, shredded

■ Rinse chicken well. Cook in water to cover in saucepan until tender; drain, reserving broth. Skim grease from broth; shred chicken, discarding skin and bones. Add bouillon, basil, salt, pepper, broccoli, onion and mushrooms to reserved broth in saucepan. Bring to a boil. Stir in mixture of cornstarch and water. Cook until thickened, stirring constantly. Layer rice, vegetable mixture, chicken and cheese in 9x13-inch baking dish sprayed with nonstick cooking spray. Bake at 375 degrees for 20 minutes or until bubbly.
Approx Per Serving: Cal 465; Prot 36 g; Carbo 33 g; Fiber 3 g; T Fat 21 g; 41% Calories from Fat; Chol 109 mg; Sod 1253 mg.

Regina Wilson, HFH Odessa R-VII Area, Odessa, MO

Chicken Murphy

Yield: 10 servings

3 pounds chicken
   breast filets
3 large yellow onions,
   thinly sliced, cut
   into halves
5 cloves of garlic,
   thinly sliced
3 tablespoons olive oil
Oregano to taste
Basil to taste
1/2 teaspoon salt

1/2 teaspoon pepper
1 8-ounce jar
   Marinara sauce
10 Italian frying
   peppers, seeded
   sliced
2 cups sliced
   mushrooms
2 large parboiled
   potatoes, cubed

■ Rinse chicken and pat dry. Cut into bite-sized pieces. Sauté onions and garlic in olive oil in large skillet until tender. Push to 1 side. Add chicken. Cook on both sides until brown. Stir in oregano, basil, salt, pepper, Marinara sauce and peppers. Cook, covered, over low heat for 20 minutes. Add mushrooms and potatoes. Cook, covered, until potatoes are tender.
Approx Per Serving: Cal 283; Prot 34 g; Carbo 17 g; Fiber 2 g; T Fat 9 g; 28% Calories from Fat; Chol 87 mg; Sod 331 mg.

Judy Cohen, Freehold Area HFH, Freehold, NJ

Chicken Salsa

Yield: 12 servings

1 10-ounce can cream
   of chicken soup
1 10-ounce can cream
   of mushroom soup
1 cup milk
1 8-ounce jar green
   chili salsa

12 corn tortillas, sliced
   into strips
4 chicken breast filets,
   cooked, chopped
8 ounces Cheddar
   cheese, shredded

■ Combine soups, milk and salsa in bowl; mix well. Alternate layers of tortilla strips, chicken and soup mixture in lightly greased 10x16-inch baking pan. Sprinkle with cheese. Bake at 350 degrees for 1 1/2 hours or until light brown and bubbly.
Approx Per Serving: Cal 258; Prot 18 g; Carbo 20 g; Fiber 2 g; T Fat 13 g; 44% Calories from Fat; Chol 49 mg; Sod 656 mg.

Mildred Moser Smith, Pomona Valley HFH, Claremont, CA

Chicken Divine

Yield: 10 servings

2 10-ounce packages
   frozen broccoli,
   cooked, drained
4 cups chopped cooked
   chicken
2 10-ounce cans
   cream of chicken
   soup

1 cup mayonnaise
1/2 teaspoon thyme
1 cup shredded
   Cheddar cheese
3 slices bread,
   crumbled
2 teaspoons melted
   butter

■ Arrange broccoli in nonstick 9x13-inch baking pan. Spoon mixture of chicken, soup, mayonnaise and thyme over broccoli. Sprinkle with cheese. Top with bread crumbs tossed with butter. Bake at 350 degrees for 30 minutes.
Approx Per Serving: Cal 407; Prot 23 g; Carbo 12 g; Fiber 2 g; T Fat 30 g; 66% Calories from Fat; Chol 82 mg; Sod 752 mg.

Cora Malone, HFH of the Kokomo Community, Kokomo, IN

Justice O'Connor's Creamed Tacos

Yield: 8 servings

12 corn tortillas
Oil for frying
Salt to taste
1 onion, chopped
2 tablespoons oil
1½ cups half and half
1 4-ounce can
  chopped green
  chilies

Pepper to taste
½ cup taco sauce
2 3-pound chickens,
  cooked, chopped
2 cups shredded
  Longhorn cheese

- Dip tortillas in hot oil in skillet to soften. Drain; sprinkle with salt. Cut into quarters. Sauté onion in 2 tablespoons oil in skillet until brown. Add half and half, green chilies, salt and pepper; mix well. Simmer until of desired consistency. Stir in taco sauce. Alternate layers of tortillas, chicken, green chili sauce and cheese in nonstick baking pan, ending with sauce and cheese. Bake at 350 degrees for 1 hour.

Approx Per Serving: Cal 639; Prot 61 g; Carbo 25 g; Fiber 4 g; T Fat 33 g; 46% Calories from Fat; Chol 198 mg; Sod 506 mg.
Nutritional information does not include oil for frying.

Maggie Craig Chrisman, HFH International Board of Directors
Paradise Valley, AZ

Cheesy Turkey Casserole

Yield: 12 servings

2 cups chopped cooked
  turkey
2 cups milk
1 10-ounce can cream
  of celery soup
1 10-ounce can cream
  of mushroom soup
¼ cup chopped onion

2 cups uncooked
  noodles, broken
1 8-ounce can
  mushrooms, drained
2 cups shredded
  Cheddar cheese
½ teaspoon salt

- Combine all ingredients in bowl; mix well. Spoon into greased 9x13-inch baking dish. Chill, covered, overnight. Bake at 350 degrees for 1 hour or until bubbly. May bake at 275 degrees for 2 hours.

Approx Per Serving: Cal 206; Prot 15 g; Carbo 10 g; Fiber 1 g; T Fat 12 g; 52% Calories from Fat; Chol 54 mg; Sod 690 mg.

Loretta Troyer, HFH International, Middlebury, IN

Slow-Cooker Turkey Olé

Yield: 10 servings

1 10-ounce can cream
  of chicken soup
1 10-ounce can cream
  of mushroom soup
1 7-ounce jar salsa
½ cup sour cream
½ cup chopped green
  bell pepper
1 cup chopped black
  olives

1 tablespoon grated
  onion
12 corn tortillas
4 cups coarsely
  chopped cooked
  turkey
1½ cups shredded
  Cheddar cheese

- Combine soups, salsa, sour cream, bell pepper, olives and onion in bowl; mix well. Cut each tortilla into 6 to 8 pieces. Alternate layers of tortillas, turkey and soup mixture in greased slow cooker until all ingredients are used. Cook on Low for 4 to 5 hours. Sprinkle with cheese. Cook for 15 to 20 minutes or until cheese melts. May substitute chicken for turkey.

Approx Per Serving: Cal 358; Prot 25 g; Carbo 23 g; Fiber 4 g; T Fat 20 g; 48% Calories from Fat; Chol 68 mg; Sod 857 mg.

Mary Richardson, HFH of Green County, Monroe, WI

Fred and Lori's Vegetarian Chili

Yield: 16 servings

1 cup dried kidney
  beans
1 cup dried garbanzo
  beans
1 cup dried pinto beans
2 teaspoons cumin
2 teaspoons oregano
2 teaspoons basil
2 teaspoons pepper
1 teaspoon paprika
4 onions, chopped
1 green bell pepper,
  chopped

4 stalks celery, chopped
3 to 4 large cloves of
  garlic, minced
3 to 4 jalepeño
  peppers, chopped
2 tablespoons olive oil
2 quarts fresh stewed
  tomatoes
2 16-ounce cans
  tomato sauce
3 to 4 tomatoes,
  peeled, chopped

- Combine first 3 ingredients with water to cover in large saucepan. Bring to a boil; remove from heat. Soak beans for 3 hours; drain. Cover with fresh water. Cook over low heat for 45 to 60 minutes or until beans are tender; drain. Sauté next 10 ingredients in olive oil in skillet until vegetables are tender. Combine with beans, stewed tomatoes and tomato sauce in large stockpot; mix well. Simmer for 30 minutes. Add chopped tomatoes. Simmer for 2 to 3 hours, stirring occasionally.

Approx Per Serving: Cal 204; Prot 12 g; Carbo 40 g; Fiber 5 g; T Fat 4 g; 13% Calories from Fat; Chol 0 mg; Sod 374 mg.

Fred Giese and Lori Sutherland, Green County HFH
Monroe, WI

Garden Lasagna

Yield: 16 servings

8 cups milk
1 clove of garlic, cut
  into halves
3/4 cup butter
1 cup flour
1 1/4 teaspoons salt
1/4 teaspoon white
  pepper
1/8 teaspoon ground
  nutmeg
1 1/3 cups grated
  Parmesan cheese
1/4 cup minced parsley
2 10-ounce packages
  frozen mixed
  vegetables, thawed,
  drained

2 10-ounce packages
  frozen chopped
  broccoli, thawed,
  drained
24 ounces lasagna
  noodles, cooked,
  rinsed, drained
2 tablespoons butter
2/3 cup grated
  Parmesan cheese

■ Heat milk and garlic in saucepan over medium heat until milk just begins to bubble. Remove from heat; discard garlic. Melt 3/4 cup butter in large saucepan over medium heat. Stir in flour, salt, pepper and nutmeg. Cook for 2 to 3 minutes or until bubbly, stirring constantly. Add hot milk, stirring until smooth; reduce heat. Simmer for 10 minutes or until thickened, stirring constantly. Stir in 1 1/3 cups Parmesan cheese and parsley. Spread 1/3 cup sauce into each of 2 greased 3-quart baking pans. Add mixed vegetables and broccoli to remaining sauce, stirring to coat. Alternate layers of noodles and vegetable-sauce mixture in each pan until all ingredients are used. Dot each with 1 tablespoon butter; sprinkle evenly with remaining Parmesan cheese. Bake at 350 degrees for 30 to 40 minutes or until bubbly.

Approx Per Serving: Cal 429; Prot 17 g; Carbo 50 g; Fiber 3 g; T Fat 18 g; 38% Calories from Fat; Chol 52 mg; Sod 515 mg.

Balinda Cakste, Clermont County HFH, Cincinnati, OH

Ralph's Deluxe Baked Ziti

Yield: 16 servings

3 large Vidalia onions,
  thinly sliced
3 to 4 tablespoons
  olive oil
6 cloves of garlic,
  minced
2 red bell peppers, cut
  into 2-inch strips
1 yellow bell pepper,
  cut into 2-inch strips
1 pound mushrooms,
  thickly sliced
1 16-ounce package
  ziti
1 26-ounce jar
  spaghetti sauce

16 ounces feta cheese,
  cubed
1 3-ounce package
  sun-dried tomatoes,
  chopped
2 6-ounce cans sliced
  black olives
1 6-ounce package
  chopped pecans
5 ounces Parmesan
  cheese, grated
16 ounces mozzarella
  cheese, shredded

■ Sauté onions in olive oil in large skillet until tender. Add garlic, red peppers and yellow pepper. Sauté until peppers are tender. Add mushrooms. Sauté for 1 to 2 minutes; set aside. Cook ziti using package directions; drain. Pour equal amounts of half the spaghetti sauce into two 9x13-inch baking pans. Layer with ziti, onion mixture and remaining sauce. Arrange feta cheese over sauce. Sprinkle with next 4 ingredients. Top with mozzarella cheese. Bake at 350 degrees for 15 minutes or until cheese is melted. Do not overcook or mozzarella cheese will become hard.

Approx Per Serving: Cal 508; Prot 20 g; Carbo 38 g; Fiber 5 g; T Fat 33 g; 56% Calories from Fat; Chol 54 mg; Sod 978 mg.

Ralph Preston, HFH of Boca-Delray, Boca Raton, FL

Brown Beans and Hot Water Corn Bread

Yield: 8 servings

1 pound dried pinto
  beans
2 ounces salt pork
1/2 cup sugar
1/2 onion, finely
  chopped
1/2 teaspoon baking
  soda
1 teaspoon each salt
  and pepper

1 cup flour
3/4 cup yellow cornmeal
1/2 cup sugar
1 egg
1 tablespoon warm
  bacon grease
Salt to taste
3/4 cup (about) hot
  water

■ Combine beans with salt pork and water to cover in slow cooker or large saucepan. Add 1/2 cup sugar, onion, baking soda, 1 teaspoon salt and pepper. Cook overnight or until tender, stirring occasionally. Combine flour, cornmeal, 1/2 cup sugar, egg, bacon grease and salt to taste in bowl. Add enough hot water to make of desired consistency. Spoon by 3 tablespoonfuls onto greased hot skillet. Bake on both sides until golden brown.

Approx Per Serving: Cal 430; Prot 18 g; Carbo 82 g; Fiber 14 g; T Fat 4 g; 9% Calories from Fat; Chol 39 mg; Sod 393 mg.

Alicia Ford, Enid HFH, Enid, OK

Yield: 20 servings
Backwoods Baked Beans

This recipe has always been a crowd pleaser in our neck of the woods!

3   16-ounce cans
     baked beans
³/₄ cup catsup
¹/₄ cup spicy brown
     mustard
¹/₂ cup packed light
     brown sugar

¹/₃ cup dried minced
     onion
1¹/₂ teaspoons liquid
     smoke
1 teaspoon
     Worcestershire sauce
8 slices bacon

■ Combine beans, catsup, mustard, brown sugar, onion, liquid smoke and Worcestershire sauce in slow cooker; mix well. Fry bacon in skillet until crisp; drain and crumble bacon, reserving drippings. Add bacon and drippings to slow cooker; mix well. Cook on High for 30 minutes, stirring frequently. Cook on Low for 1¹/₂ hours, stirring occasionally.
Approx Per Serving: Cal 122; Prot 5 g; Carbo 24 g; Fiber 2 g; T Fat 2 g; 14% Calories from Fat; Chol 2 mg; Sod 503 mg.

Jane Mallinson, Greater Manchester HFH, Derry, NH

Yield: 12 servings
Marinated Beans

This is a good make-ahead salad for busy home builders. You can use bottled Italian salad dressing for the marinade to save time.

1   16-ounce can whole
     green beans
1   16-ounce can whole
     wax beans
1   16-ounce can
     kidney beans
1   16-ounce can
     chick-peas
1 small onion, chopped

1 green bell pepper,
     chopped
²/₃ cup vinegar
¹/₃ cup olive oil
¹/₂ cup sugar
2 cloves of garlic,
     crushed
¹/₄ teaspoon pepper

■ Drain beans and chick-peas. Combine with onion and green pepper in large bowl. Combine vinegar, olive oil, sugar, garlic and pepper in small bowl; mix well. Add to salad. Marinate in refrigerator.
Approx Per Serving: Cal 182; Prot 5 g; Carbo 28 g; Fiber 4 g; T Fat 7 g; 31% Calories from Fat; Chol 0 mg; Sod 435 mg.

Patricia Keady, Mid-Hudson Valley HFH
Hopewell Junction, NY

Yield: 20 servings
Aggie's Bean Casserole

My favorite aunt always made this to serve to a crowd on her ranch.

8 slices bacon
1 large onion, chopped
1 cup packed brown
     sugar
1 teaspoon dry mustard
¹/₂ teaspoon garlic
     powder
¹/₂ cup vinegar
1 teaspoon salt
2   16-ounce cans
     butter beans

1   16-ounce can green
     beans
1   16-ounce can lima
     beans
1   16-ounce can
     kidney beans
1   16-ounce can pork
     and beans

■ Fry bacon in skillet until crisp; drain and crumble bacon, reserving drippings in skillet. Add onion. Sauté onion until tender. Add brown sugar, dry mustard, garlic powder, vinegar and salt. Cook for 20 minutes. Drain beans. Combine with brown sugar mixture and bacon in large bowl; mix well. Spoon into 10x15-inch baking pan. Bake at 350 degrees for 1 hour.
Approx Per Serving: Cal 203; Prot 7 g; Carbo 32 g; Fiber 5 g; T Fat 6 g; 25% Calories from Fat; Chol 28 mg; Sod 658 mg.

Kathy Riddelle, Northwestern University/Uptown HFH
Chicago, IL

Millard Fuller, President and
co-founder of Habitat for Humanity

B and B Salad
Yield: 12 servings

This is good for a potluck because it makes a large amount.

1 10-ounce package
   frozen peas
Flowerets of 1 medium
   head broccoli
Flowerets of 1 medium
   head cauliflower
1 medium onion,
   chopped
1 teaspoon each pepper,
   garlic salt and Beau
   Monde seasoning

2 cups mayonnaise
1 cup sour cream
1/2 cup sugar
4 ounces bacon,
   crisp-fried, crumbled
1 cup shredded
   Cheddar cheese
1/2 cup sunflower seed

■ Combine peas, broccoli, cauliflower and chopped onion in large bowl. Sprinkle with pepper, garlic salt and Beau Monde seasoning. Combine mayonnaise, sour cream, sugar, bacon, cheese and sunflower seed in bowl; mix well. Add to salad; mix well. Chill overnight to blend flavors.
Approx Per Serving: Cal 463; Prot 9 g; Carbo 19 g; Fiber 4 g; T Fat 41 g; 77% Calories from Fat; Chol 43 mg; Sod 533 mg.

Julie Richter, Sheboygan County HFH, Sheboygan, WI

Black Beans and Corn
Yield: 12 servings

2 cups dried black
   beans
1 tablespoon cumin
   seed
1 tablespoon salt
3 cups cooked corn

1/2 cup minced red
   onion
1/2 cup chopped fresh
   cilantro
2 cups chopped
   tomatoes

■ Bring beans to a boil in water to cover in saucepan; remove from heat. Let stand for 1 hour; drain. Combine with fresh water to cover in saucepan. Cook, covered, for 30 minutes. Add cumin seed and salt. Cook until tender; drain. Combine with corn, onion, cilantro and tomatoes in bowl; mix well.
Approx Per Serving: Cal 176; Prot 9 g; Carbo 35 g; Fiber 4 g; T Fat 1 g; 6% Calories from Fat; Chol 0 mg; Sod 549 mg.

Sandra Murphy, Clermont County HFH, Cincinnati, OH

Broccoli and Peanut Salad
Yield: 10 servings

1 cup plain lowfat
   yogurt
1 small onion, grated
1/4 cup red wine
   vinegar
1/3 cup sugar

Flowerets of 2 stalks
   broccoli
1 cup dry-roasted
   peanuts
1 cup raisins

■ Combine yogurt, onion, vinegar and sugar in small bowl. Combine broccoli, peanuts and raisins in serving bowl. Add dressing; toss to mix well. Chill until serving time.
Approx Per Serving: Cal 187; Prot 6 g; Carbo 27 g; Fiber 2 g; T Fat 8 g; 34% Calories from Fat; Chol 1 mg; Sod 144 mg.

Dawn Edwards Mueller, Greenville County HFH
Greenville, SC

Broccoli Goodie
Yield: 6 servings

2 teaspoons chopped
   onion
1/2 cup margarine
11/2 cups water
1 16-ounce package
   frozen chopped
   broccoli
11/2 cups uncooked
   instant rice

1 10-ounce can cream
   of celery soup
1 8-ounce jar Cheez
   Whiz
2 tablespoons
   imitation bacon bits

■ Bring onion, margarine and water to a boil in 2-quart saucepan. Add broccoli. Cook for 3 minutes; remove from heat. Stir in rice; let stand for 5 minutes. Add soup and Cheez Whiz; mix until smooth. Spoon into 21/2-quart baking dish; sprinkle with bacon bits. Bake at 325 degrees for 1 hour.
Approx Per Serving: Cal 414; Prot 13 g; Carbo 31 g; Fiber 3 g; T Fat 27 g; 58% Calories from Fat; Chol 29 mg; Sod 1046 mg.

Wilda R. Haye, HFH of Williams County, Stryker, OH

Immokalee Broccoli Casserole

Yield: 10 servings

This was a popular dish on our building trip to Immokalee, Florida, during spring break.

2 cups uncooked rice
2 10-ounce cans
  cream of mushroom
  soup
8 ounces Velveeta
  cheese, chopped

1½ large heads
  broccoli, chopped
Salt and pepper to taste

■ Cook rice until nearly tender; drain. Place in deep baking dish. Layer with remaining ingredients. Mix gently. Bake at 350 degrees for 45 minutes.
Approx Per Serving: Cal 283; Prot 9 g; Carbo 36 g; Fiber 1 g; T Fat 12 g; 37% Calories from Fat; Chol 22 mg; Sod 791 mg.

Caroline Donnelly, American University Campus Chapter
Washington, D.C.

Cabbage Slaw

Yield: 12 servings

1 head cabbage, grated
1 green bell pepper,
  finely chopped
1 onion, finely chopped

1 cup sugar
½ cup vinegar
½ cup oil
1 tablespoon sugar

■ Combine cabbage, chopped green pepper and chopped onion in large bowl. Stir in 1 cup sugar; let stand for several minutes. Bring vinegar, oil and 1 tablespoon sugar to a boil in saucepan. Pour over salad; mix well. Store in refrigerator.
Approx Per Serving: Cal 161; Prot <1 g; Carbo 21 g; Fiber 1 g; T Fat 9 g; 49% Calories from Fat; Chol 0 mg; Sod 5 mg.

Georgia C. Mason, Highlands County HFH
Avon Park, FL

Baked Corn

Yield: 12 servings

This dish is good for a picnic because it can be eaten cold.

2 eggs, slightly beaten
1 cup sour cream
½ cup melted
  margarine
1 16-ounce can whole
  kernel corn, drained

1 16-ounce can
  cream-style corn
1 8-ounce package
  corn muffin mix

■ Combine all ingredients in bowl; mix well. Spoon into 9x13-inch baking dish. Bake at 350 degrees for 35 to 40 minutes or until set and golden brown.
Approx Per Serving: Cal 217; Prot 4 g; Carbo 22 g; Fiber 1 g; T Fat 14 g; 56% Calories from Fat; Chol 44 mg; Sod 391 mg.

Dorothy Purvis, HFH of Butler County, Gibsonia, PA

Hashed Brown Casserole

Yield: 12 servings

½ cup chopped onion
½ cup melted
  margarine
1 10-ounce can cream
  of chicken soup
1 cup sour cream
1 2-pound package
  frozen hashed brown
  potatoes, thawed

2 cups shredded
  Cheddar cheese
Salt and pepper to taste
2 cups crushed
  cornflakes
¼ cup melted
  margarine

■ Sauté onion in ½ cup margarine in nonstick skillet until tender. Combine with soup and sour cream in bowl; mix well. Add potatoes, cheese, salt and pepper, stirring well. Pour into greased 9x13-inch baking dish. Bake at 350 degrees for 45 minutes. Toss cornflakes with ¼ cup melted margarine. Sprinkle over potato mixture. Bake for 15 minutes longer.
Approx Per Serving: Cal 453; Prot 10 g; Carbo 35 g; Fiber 2 g; T Fat 32 g; 64% Calories from Fat; Chol 30 mg; Sod 639 mg.

Glinda Nicodemus, HFH of St. Joseph County
Notre Dame, IN

*T**aking the five loaves and the two fish and looking up to heaven, he gave thanks and broke them. Then he gave them to the disciples to set before the people. They all ate and were satisfied, and the disciples picked up twelve basketfuls of broken pieces that were left over.*

Luke 9:16-17

Tanta Ria's Austrian Potato Salad
Yield: 12 servings

12 medium potatoes
1 cup water
2 or 3 cubes vegetable
  bouillon
1 medium onion,
  chopped
2 cloves of garlic,
  minced

1/2 teaspoon pepper
1/2 teaspoon paprika,
  dill, thyme or other
  seasoning
2 to 3 ounces vinegar
2 teaspoons chopped
  cilantro or parsley

■ Cook potatoes in water to cover in saucepan until tender; drain. Cool and peel potatoes, cut into quarters and slice. Combine 1 cup water, bouillon, onion, garlic, pepper and seasoning of choice in saucepan. Bring to a boil. Add to potatoes in large bowl; mix gently. Stir in vinegar; sprinkle with cilantro. Serve hot or chilled.
Approx Per Serving: Cal 124; Prot 3 g; Carbo 29 g; Fiber 2 g; T Fat <1 g; 2% Calories from Fat; Chol <1 mg; Sod 295 mg.

Fred Giese, HFH of Green County, Monroe, WI

Minted Marinated Rice and Vegetables
Yield: 10 servings

This recipe makes enough to feed a hungry Habitat crew.

1 tablespoon Dijon
  mustard
1/2 cup red wine vinegar
2 teaspoons sugar
1 teaspoon each salt
  and pepper
Finely chopped mint
  leaves to taste
1 cup olive oil
8 cups hot cooked rice
1 each green and red
  bell pepper, julienned
1 medium purple
  onion, chopped

6 scallions, finely
  sliced
2 shallots, finely
  chopped
1   10-ounce can peas,
  drained
1/2 cup chopped black
  olives
1 cup dried currants
1/4 cup chopped Italian
  parsley
1/2 cup chopped dill
Salt and pepper to taste

■ Whisk mustard, vinegar, sugar, 1 teaspoon salt, 1 teaspoon pepper and mint together in bowl. Add olive oil gradually, whisking constantly. Combine with hot rice in large bowl; toss to mix well. Cool to room temperature. Add bell peppers, onion, scallions, shallots, peas, olives, currants, parsley, dill and salt and pepper to taste; mix well. Serve at room temperature. Store in refrigerator.
Approx Per Serving: Cal 473; Prot 6 g; Carbo 61 g; Fiber 4 g; T Fat 24 g; 44% Calories from Fat; Chol 0 mg; Sod 365 mg.

Sue Wagner, HFH of Green County, Monroe, WI

Sauerkraut Salad
Yield: 8 servings

1   20-ounce can
  sauerkraut, drained
1 cup chopped celery
1 cup chopped green
  bell pepper

1/2 cup chopped onion
1/2 cup oil
1/4 cup cider vinegar
1 cup sugar
1/2 teaspoon salt

■ Combine sauerkraut, celery, green pepper and onion in serving bowl. Combine oil, vinegar, sugar and salt in small bowl. Add to salad; mix well. Chill, covered, for several hours to overnight.
Approx Per Serving: Cal 240; Prot 1 g; Carbo 30 g; Fiber 2 g; T Fat 14 g; 50% Calories from Fat; Chol 0 mg; Sod 617 mg.

Kenna Smith-Dunn, Ashland-Ironton Area HFH
Ashland, KY

Vegetable and Rice Salad
Yield: 6 servings

1 cup uncooked rice,
  cooked
1   16-ounce can
  kidney beans,
  drained, rinsed
1 large stalk broccoli,
  chopped
8 ounces snow peas
8 ounces mushrooms,
  sliced
1 each green and red
  bell pepper, cut into
  1/4-inch strips

1/4 cup olive oil
2 tablespoons lemon
  juice
3 tablespoons vinegar
2 large cloves of garlic,
  crushed
1 teaspoon dry mustard
3/4 teaspoon tarragon,
  crushed
1/2 teaspoon pepper

■ Combine rice, beans, broccoli, snow peas, mushrooms and bell peppers in large bowl. Combine olive oil, lemon juice, vinegar, garlic, dry mustard, tarragon and pepper in covered jar; shake to mix well. Add to salad; toss to mix. Chill for several hours or overnight. May substitute 1 cup peas for snow peas.
Approx Per Serving: Cal 297; Prot 9 g; Carbo 45 g; Fiber 9 g; T Fat 10 g; 29% Calories from Fat; Chol 0 mg; Sod 275 mg.

Lois E. Wolters, Habitat Gypsies, Columbus, NC

Marinated Vegetable Salad

Yield: 8 servings

1 11-ounce can Shoe Peg corn
1 16-ounce can French-style green beans
1 16-ounce can tiny green peas
1/4 cup chopped green onions
1/2 cup chopped celery
1/2 cup chopped green bell pepper
1/2 cup oil
1 cup vinegar
3/4 cup sugar
1 teaspoon salt
1/2 teaspoon pepper

■ Drain corn, beans and peas. Combine with green onions, celery and green pepper in medium bowl. Combine oil, vinegar, sugar, salt and pepper in saucepan. Bring to a boil. Pour over salad; mix well. Chill for up to 1 week.
Approx Per Serving: Cal 281; Prot 4 g; Carbo 38 g; Fiber 4 g; T Fat 14 g; 43% Calories from Fat; Chol 0 mg; Sod 631 mg.

Shirley J. Kopp, Grants Pass Area HFH, Grants Pass, OR

Vegetable Casserole

Yield: 8 servings

1 16-ounce can corn, drained
1 16-ounce can cut green beans
1/2 cup chopped celery
1/2 cup chopped onion
1 cup shredded Cheddar cheese
1 cup sour cream
Salt and pepper to taste
1 8-ounce package butter crackers, crushed
1/2 cup melted butter
1/2 cup slivered almonds

■ Combine corn, undrained beans, celery, onion, cheese, sour cream, salt, pepper and half the cracker crumbs, half the butter and half the almonds in bowl; mix well. Spoon into large baking dish. Top with mixture of remaining cracker crumbs, butter and almonds. Bake at 350 degrees for 45 minutes.
Approx Per Serving: Cal 470; Prot 10 g; Carbo 37 g; Fiber 3 g; T Fat 36 g; 63% Calories from Fat; Chol 59 mg; Sod 831 mg.

Mike Hoyt, Hawkins HFH, Rogersville, TN

Vegetable-Pasta Salad

Yield: 12 servings

1 16-ounce package linguine or fettucini
1 cup chopped green bell pepper
1 cup chopped broccoli
1 cup chopped cauliflower
1/2 cup sliced radishes
1/2 cup sliced green onions
2 4-ounce jars green olives, drained
1/2 cup grated Parmesan cheese
1 envelope zesty Italian salad dressing mix
1 16-ounce bottle of zesty Italian salad dressing
1 cup cherry tomatoes

■ Cook pasta using package directions; drain and cool. Combine with green pepper, broccoli, cauliflower, radishes, green onions, olives, Parmesan cheese, salad dressing mix and 3/4 of the salad dressing in large bowl; mix well. Chill for 2 hours to overnight. Add remaining salad dressing and tomatoes at serving time.
Approx Per Serving: Cal 364; Prot 7 g; Carbo 35 g; Fiber 3 g; T Fat 27 g; 59% Calories from Fat; Chol 3 mg; Sod 787 mg.

Anne Gist, Black Hills Area HFH, Rapid City, SD

Provolone Stromboli

Yield: 8 servings

You may prepare this in advance, underbake it slightly and wrap in foil.
Freeze it until needed and reheat in the oven.

2 loaves frozen bread dough
4 egg whites
2 tablespoons grated Parmesan cheese
2 teaspoons chopped parsley
1 teaspoon garlic powder
2 teaspoons oregano
1/2 teaspoon pepper
1/4 cup oil
8 ounces pepperoni, sliced
1 pound cooked ham, chopped
1 pound provolone cheese, sliced
1 egg white

■ Place bread dough on 2 baking sheets. Let thaw and rise using package directions. Roll as for pizza. Combine 4 egg whites, Parmesan cheese, chopped parsley, garlic powder, oregano, pepper and oil in bowl; mix well. Spread over surface of both loaves. Layer pepperoni, ham and provolone cheese slices down center of each loaf. Fold sides over to cover filling completely; seal edges. Turn seam side down on baking sheets. Brush with 1 egg white. Bake at 350 degrees for 30 to 35 minutes or until golden brown. Serve sliced with salad, fruit or chips.
Approx Per Serving: Cal 788; Prot 45 g; Carbo 63 g; Fiber <1 g; T Fat 42 g; 47% Calories from Fat; Chol 82 mg; Sod 2570 mg.

Suzanne Waters, Williamsport/Lycoming HFH
Williamsport, PA

Stuffed Bread

Yield: 12 servings

2 pounds ground beef
1 loaf frozen bread
   dough, thawed
1/3 cup ranch salad
   dressing

3 cups sliced onions,
   separated into rings
2 cups shredded
   American cheese
Garlic salt to taste

- Brown ground beef in skillet, stirring until crumbly; drain. Roll bread dough into rectangle on lightly floured surface. Spread with salad dressing. Layer onions, cheese and ground beef on dough. Roll up dough to enclose filling. Place on baking sheet; sprinkle with garlic salt. Bake at 375 degrees for 45 minutes or until golden brown.

Approx Per Serving: Cal 352; Prot 21 g; Carbo 23 g; Fiber <1 g; T Fat 21 g; 51% Calories from Fat; Chol 70 mg; Sod 573 mg.

Dana Hanson, Morgan County HFH, Ft. Morgan, CO

Habitat Bran Muffins

Yield: 12 servings

1/2 cup bran
1/2 cup milk
1/2 cup margarine,
   softened

1/2 cup honey
1 egg
13/4 cups flour
1 teaspoon baking soda

- Combine bran and milk in bowl; mix well. Let stand for several minutes. Cream margarine and honey in mixer bowl until light. Beat in egg. Add mixture of flour and baking soda alternately with bran mixture, mixing just until moistened after each addition; do not overmix. Spoon into greased muffin cups. Bake at 400 degrees for 20 minutes. May substitute orange juice for milk or add 1/2 cup dates or crushed pineapple.

Approx Per Serving: Cal 193; Prot 3 g; Carbo 27 g; Fiber 1 g; T Fat 9 g; 39% Calories from Fat; Chol 19 mg; Sod 169 mg.

Joan Higgins-Smith, Lincoln HFH, Lincoln, NE

Cheesy Bubble Bread

Yield: 16 servings

1 1/2 cups shredded
   Cheddar cheese
1/2 cup chopped fresh
   basil or 1 1/2
   teaspoons dried basil

2 16-ounce loaves
   frozen bread dough,
   thawed
1/2 cup melted butter

- Mix cheese and basil in bowl. Cut each loaf of dough into 32 pieces; shape into balls. Arrange 1/3 of the balls in greased bundt or tube pan. Brush with 2 tablespoons melted butter; sprinkle with 1/3 of the cheese mixture. Repeat process twice; drizzle with remaining butter. Let rise, covered with damp cloth, in warm place for 1 1/2 hours or until dough rises to top of pan. Bake at 350 degrees for 30 minutes; reduce oven temperature to 300 degrees. Bake for 15 to 20 minutes longer or until light brown and sounds hollow when tapped. Invert immediately onto serving plate. May store in foil and reheat.

Approx Per Serving: Cal 236; Prot 7 g; Carbo 31 g; Fiber <1 g; T Fat 11 g; 40% Calories from Fat; Chol 27 mg; Sod 458 mg.

Patricia Morrill, Branch County HFH, Coldwater, MI

Habitat is helping point the way to the future in the Sandtown area of Baltimore, Maryland.

Yield: 8 servings

Russian Cheese Bread

Take this to serve warm at picnics.

3¹/₂ to 4 cups flour
2 tablespoons dry yeast
1 tablespoon sugar
2 teaspoons salt
1 cup milk
¹/₂ cup butter

1¹/₂ pounds Muenster cheese, shredded
2 tablespoons butter, softened
1 egg

■ Mix 2 cups flour, yeast, sugar and salt in large bowl. Heat milk and ¹/₂ cup butter in saucepan until lukewarm. Add to flour mixture gradually, beating until smooth. Add enough remaining flour to form smooth dough, beating constantly. Knead on floured surface for 10 minutes or until smooth and elastic. Place in buttered bowl, turning to coat surface. Let rise for 1 hour or until doubled in bulk. Punch dough down. Roll to 16-inch circle on floured surface; place in foil-lined 9-inch baking pan. Combine cheese, 2 tablespoons butter and egg in bowl; mix with spoon. Spoon onto dough. Pull up edge of dough to center over cheese mixture; twist to seal. Bake at 375 degrees for 45 minutes or until golden brown.
Approx Per Serving: Cal 706; Prot 28 g; Carbo 52 g; Fiber 2 g; T Fat 42 g; 54% Calories from Fat; Chol 150 mg; Sod 1211 mg.

Joyce Klein, HFH of Knox County, Ohio , Gambier, OH

Yield: 100 servings

World-Famous Chocolate Chip Cookies

5 cups rolled oats
4 cups flour
1 teaspoon salt
2 teaspoons baking powder
2 teaspoons baking soda
2 cups butter, softened
2 cups packed brown sugar

2 cups sugar
4 eggs
2 teaspoons vanilla extract
4 cups chocolate chips
1   8-ounce chocolate bar, grated
3 cups chopped walnuts

■ Process a small amount of oats at a time in food processor until powdery. Mix flour, processed oats, salt, baking powder and baking soda together. Cream butter, brown sugar and sugar in mixer bowl until light and fluffy. Add eggs and vanilla; beat well. Add flour mixture gradually, beating well after each addition. Add chocolate chips, grated chocolate and walnuts; mix well. Drop by spoonfuls onto ungreased cookie sheet. Bake at 350 degrees for 6 minutes or until lightly browned.
Approx Per Serving: Cal 175; Prot 2 g; Carbo 22 g; Fiber 1 g; T Fat 10 g; 47% Calories from Fat; Chol 19 mg; Sod 84 mg.

Kathy Ofner, New River HFH, Scarbro, WV

Yield: 112 servings

Expensive-Lesson $250 Cookies

5 cups rolled oats
4 cups flour
1 teaspoon salt
2 teaspoons baking powder
2 teaspoons baking soda
2 cups butter, softened
2 cups packed brown sugar

2 cups sugar
4 eggs
2 teaspoons vanilla extract
4 cups chocolate chips
1   8-ounce chocolate bar, grated
3 cups chopped pecans

■ Process oats in blender container until powdery. Sift oats, flour, salt, baking powder and baking soda together. Cream butter, brown sugar and sugar in mixer bowl until light and fluffy. Add eggs and vanilla; beat well. Add flour mixture gradually, beating well after each addition. Stir in chocolate chips, grated chocolate and pecans. Shape into balls. Place 2 inches apart on nonstick cookie sheet. Bake at 375 degrees for 10 minutes or until light brown.
Approx Per Serving: Cal 156; Prot 2 g; Carbo 19 g; Fiber 1 g; T Fat 9 g; 48% Calories from Fat; Chol 17 mg; Sod 75 mg.

Mary Warboys, Morgan County HFH, Fort Morgan, CO

Best Sugar Cookie in the World

Yield: 100 servings

1 cup butter, softened
1 cup oil
1 cup confectioners'
   sugar
1 cup sugar
2 teaspoons vanilla
   extract

2 eggs, beaten
5 cups flour
1 teaspoon baking soda
1 teaspoon cream of
   tartar
1/4 teaspoon salt

■ Cream butter, oil, confectioners' sugar, sugar, vanilla and eggs in mixer bowl until light and fluffy. Add flour, baking soda, cream of tartar and salt, stirring well. Shape into small balls. Place on ungreased cookie sheet. Press flat with glass dipped in sugar. Bake at 350 degrees for 10 to 12 minutes or until light brown at edges. May substitute 1 cup sugar for confectioners' sugar and 1 teaspoon lemon extract for 1 teaspoon vanilla. May use additional 1 teaspoon each baking soda and cream of tartar.
Approx Per Serving: Cal 72; Prot 1 g; Carbo 8 g; Fiber <1 g; T Fat 4 g; 52% Calories from Fat; Chol 9 mg; Sod 31 mg.

Hazel N. Stevenson, Owensboro-Daviess County HFH
Owensboro, KY
Gail Huffman, First Presbyterian Church, Jefferson, IA

French Apple Habitarts for Humanity

Yield: 24 servings

These tarts are a hit at Habitat building sites and are a good fund-raiser at auctions.

3 sticks unsalted
   butter, chilled
3 cups flour
1/4 cup sugar
4 to 6 tablespoons ice
   water

6 firm McIntosh or
   Granny Smith apples
1/3 cup sugar
Cinnamon to taste
1/3 cup apple jelly,
   melted

■ Cut each stick of butter into halves; cut halves lengthwise into quarters. Cut quarters into 96 cubes. Add to mixture of flour and 1/4 cup sugar in bowl; toss to coat butter. Add ice water, mixing until mixture forms dough. Knead with hands until mixture is smooth. Chill for 15 minutes; dust with additional flour if mixture is sticky. Shape into 2 logs; cut each log into 12 portions. Press into foil-lined muffin cups. Cut apples into quarters, keeping wedges of each quarter together. Press each apple quarter rounded side up into prepared cup; sprinkle tarts with 1/3 cup sugar and cinnamon. Bake at 375 degrees for 10 to 17 minutes or until pastry is dark golden brown. Glaze with jelly. Serve warm with French vanilla ice cream.
Approx Per Serving: Cal 206; Prot 2 g; Carbo 24 g; Fiber 1 g; T Fat 12 g; 50% Calories from Fat; Chol 31 mg; Sod 3 mg.

Allen W. Wood, Westchester County HFH, Larchmont, NY

Carrot Cakes

Yield: 30 servings

4 eggs, beaten
2 cups sugar
2 teaspoons baking
   soda
2 teaspoons cinnamon
1 teaspoon salt
1 1/2 cups corn oil
2 1/2 cups flour
3 4-ounce jars baby
   food carrots

1 cup chopped walnuts
1 1-pound package
   confectioners' sugar
8 ounces cream cheese,
   softened
1 teaspoon vanilla
   extract
1/2 cup margarine,
   softened

■ Combine eggs, sugar, baking soda, cinnamon, salt, oil, flour, carrots and walnuts in bowl; mix well. Pour into 2 nonstick 10x13-inch cake pans. Bake at 350 degrees for 30 minutes or until cakes test done. Combine confectioners' sugar, cream cheese, vanilla and margarine in bowl. Beat until of spreading consistency. Spread over cooled cakes.
Approx Per Serving: Cal 349; Prot 3 g; Carbo 41 g; Fiber 1 g; T Fat 20 g; 50% Calories from Fat; Chol 37 mg; Sod 200 mg.

Kim Merchant, Jubilee HFH, Jacksonville, IL

Texas Fudge Cake

Yield: 24 servings

2 cups flour
1/2 teaspoon salt
2 cups sugar
1 cup margarine
1 cup water
3 tablespoons baking cocoa
2 eggs
1/2 cup buttermilk
1 teaspoon vanilla extract

1 teaspoon baking soda
1/2 cup margarine
6 tablespoons milk
3 tablespoons baking cocoa
1   1-pound package confectioners' sugar
1 cup chopped pecans
1 teaspoon vanilla extract

■ Mix flour, salt and sugar in large bowl. Bring 1 cup margarine, water and 3 tablespoons baking cocoa to a boil in saucepan. Pour over flour mixture; mix well. Add eggs, buttermilk, 1 teaspoon vanilla and baking soda; mix well. Pour into greased 11x17-inch cake pan. Bake at 350 degrees for 20 minutes. Melt 1/2 cup margarine with milk and 3 tablespoons baking cocoa in saucepan. Remove from heat. Add confectioners' sugar, pecans and 1 teaspoon vanilla. Beat until of spreading consistency. Spread over cooled cake.
Approx Per Serving: Cal 339; Prot 3 g; Carbo 49 g; Fiber 1 g; T Fat 16 g; 41% Calories from Fat; Chol 19 mg; Sod 226 mg.

Paulette House, Rogue Valley HFH, Medford, OR

Frosty Cream Cake

Yield: 24 servings

1 cup raisins
1/2 cup margarine, softened
1 1/2 cups sugar
2 eggs
2 1/2 cups flour

1 teaspoon baking soda
1 teaspoon cinnamon
1/2 teaspoon nutmeg
1/2 teaspoon salt
1 cup chopped walnuts

■ Cook raisins in water to cover in saucepan for 3 to 4 minutes. Drain, reserving 1 cup cooking liquid; cool to room temperature. Cream margarine and sugar in mixer bowl until light and fluffy. Beat in eggs. Mix next 5 ingredients together. Add to batter alternately with reserved cooking liquid. Fold in raisins and walnuts. Spoon into greased and floured 10x15-inch cake pan. Bake at 350 degrees for 20 minutes. Frost with confectioners' sugar frosting.
Approx Per Serving: Cal 189; Prot 3 g; Carbo 29 g; Fiber 1 g; T Fat 8 g; 35% Calories from Fat; Chol 18 mg; Sod 131 mg.

Nellie Wall, Morgan County HFH, Ft. Morgan, CO

Colonial Seed Cakes

Yield: 24 servings

1/2 cup poppy seed
3/4 cup milk
3/4 cup margarine, softened
3 eggs, at room temperature

1 1/4 cups sugar
2 cups sifted flour
2 teaspoons baking powder
1 teaspoon vanilla extract

■ Mix poppy seed and milk in large bowl; let stand at room temperature for 3 to 4 hours. Add remaining ingredients to poppy seed mixture; beat at medium speed for 1 minute, scraping side of bowl occasionally. Spoon into 2 greased and floured loaf pans. Bake at 350 degrees for 1 1/4 hours or until top springs back when lightly touched. Cool in pans for 5 minutes. Loosen edges; remove to wire rack to cool completely.
Approx Per Serving: Cal 157; Prot 3 g; Carbo 19 g; Fiber <1 g; T Fat 8 g; 46% Calories from Fat; Chol 28 mg; Sod 107 mg.

Pat Andrews, Pemi-Valley Habitat, Plymouth, NH

Delicious Strawberry Pies

Yield: 12 servings

2 pints whole strawberries, stemmed
2 cups water
2 cups sugar
6 tablespoons cornstarch
1   3-ounce package strawberry gelatin

1 1/2 teaspoons almond flavoring
1 teaspoon red food coloring
2 baked 9-inch pie shells

■ Mix water, sugar and cornstarch in saucepan. Cook over medium heat until thickened, stirring constantly. Remove from heat. Stir in gelatin, flavoring and food coloring. Cool. Add strawberries. Spoon into pie shells. Chill for 3 hours.
Approx Per Serving: Cal 334; Prot 3 g; Carbo 60 g; Fiber 2 g; T Fat 10 g; 27% Calories; from Fat; Chol 0 mg; Sod 207 mg.

Gail Bullington, Albany Area HFH, Albany, GA

Pizza Fruit Pie

Yield: 16 servings

1 2-layer yellow cake mix
1/2 cup coconut
1/2 cup margarine
1 egg
1 4-ounce package lemon instant pudding mix

1 cup milk
8 ounces cream cheese, softened
1/2 cup sliced strawberries
1/2 cup bananas
1/2 cup sliced grapes
1/2 cup sliced kiwifruit

- Combine cake mix and coconut in bowl. Cut in margarine until crumbly. Stir in egg. Press over bottom of pizza pan. Bake at 350 degrees for 15 minutes or until light brown. Cool. Beat pudding mix, milk and cream cheese in bowl. Spread over cooled crust. Arrange fruit over top.

Approx Per Serving: Cal 300; Prot 4 g; Carbo 39 g; Fiber 1 g; T Fat 15 g; 44% Calories; from Fat; Chol 31 mg; Sod 353 mg.

Marilyn Veley, Charlotte County HFH, Port Charlotte, FL

Garbage Snack

Yield: 64 servings

3 cups Cheerios
3 cups crisp rice cereal
1 12-ounce jar dry-roasted peanuts

1 9-ounce package pretzel sticks
2 pounds white chocolate disks

- Combine first 4 ingredients in bowl; mix well. Melt white chocolate in top of double boiler. Pour over mix, stirring to coat. Drop by tablespoonfuls onto waxed paper; cool.

Approx Per Serving: Cal 125; Prot 3 g; Carbo 14 g; Fiber >1 g; T Fat 7 g; 49% Calories from Fat; Chol 3 mg; Sod 145 mg.

Joanne Saul, HFH of Butler County, Mars, PA

Granola

Yield: 20 servings

1/2 cup oil
1/2 cup water
1/2 cup honey
6 cups oats
1/2 to 1 cup wheat germ

1/2 cup whole wheat flour
1 cup flaked coconut
1 cup raisins
1 cup chopped dates

- Combine oil, water and honey in saucepan. Bring to a boil; cool. Mix with oats, wheat germ, flour and coconut in 9x13-inch baking pan. Bake at 225 degrees for 1 hour, stirring every 20 to 30 minutes. Stir in raisins and dates. Bake for 1 hour longer, stirring every half hour; cool. May add chopped nuts.

Approx Per Serving: Cal 257; Prot 6 g; Carbo 42 g; Fiber 5 g; T Fat 9 g; 29% Calories from Fat; Chol 0 mg; Sod 3 mg.

Margaret Bateman
Tuscola United Methodist Church Work Camps, Tuscola, IL

Uncle Will's Granola

Yield: 16 servings

I have used this for over 20 years with my family of 6 children. All their friends ask for the recipe. It is from my uncle, who is now approaching the age of 90.

1/4 teaspoon cinnamon
1/4 cup oil
1/2 cup honey
1/4 cup warm water
1/2 teaspoon vanilla extract

3 cups slow-cooking oats
1 cup sunflower seed
1/2 cup wheat germ
1/2 cup unsalted cashews
1 cup raisins

- Mix first 5 ingredients in small bowl. Add oats, sunflower seed, wheat germ and cashews in large bowl; mix well. Spoon into 12x15-inch baking pan. Bake at 250 to 275 degrees for 45 minutes or until browned, stirring every 15 minutes; cool on brown paper. Stir in raisins. Store in refrigerator.

Approx Per Serving: Cal 235; Prot 6 g; Carbo 31 g; Fiber 4 g; T Fat 11 g; 40% Calories from Fat; Chol 0 mg; Sod 3 mg.

Sandy Newman, Mooresville/Lake Norman HFH
Davidson, NC

*H*abitat for Humanity has chosen to witness to Jesus Christ's Gospel by working with God's people in need everywhere to create a better habitat in which to live and work.

No-Bake Cookies

Yield: 48 servings

½ cup light syrup
½ cup sugar
1 cup peanut butter
3 cups crisp rice cereal

1 cup chocolate chips
1 cup butterscotch
chips

■ Combine syrup and sugar in heavy saucepan. Cook over medium heat until mixture begins to boil; remove from heat. Add peanut butter, mixing well. Stir in cereal. Press into greased 9x12-inch pan. Melt chocolate and butterscotch chips in saucepan, stirring to mix. Spoon over mixture. Let stand until topping is set. Cut into bars.
Approx Per Serving: Cal 87; Prot 2 g; Carbo 11 g; Fiber <1 g; T Fat 5 g; 46% Calories from Fat; Chol 0 mg; Sod 48 mg.

Evelene Meininger, Morgan County HFH
Fort Morgan, CO

Peanut Butter Toast

Yield: variable

Zwieback toast
Peanut butter

Sliced canned pears or
peaches

■ Spread toast with peanut butter; top with fruit. Place in front of small child. Watch for proper chewing and swallowing—and lots of smiles.
Nutritional information for this recipe is not available.

Nicholas and Nathaniel Kostecki, Northern Straits HFH
Cedarville, MI

Burnt Sugar Peanuts

Yield: 8 servings

½ cup water
1 cup sugar

2 cups raw peanuts
Salt to taste

■ Cook water, sugar and peanuts in saucepan over medium heat for 15 minutes or until peanuts crystallize, stirring frequently. Spread out on baking sheet; sprinkle with salt. Bake at 300 degrees for 15 minutes; remove from oven. Sprinkle with salt and stir. Bake for 15 to 30 minutes longer or until peanuts are crisp, stirring occasionally.
Approx Per Serving: Cal 307; Prot 9 g; Carbo 32 g; Fiber 3 g; T Fat 18 g; 49% Calories from Fat; Chol 0 mg; Sod 4 mg.

Nellie C. Neuffer, Oregon Trail HFH, Hermiston, OR

Peanut Crispy Bars

Yield: 48 servings

1 cup light corn syrup
1 cup peanut butter
½ cup packed brown
sugar

7 cups crisp rice cereal
1 cup chocolate chips

■ Combine corn syrup, peanut butter and brown sugar in heavy saucepan. Cook over medium heat until bubbly, stirring constantly. Pour over cereal in large bowl, stirring to coat. Add chocolate chips; mix. Press into greased 11x17-inch pan; cool. Cut into bars.
Approx Per Serving: Cal 96; Prot 2 g; Carbo 14 g; Fiber 1 g; T Fat 4 g; 36% Calories from Fat; Chol 0 mg; Sod 76 mg.

Sally Erdahl, HFH of South Central Minnesota
Mankato, MN

Basil Popcorn

Yield: 16 servings

¼ cup melted
margarine
1 teaspoon basil
2 tablespoons minced
onion

1 tablespoon soy sauce
1 teaspoon garlic
powder
4 quarts popped
popcorn

■ Mix first 5 ingredients in bowl. Pour over popped popcorn in large bowl, tossing to coat.
Approx Per Serving: Cal 54; Prot 1 g; Carbo 6 g; Fiber 1 g; T Fat 3 g; 50% Calories from Fat; Chol 0 mg; Sod 82 mg.

Anni Powell, Oregon Trail HFH, Hermiston, OR

Caramel-Nut Corn

Yield: 32 servings

2 cups packed brown
   sugar
1 cup margarine
1/2 cup corn syrup
1/4 teaspoon cream of
   tartar

1 teaspoon baking soda
8 quarts popped
   popcorn
2 cups pecan halves

▪ Combine first 4 ingredients in heavy saucepan. Bring to a boil, stirring constantly. Cook for 2 minutes; remove from heat. Stir in baking soda. Pour over mixture of popcorn and pecans in large bowl, stirring to mix. Spread on greased baking sheets. Bake at 250 degrees for 15 minutes; stir. Bake for 10 to 15 minutes longer or until golden brown.
Approx Per Serving: Cal 204; Prot 2 g; Carbo 28 g; Fiber 2 g; T Fat 11 g; 45% Calories from Fat; Chol 0 mg; Sod 103 mg.

Sally Chronister, Greater East Liverpool HFH
East Liverpool OH

Caramel Popcorn

Yield: 24 servings

1 cup margarine
2 cups packed brown
   sugar
1/4 cup dark corn syrup

1/2 teaspoon baking
   soda
6 quarts popped
   popcorn

▪ Combine margarine, brown sugar and corn syrup in heavy saucepan. Bring to a boil. Cook for 5 minutes, stirring constantly; remove from heat. Stir in baking soda. Pour over popped popcorn in large bowl, tossing to coat. Spread on buttered baking sheets. Bake at 250 degrees for 1 hour, stirring occasionally; cool. Break apart and store in airtight container.
Approx Per Serving: Cal 193; Prot 1 g; Carbo 31 g; Fiber 1 g; T Fat 8 g; 36% Calories from Fat; Chol 0 mg; Sod 119 mg.

Linda K. Gehl, Orleans County HFH, Albion, NY

Party Mix Popcorn

Yield: 8 servings

6 tablespoons melted
   butter
1 tablespoon
   Worcestershire sauce
1 teaspoon seasoned
   salt
1/2 teaspoon garlic
   powder
1 quart unseasoned
   popped popcorn

1 1/2 cups chow mein
   noodles
1 1/2 cups miniature
   shredded wheat
1 cup pecan halves
1 teaspoon minced
   basil

▪ Mix butter, Worcestershire sauce, seasoned salt and garlic powder in small bowl. Pour over mixture of popcorn, chow mein noodles, shredded wheat and pecan halves, tossing to coat. Sprinkle with basil, tossing to mix. Spread on baking sheet. Bake at 250 degrees for 45 minutes, stirring every 15 minutes. Store in airtight container in refrigerator.
Approx Per Serving: Cal 253; Prot 4 g; Carbo 17 g; Fiber 3 g; T Fat 20 g; 69% Calories from Fat; Chol 24 mg; Sod 339 mg.

Elizabeth J. Richardson, HFH of Freeborn/Mower, Austin, MN

Peanut Butter Popcorn

Yield: 24 servings

This is good the next day, if you can keep people out of it! Good snack to take on hikes,
or to enjoy while watching a movie, after school or at a habitat work site.

1/2 cup sugar
1/4 cup light corn syrup
1/4 cup honey
1/2 cup chunky peanut
   butter

1/2 teaspoon vanilla
   extract
6 quarts popped
   popcorn

▪ Combine sugar, corn syrup and honey in small saucepan. Bring to a rolling boil, stirring often; remove from heat. Stir in peanut butter and vanilla. Pour over popcorn, tossing to coat.
Approx Per Serving: Cal 98; Prot 2 g; Carbo 17 g; Fiber 1 g; T Fat 3 g; 27% Calories from Fat; Chol 0 mg; Sod 28 mg.

Christine Rinne, HFH of San Joaquin County, Stockton, CA

Pecan Snackers

Yield: 6 servings

Addictive!!

1 egg white, stiffly beaten
3/4 cup packed brown sugar
2 tablespoons self-rising flour
1/2 teaspoon vanilla extract
11/2 cups pecan halves

- Mix beaten egg white with brown sugar, flour and vanilla gently in bowl. Fold in pecan halves. Place coated pecans 1 at a time on foil-lined baking sheet. Bake at 250 degrees for 30 minutes. Turn off oven; do not open door. Let stand in oven for 30 minutes. Store in airtight container.
  Approx Per Serving: Cal 320; Prot 3 g; Carbo 40 g; Fiber 2 g; T Fat 18 g; 49% Calories from Fat; Chol 0 mg; Sod 52 mg.

Jo Pendleton, Waco HFH, Waco, TX

Snack Balls

Yield: 20 servings

1/2 cup baking cocoa
1/2 cup honey
1/2 cup crunchy peanut butter
1/2 cup sunflower seed kernels
1/2 cup sesame seed
1/2 cup oats
1/2 cup flaked coconut

- Combine baking cocoa, honey, peanut butter, sunflower seed, sesame seed and oats in bowl; mix well. Shape into bite-sized balls. Roll in coconut. Store in airtight container in refrigerator. May substitute carob powder for baking cocoa.
  Approx Per Serving: Cal 128; Prot 5 g; Carbo 12 g; Fiber 2 g; T Fat 8 g; 54% Calories from Fat; Chol 0 mg; Sod 5 mg.

Mike Abts, Crawford County HFH, Leavenworth, IN

Apple Nectar

Yield: 20 servings

2 quarts apple juice, chilled
2 6-ounce cans frozen orange juice concentrate, thawed
2 tablespoons lemon juice
2 12-ounce cans apricot nectar, chilled

- Combine all ingredients in bowl; mix well. Serve over ice garnished with slices of lemon and orange.
  Approx Per Serving: Cal 93; Prot 1 g; Carbo 23 g; Fiber 1 g; T Fat <1 g; 2% Calories from Fat; Chol 0 mg; Sod 4 mg.

Claire Martindale, Habitat East, Bridgewater, VA

Celi's Instant Cappucino

Yield: 50 servings

This is available in the Religious Life Center of the Chaplain's Office for students to enjoy.

1 16-ounce package Nestle's Quik
1 cup instant coffee granules
2 cups confectioners' sugar
2 3-quart packages nonfat dry milk powder
1 8-ounce jar Amaretto-flavored non-dairy creamer

- Combine all ingredients in bowl; mix well. Use 1/4 cup mix with 1 cup hot water for cappucino. Store in airtight container.
  Approx Per Serving: Cal 163; Prot 12 g; Carbo 27 g; Fiber <1 g; T Fat 1 g; 8% Calories from Fat; Chol 6 mg; Sod 192 mg.

Celi Stoutamire, Roanoke College Campus Chapter
Salem, VA

Cranberry Sparkler

Yield: 10 servings

4 cups cranberry juice cocktail
1 6-ounce can frozen lemonade concentrate, thawed
1 6-ounce can frozen limeade concentrate, thawed
1/4 cup sugar
4 cups club soda

- Mix first 4 ingredients in bowl. Stir in club soda. Pour into ice-filled glasses.
  Approx Per Serving: Cal 140; Prot <1 g; Carbo 36 g; Fiber <1 g; T Fat <1 g; 1% Calories from Fat; Chol 0 mg; Sod 23 mg.

Patricia J. Wagner, Barry County HFH, Middleville, MI

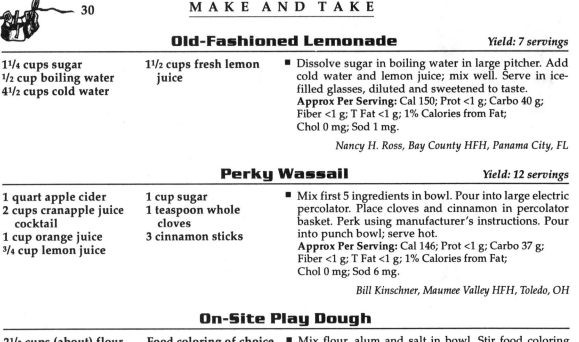
Old-Fashioned Lemonade

Yield: 7 servings

1¼ cups sugar
½ cup boiling water
4½ cups cold water

1½ cups fresh lemon
juice

■ Dissolve sugar in boiling water in large pitcher. Add cold water and lemon juice; mix well. Serve in ice-filled glasses, diluted and sweetened to taste.
Approx Per Serving: Cal 150; Prot <1 g; Carbo 40 g; Fiber <1 g; T Fat <1 g; 1% Calories from Fat; Chol 0 mg; Sod 1 mg.

Nancy H. Ross, Bay County HFH, Panama City, FL

Perky Wassail

Yield: 12 servings

1 quart apple cider
2 cups cranapple juice
cocktail
1 cup orange juice
¾ cup lemon juice

1 cup sugar
1 teaspoon whole
cloves
3 cinnamon sticks

■ Mix first 5 ingredients in bowl. Pour into large electric percolator. Place cloves and cinnamon in percolator basket. Perk using manufacturer's instructions. Pour into punch bowl; serve hot.
Approx Per Serving: Cal 146; Prot <1 g; Carbo 37 g; Fiber <1 g; T Fat <1 g; 1% Calories from Fat; Chol 0 mg; Sod 6 mg.

Bill Kinschner, Maumee Valley HFH, Toledo, OH

On-Site Play Dough

2½ cups (about) flour
1 tablespoon
powdered alum
½ cup salt

Food coloring of choice
3 tablespoons corn oil
2 cups boiling water

■ Mix flour, alum and salt in bowl. Stir food coloring and oil into boiling water in saucepan. Add to flour mixture; mix well, adding additional flour if needed for desired consistency. Knead until smooth. Store in ziplock bags in refrigerator for several weeks.

Mary Boyer, Black Hills Area HFH, Rapid City, SD

Recipe for Humanity

Yield: unlimited

This favorite recipe is enjoyed by all who participate and especially by this partner family.

- Take a family in need, knowing you'll help someone who wants to succeed.

- Mix that up with volunteers young and old, a pinch that adds all kinds of soul.

- Make sure you have people of all races, for without that this recipe would be tasteless.

- Then you add donations, tears of joy, togetherness, property, tools, faith and pride.

- Make sure you have all these ingredients right by your side.

- Add pounds and pounds of love, patience and a big smile.

- Then you stir it up and let it sit for a while.

- The most important ingredient, which is really first as well as last,

- Is thanks to the Lord for the future as well as the past.

- Stir slowly to make sure it's all blended.

- Don't give up until the project is ended.

Crystal Shepherd, Central HFH Partner Family
Cleveland, OH

APPETIZERS SOUP – SALADS

". . . I laid a foundation as an expert builder, and someone else is building on it. But each one should be careful how he builds. For no one can lay any foundation other than the one already laid, which is Jesus Christ."

I Corinthians 3:10

Apricot Brie en Croûte

Yield: 28 servings

1 package frozen puff
  pastry shells, thawed
1   2-pound round Brie
  cheese

2 tablespoons apricot
  preserves
1 egg yolk
1 tablespoon water

- Roll out pastry large enough to cover bottom and side of cheese. Place on buttered baking sheet; place cheese in center. Spread apricot preserves over top of cheese up to ¹/₂ inch from edge. Fold pastry up side of cheese. Trim remaining pastry to fit over top of cheese; seal edge. Make braid with excess pastry to cover seam. Brush with mixture of egg yolk and water. Bake at 400 degrees for 10 minutes. Reduce oven temperature to 325 degrees. Bake for 20 minutes longer or until golden brown. Let stand at room temperature for 2 hours before serving.

  Approx Per Serving: Cal 190; Prot 8 g; Carbo 8 g; Fiber <1 g; T Fat 14 g; 67% Calories from Fat; Chol 40 mg; Sod 287 mg.

Sallie Wakefield Baggett, HFH of Montgomery County
Clarksville, TN

Cream Cheese Burrito

Yield: 36 servings

16 ounces cream
  cheese, softened
¹/₄ cup chopped green
  chilies
¹/₂ cup chopped
  pimentos

¹/₂ cup chopped black
  olives
4 large flour tortillas

- Combine cream cheese, green chilies, chopped pimentos and olives in bowl; mix well. Spread over tortillas. Roll up to enclose filling. Chill in refrigerator. Cut into ¹/₄-inch slices.

  Approx Per Serving: Cal 68; Prot 1 g; Carbo 4 g; Fiber <1 g; T Fat 5 g; 69% Calories from Fat; Chol 14 mg; Sod 79 mg.

Jeanne Dodge, Morgan County HFH, Fort Morgan, CO

Buffalo-Style Chicken Wings

Yield: 15 servings

2¹/₂ pounds chicken
  wings
Garlic salt and pepper
  to taste

6 tablespoons Durkee
  Red Hot Sauce
¹/₂ cup butter, softened

- Rinse chicken wings and pat dry. Joint, discarding tips. Place on baking sheet; sprinkle with garlic salt and pepper. Bake at 425 degrees for 1 hour, turning once. Mix hot sauce and butter in small bowl. Dip chicken wings in sauce to coat completely. Place in slow cooker to serve; pour remaining sauce over wings. Heat on Low.

  Approx Per Serving: Cal 219; Prot 15 g; Carbo <1 g; Fiber 0 g; T Fat 17 g; 72% Calories from Fat; Chol 65 mg; Sod 123 mg.

Bev Bever, Morgan County HFH, Brush, CO

Tango Wings

Yield: 30 servings

5 pounds chicken
  wings
1 envelope onion soup
  mix
1   8-ounce bottle of
  Russian salad
  dressing

1   4-ounce jar apple
  jelly
1   8-ounce bottle of
  barbecue sauce
2 teaspoons Tabasco
  sauce

- Rinse chicken wings and pat dry. Disjoint chicken wings, discarding tips. Place in shallow roasting pan. Combine onion soup mix, salad dressing, jelly, barbecue sauce and Tabasco sauce in bowl; mix well. Pour over chicken wings, turning to coat. Roast at 350 degrees for 45 minutes.

  Approx Per Serving: Cal 218; Prot 15 g; Carbo 4 g; Fiber <1 g; T Fat 15 g; 63% Calories from Fat; Chol 53 mg; Sod 197 mg.

Adriana Mendes, Riner College HFH, Nashua, NH

Almond Fruited Cheese Ball

Yield: 16 servings

8 ounces cream cheese,
  softened
1/3 cup flaked coconut
1 teaspoon almond
  extract
1/3 cup raisins

1 8-ounce can crushed
   pineapple, drained
2 cups Almond
  Delight cereal,
  crushed

■ Combine cream cheese, coconut, almond extract,
raisins, pineapple and half the cereal in bowl; mix
well. Chill for 30 minutes. Shape into ball. Roll in
remaining cereal; place on serving plate.
Approx Per Serving: Cal 93; Prot 2 g; Carbo 10 g;
Fiber 1 g; T Fat 6 g; 54% Calories from Fat;
Chol 16 mg; Sod 76 mg.

Joy Martin, Albuquerque, NM

Shrimp-Cheese Balls

Yield: 16 servings

8 ounces cream cheese,
  softened
1 1/2 teaspoons dry
  mustard
1 teaspoon grated
  onion
1 teaspoon lemon juice

Cayenne pepper and
  salt to taste
1 4-ounce can tiny
   shrimp, drained
2/3 cup chopped
  walnuts

■ Beat cream cheese, mustard, onion, lemon juice,
cayenne pepper and salt in bowl until light and fluffy.
Fold in shrimp. Chill until firm. Shape into 1-inch
balls; roll in walnuts. Chill in refrigerator.
Approx Per Serving: Cal 92; Prot 3 g; Carbo 2 g;
Fiber <1 g; T Fat 8 g; 79% Calories from Fat;
Chol 28 mg; Sod 54 mg.

Norma P. Curtis, HFH of Wausau, Wausau, WI

Plains Special Cheese Ring

Yield: 8 servings

1 pound sharp
  Cheddar cheese,
  shredded
1 cup mayonnaise
1 small onion, grated

1 cup chopped pecans
Cayenne pepper and
  black pepper to taste
1 8-ounce jar
   strawberry preserves

■ Combine cheese, mayonnaise, onion, pecans, cayenne
pepper and black pepper in bowl; Mix well with
hands. Press into ring mold. Chill until firm. Unmold
onto serving plate; fill with preserves. Serve as
appetizer or as complement to main dish.
Approx Per Serving: Cal 606; Prot 16 g; Carbo 25 g;
Fiber 1 g; T Fat 51 g; 74% Calories from Fat;
Chol 76 mg; Sod 511 mg.

Jimmy and Rosalynn Carter, Plains, GA

Jimmy and Rosalynn Carter

*B*uilding a
Habitat house
transforms not
only one family,
it transforms a
whole community.

**Former First Lady
Rosalynn Carter**

Clams Casino

Yield: 18 servings

1/4 cup margarine
1 to 2 hot peppers, chopped
Mrs. Dash spicy seasoning to taste
8 ounces butter crackers, crushed
1 ounce sharp Cheddar cheese, chopped

1 egg, beaten
18 small clams, cleaned, opened, tops removed
3 slices bacon, cut into 1-inch pieces

■ Stir-fry peppers, spicy seasoning and cracker crumbs in margarine in skillet for 1 minute. Add cheese. Cook over low heat until cheese is melted; remove from heat. Whisk in egg. Place clams on baking sheet. Spoon mixture on top of clams; top with bacon. Bake at 350 degrees for 15 to 20 minutes or until bacon is crisp.
Approx Per Serving: Cal 108; Prot 3 g; Carbo 9 g; Fiber <1 g; T Fat 8 g; 59% Calories from Fat; Chol 17 mg; Sod 190 mg.

Kim Marzilli, Rehoboth, MA

Cheese and Crab Soufflé

Yield: 12 servings

1 6-ounce can crab meat, drained, flaked
10 ounces Cheddar cheese, shredded
1 tablespoon minced onion
1 cup mayonnaise

1 teaspoon Worcestershire sauce
3 drops of Tabasco sauce
1/2 teaspoon salt
1/2 teaspoon pepper
1/2 teaspoon sugar

■ Combine all ingredients in bowl; mix well. Spoon into baking dish. Garnish with paprika. Bake at 350 degrees for 20 minutes. Serve with assorted crackers.
Approx Per Serving: Cal 242; Prot 9 g; Carbo 1 g; Fiber <1 g; T Fat 23 g; 83% Calories from Fat; Chol 48 mg; Sod 391 mg.

Lorrayne P. Masher, Pemi-Valley Habitat, Campton, NH

Crab Paté

Yield: 25 servings

1 10-ounce can cream of mushroom soup
1 envelope unflavored gelatin
3 tablespoons cold water
3/4 cup mayonnaise

8 ounces cream cheese, softened
1 6-ounce can crab meat, drained, flaked
1 small onion, grated
1 cup finely chopped celery

■ Heat soup in medium saucepan over low heat; remove from heat. Dissolve gelatin in cold water. Stir into soup. Add mayonnaise, cream cheese, crab meat, onion and celery; mix well. Spoon into greased 4-cup mold. Chill for 3 hours or until firm. Unmold onto serving plate; serve with crackers or party bread.
Approx Per Serving: Cal 101; Prot 3 g; Carbo 2 g; Fiber <1 g; T Fat 9 g; 83% Calories from Fat; Chol 20 mg; Sod 183 mg.

Gail Bullington, Albany Area HFH, Albany, GA

Crab Puffs

Yield: 12 servings

1 5-ounce jar Old English cheese
1/2 cup margarine, softened
1 6-ounce can crab meat, drained, flaked

11/2 tablespoons mayonnaise
Garlic powder to taste
6 English muffins, split

■ Combine first 5 ingredients in bowl; mix well. Spread over English muffin halves; place on baking sheet. Bake at 450 degrees for 8 to 10 minutes or until brown.
Approx Per Serving: Cal 202; Prot 7 g; Carbo 14 g; Fiber 1 g; T Fat 13 g; 57% Calories from Fat; Chol 22 mg; Sod 474 mg.

Alberta Julian, HFH of Evansville, Evansville, IN

Dandelion Wine

Yield: 32 servings

1 quart dandelion blossoms
31/2 pounds sugar

1 lemon, sliced
1 gallon boiling water
1 cake yeast

■ Combine dandelion blossoms, sugar and lemon slices in stone crock. Pour in boiling water, stirring until sugar is dissolved. Dissolve yeast in a small amount of warm water; add to mixture. Let stand for 4 to 5 days, stirring twice each day. Pour into sterilized wine bottles. Leave bottles open so foam can escape; refill from time to time from another bottle.
Nutritional information for this recipe is not available.

Roger R. Schwartz, Northern Kentucky HFH, Ft. Wright, KY

Yield: 12 servings

Caramel Apple Dip

8 ounces cream cheese, softened
3/4 cup packed dark brown sugar

1/4 cup sugar
Vanilla extract to taste
2 tablespoons chopped peanuts

■ Beat cream cheese, brown sugar and sugar in mixer bowl until light and fluffy. Stir in vanilla and peanuts; spoon into serving bowl. Serve with sliced fresh apples. May use all brown sugar and omit peanuts.
Approx Per Serving: Cal 160; Prot 2 g; Carbo 22 g; Fiber <1 g; T Fat 7 g; 40% Calories from Fat; Chol 21 mg; Sod 64 mg.

Candy Ockert, North Bradley Church of God, Coleman, MI
Nancy Carlsrud, Fergus Falls Area HFH, Flandreau, SD

Yield: 80 servings

Fruit Dip

1 13-ounce jar marshmallow creme
8 ounces cream cheese, softened

8 ounces whipped topping

■ Combine marshmallow creme, cream cheese and whipped topping in bowl; mix well. Serve dip with fresh fruit.
Approx Per Serving: Cal 34; Prot <1 g; Carbo 4 g; Fiber 0 g; T Fat 2 g; 45% Calories from Fat; Chol 3 mg; Sod 12 mg.

Kenna Smith-Dunn, Ashland-Ironton HFH, Ashland, KY

Yield: 24 servings

Deviled Egg-Chick

12 hard-boiled eggs
1 tablespoon mayonnaise
1 tablespoon mustard

1 teaspoon salt
1 tablespoon chili powder

■ Slice eggs lengthwise. Remove yolks carefully; reserve whites. Combine yolks, mayonnaise, mustard and salt in small bowl; mix well. Spoon into reserved egg whites; sprinkle with chili powder. Arrange deviled eggs on serving tray.
Approx Per Serving: Cal 45; Prot 3 g; Carbo 1 g; Fiber <1 g; T Fat 3 g; 67% Calories from Fat; Chol 107 mg; Sod 136 mg.

Rosa Chapa, HFH of Wichita Falls, Wichita Falls, TX

Yield: 8 servings

Avocadomole

1 tomato, finely chopped
1 onion, finely chopped

1/2 teaspoon lemon juice
1 avocado, mashed

■ Combine tomato, onion and lemon juice in small bowl; stir in mashed avocado. Serve with chips.
Approx Per Serving: Cal 50; Prot 1 g; Carbo 4 g; Fiber 3 g; T Fat 4 g; 64% Calories from Fat; Chol 0 mg; Sod 4 mg.

Diana Ramos, HFH of Wichita Falls, Wichita Falls, TX

Yield: 20 servings

Guacamole Supreme

2 ripe avocados, peeled
2 tablespoons lemon juice
1/2 teaspoon salt
1/4 teaspoon pepper
1 cup sour cream
1/2 cup mayonnaise
1 envelope taco seasoning mix

2 10-ounce cans bean dip
1 cup chopped green onions
2 cups chopped tomatoes
2 4-ounce cans chopped black olives
1/2 cup shredded sharp Cheddar cheese

■ Mash avocados with lemon juice, salt and pepper in bowl; set aside. Mix sour cream, mayonnaise and taco seasoning mix in medium bowl. Layer bean dip, avocado mixture, sour cream mixture, onions, tomatoes, olives and cheese on 12-inch round platter. Serve with tortilla chips.
Approx Per Serving: Cal 173; Prot 4 g; Carbo 8 g; Fiber 3 g; T Fat 15 g; 74% Calories from Fat; Chol 12 mg; Sod 537 mg.

Janet Cornell, Westchester County HFH, Valhalla, NY

Hot Cheesy Bean Dip

Yield: 12 servings

8 ounces cream cheese, softened
1 cup sour cream
1 16-ounce can refried beans
1/2 envelope enchilada seasoning mix

20 drops of hot pepper sauce
4 ounces Cheddar cheese, shredded
4 ounces Monterey Jack cheese, shredded

■ Combine cream cheese, sour cream, refried beans, enchilada seasoning mix and hot pepper sauce in bowl; mix well. Spoon into two 8-inch round pie plates. Top with mixture of Cheddar and Monterey Jack cheeses. Bake at 350 degrees for 15 to 20 minutes or until cheese is melted. Serve with tortilla chips.
Approx Per Serving: Cal 228; Prot 9 g; Carbo 10 g; Fiber 3 g; T Fat 17 g; 67% Calories from Fat; Chol 48 mg; Sod 496 mg.

Dolores Le, HFH of Green County, Monroe, WI

Patti's Bean Dip

Yield: 15 servings

1 cup cooked pinto beans
1 envelope chili seasoning mix
8 ounces cream cheese, softened
1 cup sour cream
Tabasco sauce to taste

Garlic to taste
1/2 cup shredded Cheddar cheese
2 tomatoes, chopped
1 4-ounce can chopped black olives, drained

■ Combine beans, seasoning mix, cream cheese, sour cream, Tabasco sauce and garlic in blender container. Process until smooth. Spoon into small baking dish. Top with cheese, tomatoes and olives. Bake at 350 degrees for 20 minutes or until bubbly.
Approx Per Serving: Cal 134; Prot 4 g; Carbo 5 g; Fiber 2 g; T Fat 12 g; 74% Calories from Fat; Chol 27 mg; Sod 146 mg.

Frances E. Sosadeeter, Northern Straits HFH, St. Ignace, MI

Crab Dip

Yield: 12 servings

8 ounces cream cheese, softened
3/4 cup mayonnaise
2 tablespoons minced onion
1/8 teaspoon seasoned salt
1 teaspoon horseradish

Lemon juice to taste
Worcestershire sauce to taste
1 6-ounce can crab meat, drained
1/2 cup slivered almonds

■ Combine first 7 ingredients in bowl; mix well. Fold in crab meat gently. Spoon into casserole. Sprinkle with almonds. Bake at 325 degrees for 25 minutes. Serve warm with crackers.
Approx Per Serving: Cal 212; Prot 6 g; Carbo 2 g; Fiber 1 g; T Fat 21 g; 86% Calories from Fat; Chol 41 mg; Sod 196 mg.

Jennifer Johnson, Lima Area HFH, Lima, OH

Creamy Nacho-Chili Dip

Yield: 16 servings

1 15-ounce can chili without beans
1 10-ounce can nacho cheese soup

8 ounces cream cheese, softened
1 12-ounce package corn chips

■ Combine chili, soup and cream cheese in saucepan. Cook over low heat until heated through, stirring frequently. Serve in slow cooker or chafing dish.
Approx Per Serving: Cal 230; Prot 5 g; Carbo 15 g; Fiber 1 g; T Fat 17 g; 65% Calories from Fat; Chol 18 mg; Sod 506 mg.

Maxine Wood, Sisters HFH, Sisters, OR

Mexican Dip

Yield: 15 servings

16 ounces cream cheese, softened
1 cup mayonnaise
1 8-ounce jar hot taco sauce
1/2 head lettuce, shredded
1 bunch green onions, chopped

1 4-ounce can chopped black olives, drained
2 to 3 tomatoes, chopped
12 ounces Cheddar cheese, shredded
1 8-ounce jar mild taco sauce

■ Beat cream cheese and mayonnaise in bowl until smooth. Spoon into 9x13-inch dish; spread with hot taco sauce. Layer with lettuce, green onions, olives, tomatoes and cheese 1/2 at a time until all ingredients are used. Top with mild taco sauce. Chill for 8 to 12 hours. Serve with corn chips or taco chips.
Approx Per Serving: Cal 343; Prot 9 g; Carbo 7 g; Fiber 1 g; T Fat 33 g; 82% Calories from Fat; Chol 66 mg; Sod 615 mg.

Cathy Sheffield, Durham County HFH, Durham, NC

Mexican Layered Dip

Yield: 16 servings

1 16-ounce can refried beans
3 to 4 ripe avocados, mashed
1 cup sour cream
1 envelope taco seasoning mix
1 cup mayonnaise
1 6-ounce can chopped black olives, drained
1 tomato, chopped
16 ounces Cheddar cheese, shredded

■ Spread refried beans in 9x13-inch dish; top with avocados. Mix sour cream, taco seasoning mix and mayonnaise in bowl. Spread over avocados. Top with olives, chopped tomato and shredded cheese. Serve with tortilla chips.
Approx Per Serving: Cal 384; Prot 11 g; Carbo 13 g; Fiber 8 g; T Fat 34 g; 76% Calories from Fat; Chol 44 mg; Sod 686 mg.

Sharon Harwood, Milton-Freewater, OR

Salsa Cream Dip

Yield: 6 servings

This is a favorite for special occasions at home or around the office.

8 ounces cream cheese
3/4 to 1 cup thick medium salsa sauce
3/4 cup shredded Cheddar cheese

■ Press cream cheese evenly onto platter. Spread salsa sauce over top. Sprinkle with Cheddar cheese. Microwave on medium-high for 2 1/2 minutes or until center is warm.
Approx Per Serving: Cal 202; Prot 6 g; Carbo 4 g; Fiber 0 g; T Fat 18 g; 80% Calories from Fat; Chol 56 mg; Sod 436 mg.

Linda Fuller, HFH International, Americus, GA

Yum-Yum Dip

Yield: 68 servings

This dip can be served with chips or fresh vegetables, as dressing on green salad, or as topping for baked potatoes. May store for several weeks in refrigerator.

4 cups chilled mayonnaise
4 cups buttermilk
2 tablespoons minced onion
5 tablespoons dried parsley
1 teaspoon MSG
2 teaspoons garlic powder

■ Combine mayonnaise, buttermilk, onion, parsley, MSG and garlic powder in large bowl; mix well. Chill for 1 hour before serving.
Approx Per Serving: Cal 99; Prot 1 g; Carbo 1 g; Fiber <1 g; T Fat 10 g; 93% Calories from Fat; Chol 8 mg; Sod 152 mg.

Donna L. Golden, Southeast Region HFH, Leesburg, GA

Three-Cheese Fondue

Yield: 32 servings

This is good to make the day before and store in the refrigerator. Warm over low heat and pour into the fondue pot.

1/3 cup finely chopped onion
3 tablespoons butter
3 tablespoons flour
1 1/2 cups milk
4 cups shredded sharp Cheddar cheese
8 ounces cream cheese, softened
3 ounces bleu cheese, crumbled
3 drops of red pepper sauce

■ Sauté onion in butter in medium saucepan for 5 minutes or until tender. Stir in flour. Cook over medium heat for 3 minutes. Stir in milk. Bring to a boil. Cook until thickened, stirring constantly; reduce heat to low. Add cheeses and pepper sauce. Cook over very low heat until cheeses are melted, stirring constantly. Pour into fondue pot. Serve with assorted fresh vegetables and French bread cubes.
Approx Per Serving: Cal 111; Prot 5 g; Carbo 2 g; Fiber <1 g; T Fat 9 g; 76% Calories from Fat; Chol 29 mg; Sod 160 mg.

Janice Rinne, HFH of San Joaquin County, Stockton, CA

I will show you what he is like who comes to me and hears my words and puts them into practice. He is like a man building a house, who dug down deep and laid the foundation on rock. When a flood came, the torrent struck that house but could not shake it, because it was well built.

Luke 6:47-48

Egg Rolls
Yield: 60 servings

2 pounds ground pork
3 tablespoons salt
2 tablespoons black
  pepper
1 tablespoon MSG
14 ounces bean thread
  vermicelli, cooked
16 ounces onions,
  chopped
1 head cabbage, finely
  chopped
8 ounces mushrooms,
  chopped
2 pounds bean sprouts,
  finely chopped

1 bunch green onions,
  chopped
12 eggs, beaten
60 egg roll wrappers
4 egg yolks, beaten
Oil for deep frying
2 cups sugar
3 cups water
6 ounces ground
  peanuts
1 teaspoon salt
Chili pepper to taste

- Brown ground pork in skillet, stirring until crumbly. Season with 3 tablespoons salt, pepper and MSG. Add cooked vermicelli, onions, cabbage, mushrooms, bean sprouts and green onions; mix well. Sauté until heated through, stirring constantly; remove from heat. Stir in eggs. Spoon a small amount of filling in center of lower part of each egg roll wrapper. Follow direction on package for rolling. Deep-fry in hot oil in wok until golden brown; drain. Heat sugar in saucepan until caramelized. Stir in water, peanuts, salt and chili pepper, mixing well. Spoon into serving bowl; dip egg rolls into sauce.

Approx Per Serving: Cal 195; Prot 10 g; Carbo 26 g; Fiber 1 g; T Fat 6 g; 27% Calories from Fat; Chol 68 mg; Sod 733 mg.

Jai Lor, Twin Cities HFH Homeowner, St. Paul, MN

New Jersey Shore Hot Crab Fondue
Yield: 20 servings

A favorite of my family on the east coast, this recipe is one which I brought with me to Colorado when I came to work here as a VISTA volunteer for Habitat for Humanity.

1 5-ounce jar Cheez
  Whiz
8 ounces cream cheese,
  softened
1 8-ounce package
  crab meat, drained,
  flaked
1/4 cup light cream

1/2 teaspoon
  Worcestershire sauce
1/4 teaspoon garlic salt
Cayenne pepper to
  taste
2 tablespoons cooking
  sherry

- Combine Cheez Whiz and cream cheese in saucepan. Cook over medium heat until cheeses are melted, stirring often. Add remaining ingredients. Cook until smooth, stirring constantly. Serve in fondue pot with toasted cubed French or Italian bread.

Approx Per Serving: Cal 77; Prot 4 g; Carbo 1 g; Fiber 0 g; T Fat 6 g; 73% Calories from Fat; Chol 30 mg; Sod 182 mg.

Corinne Le Baron, Morgan County HFH, Fort Morgan, CO

Stuffed Mushrooms
Yield: 25 servings

25 small mushrooms
2 to 3 tablespoons
  melted butter
3 ounces cream cheese,
  softened

1/2 cup grated
  Parmesan cheese
2 tablespoons milk
25 almond slices

- Remove stems from mushrooms and discard. Brush caps with melted butter inside and out. Beat cream cheese with Parmesan cheese and milk in mixer bowl until light and fluffy. Fill caps with mixture; top each mushroom with almond slice. Place on buttered baking sheet. Bake at 350 degrees for 15 minutes or until light brown.

Approx Per Serving: Cal 36; Prot 1 g; Carbo 1 g; Fiber <1 g; T Fat 3 g; 77% Calories from Fat; Chol 9 mg; Sod 53 mg.

Rusleen Maurice, Bryan-College Station HFH, Bryan, TX

Crab-Stuffed Mushroom Caps
Yield: 15 servings

1 7-ounce can crab
  meat, drained, flaked
1/4 cup oil
1 egg, beaten
2 tablespoons
  mayonnaise-type
  salad dressing
2 tablespoons finely
  chopped onion

2 teaspoons lemon juice
2 cups fine bread
  crumbs
2 tablespoons melted
  butter
1 pound large
  mushrooms, stems
  removed

- Combine crab meat, oil, egg, salad dressing, onion, lemon juice, bread crumbs and butter in bowl; mix well. Stuff mushroom caps with mixture. Place on baking sheet. Bake at 375 degrees for 15 minutes.

Approx Per Serving: Cal 130; Prot 5 g; Carbo 12 g; Fiber 1 g; T Fat 7 g; 49% Calories from Fat; Chol 31 mg; Sod 175 mg.

Stephanie Grove, HFH of Butler County, Mars, PA

Dilly Onion

Yield: 20 servings

1 large mild onion,
  thinly sliced
1/3 cup sugar
2 teaspoons salt
1 teaspoon dillseed

1/2 cup white vinegar
1/4 cup water
20 slices party rye
  bread

- Arrange onion slices in dish. Combine sugar, salt, dillseed, vinegar and water in saucepan. Bring to a boil, stirring often. Pour over onion. Chill, covered, for 5 hours; drain. Chop onion and spoon 1 tablespoon mixture on each party rye bread slice. May use sliced in marinade as side dish for barbecue.

Approx Per Serving: Cal 34; Prot 1 g; Carbo 7 g; Fiber 1 g; T Fat <1 g; 7% Calories from Fat; Chol 0 mg; Sod 260 mg.

Dianne Kinzer, Jubilee HFH, Jacksonville, IL

Pico de Gallo

Yield: 32 servings

2 jalapeño peppers,
  finely chopped
2 yellow chili peppers,
  finely chopped
1 small Bermuda
  onion, finely
  chopped
1 small yellow onion,
  finely chopped

3 tomatoes, finely
  chopped
1/2 teaspoon garlic
  powder
1/2 teaspoon salt
1 tablespoon chopped
  cilantro
Juice of 2 limes

- Combine jalapeño peppers, chili peppers, onions and tomatoes in bowl; mix well. Stir in garlic powder, salt, cilantro and lime juice. Chill, covered, in refrigerator until serving time.

Approx Per Serving: Cal 7; Prot <1 g; Carbo 2 g; Fiber <1 g; T Fat <1 g; 6% Calories from Fat; Chol 0 mg; Sod 35 mg.

Anthony Mendoza, Las Vegas, New Mexico HFH
Las Vegas, NM

Salsa Cheesecake

Yield: 15 servings

2 tablespoons melted
  margarine
1/2 cup bread crumbs
12 ounces cream
  cheese, softened
4 ounces Roquefort
  cheese, softened

1 cup sour cream
2 tablespoons flour
1 cup grated Parmesan
  cheese
1/2 cup salsa
4 eggs, beaten

- Brush side and bottom of 9-inch springform pan with melted margarine. Sprinkle with half the bread crumbs. Combine cream cheese, Roquefort cheese, sour cream, flour, Parmesan cheese and half the salsa in bowl; mix well. Beat in eggs. Spoon into prepared pan; sprinkle with remaining bread crumbs. Bake at 350 degrees for 1 1/4 hours. Cool in oven with door partially open for 1 hour. Drizzle with remaining salsa; serve warm.

Approx Per Serving: Cal 219; Prot 8 g; Carbo 6 g; Fiber <1 g; T Fat 18 g; 75% Calories from Fat; Chol 100 mg; Sod 421 mg.

Chere Anderson, HFH of Northern Fox Valley
Sleepy Hollow, IL

California Pizelles

Yield: 16 servings

1/2 cup sour cream
1/2 cup softened cream
  cheese
1/4 cup chopped green
  onions
4 flour tortillas
1/2 cup chopped
  artichokes, drained
1/2 cup chopped
  mushrooms
1/2 cup chopped
  tomatoes

1/2 cup chopped
  avocado
1 cup chopped cooked
  chicken
1/2 cup shredded
  Monterey Jack
  cheese
1/2 cup shredded Swiss
  cheese

- Beat sour cream and cream cheese in bowl until smooth. Fold in green onions. Spread over tortillas. Top each tortilla with equal portion of artichokes, mushrooms, tomatoes, avocado, chicken and cheeses. Place on baking sheet. Bake at 325 degrees for 10 to 15 minutes or until cheese melts. Cut each tortilla into 4 wedges; serve hot. May substitute chopped cooked shrimp for chicken.

Approx Per Serving: Cal 123; Prot 6 g; Carbo 7 g; Fiber 2 g; T Fat 8 g; 57% Calories from Fat; Chol 26 mg; Sod 103 mg.

Diane W. Kirkpatrick, HFH of Metro Louisville
Louisville, KY

Vegetable Pizza

Yield: 15 servings

1 8-count can crescent rolls
1/2 cup mayonnaise
1/2 envelope ranch dressing mix
8 ounces cream cheese, softened

1 cup chopped carrots
1 cup chopped broccoli
1 cup chopped cauliflower

- Spread crescent roll dough on baking sheet, sealing perforations. Bake at 350 degrees using package directions; cool. Combine mayonnaise, ranch dressing mix and cream cheese in bowl; mix well. Spread over cooled crust. Top with carrots, broccoli and cauliflower. Slice into serving pieces.

Approx Per Serving: Cal 166; Prot 2 g; Carbo 8 g; Fiber 1 g; T Fat 14 g; 75% Calories from Fat; Chol 21 mg; Sod 278 mg.

Lori Gill, Northern Straits HFH, St. Ignace, MI

Dilly Vegetable Pizza

Yield: 15 servings

2 8-count cans crescent rolls
16 ounces cream cheese, softened
1 cup mayonnaise-type salad dressing
1 1/2 teaspoons dillweed
1 1/2 teaspoons onion salt
1/2 cup chopped carrot
1/2 cup chopped green bell pepper
1/2 cup sliced celery

1/4 cup sliced black olives
1/4 cup sliced green olives
1/4 cup sliced radishes
1/2 cup sliced mushrooms
1/2 cup chopped broccoli
1/2 cup chopped cauliflower
1 cup shredded Cheddar cheese

- Spread both cans of crescent rolls on baking pan, sealing perforations. Bake at 400 degrees for 10 minutes or until golden brown; cool. Mix cream cheese, salad dressing, dillweed and onion salt in bowl; spread over cooled crust. Sprinkle with carrot, green pepper, celery, olives, radishes, mushrooms, broccoli and cauliflower; top with cheese. Cut into serving pieces.

Approx Per Serving: Cal 317; Prot 6 g; Carbo 18 g; Fiber 1 g; T Fat 25 g; 70% Calories from Fat; Chol 45 mg; Sod 747 mg.

Charlotte Rhoades, Habitat Gypsy, Middleville, MI

Saganaki

Yield: 4 servings

8 ounces Kefalotiri cheese, sliced 1/4-inch thick
1 tablespoon flour

1 to 2 tablespoons olive oil
1 ounce brandy
Juice of 1/2 lemon

- Dust cheese slices with flour. Heat oil in skillet over medium-high heat. Fry cheese slices on each side in hot oil until golden brown; remove from heat. Pour brandy over cheese and ignite. Squeeze lemon juice over cheese to extinguish flames. Serve immediately. Kefalotiri cheese does not melt when properly prepared. There is no good substitute for it to use in this recipe.

Approx Per Serving: Cal 235; Prot 9 g; Carbo 7 g; Fiber <1 g; T Fat 19 g; 73% Calories from Fat; Chol 50 mg; Sod 631 mg.

Dan Bronk, HFH of Wausau, Wausau, WI

Spinach-Cheese Squares

Yield: 36 servings

1/3 cup melted butter
3 eggs, beaten
1 cup flour
1 cup milk
1 teaspoon salt
1 teaspoon baking powder

16 ounces Monterey Jack cheese, shredded
3 cups drained, thawed chopped frozen spinach leaves

- Coat 9x13-inch baking dish with melted butter. Beat eggs, flour, milk, salt and baking powder in bowl. Stir in cheese and spinach. Spoon mixture into prepared dish. Bake at 350 degrees for 35 to 45 minutes or until edges are slightly brown; cool. Cut into small squares to serve.

Approx Per Serving: Cal 90; Prot 5 g; Carbo 4 g; Fiber 1 g; T Fat 6 g; 62% Calories from Fat; Chol 35 mg; Sod 172 mg.

Shirley Kelel, Northern Straits HFH, St. Ignace, MI

Salmon Spread

Yield: 15 servings

1   7-ounce can red
salmon, drained,
flaked
8 ounces cream cheese,
softened
1 tablespoon lemon
juice

1 teaspoon prepared
horseradish
1/2 teaspoon liquid
smoke
Salt and pepper to taste

■ Combine salmon, cream cheese, lemon juice, horse-radish, liquid smoke, salt and pepper in bowl; mix well. Shape into ball. Chill, covered, overnight. Serve with crackers.
Approx Per Serving: Cal 72; Prot 4 g; Carbo 1 g; Fiber <1 g; T Fat 6 g; 76% Calories from Fat; Chol 23 mg; Sod 118 mg.

Linda Richards, Southwest Iowa HFH, Shenandoah, IA

Hot Shrimp Spread

Yield: 16 servings

8 ounces cream cheese,
softened
1/4 cup mayonnaise
1/4 cup chopped onion
1   8-ounce can tiny
shrimp, drained,
chopped

2 hard-boiled eggs,
finely chopped

■ Beat cream cheese and mayonnaise in bowl until smooth. Fold in onion. Spread half the mixture in 8-inch round baking dish. Top with shrimp and half the eggs. Cover with remaining cheese mixture and sprinkle with remaining egg. Bake at 325 degrees for 45 to 60 minutes or until firm. Serve with crackers.
Approx Per Serving: Cal 102; Prot 5 g; Carbo 1 g; Fiber <1 g; T Fat 9 g; 76% Calories from Fat; Chol 69 mg; Sod 94 mg.

Joanne Vosmek, HFH of Wausau, Wausau, WI

Vietnamese Spring Rolls

Yield: 20 servings

1   2-ounce package
green bean thread
vermicelli
1/2 teaspoon sesame oil
1 pound ground beef
1 teaspoon hoisen
sauce
1/2 teaspoon
confectioners' sugar
1/2 teaspoon sesame oil

3 tablespoons
applesauce
5 leaf lettuce leaves,
cut into 1/2-inch strips
1   14-ounce package
rice sheets (Lumpia
paper or Bánh Tráng)
40   8-inch long pieces
of chives or onion
grass

■ Cook vermicelli in boiling water for 60 to 80 seconds; drain and set aside. Brush 1/2 teaspoon oil in 8x10-inch baking pan. Pack ground beef firmly in pan. Bake at 350 degrees for 20 minutes. Slice into 1/2-inch strips. Combine hoisen sauce, confectioners' sugar, 1/2 teaspoon sesame oil and applesauce in small bowl; mix well. Brush lettuce strips with mixture using pastry brush. Plunge rice sheets 1 at a time into pan of hot water; place on flat surface. Layer each sheet with lettuce, ground beef strips, vermicelli and chives; roll up to enclose filling. Place on serving plate. May substitute ground pork, chicken or shrimp for ground beef, black bean-garlic sauce for hoisen sauce and plum sauce for applesauce.
Approx Per Serving: Cal 126; Prot 6 g; Carbo 17 g; Fiber <1 g; T Fat 4 g; 27% Calories from Fat; Chol 15 mg; Sod 16 mg.

Herbert C. Mortz, Benton HFH, Corvallis, OR

Beef Sticks

Yield: 20 servings

5 pounds ground beef
5 teaspoons Tender-
Quick salt
2 teaspoons liquid
smoke
21/2 teaspoons mustard
seed

21/2 teaspoons coarse
pepper
21/2 teaspoons garlic
salt

■ Combine ground beef, salt, liquid smoke, mustard seed, pepper and garlic salt in bowl; mix well. Chill, covered, for 3 days, kneading mixture once each day. Shape into 5 rolls. Place on rack in broiler pan. Bake at 150 degrees for 8 hours. Cool; store, wrapped in plastic wrap, in refrigerator. Serve, sliced, with crackers.
Approx Per Serving: Cal 231; Prot 21 g; Carbo <1 g; Fiber 0 g; T Fat 16 g; 63% Calories from Fat; Chol 74 mg; Sod 854 mg.

Berniece Haverstock, Crawford County HFH, Marengo, IN

Avocado Soup

Yield: 6 servings

1 tomato, peeled,
    seeded and chopped
1 tablespoon minced
    onion
4 cups chicken broth
1/2 cup whipping cream

1 teaspoon lemon juice
2 large ripe avocados,
    peeled, mashed
1/4 cup dry sherry
Salt and pepper to taste
1 banana, thinly sliced

■ Process tomato, onion, chicken broth, cream and lemon juice in blender until puréed. Pour into saucepan. Simmer for several minutes. Stir in mashed avocados, sherry, salt and pepper. Cook over low heat until heated through; do not boil. Serve hot or cold with banana slices floating on top.
Approx Per Serving: Cal 237; Prot 6 g; Carbo 12 g; Fiber 7 g; T Fat 19 g; 71% Calories from Fat; Chol 28 mg; Sod 535 mg.

Anna Marie Palmer, Fort Bend HFH, Sugarland, TX

Ham and Bean Soup

Yield: 10 servings

Our church school class prepares a meal for the Community Soup Kitchen the 3rd Saturday of March. We serve this soup along with corn bread, fruit gelatin and cookies.

2 pounds dried navy
    beans
3 to 4 quarts water
2 pounds smoked
    turkey ham, cubed
2 onions, chopped

4 carrots, chopped
1   32-ounce can
    vegetable juice
    cocktail
Salt to taste

■ Soak beans in water overnight; drain and rinse. Place in 6-quart kettle with 2 to 3 quarts water. Add turkey, onions and carrots. Simmer for 1 1/2 hours or until beans are tender, adding more water as needed. Stir in vegetable juice cocktail. Simmer for 30 minutes longer. Season with salt.
Approx Per Serving: Cal 462; Prot 38 g; Carbo 67 g; Fiber 4 g; T Fat 6 g; 12% Calories from Fat; Chol 51 mg; Sod 1225 mg.

Thelma M. Battershell, Painesville Area HFH, Painesville, OH

Super Bean Soup

Yield: 4 servings

1 1/2 cups mixed dried
    beans
2 ounces ham, cut into
    1/2-inch cubes
1/2 onion, chopped
1   16-ounce can
    tomatoes
1   8-ounce can tomato
    sauce

1 clove of garlic,
    chopped
1/4 teaspoon red pepper
1/2 teaspoon chili
    powder
1 tablespoon lemon
    juice
1/2 teaspoon sugar
Salt and pepper to taste

■ Rinse beans in cold water; place in 3-quart saucepan. Cover with boiling water to 1 inch above beans. Soak for 4 hours; drain. Cover with water to 1 inch above beans. Cook over medium heat until beans begin to simmer; reduce heat slightly. Add ham. Simmer for 3 hours, stirring occasionally. Add remaining ingredients. Simmer for 30 minutes longer. Serve with toasted brown bread and green salad.
Approx Per Serving: Cal 323; Prot 22 g; Carbo 57 g; Fiber 11 g; T Fat 2 g; 5% Calories from Fat; Chol 8 mg; Sod 729 mg.

Lucia H. Glenn, Mid-Yellowstone Valley HFH, Billings, MT

Billi Bi

Yield: 4 servings

2 pounds mussels,
    scrubbed
2 shallots, coarsely
    chopped
2 small onions, cut
    into quarters
Salt, freshly ground
    black pepper and
    cayenne pepper to
    taste

2 sprigs of parsley
1 cup dry white wine
2 tablespoons butter
1/2 bay leaf
1/2 teaspoon thyme
2 cups whipping cream
1 egg yolk, slightly
    beaten

■ Combine first 11 ingredients in large kettle; cover. Bring to a boil; reduce heat. Simmer for 5 to 10 minutes or until mussels open; remove mussels to serving bowl. Strain liquid through double thickness of cheesecloth into saucepan. Bring to a boil. Stir in cream. Bring to a boil, stirring constantly; remove from heat. Whisk in egg yolk. Simmer until thickened, stirring constantly; do not boil. Serve hot or cold with individual servings of mussels.
Approx Per Serving: Cal 879; Prot 48 g; Carbo 28 g; Fiber 1 g; T Fat 60 g; 64% Calories from Fat; Chol 334 mg; Sod 771 mg.

Margaret Mahoney, HFH of Oshkosh, Oshkosh, WI

Broccoli, Potato and Cheese Soup

Yield: 8 servings

4 cups water
1 cup chopped celery
1 cup chopped onion
2 chicken bouillon
  cubes
2 beef bouillon cubes
Flowerets of 1 bunch
  broccoli

2 10-ounce cans
  cream of chicken
  soup
16 ounces Velveeta
  cheese, cubed
4 to 5 cooked cubed
  potatoes

■ Combine water, celery, onion, bouillon cubes and broccoli in saucepan. Bring to a boil. Cook for 20 minutes, stirring occasionally. Stir in soup, Velveeta cheese and potatoes. Cook over low heat for 20 minutes or until potatoes are tender and cheese is melted, stirring occasionally.

Approx Per Serving: Cal 375; Prot 18 g; Carbo 28 g; Fiber 3 g; T Fat 22 g; 52% Calories from Fat; Chol 60 mg; Sod 1902 mg.

Judy Speakman, Jubilee HFH, Jacksonville, IL

Cabbage Soup

Yield: 8 servings

2 pounds ground beef
1 onion, chopped
2 15-ounce cans
  stewed tomatoes
1 teaspoon onion
  powder
1 teaspoon garlic
  powder

¹/₂ teaspoon pepper
2 teaspoons salt
2¹/₂ to 3¹/₂ pounds
  cabbage, sliced
1 32-ounce can
  vegetable juice
  cocktail

■ Brown ground beef and onion in skillet, stirring until crumbly; drain. Combine with tomatoes, onion powder, garlic powder, pepper, salt, cabbage and vegetable juice cocktail in large saucepan. Simmer for 2 hours, stirring occasionally.

Approx Per Serving: Cal 337; Prot 25 g; Carbo 26 g; Fiber 6 g; T Fat 17 g; 42% Calories from Fat; Chol 74 mg; Sod 1388 mg.

Rev. Joe Tripp, Fall River, MA

Cheddar-Spinach Soup

Yield: 6 servings

1 cup water
2 chicken bouillon
  cubes
¹/₄ cup flour
¹/₄ cup margarine
¹/₄ cup finely chopped
  onion
1 teaspoon
  Worcestershire sauce

2 cups skim milk
¹/₈ teaspoon oregano
2 cups low-fat Cheddar
  cheese, cubed
1 10-ounce package
  frozen chopped
  spinach, thawed,
  drained

■ Mix water, bouillon cubes and flour in slow cooker. Add margarine, onion, Worcestershire sauce, milk, oregano, cheese and spinach. Cook on Low for 4 hours, stirring occasionally.

Approx Per Serving: Cal 243; Prot 16 g; Carbo 13 g; Fiber 1 g; T Fat 15 g; 53% Calories from Fat; Chol 22 mg; Sod 767 mg.

Cindy and Kurt Fienhaber, Rocky Mountain Habitat
Louisville, CO

Grandma's Chicken and Dumpling Soup

Yield: 10 servings

1 3-pound chicken,
  cut up
6 cups cold water
3 chicken bouillon
  cubes
1 10-ounce can
  chicken broth
1 10-ounce can cream
  of chicken soup
1 10-ounce can cream
  of mushroom soup
1 cup chopped celery
1¹/₂ cups chopped
  carrots
¹/₄ cup chopped onion
1 cup chopped potatoes

1 small bay leaf
1 cup fresh or frozen
  peas
1 teaspoon seasoned
  salt
2 cups flour
1 teaspoon salt
¹/₄ teaspoon white or
  black pepper
4 teaspoons baking
  powder
1 egg, beaten
2 tablespoons melted
  butter
²/₃ cup milk

■ Rinse chicken. Combine with water and bouillon cubes in large kettle. Bring to a boil; reduce heat. Simmer for 1¹/₂ hours or until chicken is tender. Remove chicken; set aside to cool. Chop into bite-sized pieces, discarding skin and bones. Skim fat from broth and strain into large saucepan. Add chicken, chicken broth, chicken and mushroom soups, celery, carrots, onion, potatoes, bay leaf, peas and seasoned salt. Simmer, covered, for 2 to 3 hours. Sift flour, salt, pepper and baking powder into large bowl. Add egg, melted butter and enough milk to make moist, stiff batter. Drop by teaspoonfuls into boiling chicken mixture. Cook, covered, for 18 to 20 minutes or until dumplings are done. Discard bay leaf before serving.

Approx Per Serving: Cal 355; Prot 27 g; Carbo 32 g; Fiber 2 g; T Fat 13 g; 33% Calories from Fat; Chol 94 mg; Sod 1471 mg.

Pam Hinojos, Morgan County HFH, Snyder, CO

Fran's Favorite Chicken-Corn Chowder

Yield: 6 servings

5 slices bacon, chopped
3/4 cup sliced celery
3/4 cup chopped onion
2 10-ounce cans cream of chicken soup
1 17-ounce can cream-style corn
1 8-ounce can whole kernel corn, drained

1 4-ounce can mushrooms
3 cups skim milk
1 cup chopped cooked potato
1/2 teaspoon basil
1/2 teaspoon salt
Pepper to taste

- Fry bacon in skillet until crisp; drain, reserving 2 tablespoons pan drippings. Sauté celery and onion in reserved pan drippings until tender. Combine bacon, celery, onion, soup, corn, undrained mushrooms, milk, potato, basil, salt and pepper in 4-quart saucepan. Cook over medium heat until heated through, stirring frequently; do not boil.

Approx Per Serving: Cal 283; Prot 12 g; Carbo 42 g; Fiber 4 g; T Fat 9 g; 28% Calories from Fat; Chol 14 mg; Sod 1480 mg.

Jeanette Johnson, HFH of Wausau, Wausau, WI

Clam Chowder

Yield: 8 servings

1 cup finely chopped onion
1 cup finely chopped celery
1 cup finely chopped potatoes
3/4 cup butter
3/4 cup flour
1/2 teaspoon sugar

1 teaspoon salt
Pepper to taste
4 cups milk
2 7-ounce cans minced clams, drained
1 to 2 teaspoons vinegar

- Simmer onion, celery and potatoes in a small amount of water in large saucepan until tender. Melt butter in small saucepan over medium heat. Blend in flour, sugar, salt and pepper. Stir in milk gradually. Cook until thickened, stirring constantly. Stir into vegetable mixture; add clams and vinegar. Cook over low heat until heated through.

Approx Per Serving: Cal 368; Prot 19 g; Carbo 23 g; Fiber 1 g; T Fat 23 g; 55% Calories from Fat; Chol 96 mg; Sod 533 mg.

Pauline R. Powell, Oregon Trail HFH, Pendleton, OR

Bahamian Conch Chowder

Yield: 4 servings

Pioneers of the Florida Keys devised many ways to use the native seafoods. Conch was plentiful and could be kept in ocean-side pens until ready to eat.

3 conchs, cleaned
1/3 pound salt pork, chopped
2 tablespoons flour
1 32-ounce can tomatoes
2 potatoes, cubed
1 onion, chopped

1 green bell pepper, chopped
1 teaspoon Worcestershire sauce
2 drops of Tabasco sauce
Salt to taste
6 cups water

- Grind conch and set aside. Brown salt pork in large kettle; add flour. Cook until thickened, stirring constantly. Add tomatoes, potatoes, onion, green pepper, Worcestershire sauce, Tabasco sauce, salt and water. Cook for 20 minutes or until potatoes are tender. Add conch. Cook for 25 minutes longer, stirring occasionally.

Approx Per Serving: Cal 290; Prot 22 g; Carbo 36 g; Fiber 4 g; T Fat 7 g; 22% Calories from Fat; Chol 82 mg; Sod 823 mg.

Lenora Albury, HFH of the Upper Keys, Key Largo, FL

Key Conch Chowder

Yield: 4 servings

An old Florida Keys recipe

1 large conch, cleaned
2 large onions, chopped
3 cloves of garlic, minced
1 green bell pepper, chopped
1 8-ounce can tomato sauce

1 6-ounce can tomato paste
3 potatoes, cubed
1 tablespoon oregano
1 1/2 teaspoons salt
1/8 teaspoon pepper
Tabasco sauce to taste

- Process conch in food processor until finely chopped. Place in saucepan with water to cover. Cook for 30 minutes. Stir in onions, garlic, green pepper, tomato sauce, tomato paste, potatoes, oregano, salt, pepper and Tabasco sauce. Simmer until potatoes are tender, adding additional water for desired consistency.

Approx Per Serving: Cal 219; Prot 13 g; Carbo 43 g; Fiber 6 g; T Fat 1 g; 5% Calories from Fat; Chol 36 mg; Sod 1306 mg.

Margaret Stevens, HFH of the Upper Keys, Islamorada, FL

Corn Chowder

Yield: 6 servings

2 cups cream
1 cup milk
2 stalks celery, chopped
2 potatoes, peeled, cubed

1 small onion, chopped
2 17-ounce cans cream-style corn
Salt and pepper to taste

■ Combine cream, milk, celery, potatoes, onion, corn, salt and pepper in slow cooker; mix well. Cook on Medium for 4 to 5 hours, stirring occasionally.
Approx Per Serving: Cal 294; Prot 8 g; Carbo 45 g; Fiber 5 g; T Fat 11 g; 33% Calories from Fat; Chol 35 mg; Sod 522 mg.

Rick Kuharske, HFH of Wausau, Wausau, WI

Creamy Fish Chowder

Yield: 4 servings

1 envelope leek soup mix
2 cups water
8 ounces cod, cut into cubes

1 cup half and half
Pepper to taste

■ Whisk soup mix into water in 2-quart saucepan. Bring to a boil over medium-high heat, stirring constantly; reduce heat to low. Simmer, partially covered, for 5 minutes, stirring occasionally. Add cod. Simmer for 5 minutes longer or until fish flakes easily. Stir in half and half. Cook over low heat until heated through, stirring constantly. Stir in pepper. Garnish with chopped parsley or chives and sherry. May substitute mocha mix or milk for half and half.
Approx Per Serving: Cal 174; Prot 14 g; Carbo 10 g; Fiber <1 g; T Fat 9 g; 45% Calories from Fat; Chol 49 mg; Sod 715 mg.

Virginia Butler, Mesilla Valley HFH, Las Cruces, NM

California Fish Soup

Yield: 12 servings

1 large onion, thinly sliced
1 stalk of celery, thinly sliced
1 red bell pepper, chopped
2 cloves of garlic, minced
1/2 teaspoon dried crushed red pepper
1/2 teaspoon dried thyme
1/4 teaspoon dried sage
1/4 teaspoon dried basil
3 tablespoons olive oil
2 14-ounce cans chicken broth

1 28-ounce can stewed tomatoes, chopped
1/2 cup tomato paste
1 cup dry white wine
1 7-ounce package cheese-filled tortellini
1 1/2 pounds halibut, cut into 1-inch strips
8 ounces small shrimp, peeled
1/2 cup chopped fresh parsley
Salt and Parmesan cheese to taste

■ Sauté onion, celery, bell pepper, garlic, red pepper, thyme, sage and basil in olive oil in large 4-quart kettle until onion is tender. Add tomato paste, undrained tomatoes, chicken broth and wine. Simmer for 30 minutes, stirring occasionally. Cook tortellini using package directions; drain and set aside. Bring soup mixture to a boil. Add halibut and shrimp. Cook for 3 to 5 minutes or until fish begins to flake. Add tortellini, parsley and salt. Simmer for 1 to 2 minutes longer. Ladle into soup bowls; top with cheese.
Approx Per Serving: Cal 215; Prot 20 g; Carbo 17 g; Fiber 1 g; T Fat 7 g; 29% Calories from Fat; Chol 53 mg; Sod 558 mg.

Marge Best, HFH of Chico, Chico, CA

Gazpacho

Yield: 6 servings

2 16-ounce cans whole tomatoes
2 tablespoons vinegar
2 tablespoons olive oil
1 teaspoon cayenne pepper

Garlic and salt to taste
2 to 3 green bell peppers, chopped
2 cucumbers, peeled, chopped
1 sweet onion, chopped

■ Combine tomatoes, vinegar, oil, cayenne pepper, garlic, salt, bell peppers, cucumbers and onion in food processor. Process until vegetables are finely chopped but not puréed. Chill until serving time.
Approx Per Serving: Cal 101; Prot 3 g; Carbo 14 g; Fiber 4 g; T Fat 5 g; 42% Calories from Fat; Chol 0 mg; Sod 249 mg.

Lisa Verploegh, HFH International, Americus, GA

Gazpacho Andaluz

Yield: 8 servings

This is an authentic recipe from Andalusia in the south of Spain.

3 to 4 large ripe
  tomatoes, peeled,
  chopped
1 large cucumber,
  peeled, chopped
1 large yellow onion,
  chopped
1 large green bell
  pepper, chopped

2 cloves of garlic,
  peeled
1 loaf French bread
3 tablespoons olive oil
3 tablespoons red wine
  vinegar
Salt to taste
10 to 12 ice cubes

■ Combine tomatoes, half the cucumber, half the onion, half the green pepper and garlic in food processor. Process until puréed. Soak ¾ of the French bread in a small amount of water. Add a little at a time to puréed mixture, processing until smooth. Add olive oil, vinegar and salt. Process until blended. Pour into large bowl with ice cubes; chill until serving time. Cube remaining bread. Serve soup cold, topped with remaining chopped vegetables and cubed bread.
Approx Per Serving: Cal 234; Prot 6 g; Carbo 35 g; Fiber 3 g; T Fat 8 g; 29% Calories from Fat; Chol 0 mg; Sod 335 mg.

Amy Bejarano, Homestead HFH, Homestead, FL

Hamburger Soup

Yield: 14 servings

1 pound lean ground
  beef
1 large onion, chopped
3 stalks celery, chopped
4 carrots, chopped
3 potatoes, chopped
8 cups water

2 beef bouillon cubes
1 28-ounce can
  tomatoes
1 teaspoon salt
½ teaspoon pepper
1 16-ounce can Shoe
  Peg corn, drained

■ Brown ground beef in 4-quart saucepan, stirring until crumbly; drain. Add onion, celery, carrots, potatoes, water, bouillon cubes and tomatoes; mix well. Simmer for 2 hours, stirring occasionally. Add salt, pepper and corn. Simmer until heated through. Serve with coleslaw and corn bread.
Approx Per Serving: Cal 143; Prot 8 g; Carbo 18 g; Fiber 2 g; T Fat 5 g; 31% Calories from Fat; Chol 21 mg; Sod 478 mg.

*Emily Rothrock Durban, First Presbyterian Church
Reidsville, NC*

Hodgepodge

Yield: 16 servings

2 pounds lean ground
  beef
1 onion, chopped
1 32-ounce can
  vegetable juice
  cocktail
1 28-ounce can pork
  and beans
2 10-ounce cans
  minestrone soup

1 16-ounce can mixed
  vegetables
1½ cups small shell
  pasta
3 to 4 tablespoons
  brown sugar
1 tablespoon
  Worcestershire sauce
1 teaspoon garlic powder

■ Brown ground beef and onion in large stock pot, stirring until ground beef is crumbly; drain. Add remaining ingredients; mix well. Simmer for 45 minutes, stirring occasionally. Add additional water for desired consistency.
Approx Per Serving: Cal 255; Prot 16 g; Carbo 27 g; Fiber 5 g; T Fat 10 g; 33% Calories from Fat; Chol 41 mg; Sod 723 mg.

Sandy Boersen, Lakeshore HFH, Zeeland, MI

Williamsburg Inn Mushroom Soup

Yield: 16 servings

1 large Bermuda
  onion, chopped
3 cups chopped leeks
16 ounces fresh
  mushrooms, chopped
⅛ cup chopped
  shallots
1 tablespoon chopped
  garlic

2 tablespoons thyme
4 large bay leaves
1 cup butter
¾ cup flour
2 quarts chicken stock
2 cups whipping cream
Salt and white pepper
  to taste

■ Sauté first 7 ingredients in butter in large stockpot until onion is tender. Stir in flour. Cook for several minutes or until thickened, stirring constantly. Add chicken stock. Simmer for 20 to 30 minutes or until soup is creamy. Discard bay leaves. Purée mixture in food processor; return to stockpot. Add cream, salt and pepper. Cook over low heat until heated through, stirring constantly.
Approx Per Serving: Cal 270; Prot 5 g; Carbo 11 g; Fiber 1 g; T Fat 24 g; 77% Calories from Fat; Chol 72 mg; Sod 502 mg.

Carrie Brost, Sheboygan HFH, Sheboygan, WI

Fresh Mushroom Soup

Yield: 6 servings

6 cups sliced fresh
  mushrooms
1/2 cup finely chopped
  onion
1/2 cup finely chopped
  celery
1/4 to 1/2 cup margarine

6 tablespoons flour
1 teaspoon crushed
  dried basil
1/2 teaspoon salt
1/4 teaspoon pepper
3 cups chicken broth
3 cups milk

■ Sauté mushrooms, onion and celery in margarine in saucepan until tender-crisp. Stir in flour, basil, salt and pepper. Simmer for 1 minute or until smooth, stirring constantly. Add chicken broth and milk gradually. Cook until slightly thickened, stirring constantly; do not boil.
Approx Per Serving: Cal 282; Prot 9 g; Carbo 17 g; Fiber 2 g; T Fat 20 g; 64% Calories from Fat; Chol 17 mg; Sod 807 mg.

Nancy MacLeod, HFH of Green County, Monroe, WI

Sybil's French Onion Soup

Yield: 6 servings

2 to 4 large onions,
  thinly sliced
2 tablespoons butter
2 14-ounce cans beef
  broth
1 broth can water

1 teaspoon
  Worcestershire sauce
Salt and pepper to taste
1 cup toasted croutons
6 slices Swiss or
  Provolone cheese

■ Sauté onions in butter in deep saucepan until tender but not browned. Add beef broth, water, Worcestershire sauce, salt and pepper. Simmer, covered, for 20 minutes, stirring occasionally. Pour into 6 ovenproof mugs; place on baking sheet. Float croutons on top of soup; cover with slice of cheese. Broil 4 inches from heat source for 4 minutes or until cheese begins to melt and brown.
Approx Per Serving: Cal 205; Prot 12 g; Carbo 13 g; Fiber 2 g; T Fat 12 g; 54% Calories from Fat; Chol 37 mg; Sod 614 mg.

Jenifer Kostecki, Northern Straits HFH, Cedarville, MI

Simple Gourmet Split Pea Soup

Yield: 8 servings

1 16-ounce package
  dried split peas,
  rinsed
1 stalk celery, sliced
1 onion, chopped
1 tablespoon chopped
  parsley
1 teaspoon basil

1 1/2 pounds Kielbasa
  sausage, sliced
9 cups boiling water
Salt and pepper to taste
4 carrots, sliced
2 potatoes, cut into
  1/2-inch cubes

■ Combine split peas, celery, onion, parsley, basil and Kielbasa sausage in 6-quart saucepan. Add boiling water. Simmer for 1 hour, stirring occasionally. Add salt and pepper. Simmer for 1 hour longer. Add carrots and potatoes. Simmer for 30 minutes longer, adding additional water for desired consistency.
Approx Per Serving: Cal 370; Prot 21 g; Carbo 47 g; Fiber 10 g; T Fat 12 g; 28% Calories from Fat; Chol 26 mg; Sod 458 mg.

Miles White, Cape Area HFH, Cape Girardeau, MO

Portuguese Sausage Soup

Yield: 18 servings

2 onions, chopped
1 clove of garlic,
  minced
1/4 cup olive oil
1 28-ounce can
  crushed tomatoes
3 carrots, sliced
1/2 medium head
  cabbage, coarsely
  chopped

2 quarts beef stock
1 1/2 pounds Italian
  sausage
1/4 teaspoon cayenne
  pepper
1 teaspoon salt
1/2 teaspoon black
  pepper
1 15-ounce can red
  kidney beans

■ Sauté onions and garlic in olive oil in stockpot until golden brown. Add tomatoes, carrots, cabbage and beef stock. Simmer for 10 minutes, stirring occasionally. Remove casing from sausage and chop. Add to soup mixture with cayenne pepper, salt and black pepper. Simmer, covered, for 1 3/4 hours, stirring occasionally. Stir in kidney beans. Simmer for 15 minutes longer.
Approx Per Serving: Cal 132; Prot 7 g; Carbo 9 g; Fiber 3 g; T Fat 8 g; 54% Calories from Fat; Chol 14 mg; Sod 789 mg.

Mary Shreders, Highlands County HFH, Sebring, FL

Posole

Yield: 6 servings

A delicious stew-like soup

2 onions, chopped
4 to 5 cloves of garlic, chopped
2 teaspoons oil
2 pounds pork tenderloin, cubed
2 15-ounce cans Mexican-style stewed tomatoes

2 14-ounce cans chicken broth
1 30-ounce can hominy, drained
1 4-ounce can chopped green chilies, drained
Chili powder and cumin to taste

- Sauté onions and garlic in oil in large saucepan until tender; remove and set aside. Brown tenderloin cubes on all sides in same saucepan; add onions and garlic. Stir in stewed tomatoes, chicken broth, hominy, green chilies, chili powder and cumin. Simmer for 30 minutes, stirring occasionally. Serve with fresh warm flour tortillas.

Approx Per Serving: Cal 396; Prot 37 g; Carbo 34 g; Fiber 1 g; T Fat 13 g; 29% Calories from Fat; Chol 93 mg; Sod 1496 mg.

Sallie Wakefield Baggett, HFH of Montgomery County Clarksville, TN

Golden Potato Soup

Yield: 10 servings

6 cups cubed red potatoes
2 cups water
1 cup sliced celery
1 cup thinly sliced carrots
1/2 cup finely chopped onion
2 chicken bouillon cubes

2 teaspoons dried parsley flakes
1 teaspoon salt
1/2 teaspoon pepper
1/4 cup flour
3 cups milk
12 ounces process American cheese, cubed

- Combine potatoes, water, celery, carrots, onion, bouillon cubes, parsley flakes, salt and pepper in 4-quart saucepan. Bring to a boil; reduce heat to low. Simmer, covered, for 8 to 10 minutes or until potatoes are tender. Blend flour into 1/4 cup milk to form a smooth paste. Stir into soup. Add remaining milk and cheese. Cook over medium heat until thickened, stirring frequently. Serve with crackers or corn muffins.

Approx Per Serving: Cal 263; Prot 12 g; Carbo 25 g; Fiber 2 g; T Fat 13 g; 45% Calories from Fat; Chol 42 mg; Sod 978 mg.

Lucile C. Furgerson, Starkville HFH, Starkville, MS

Potato-Carrot Soup

Yield: 4 servings

1 carrot, chopped
1/4 cup chopped onion
3 tablespoons butter
2 tablespoons flour
1 chicken bouillon cube
4 cups milk

6 cooked potatoes, peeled, cubed
2 tablespoons chopped parsley
1 teaspoon salt
1/2 teaspoon seasoned salt

- Sauté carrot and onion in butter in large saucepan until tender. Stir in flour. Cook until bubbly, stirring constantly. Add bouillon cube and milk gradually. Cook until thickened, stirring constantly. Add half the potatoes. Mash remaining potatoes; add with parsley, salt and seasoned salt. Cook until heated through. Serve hot, garnished with butter.

Approx Per Serving: Cal 433; Prot 13 g; Carbo 58 g; Fiber 4 g; T Fat 17 g; 35% Calories from Fat; Chol 57 mg; Sod 1174 mg.

Sue Dean, Highlands County HFH, Sebring, FL

Boca Shrimp Bisque

Yield: 12 servings

1/2 cup sliced carrot
1 cup chopped celery
1/2 cup chopped green bell pepper
1/2 cup chopped white onion
1 tablespoon olive oil
4 cloves of garlic, minced

5 cups chopped shrimp
Coarsely ground pepper to taste
2 10-ounce cans cream of mushroom soup
2 soup cans milk
4 cups cooked chopped potatoes

- Sauté carrot, celery, green pepper and onion separately in oil in saucepan until tender; reduce heat to medium-low. Add garlic. Sauté until tender. Add shrimp. Sauté until pink. Add sautéed vegetables, pepper, soup, milk and potatoes. Simmer for 40 minutes, stirring frequently.

Approx Per Serving: Cal 200; Prot 18 g; Carbo 16 g; Fiber 1 g; T Fat 7 g; 32% Calories from Fat; Chol 139 mg; Sod 566 mg.

John A. Truesdell, HFH of Boca-Delray, Boca Raton, FL

Italian Vegetable Soup

Yield: 12 servings

1 pound ground beef
1 cup chopped onion
1 cup sliced carrots
1 cup sliced celery
2 cloves of garlic, minced
1 16-ounce can tomatoes
1 15-ounce can tomato sauce
1 15-ounce can kidney beans, drained
2 cups water

5 teaspoons instant beef bouillon
1 tablespoon parsley flakes
1 teaspoon salt
1/2 teaspoon oregano
1/2 teaspoon basil
1/4 teaspoon pepper
2 cups shredded cabbage
1 cup green beans
1/2 cup uncooked elbow macaroni

■ Brown ground beef in large kettle, stirring until crumbly; drain. Add onion, carrots, celery, garlic, tomatoes, tomato sauce, kidney beans, water, beef bouillon, parsley, salt, oregano, basil and pepper; mix well. Bring to a boil; reduce heat. Simmer for 20 minutes, stirring occasionally. Add cabbage, green beans and macaroni. Bring to a boil; reduce heat. Simmer until vegetables are tender, stirring frequently. Garnish with grated Parmesan cheese.
Approx Per Serving: Cal 150; Prot 11 g; Carbo 15 g; Fiber 5 g; T Fat 6 g; 34% Calories from Fat; Chol 25 mg; Sod 972 mg.

Mrs. Wesley J. Hudson, Morgan County HFH
Fort Morgan, CO

Short-Cut Vegetable-Beef Soup

Yield: 16 servings

2 pounds lean stew beef, cubed
8 ounces tomato sauce
2 16-ounce cans stew vegetables, drained
1 6-ounce can mixed vegetables, drained
2 teaspoons Worcestershire sauce
1 teaspoon salt

1 teaspoon pepper
2 6-ounce cans stewed tomatoes
1 4-ounce can corn, drained
1 4-ounce can green beans, drained
1 4-ounce can peas, drained
1 cup catsup

■ Cook beef in tomato sauce in large saucepan for 15 minutes. Add stew vegetables, mixed vegetables and Worcestershire sauce. Bring to a boil. Add salt, pepper, stewed tomatoes, corn, green beans and peas. Simmer for 40 minutes, stirring occasionally. Stir in catsup. Simmer for 20 minutes longer.
Approx Per Serving: Cal 148; Prot 14 g; Carbo 16 g; Fiber 4 g; T Fat 4 g; 22% Calories from Fat; Chol 32 mg; Sod 639 mg.

Barnetta Phillips, HFH of Wichita Falls, Wichita Falls, TX

Tomato Soup

Yield: 4 servings

1 quart canned tomatoes
1 stalk celery, sliced
1/2 onion, chopped
1/2 cup water
2 bay leaves
1 whole clove
1 sprig of parsley

2 tablespoons water
1 tablespoon butter
1 tablespoon flour
1 tablespoon sugar
1/2 teaspoon salt
Red and black pepper to taste

■ Purée tomatoes, celery and onion in blender. Pour into saucepan. Rinse blender with 1/2 cup water and add to saucepan. Add bay leaves, clove and parsley. Bring to a boil, stirring frequently. Combine remaining ingredients in small bowl; mix well. Stir into soup. Simmer until thickened, stirring constantly. Discard bay leaves and clove before serving.
Approx Per Serving: Cal 106; Prot 3 g; Carbo 18 g; Fiber 3 g; T Fat 4 g; 28% Calories from Fat; Chol 8 mg; Sod 687 mg.

Jean C. Roeding, Northwest Nebraska HFH, Chadron, NE

Cheese Tortellini Soup

Yield: 6 servings

1 clove of garlic, chopped
1 medium onion, chopped
3 tablespoons olive oil
3 carrots, coarsely chopped
2 stalks celery, coarsely chopped

2 cups crushed tomatoes
5 cups chicken broth
1 1/2 cups cheese tortellini
2 teaspoons dried basil
1/2 cup Parmesan cheese

■ Sauté garlic and onion in olive oil in skillet. Add carrots and celery. Cook, covered, for 20 minutes. Add tomatoes and broth. Bring to a boil; reduce heat. Simmer for 20 minutes. Add tortellini and basil. Simmer until tortellini is cooked. Sprinkle each bowl of soup with Parmesan cheese. This soup is better made a day ahead so that the flavors can blend.
Approx Per Serving: Cal 254; Prot 13 g; Carbo 24 g; Fiber 3 g; T Fat 12 g; 43% Calories from Fat; Chol 20 mg; Sod 1032 mg.

Janet McSweeney, Greater Lawrence HFH, Andover, MA

Ambrosia Salad

Yield: 8 servings

1 cup sour cream
1 cup whipping cream, whipped
1 16-ounce can crushed pineapple, drained

1 11-ounce can mandarin oranges, drained
2 cups miniature marshmallows

▪ Blend sour cream and whipped cream in bowl. Add pineapple, mandarin oranges and marshmallows; mix gently. Chill for 2 hours or longer.
Approx Per Serving: Cal 262; Prot 2 g; Carbo 28 g; Fiber 1 g; T Fat 17 g; 56% Calories from Fat; Chol 54 mg; Sod 42 mg.

Kim Marzilli, Rehoboth, MA

Cherry and Pineapple Salad

Yield: 12 servings

1 21-ounce can cherry pie filling
2/3 cup evaporated milk
8 ounces whipped topping

2 cups miniature marshmallows
1 20-ounce can pineapple tidbits, drained

▪ Combine pie filling and evaporated milk in bowl; mix well. Add whipped topping, marshmallows and pineapple; mix well. Spoon into serving bowl. Chill for several hours to overnight.
Approx Per Serving: Cal 181; Prot 2 g; Carbo 32 g; Fiber 1 g; T Fat 6 g; 28% Calories from Fat; Chol 4 mg; Sod 43 mg.

Julie Strusz, HFH of South Central Minnesota, Mankato, MN

Cranberry Mold

Yield: 8 servings

2 3-ounce packages raspberry gelatin
2 cups boiling water
1 cup cold water
8 ounces cream cheese, softened
1/2 cup sugar
1 teaspoon vanilla extract

1 cup evaporated milk
1 envelope unflavored gelatin
1/2 cup cold water
1/2 cup chopped pecans
1/4 cup sugar
1 cup ground cranberries

▪ Dissolve raspberry gelatin in boiling water in medium bowl. Stir in 1 cup cold water. Pour 1 1/2 cups of the mixture into oiled 6-cup mold. Chill until set. Beat cream cheese and 1/2 cup sugar in mixer bowl until light. Add vanilla and evaporated milk and gradually, beating constantly. Soften unflavored gelatin in 1/2 cup cold water in saucepan for 5 minutes. Heat over low heat until completely dissolved. Stir into cream cheese mixture. Fold in pecans. Spread over congealed layer. Chill until nearly set. Add 1/4 cup sugar and cranberries to remaining raspberry gelatin mixture; mix well. Spread over cream cheese layer. Chill, covered, for 4 hours to overnight. Unmold salad onto lettuce-lined serving plate.
Approx Per Serving: Cal 357; Prot 8 g; Carbo 46 g; Fiber 2 g; T Fat 17 g; 42% Calories from Fat; Chol 40 mg; Sod 186 mg.

Mary Bullock, Laurel County HFH, London, KY

Frozen Fruit Salad

Yield: 15 servings

2 bananas
1 tablespoon lemon juice
1/2 10-ounce jar maraschino cherries, drained, cut into quarters
2 tablespoons sugar

1 8-ounce can crushed pineapple, drained
1/2 10-ounce package miniature marshmallows
5 cups whipped topping

▪ Mash bananas with lemon juice in bowl. Add maraschino cherries, sugar, pineapple, marshmallows and whipped topping; mix gently. Spoon into large mold. Freeze overnight. Place mold in warm water for a short time; run knife around edge. Unmold salad onto serving plate. Chill for 1 hour.
Approx Per Serving: Cal 149; Prot 1 g; Carbo 24 g; Fiber 1 g; T Fat 6 g; 37% Calories from Fat; Chol 0 mg; Sod 15 mg.

Mary Faber, Battle Creek Area HFH, Battle Creek, MI

Fruit Salad

Yield: 16 servings

You may vary the amount and type of fruit in order to take advantage of seasonal harvests.

2 3-ounce packages
   lemon gelatin
1 cup boiling water
1 12-ounce can frozen
   lemonade
   concentrate, thawed
1 12-ounce can ginger
   ale

2 cups strawberries
2 cups bite-sized
   cantaloupe
2 cups bite-sized
   honeydew
2 cups seedless grapes
1 cup blueberries
1 cup sliced peaches

■ Dissolve gelatin in boiling water in large bowl. Stir in lemonade concentrate and ginger ale. Add strawberries, cantaloupe, honeydew, seedless grapes, blueberries and peaches; mix gently. Chill for 4 hours to overnight.

Approx Per Serving: Cal 129; Prot 2 g; Carbo 32 g; Fiber 1 g; T Fat <1 g; 2% Calories from Fat; Chol 0 mg; Sod 41 mg.

Kathy Grossman, HFH of Butler County, Butler, PA

Junk Salad

Yield: 20 servings

24 ounces cottage
   cheese
16 ounces whipped
   topping
1 6-ounce package
   orange gelatin
2 bananas, sliced

1 15-ounce can
   mandarin oranges,
   drained
1 16-ounce can
   pineapple tidbits,
   drained
1 cup chopped pecans

■ Combine cottage cheese, whipped topping and dry gelatin in large bowl; mix well. Add bananas, mandarin oranges, pineapple and pecans; mix gently. Chill until serving time.

Approx Per Serving: Cal 213; Prot 6 g; Carbo 24 g; Fiber 1 g; T Fat 11 g; 46% Calories from Fat; Chol 5 mg; Sod 172 mg.

Tahnee Bowman, McPherson Area HFH, McPherson, KS

Lime Gelatin Salad

Yield: 12 servings

8 ounces cream cheese,
   softened
1/3 cup
   mayonnaise-type
   salad dressing
8 ounces whipped
   topping
1 stalk celery, finely
   chopped

1 20-ounce can
   crushed pineapple,
   drained
1/2 cup chopped pecans
1 3-ounce package
   lime gelatin
1 cup boiling water
1 cup cold water

■ Beat cream cheese in mixer bowl until light. Add salad dressing; beat until smooth. Add whipped topping; mix well. Stir in celery, pineapple and pecans. Dissolve gelatin in boiling water in bowl. Stir in cold water. Add to pineapple mixture; mix well. Spoon into 9x13-inch dish. Chill until serving time.

Approx Per Serving: Cal 236; Prot 3 g; Carbo 20 g; Fiber 1 g; T Fat 17 g; 62% Calories from Fat; Chol 22 mg; Sod 133 mg.

Ida Miller, Ashland-Ironton Area HFH, Ashland, KY

Orange Cream Salad

Yield: 10 servings

1 20-ounce can
   pineapple tidbits
1 16-ounce can sliced
   peaches
1 11-ounce can
   mandarin oranges
3 medium bananas,
   sliced
2 medium apples,
   chopped

1 4-ounce package
   vanilla instant
   pudding mix
1 cup milk
1/2 6-ounce can frozen
   orange juice
   concentrate, thawed
3/4 cup sour cream

■ Drain pineapple, peaches and mandarin oranges. Combine drained fruits with bananas and apples in large bowl. Beat pudding mix and milk in bowl until smooth. Stir in orange juice concentrate and sour cream. Fold into fruit mixture. Chill, covered, until serving time.

Approx Per Serving: Cal 226; Prot 3 g; Carbo 47 g; Fiber 3 g; T Fat 5 g; 18% Calories from Fat; Chol 11 mg; Sod 101 mg.

Janet Love, Genesee Valley HFH, Alfred Station, NY

*H*abitat for Humanity is an excellent example of Americans working together for the good of our nation. I commend the many volunteers who roll up their sleeves to build houses so that other families can have a decent place to live. Your generous efforts reflect the kind of commitment to volunteerism and service that is needed to change America for the better.

President Bill Clinton

Picture Glass Salad

Yield: 16 servings

1   3-ounce package
   each lime, cherry
   and orange gelatin
3 cups boiling water
1¹/₂ cups cold water
1 cup pineapple juice

¹/₄ cup sugar
1   3-ounce package
   lemon gelatin
¹/₂ cup cold water
8 ounces whipped
   topping

■ Dissolve lime gelatin in 1 cup boiling water in 8x8-inch dish. Stir in ¹/₂ cup cold water. Repeat process with cherry and orange gelatins, using separate dishes. Chill until firm. Cut each layer into ¹/₂-inch cubes. Bring pineapple juice to a boil in saucepan. Stir in sugar and lemon gelatin until dissolved. Stir in ¹/₂ cup cold water. Chill until syrupy. Fold in whipped topping and gelatin cubes. Spoon into large mold. Chill until firm. Unmold onto serving plate.
Approx Per Serving: Cal 145; Prot 2 g; Carbo 27 g; Fiber <1 g; T Fat 4 g; 22% Calories from Fat; Chol 0 mg; Sod 71 mg.

Lois Jordan, Newaygo HFH, Fremont, MI

Pineapple Salad

Yield: 8 servings

1   20-ounce can
   juice-pack crushed
   pineapple
2¹/₂ teaspoons
   cornstarch
2 tablespoons sugar
2 eggs, beaten

2 cups seedless grapes
3 bananas, sliced
1¹/₂ cups miniature
   marshmallows
1 cup maraschino
   cherries, cut into
   thirds

■ Drain pineapple, reserving juice. Blend a small amount of reserved pineapple juice with cornstarch in double boiler. Stir in remaining pineapple juice, sugar and eggs. Cook until thickened, stirring constantly. Cool to room temperature. Add pineapple, grapes, bananas, marshmallows and maraschino cherries. May prepare salad in advance and add bananas just before serving.
Approx Per Serving: Cal 212; Prot 3 g; Carbo 49 g; Fiber 2 g; T Fat 2 g; 8% Calories from Fat; Chol 53 mg; Sod 29 mg.

Ione Sandene, Omaha HFH, Omaha, NE

Pistachio Salad

Yield: 12 servings

2   20-ounce cans
   crushed pineapple
2   4-ounce packages
   pistachio instant
   pudding mix

2 cups miniature
   marshmallows
12 ounces whipped
   topping

■ Drain pineapple, reserving juice. Combine reserved juice with pudding mix in bowl; mix well. Add marshmallows, whipped topping and pineapple; mix gently. Chill until serving time.
Approx Per Serving: Cal 264; Prot 1 g; Carbo 51 g; Fiber 1 g; T Fat 7 g; 24% Calories from Fat; Chol 0 mg; Sod 143 mg.

Debbie Luepnitz, Northern Straits HFH, Moran, MI

Pretzel-Berry Salad

Yield: 12 servings

2¹/₂ cups crushed
   pretzels
³/₄ cup melted
   margarine
1 cup sugar
8 ounces cream cheese,
   softened
1 envelope whipped
   topping mix

¹/₂ cup cold milk
1 teaspoon vanilla
   extract
1   6-ounce package
   strawberry gelatin
2 cups boiling water
2   10-ounce packages
   frozen strawberries

■ Mix pretzels, margarine and 2 tablespoons of the sugar in bowl. Press into 9x13-inch baking dish. Bake at 375 degrees for 10 minutes. Cool to room temperature. Blend remaining sugar and cream cheese in mixer bowl. Combine topping mix, milk and vanilla in deep mixer bowl; beat until stiff peaks form. Fold into cream cheese mixture. Spread evenly over pretzel layer. Chill for 2 hours or longer. Dissolve gelatin in boiling water in bowl. Add strawberries, stirring until thawed. Spread over cream cheese layer. Chill until set. Cut into squares. Serve in lettuce cups.
Approx Per Serving: Cal 378; Prot 5 g; Carbo 50 g; Fiber 2 g; T Fat 20 g; 44% Calories from Fat; Chol 22 mg; Sod 525 mg.

Carole Meek, Augusta HFH, Martinez, GA

Raspberry Salad

Yield: 9 servings

1 8-ounce can crushed
   pineapple
1/2 cup water
1 3-ounce package
   raspberry gelatin

1 cup cottage cheese
4 ounces whipped
   topping

■ Bring undrained pineapple and water to a boil in saucepan. Add gelatin, stirring until dissolved. Boil for 3 minutes. Cool until slightly thickened. Fold in cottage cheese and whipped topping. Spoon into 9x9-inch dish. Chill until set.

Approx Per Serving: Cal 119; Prot 4 g; Carbo 17 g; Fiber <1 g; T Fat 4 g; 31% Calories from Fat; Chol 3 mg; Sod 128 mg.

Jo McKeown, Southwest Iowa HFH, Shenandoah, IA

Rhubarb Salad

Yield: 6 servings

2 cups chopped
   rhubarb
1/2 cup water
1 3-ounce package
   strawberry gelatin

1 cup sugar
1/2 cup applesauce
1 8-ounce can crushed
   pineapple

■ Cook rhubarb in water in saucepan until tender. Add gelatin and sugar, stirring until dissolved; remove from heat. Add applesauce and pineapple; mix well. Spoon into serving dish. Chill for 1 hour.

Approx Per Serving: Cal 235; Prot 2 g; Carbo 59 g; Fiber 2 g; T Fat <1 g; 1% Calories from Fat; Chol 0 mg; Sod 49 mg.

Patsy Lambert, Almost Heaven HFH, Riverton, WV

Ribbon Salad

Yield: 15 servings

1 3-ounce package
   lime gelatin
1 cup boiling water
1/2 cup cold water
2 envelopes
   unflavored gelatin
1/2 cup cold water
2 cups milk
1 cup sugar

2 cups sour cream
2 teaspoons vanilla
   extract
1 3-ounce package
   each raspberry,
   lemon and orange
   gelatin
3 cups boiling water
1 1/2 cups cold water

■ Dissolve lime gelatin in 1 cup boiling water. Stir in 1/2 cup cold water. Spoon into lightly greased 9x13-inch dish. Chill until firm. Soften unflavored gelatin in 1/2 cup cold water. Bring milk to a boil in saucepan. Add softened gelatin and sugar, stirring until dissolved. Fold in sour cream and vanilla. Spread 1 3/4 cups of the mixture over lime gelatin. Prepare raspberry, lemon and orange gelatins and repeat process, alternating each color with half of the remaining sour cream mixture and chilling each layer until firm before adding the next layer.

Approx Per Serving: Cal 224; Prot 5 g; Carbo 36 g; Fiber <1 g; T Fat 8 g; 29% Calories from Fat; Chol 18 mg; Sod 103 mg.

Karen Malte, Orleans County HFH, Medina, NY

Sawdust Salad

Yield: 15 servings

I thought that the name of this salad, derived from the cinnamon on top, made it ideal for Habitat volunteers.

1 3-ounce package
   orange gelatin
1 3-ounce package
   lemon gelatin
2 cups boiling water
2 cups cold water
1 15-ounce can
   crushed pineapple,
   drained
1 10-ounce package
   miniature
   marshmallows

2 eggs, beaten
2 tablespoons flour
1 cup sugar
2 cups pineapple juice
2 envelopes whipped
   topping mix
8 ounces cream cheese
1 cup milk
Cinnamon to taste

■ Dissolve orange and lemon gelatins in boiling water in large bowl. Stir in cold water. Fold in pineapple and marshmallows. Spoon into 9x13-inch dish. Chill until set. Blend eggs, flour, sugar and pineapple juice together in saucepan. Cook over medium heat until thickened, stirring constantly. Cool to room temperature. Spread over congealed layer. Chill. Beat whipped topping mix, cream cheese and milk in bowl until smooth. Spread over top of salad; sprinkle with cinnamon. Chill until serving time.

Approx Per Serving: Cal 282; Prot 5 g; Carbo 51 g; Fiber <1 g; T Fat 8 g; 24% Calories from Fat; Chol 47 mg; Sod 116 mg.

Erin Bunting, Firelands HFH, Huron, OH

Seafoam Salad

Yield: 15 servings

1 3-ounce package
  lemon gelatin
1 3-ounce package
  lime gelatin
2 cups boiling water
1 16-ounce can
  crushed pineapple
1 cup cottage cheese

1 cup mayonnaise-type
  salad dressing
1 12-ounce can
  evaporated milk
1 tablespoon ground
  horseradish
1 cup chopped walnuts

■ Dissolve lemon and lime gelatins in boiling water in bowl. Cool until mixture begins to thicken. Combine next 5 ingredients in bowl; mix well. Add to gelatin; mix well. Spoon into 9x13-inch dish; sprinkle with chopped walnuts. Chill for 3 hours or until set. May omit ground horseradish.
Approx Per Serving: Cal 223; Prot 6 g; Carbo 24 g; Fiber 1 g; T Fat 13 g; 49% Calories from Fat; Chol 13 mg; Sod 229 mg.

Lois Sampson, Black Hills Area HFH, Rapid City, SD

Strawberry and Walnut Salad

Yield: 12 servings

2 3-ounce packages
  strawberry gelatin
1 cup boiling water
2 medium bananas,
  mashed
1 20-ounce can
  crushed pineapple,
  drained

2 10-ounce packages
  frozen strawberries,
  thawed
1 cup coarsely chopped
  walnuts
2 cups sour cream

■ Dissolve gelatin in boiling water in large bowl. Stir in bananas, pineapple, strawberries and walnuts. Spoon half the mixture into 9x13-inch dish. Chill for 1½ hours or until set. Stir sour cream into remaining gelatin mixture. Spread over congealed layer. Chill in refrigerator overnight.
Approx Per Serving: Cal 257; Prot 5 g; Carbo 31 g; Fiber 3 g; T Fat 14 g; 48% Calories from Fat; Chol 17 mg; Sod 68 mg.

Diane McAninch, Mosinee, WI

Marinated Beef Salad

Yield: 4 servings

1 1 to 1¼-pound
  flank steak
¼ cup fresh lemon
  juice
¼ cup chili sauce
¼ cup oil
1 tablespoon brown
  sugar
¼ teaspoon each garlic
  powder, ground
  ginger and pepper

2 cups thinly sliced
  carrots
1 8-ounce can sliced
  water chestnuts,
  drained
1 medium sweet
  onion, sliced into
  rings
1 6-ounce package
  frozen pea pods

■ Broil steak for 5 minutes on each side or until done to taste; slice diagonally into thin strips. Mix next 7 ingredients in large bowl. Add beef, carrots, water chestnuts and onion; mix well. Marinate, covered, in refrigerator for 8 hours to overnight, stirring occasionally. Add pea pods at serving time. Serve on lettuce-lined serving plates; garnish with tomato wedges. May substitute 4 ounces fresh pea pods for frozen pea pods.
Approx Per Serving: Cal 416; Prot 30 g; Carbo 26 g; Fiber 5 g; T Fat 22 g; 48% Calories from Fat; Chol 80 mg; Sod 293 mg.

Alicia Woodard, HFH of Wichita Falls, Wichita Falls, TX

Chinese Chicken Salad

Yield: 8 servings

3 chicken breasts,
  skinned, cooked,
  shredded
1 head Chinese Napa
  cabbage, shredded
4 onions, chopped
1 8-ounce can
  Chinese noodles
⅓ to ½ cup sliced
  almonds

¼ cup sesame seed
¾ cup peanut oil
¼ cup packed brown
  sugar
6 tablespoons rice
  wine vinegar
2 tablespoons soy sauce
1 tablespoon chopped
  green bell pepper
½ teaspoon salt

■ Combine chicken, cabbage, onions, noodles, almonds and sesame seed in salad bowl. Combine peanut oil, brown sugar, rice wine vinegar, soy sauce, green pepper and salt in food processor container; process until smooth. Add to chicken mixture at serving time; toss gently to mix.
Approx Per Serving: Cal 500; Prot 18 g; Carbo 34 g; Fiber 4 g; T Fat 34 g; 60% Calories from Fat; Chol 30 mg; Sod 706 mg.

Charlene Durand

Chicken and Cucumber Salad

Yield: 4 servings

1 cup uncooked
  macaroni
3/4 cup mayonnaise
1 tablespoon finely
  chopped onion
1/2 teaspoon salt

1/4 teaspoon pepper
1 1/2 cups chopped
  cooked chicken
1 cup chopped
  cucumber

- Cook macaroni using package directions; rinse and drain. Combine mayonnaise, onion, salt and pepper in bowl; mix well. Add pasta, chicken and cucumber; mix gently. Chill, covered, for 2 hours or longer.
Approx Per Serving: Cal 181; Prot 17 g; Carbo 13 g; Fiber 1 g; T Fat 6 g; 31% Calories from Fat; Chol 48 mg; Sod 328 mg.

Marnee Ballay, Habitat Gypsy, Livingston, TX

Arkansas Aloha Chicken Salad

Yield: 4 servings

Many thanks. I received the first house built by the Pulaski County Habitat for Humanity and made some wonderful new friends as well.

1 20-ounce can
  crushed pineapple
4 medium chicken
  breasts, skinned
1 cup chopped pecans

1 medium sweet red or
  Vidalia onion,
  chopped
1 cup light mayonnaise

- Drain pineapple, reserving juice. Rinse chicken and pat dry. Cook chicken in reserved juice in large covered skillet for 30 minutes or until cooked through. Cool and chop chicken, discarding skin and bones. Combine chicken with pineapple, pecans, onion and mayonnaise in large bowl; mix well. Chill, covered, until serving time. Serve on spinach-lined serving plates or on toasted rolls with hot soup.
Approx Per Serving: Cal 603; Prot 30 g; Carbo 45 g; Fiber 4 g; T Fat 35 g; 52% Calories from Fat; Chol 88 mg; Sod 366 mg.

Anne Hefner, HFH of Pulaski County, Little Rock, AR

Oriental Shrimp Salad

Yield: 6 servings

3 cups cooked rice
1 10-ounce package
  frozen green peas,
  cooked
1 1/2 pounds shrimp,
  cooked, peeled
1 1/2 cups thinly sliced
  celery
1/2 cup chopped green
  onions
1/2 cup oil

2 tablespoons cider
  vinegar
2 tablespoons lemon
  juice
1 tablespoon soy sauce
1 tablespoon sugar
1/2 teaspoon celery seed
1 teaspoon curry
  powder
1 teaspoon salt

- Combine rice, peas, shrimp, celery and green onions in salad bowl. Combine oil, vinegar, lemon juice, soy sauce, sugar, celery seed, curry powder and salt in bowl; mix well. Add to salad; toss gently. Chill, covered, overnight. Garnish with toasted almonds. May also add almonds to salad.
Approx Per Serving: Cal 390; Prot 21 g; Carbo 33 g; Fiber 2 g; T Fat 19 g; 45% Calories from Fat; Chol 158 mg; Sod 737 mg.

Nancy H. Ross, Bay County HFH, Panama City, FL

Sesame Pork Salad

Yield: 6 servings

1 1/2 cups slivered
  cooked pork
3 cups cooked rice
4 ounces fresh snow
  peas, trimmed,
  julienned
1 medium cucumber,
  peeled, seeded,
  julienned
1 medium red bell
  pepper, julienned

1/2 cup sliced green
  onions
2 tablespoons sesame
  seed, toasted
1/4 cup chicken broth
3 tablespoons rice or
  white wine vinegar
3 tablespoons soy sauce
1 tablespoon peanut oil
1 teaspoon sesame oil

- Combine pork, rice, snow peas, cucumber, bell pepper, green onions and sesame seed in large bowl. Combine chicken broth, rice wine vinegar, soy sauce, peanut oil and sesame oil in small covered jar; shake to mix well. Add to salad; toss lightly. Serve slightly chilled or at room temperature. May substitute chicken for pork if desired.
Approx Per Serving: Cal 248; Prot 14 g; Carbo 30 g; Fiber 2 g; T Fat 8 g; 29% Calories from Fat; Chol 28 mg; Sod 573 mg.

Paul Carpenter, Mahoning County HFH, Youngstown, OH

Taco Salad

Yield: 8 servings

2 pounds ground chuck
1 small onion, chopped
1 envelope taco
    seasoning mix
Seasoned salt and
    pepper to taste
1 large head lettuce,
    chopped
3 cups shredded
    Cheddar cheese

2 to 3 medium
    tomatoes, chopped
1 envelope taco
    seasoning mix
12 ounces tortilla chips
1   24-ounce bottle of
    Catalina salad
    dressing

■ Brown ground chuck with onion in skillet, stirring until ground beef is crumbly; drain. Add 1 envelope taco seasoning mix, seasoned salt and pepper; mix well. Layer lettuce, cheese, tomatoes and beef mixture in large bowl. Sprinkle with 1 envelope taco seasoning mix. Chill, covered, until serving time. Top with tortilla chips and salad dressing; mix well.
Approx Per Serving: Cal 1064; Prot 36 g; Carbo 59 g; Fiber 3 g; T Fat 76 g; 64% Calories from Fat; Chol 119 mg; Sod 2452 mg.

Mary E. Crecelius, Crawford County HFH, English, IN

Tuna-on-a-Shoestring Salad

Yield: 6 servings

1   7-ounce can tuna,
    drained
2 cups grated carrots
1 cup sliced celery
1/4 cup minced onion

3/4 to 1 cup light
    mayonnaise
1   4-ounce can
    shoestring potatoes

■ Separate tuna into large chunks. Combine with carrots, celery, onion and mayonnaise in large bowl; mix gently. Chill, covered, overnight. Add shoestring potatoes at serving time; toss lightly. May substitute Chinese noodles for potatoes.
Approx Per Serving: Cal 261; Prot 12 g; Carbo 20 g; Fiber 2 g; T Fat 15 g; 52% Calories from Fat; Chol 29 mg; Sod 379 mg.

Miriam Lidell, Benton HFH, Corvallis, OR

Macaroni Salad

Yield: 10 servings

11/2 cups uncooked
    macaroni
Salt to taste
1 cup chopped celery
1/4 cup chopped green
    bell pepper

1/2 cup thinly sliced
    radishes
1 cup mayonnaise-type
    salad dressing
1 tablespoon prepared
    mustard

■ Cook macaroni in salted water in saucepan until tender; rinse and drain. Combine remaining ingredients in serving bowl. Add macaroni; mix gently. Chill until serving time.
Approx Per Serving: Cal 127; Prot 1 g; Carbo 13 g; Fiber 1 g; T Fat 8 g; 56% Calories from Fat; Chol 6 mg; Sod 198 mg.

Marjorie Orman, Morgan County HFH, Ft. Morgan, CO

Pasta-Vegetable Salad

Yield: 6 servings

11/2 cups uncooked
    pasta
2 tomatoes, chopped
2 cups chopped
    broccoli

1 cup shredded carrot
1/2 cup sliced black
    olives
1 cup Italian salad
    dressing

■ Cook pasta using package directions; drain. Arrange pasta, tomatoes, broccoli, carrot and olives in concentric circles on platter lined with salad greens. Drizzle with salad dressing. Serve immediately.
Approx Per Serving: Cal 283; Prot 4 g; Carbo 20 g; Fiber 3 g; T Fat 27 g; 72% Calories from Fat; Chol 0 mg; Sod 317 mg.

Tonia Chapa, HFH of Wichita Falls, Wichita Falls, TX

Spaghetti Salad

Yield: 8 servings

1   16-ounce package
    spaghetti
1/2 cup chopped red
    bell pepper
1/2 cup sliced radishes
1 cup chopped broccoli

1 cup chopped
    cucumbers
1   3-ounce jar salad
    seasoning
1   16-ounce bottle of
    Italian salad dressing

■ Cook spaghetti using package directions; drain. Combine with bell pepper, radishes, broccoli, cucumbers, salad seasoning and salad dressing in large bowl; mix well. Chill for 2 hours or longer.
Approx Per Serving: Cal 509; Prot 13 g; Carbo 52 g; Fiber 4 g; T Fat 36 g; 56% Calories from Fat; Chol 0 mg; Sod 770 mg.

Charlene Orton, Swansea, MA

Rice Salad with Sherry Dressing

Yield: 8 servings

1¹/₂ cups uncooked rice
1¹/₂ teaspoons salt
3¹/₃ cups boiling water
2 medium carrots,
  sliced diagonally
¹/₂ cup oil
¹/₄ cup dry sherry
1 small yellow squash,
  cut into ¹/₄x1-inch
  strips

1 cup broccoli
  flowerets
8 to 10 cherry
  tomatoes, cut into
  halves
¹/₂ cup sliced radishes
¹/₄ cup cider vinegar
1 clove of garlic,
  minced
1 teaspoon sugar

■ Stir rice and salt into boiling water in medium saucepan. Simmer, covered, for 20 minutes. Let stand, covered, for 5 minutes or until water is absorbed. Place in large bowl; cool to room temperature. Cook carrots in 1 teaspoon oil and 1 teaspoon wine in skillet for 1 to 2 minutes, stirring frequently. Add squash and broccoli. Cook for 1 minute or until vegetables are tender-crisp, stirring frequently. Add to rice with tomatoes and radishes; mix well. Combine remaining oil, remaining wine, vinegar, garlic and sugar in small bowl; mix well. Add to salad; mix well. Chill, covered, for several hours.
Approx Per Serving: Cal 278; Prot 3 g; Carbo 33 g; Fiber 2 g; T Fat 14 g; 46% Calories from Fat; Chol 0 mg; Sod 415 mg.

Dorothy Gilliam, Pinellas HFH, St. Petersburg, FL

Egg and Rice Salad

Yield: 10 servings

2 cups cooked brown
  rice
¹/₄ cup minced green
  onions
1 cup chopped celery

6 hard-boiled eggs,
  chopped
¹/₄ cup chopped pickles
³/₄ cup mayonnaise
Salt to taste

■ Combine rice, green onions, celery, eggs, pickles, mayonnaise and salt in bowl; mix gently. Serve in lettuce-lined salad bowl; garnish with tomato wedges and radish roses or sliced stuffed olives.
Approx Per Serving: Cal 215; Prot 5 g; Carbo 11 g; Fiber 1 g; T Fat 17 g; 70% Calories from Fat; Chol 138 mg; Sod 180 mg.

Jeanie Blythe, University of Kentucky Campus Chapter
Lexington, KY

Tabouli with White Beans

Yield: 6 servings

1¹/₂ cups uncooked
  bulgur
3 cups water
¹/₂ cup cooked white
  beans
2 tomatoes, chopped
2 tablespoons chopped
  chives

2 teaspoons chopped
  fresh mint
¹/₄ cup chopped parsley
Chopped garlic to taste
1¹/₂ tablespoons oil
Juice of 2 lemons
¹/₄ teaspoon salt
Pepper to taste

■ Cook bulgur in water in saucepan for 5 minutes. Let stand, covered, for 2 hours; drain. Chill in refrigerator. Combine with beans, tomatoes, chives, mint, parsley, garlic, oil, lemon juice, salt and pepper in bowl; mix well. Serve on lettuce-lined salad plates. May substitute vegetable stock for water.
Approx Per Serving: Cal 214; Prot 7 g; Carbo 39 g; Fiber 10 g; T Fat 4 g; 17% Calories from Fat; Chol 0 mg; Sod 95 mg.

William and Marian Hall, HFH of Wausau, Wausau, WI

Tabouli

Yield: 8 servings

1¹/₂ cups boiling water
1 cup uncooked bulgur
1 teaspoon salt
¹/₄ cup lemon juice
1 clove of garlic,
  crushed

¹/₄ cup olive oil
2 tomatoes, chopped
1 cup chopped parsley
4 green onions,
  chopped

■ Pour boiling water over bulgur and salt in bowl. Let stand, covered, for 30 minutes. Stir in lemon juice, garlic and olive oil. Chill for 2 hours. Add tomatoes, parsley and green onions; mix well. Serve on lettuce-lined serving plate. May also serve as dip with chips or crackers.
Approx Per Serving: Cal 147; Prot 3 g; Carbo 19 g; Fiber 5 g; T Fat 7 g; 42% Calories from Fat; Chol 0 mg; Sod 273 mg.

Allen Laird, Waco HFH, Waco, TX

Wheat Berry Salad
Yield: 6 servings

1 cup uncooked wheat
  berries
2 cups water
1 green bell pepper,
  chopped
2 large carrots, grated

1 cucumber, chopped
1 onion, chopped
1 cup chopped parsley
Salt and pepper to taste
1/3 cup olive oil
1/3 cup lemon juice

- Bring wheat berries to a boil in water in saucepan. Simmer for 45 minutes. Let stand, covered, for 1 hour to absorb water; drain. Combine with green pepper, carrots, cucumber and onion in bowl; mix well. Add parsley, salt and pepper. Stir in mixture of olive oil and lemon juice. Chill until serving time.
  Approx Per Serving: Cal 241; Prot 4 g; Carbo 30 g; Fiber 8 g; T Fat 13 g; 46% Calories from Fat; Chol 0 mg; Sod 16 mg.

Stephen M. Senesi, Kalamazoo Valley HFH, Kalamazoo, MI

Best Broccoli Salad
Yield: 10 servings

1 large head broccoli,
  chopped
1/2 medium Bermuda
  onion, chopped
1 cup seedless red
  grapes
3 ounces sunflower
  seed

1 cup raisins
10 slices bacon,
  crisp-fried, crumbled
1/2 cup mayonnaise
1/4 cup sugar
1 tablespoon red wine
  vinegar

- Combine broccoli, onion, grapes, sunflower seed, raisins and bacon in salad bowl. Mix mayonnaise, sugar and vinegar in small bowl. Add to salad; mix well. Chill until serving time.
  Approx Per Serving: Cal 251; Prot 5 g; Carbo 24 g; Fiber 2 g; T Fat 16 g; 55% Calories from Fat; Chol 12 mg; Sod 170 mg.

Cathy Todd, Mooresville/Lake Norman HFH
Huntersville, NC

Broccoli Salad with Cooked Dressing
Yield: 10 servings

1 egg
1 egg yolk
1/2 cup sugar
11/2 teaspoons
  cornstarch
1 teaspoon dry mustard
1/4 cup light vinegar
1/4 cup water
3 tablespoons melted
  butter
1/4 cup mayonnaise

4 cups chopped
  broccoli
1/2 cup golden raisins
8 ounces bacon,
  crisp-fried, crumbled
2 cups sliced
  mushrooms
1/2 cup chopped pecans
1/2 cup thinly sliced
  red onion

- Whisk egg, egg yolk, sugar, cornstarch and dry mustard in double boiler. Add vinegar and water; mix well. Cook over simmering water until thickened, stirring constantly. Beat in butter and mayonnaise. Chill in refrigerator. Combine remaining ingredients in serving bowl. Add dressing; mix well. Chill for 1 hour or longer. May serve in lettuce cups.
  Approx Per Serving: Cal 245; Prot 5 g; Carbo 22 g; Fiber 3 g; T Fat 17 g; 58% Calories from Fat; Chol 61 mg; Sod 188 mg.

Marlene Dominick, Rapidan HFH, Locust Grove, VA

Broccoli and Grape Salad
Yield: 10 servings

1 cup mayonnaise
1 tablespoon vinegar
2 tablespoons sugar
1 bunch broccoli,
  chopped
11/2 cups sliced
  seedless grapes

11/2 cups chopped
  celery
1/2 cup chopped green
  onions
8 ounces bacon,
  crisp-fried, crumbled
1/4 cup toasted almonds

- Combine mayonnaise, vinegar and sugar in bowl; mix well. Add broccoli, grapes, celery, and green onions; mix well. Marinate, covered, in refrigerator overnight. Sprinkle with bacon and almonds at serving time.
  Approx Per Serving: Cal 275; Prot 5 g; Carbo 15 g; Fiber 3 g; T Fat 23 g; 72% Calories from Fat; Chol 19 mg; Sod 261 mg.

Miriam Sater, Oregon Trail HFH, Hermiston, OR

Easy Broccoli Salad
Yield: 8 servings

1 large bunch broccoli,
  chopped
1/2 cup chopped purple
  onion
5 slices bacon, crisp-
  fried, crumbled

1/2 cup golden raisins
3/4 cup sunflower seed
3/4 cup mayonnaise
11/2 tablespoons
  vinegar
1/4 cup sugar

- Combine broccoli, onion, bacon, raisins and sunflower seed in salad bowl. Mix mayonnaise, vinegar and sugar in small bowl. Add to salad; mix well.
  Approx Per Serving: Cal 318; Prot 6 g; Carbo 21 g; Fiber 3 g; T Fat 25 g; 68% Calories from Fat; Chol 16 mg; Sod 194 mg.

Susanne Sims, Gulf Breeze, FL

Fresh Broccoli Salad

Yield: 8 servings

1 large head broccoli,
  chopped
1/4 medium red onion,
  chopped
8 ounces Cheddar
  cheese, cubed
1 cup raisins

1 cup peanuts
6 slices bacon, crisp-
  fried, crumbled
1 1/2 cups mayonnaise
1 tablespoon vinegar
1 tablespoon sugar
2 tablespoons milk

- Combine broccoli, onion, cheese, raisins and peanuts in large salad bowl; mix well. Top with bacon. Mix mayonnaise, vinegar, sugar and milk in small bowl. Add to salad; toss to mix well.
  Approx Per Serving: Cal 619; Prot 15 g; Carbo 24 g; Fiber 4 g; T Fat 54 g; 75% Calories from Fat; Chol 59 mg; Sod 498 mg.

Judy Pierce, Morgan County HFH, Ft. Morgan, CO

Oriental Cabbage Salad

Yield: 12 servings

1 head cabbage,
  chopped
1 7-ounce can water
  chestnuts, drained,
  chopped
3 green onions, sliced
1/4 cup sesame seed,
  toasted
4 ounces slivered
  almonds, toasted

2 3-ounce packages
  chicken-flavored
  ramen noodles,
  crushed
1/2 cup sugar
1/2 cup red wine
  vinegar
1 cup oil
1 teaspoon salt
Pepper to taste

- Combine cabbage, water chestnuts, green onions, sesame seed, almonds and noodles in salad bowl. Combine seasoning packet from noodles, sugar, vinegar, oil, salt and pepper in small bowl; mix well. Add to salad; toss to mix. Chill for several hours to several days.
  Approx Per Serving: Cal 350; Prot 5 g; Carbo 23 g; Fiber 2 g; T Fat 28 g; 69% Calories from Fat; Chol 0 mg; Sod 442 mg.

Susan K. Dionne, Northern Straits HFH, St. Ignace, MI

Never-Fail Coleslaw

Yield: 6 servings

4 cups shredded
  cabbage
1/4 cup chopped onion
1/4 cup mayonnaise
1/2 cup sour cream

1/2 teaspoon dry
  mustard
1/2 teaspoon each salt
  and pepper

- Mix cabbage and onion in bowl. Add mixture of remaining ingredients to cabbage and onion; mix well. Garnish with paprika.
  Approx Per Serving: Cal 121; Prot 1 g; Carbo 4 g; Fiber 1 g; T Fat 12 g; 82% Calories from Fat; Chol 14 mg; Sod 248 mg.

Sue Pratt, Mountain Country HFH, Branson, MO

Corn Salad

Yield: 10 servings

4 8-ounce cans Shoe
  Peg corn, drained
1 medium red onion,
  chopped
3 medium tomatoes,
  chopped

1 green bell pepper,
  chopped
7 tablespoons
  mayonnaise
Salt and pepper to taste

- Combine corn, onion, tomatoes and green pepper in bowl. Add mayonnaise, salt and pepper; mix well. Chill for 30 minutes.
  Approx Per Serving: Cal 156; Prot 3 g; Carbo 20 g; Fiber 2 g; T Fat 9 g; 46% Calories from Fat; Chol 6 mg; Sod 268 mg.

Larry Bell, Starkville HFH, Starkville, MS

I have learned more about the needy than I ever did as a governor, as a candidate, or as a president. The sacrifice I thought I would be making turned out to be one of the greatest blessings of my life . . . I don't know of anything I've seen that more vividly demonstrates love in action than Habitat for Humanity.

Former President Jimmy Carter

Cheesy Pea Salad

Yield: 8 servings

1   16-ounce package
    frozen peas, thawed
1 cup shredded
    Cheddar cheese

1 cup bacon bits
1 cup mayonnaise-type
    salad dressing

■ Combine peas, cheese, bacon bits and salad dressing in bowl; mix well. Chill until serving time.
Approx Per Serving: Cal 275; Prot 13 g; Carbo 19 g; Fiber 3 g; T Fat 17 g; 54% Calories from Fat; Chol 22 mg; Sod 620 mg.

Teresa Sillings, Crawford County HFH, Taswell, IN

Herbed Carrot and Potato Salad

Yield: 6 servings

2 medium potatoes
1 cup thinly sliced
    carrots
1/4 cup thinly sliced
    celery
4 or 5 black olives,
    sliced
1/4 cup mayonnaise
1/4 cup plain yogurt
1 teaspoon lemon juice

1 teaspoon
    Worcestershire sauce
1 1/2 teaspoons chopped
    chives
1/8 teaspoon dried
    dillweed
1/8 teaspoon dry
    mustard
1/4 teaspoon salt
Pepper to taste

■ Cook potatoes, covered, in boiling water in saucepan for 25 minutes or until tender; drain. Peel and slice potatoes. Simmer carrots in a small amount of water in saucepan for 4 minutes; rinse with cold water and drain. Combine potatoes, carrots, celery and olives in large bowl; mix well. Combine remaining ingredients in small bowl. Add to potato mixture; mix gently. Chill, covered, for several hours.
Approx Per Serving: Cal 125; Prot 2 g; Carbo 12 g; Fiber 1 g; T Fat 9 g; 60% Calories from Fat; Chol 7 mg; Sod 194 mg.

*Charles and Melody Lenkner, HFH of the Magic Valley
Twin Falls, ID*

Cucumber-Gelatin Salad

Yield: 6 servings

1   3-ounce package
    lime gelatin
1 teaspoon salt
1 cup boiling water
1 tablespoon vinegar
1 teaspoon grated
    onion

Pepper to taste
1 cup sour cream
1/4 cup mayonnaise
1 cup drained
    shredded cucumber

■ Dissolve gelatin and salt in boiling water in bowl. Add vinegar, onion and pepper. Chill until slightly thickened. Fold in sour cream, mayonnaise and cucumber. Spoon into 8x8-inch dish. Chill until firm.
Approx Per Serving: Cal 214; Prot 3 g; Carbo 18 g; Fiber 1 g; T Fat 16 g; 63% Calories from Fat; Chol 22 mg; Sod 475 mg.

Kay Gunderson, HFH of Metro Louisville, Louisville, KY

Orange and Romaine Salad

Yield: 8 servings

The dressing in this recipe can be prepared in advance and stored in the refrigerator for weeks.

1 pound romaine
    lettuce, torn
8 scallions, sliced
Sections of 2 navel
    oranges, cut into
    chunks
1/2 cup pecans, toasted

1/2 cup oil
2 tablespoons red wine
    vinegar
2 tablespoons sugar
1 teaspoon Dijon
    mustard
1/2 teaspoon salt

■ Combine lettuce, scallions, oranges and pecans in salad bowl. Combine oil, vinegar, sugar, mustard and salt in blender; process until smooth. Add to salad; toss to mix well.
Approx Per Serving: Cal 217; Prot 2 g; Carbo 12 g; Fiber 3 g; T Fat 19 g; 75% Calories from Fat; Chol 0 mg; Sod 155 mg.

Jane Mihalik, HFH of Shenandoah Valley, Basye, VA

Hot Potato Salad

Yield: 6 servings

1 tablespoon flour
1/4 cup rice vinegar
1 to 2 tablespoons
    sliced green onions
1 tablespoon bacon bits
1/2 cup water

1 tablespoon sugar
1 teaspoon celery seed
1 1/2 teaspoons salt
1/2 teaspoon pepper
4 cups chopped cooked
    potatoes

■ Blend flour and vinegar in 1-quart saucepan. Add next 7 ingredients; mix well. Cook for 5 minutes, stirring constantly. Add to potatoes in bowl; mix lightly. Spoon into serving bowl.
Approx Per Serving: Cal 97; Prot 2 g; Carbo 22 g; Fiber 1 g; T Fat <1 g; 2% Calories from Fat; Chol 0 mg; Sod 560 mg.

Jo Schwaller, HFH of Gallatin Valley, Bozeman, MT

Seven-Layer Salad

Yield: 8 servings

1 head lettuce, torn
1 cup chopped celery
1 cup sliced red onion
1   10-ounce package
   frozen green peas,
   thawed

4 ounces bacon,
   crisp-fried, crumbled
1 cup shredded
   Cheddar cheese
1/4 to 1/2 cup
   mayonnaise

■ Layer lettuce, celery, onion, peas, bacon and cheese in large salad bowl. Spread with mayonnaise, sealing to edge of bowl. Chill, covered, overnight. Toss at serving time.
Approx Per Serving: Cal 218; Prot 7 g; Carbo 8 g; Fiber 3 g; T Fat 18 g; 73% Calories from Fat; Chol 27 mg; Sod 289 mg.

Rosalie Spencer, Greater East Liverpool HFH
East Liverpool, OH

Fresh Spinach Salad

Yield: 6 servings

12 ounces spinach, torn
6 to 8 ounces bean
   sprouts
1   7-ounce can sliced
   water chestnuts,
   drained
4 green onions, thinly
   sliced
1/4 cup oil
1/4 cup light vinegar

2 tablespoons catsup
Salt and pepper to taste
8 slices bacon,
   crisp-fried, crumbled
1   11-ounce can
   mandarin oranges,
   drained
3 tablespoons
   sunflower seed,
   toasted

■ Combine spinach, bean sprouts, water chestnuts and green onions in salad bowl. Chill, covered, for up to 4 hours. Combine oil, vinegar, catsup, salt and pepper in small bowl; mix well. Add bacon and dressing to salad; toss gently. Top with mandarin orange sections and sunflower seed. May substitute 2 sliced hard-boiled eggs for mandarin oranges if preferred.
Approx Per Serving: Cal 235; Prot 7 g; Carbo 20 g; Fiber 4 g; T Fat 16 g; 57% Calories from Fat; Chol 7 mg; Sod 247 mg.

Betty Jabusch, Foothills HFH, Newcastle, CA

Spinach and Black Olive Salad

Yield: 8 servings

1/2 cup oil
1/3 cup vinegar
1 teaspoon each dry
   mustard, oregano
   and basil
1 clove of garlic,
   minced
8 ounces Colby cheese,
   cut into 1/2-inch
   cubes

8 ounces corkscrew
   pasta, cooked
3 green onions,
   chopped
1 red bell pepper,
   chopped
1/3 cup sliced black
   olives
3 cups torn spinach

■ Combine oil, vinegar, dry mustard, oregano, basil and garlic in salad bowl; mix well. Add cheese, pasta, green onions, bell pepper and olives; mix well. Chill for 3 hours to overnight. Add spinach at serving time; toss to mix.
Approx Per Serving: Cal 360; Prot 11 g; Carbo 25 g; Fiber 2 g; T Fat 25 g; 61% Calories from Fat; Chol 27 mg; Sod 242 mg.

Josina Bakker, Fluvanna County HFH, Palmyra, VA

State Fair Spinach Salad

Yield: 6 servings

This recipe won a blue ribbon at the 1991 South Carolina State Fair.

1 Granny Smith apple,
   thinly sliced
1 cup orange juice
10 ounces fresh
   spinach, torn, chilled
1 medium tomato, cut
   into wedges

4 slices bacon,
   crisp-fried, crumbled
1/3 cup chopped
   walnuts
1 cup mayonnaise

■ Combine apple slices with orange juice in bowl. Place spinach in large salad bowl. Drain apple slices, reserving 1/2 cup orange juice. Arrange tomato wedges and apple slices over spinach. Sprinkle bacon and walnuts in center. Blend reserved orange juice with mayonnaise in bowl. Drizzle over salad.
Approx Per Serving: Cal 375; Prot 4 g; Carbo 12 g; Fiber 3 g; T Fat 36 g; 83% Calories from Fat; Chol 25 mg; Sod 315 mg.

Myrna J. Ives, Central South Carolina HFH, Columbia, SC

W e thank and praise God for [our house]. I know this is God's house. He's just loaning it to us while we're here. I thank and praise God for the love of the people who want to help people in need.

Mary Mathis, Habitat Homeowner

Stuffing Salad
Yield: 8 servings

3/4 cup oil
1/3 cup vinegar
1/3 cup sugar
1 tablespoon prepared
  mustard
1 tablespoon celery
  seed
8 slices bacon, crisp-
  fried, crumbled

1/2 16-ounce package
  stuffing mix
1 purple onion, thinly
  sliced
4 hard-boiled eggs,
  sliced
1 head lettuce, torn

■ Combine oil, vinegar, sugar, mustard and celery seed
in covered jar; shake to mix well. Chill in refrigerator.
Combine bacon, stuffing mix, onion, eggs and lettuce
in salad bowl. Chill for 3 hours or longer. Add dress-
ing at serving time; toss to mix well.
Approx Per Serving: Cal 410; Prot 9 g; Carbo 32 g;
Fiber 1 g; T Fat 28 g; 60% Calories from Fat;
Chol 112 mg; Sod 540 mg.

Flogene Bloomer, Hawkins HFH, Rogersville, TN

Herbed Tomatoes
Yield: 6 servings

2/3 cup oil
1/4 cup vinegar
1/4 cup chopped parsley
1/4 cup sliced green
  onions
1 clove of garlic,
  minced

2 teaspoons chopped
  thyme
1 teaspoon salt
1/4 teaspoon pepper
6 medium tomatoes,
  coarsely chopped

■ Combine oil, vinegar, parsley, green onions, garlic,
thyme, salt and pepper in bowl; mix well. Add
tomatoes; mix to coat well. Chill for several hours.
Approx Per Serving: Cal 242; Prot 1 g; Carbo 7 g;
Fiber 2 g; T Fat 25 g; 88% Calories from Fat;
Chol 0 mg; Sod 367 mg.

Barbara Vosmek, HFH of Wausau, Wausau, WI

Marinated Tomato and Cucumber Salad
Yield: 8 servings

4 cups chopped
  tomatoes
1 cup sliced cucumbers
1 cup chopped onion
3/4 cup vinegar

1/2 cup oil
1/4 cup sugar
2 tablespoons poppy
  seed
1 tablespoon salt

■ Combine tomatoes, cucumbers and onion in large
bowl; toss lightly. Combine vinegar, oil, sugar, poppy
seed and salt in covered jar; shake to mix well. Add to
vegetables; mix well. Marinate, covered, in refrigerator
for 3 hours or longer.
Approx Per Serving: Cal 185; Prot 2 g; Carbo 14 g;
Fiber 2 g; T Fat 15 g; 69% Calories from Fat;
Chol 0 mg; Sod 809 mg.

Celena Spiva, HFH of Montgomery County, Clarksville, TN

Bleu Cheese Salad Dressing
Yield: 8 servings

2 cups sour cream
1/2 cup mayonnaise
1 teaspoon sugar
1 tablespoon vinegar
Garlic powder to taste

1/2 teaspoon each
  celery salt, garlic salt
  and pepper
8 ounces bleu cheese,
  crumbled

■ Combine sour cream, mayonnaise, sugar, vinegar, garlic powder, celery salt, garlic salt and pepper in bowl;
mix by hand. Add bleu cheese; mix well. Chill in
refrigerator for 2 hours to several days. May serve as
dip if desired.
Approx Per Serving: Cal 324; Prot 8 g; Carbo 4 g;
Fiber 0 g; T Fat 31 g; 85% Calories from Fat;
Chol 55 mg; Sod 726 mg.

Brigitta H. Bradley, Transylvania HFH, Brevard, NC

French Dressing
Yield: 32 servings

1 cup canned tomato
  purée
1 cup oil
1/2 cup packed brown
  sugar
3/4 cup vinegar
1 tablespoon
  Worcestershire sauce

1/2 tablespoon grated
  onion
1/2 clove of garlic,
  minced
1 tablespoon dry
  mustard
1 tablespoon salt

■ Combine tomato purée, oil, brown sugar, vinegar,
Worcestershire sauce, onion, garlic, dry mustard and
salt in 1-quart jar with tight-fitting lid; shake to mix
well. Chill in refrigerator for several hours. Serve over
mixed greens.
Approx Per Serving: Cal 82; Prot <1 g; Carbo 5 g;
Fiber <1 g; T Fat 7 g; 73% Calories from Fat;
Chol 0 mg; Sod 208 mg.

Dianne S. Smith, HFH in Cleveland County, Shelby, NC

MEATS

"By wisdom a house is built, and through understanding it is established."

Proverbs 24:3

No-Peek Casserole

Yield: 4 servings

1½ pounds 1-inch beef cubes
1 envelope onion soup mix
1 10-ounce can cream of mushroom soup

1 4-ounce can mushrooms
½ cup red wine
1 medium onion, chopped

■ Combine beef cubes, soup mix, soup, undrained mushrooms, wine and onion in baking dish; stir slightly. Bake, covered, at 300 degrees for 3 hours. Serve over rice or noodles.
Approx Per Serving: Cal 342; Prot 34 g; Carbo 11 g; Fiber 1 g; T Fat 15 g; 43% Calories from Fat; Chol 97 mg; Sod 906 mg.

Wanda L. Schulze, Walker County HFH, Huntsville, TX

Beef Burgundy

Yield: 6 servings

2 pounds 1-inch beef cubes
1 envelope onion soup mix

1 10-ounce can cream of mushroom soup
1½ cups Burgundy

■ Place beef cubes in large baking dish. Sprinkle soup mix evenly over top. Spread with undiluted soup. Pour wine over layers. Bake, covered, at 300 degrees for 3 hours. Serve over rice or noodles.
Approx Per Serving: Cal 293; Prot 29 g; Carbo 5 g; Fiber <1 g; T Fat 12 g; 38% Calories from Fat; Chol 86 mg; Sod 536 mg.

Marva Mehaffey, HFH of Boca-Delray, Boca Raton, FL

Citrus-Chili Beef Sirloin

Yield: 8 servings

1 10-ounce jar preserved kumquats
2 tablespoons chopped green chilies
1 cup fresh orange juice
2 tablespoons fresh lemon juice

¼ cup honey
1 teaspoon salt
½ teaspoon lemon pepper
1 tablespoon cornstarch
2 pounds boneless top sirloin steak

■ Chop kumquats, discarding seed and reserving juice. Combine with chilies, orange juice, lemon juice, honey, salt, lemon pepper and cornstarch in saucepan; mix well. Bring to a boil. Simmer for 5 minutes or until sauce is slightly thickened, stirring constantly. Place steak in greased baking dish. Pour sauce over top, stirring gently with fork to coat meat. Bake, covered, at 375 degrees for 30 minutes or until meat is medium-rare, basting occasionally. Remove cover. Bake until of desired degree of doneness. Cut steak across the grain. Place on warm platter with any remaining sauce. Garnish with parsley, lemon and orange slices.
Approx Per Serving: Cal 187; Prot 19 g; Carbo 13 g; Fiber <1 g; T Fat 6 g; 29% Calories from Fat; Chol 51 mg; Sod 378 mg.
Nutritional information does not include kumquats.

Emmett J. Ryan, HFH of Gallatin Valley, Bozeman, MT

Italian Beef

Yield: 8 servings

2½ pounds rump roast
1 envelope onion soup mix
2 cups water
½ teaspoon garlic salt

½ teaspoon onion salt
½ teaspoon Italian seasoning
½ teaspoon basil
½ teaspoon oregano

■ Place roast in Dutch oven with soup mix and water. Bake, covered, at 375 degrees for 2 hours or until tender. Remove roast to warm platter. Cool pan juices; skim fat. Slice meat. Return to pan. Add garlic salt, onion salt, Italian seasoning, basil and oregano; mix well. Simmer for 5 minutes.
Approx Per Serving: Cal 189; Prot 27 g; Carbo 1 g; Fiber <1 g; T Fat 8 g; 40% Calories from Fat; Chol 80 mg; Sod 349 mg.

Albert Messer, Stroud HFH, Stroud, OK

Pulgogi (Korean Barbecue Beef)

Yield: 4 servings

Pulgogi is a popular Korean dish served with rice and Kimchi, which is pickled spicy cabbage.

1 pound boneless
  sirloin steak
1/4 cup soy sauce
1 tablespoon sesame oil
1/2 teaspoon sesame
  seed
1/2 teaspoon crushed
  garlic

1/4 teaspoon pepper
1 large green onion,
  chopped
2 tablespoons cooking
  wine
1 tablespoon sugar
Sesame oil for frying

■ Slice beef into 1/8-inch thick strips. Mix soy sauce, 1 tablespoon sesame oil, and next 5 ingredients in shallow glass bowl. Add beef. Marinate in refrigerator for 2 to 3 hours. Stir-fry beef in additional sesame oil in wok for 5 to 10 minutes or until beef is brown.
Approx Per Serving: Cal 197; Prot 20 g; Carbo 5 g; Fiber <1 g; T Fat 9 g; 46% Calories from Fat; Chol 51 mg; Sod 1075 mg.
Nutritional information does not include oil for frying.

Moo Hyung and Kaesook Chung, McLean, VA

Coffee-Flavored Pot Roast

Yield: 6 servings

Doesn't have to be watched. Ready when you are.

1 envelope instant
  meat marinade
2/3 cup cold coffee
1 medium clove of
  garlic, minced
1/4 teaspoon basil

3 to 4-pound beef pot
  roast
1 10-ounce can cream
  of mushroom soup
1 large onion, sliced

■ Combine marinade, coffee, garlic and basil in large saucepan. Pierce pot roast with fork. Place in saucepan, turning to coat with marinade. Marinate for 15 minutes, turning several times. Stir in soup and onion. Simmer, covered, for 2 to 2 1/2 hours. Remove pot roast to warm platter. Serve gravy separately.
Approx Per Serving: Cal 455; Prot 58 g; Carbo 6 g; Fiber 1 g; T Fat 21 g; 43% Calories from Fat; Chol 171 mg; Sod 476 mg.
Nutritional information does not include instant meat marinade.

Allyse Kent, Grants Pass Area HFH, Grants Pass, OR

Roast Beef Au Jus

Yield: 6 servings

1 5-pound standing
  rib roast

Garlic salt to taste
Pepper to taste

■ Let roast stand at room temperature for 1 hour. Rub roast with garlic salt and pepper. Place fat side up in 9x13-inch roasting pan. Roast at 375 degrees for 1 hour; turn off oven. Let stand in oven for 4 to 5 hours; do not open oven door. Reheat roast for 30 minutes before serving.
Approx Per Serving: Cal 496; Prot 71 g; Carbo 0 g; Fiber 0 g; T Fat 22 g; 41% Calories from Fat; Chol 213 mg; Sod 115 mg.

Charlotte Nagel, Fayetteville Area HFH, Fayetteville, NC

Perfect Roast Beef

Yield: 6 servings

1 5-pound standing
  rib roast
2 tablespoons onion
  salt
2 tablespoons
  seasoned salt

1 tablespoon lemon
  pepper
1 tablespoon paprika
1/4 tablespoon garlic
  salt
2 to 3 tablespoons oil

■ Let roast stand at room temperature for 1 hour. Combine next 5 ingredients in bowl; mix well. Sprinkle small amount of mixture over roast; rub with oil. Coat with remaining mixture. Preheat oven to 375 degrees. Place roast fat side up in roasting pan. Roast for 1 hour; turn off oven. Let stand in oven for several hours; do not open oven door. Reheat for 35 to 40 minutes before serving. For well done roast, increase cooking time by 15 to 30 minutes.
Approx Per Serving: Cal 569; Prot 71 g; Carbo 2 g; Fiber 0 g; T Fat 29 g; 47% Calories from Fat; Chol 213 mg; Sod 3667 mg.

Josiah B. Rutter, Homestead HFH, Homestead, FL

Elegant Slow-Cooker Steak

Yield: 8 servings

2 pounds round steak,
    fat trimmed
1/4 cup flour
Salt and pepper to taste
1 onion, chopped

1 8-ounce can
    prepared beef gravy
2 teaspoons
    Worcestershire sauce

■ Slice steak into 1/2x3-inch strips. Toss in mixture of flour, salt and pepper; place in slow cooker. Pour in onion, gravy and Worcestershire sauce. Cook on Low for 7 to 8 hours or until steak is tender.
Approx Per Serving: Cal 186; Prot 23 g; Carbo 6 g; Fiber <1 g; T Fat 7 g; 36% Calories from Fat; Chol 65 mg; Sod 62 mg.

Mrs. Don Freeman, Hawkins HFH, Rogersville, TN

Doh-Moh-Dah (Gambian Beef Stew)

Yield: 8 servings

2 pounds lean stew
    beef, cut into
    1 1/2-inch cubes
1 28-ounce can
    tomatoes
1 red or green bell
    pepper, cut into
    strips
1 stalk celery, sliced
    diagonally
1 potato, cubed
1 large carrot, sliced
    diagonally

1 yellow onion, sliced
1 sweet potato, cubed
1 teaspoon salt
6 tablespoons tomato
    paste
1/2 teaspoon cayenne
    pepper
1/2 cup creamy peanut
    butter
1/2 cup frozen peas,
    thawed

■ Combine beef, tomatoes, bell pepper, celery, potato, carrot, onion, sweet potato, salt and tomato paste in 5-quart saucepan; mix well. Bring to a boil; reduce heat. Simmer, covered, for 1 hour, adding water if necessary. Stir in cayenne pepper and peanut butter. Simmer for 1 hour longer or until vegetables and beef are tender. Add peas. Simmer for 5 minutes. Ladle onto large platter. Garnish with red, green and yellow bell pepper slices and parsley. Serve over rice.
Approx Per Serving: Cal 329; Prot 29 g; Carbo 21 g; Fiber 5 g; T Fat 15 g; 41% Calories from Fat; Chol 64 mg; Sod 557 mg.

Laurette R. Ryan, HFH of Gallatin Valley, Bozeman, MT

Baked Reuben

Yield: 8 servings

1 27-ounce can
    sauerkraut, drained
2 12-ounce cans
    corned beef,
    crumbled
3 cups shredded Swiss
    cheese

1 cup prepared
    Thousand Island
    dressing
3 cups buttered toasted
    bread crumbs

■ Layer sauerkraut, corned beef and cheese in 9x12-inch baking dish. Spread dressing evenly over top; sprinkle with bread crumbs. Bake at 325 degrees for 1 hour.
Approx Per Serving: Cal 655; Prot 41 g; Carbo 38 g; Fiber 3 g; T Fat 38 g; 52% Calories from Fat; Chol 122 mg; Sod 2094 mg.

Marilyn J. Freitag, HFH of Green County, Monroe, WI

English Stew

Yield: 6 servings

2 pounds beef sirloin
    tips
1/4 cup flour
1 large onion, cut into
    quarters
1 tablespoon margarine
2 pounds potatoes, cut
    into halves

2 16-ounce cans
    tomatoes
3 to 4 large carrots,
    sliced
2 cups beef bouillon

■ Dust sirloin tips with flour. Brown in 6-quart Dutch oven with onion and margarine. Add potatoes, tomatoes, carrots and bouillon. Bake, covered, at 350 degrees for 2 hours.
Approx Per Serving: Cal 429; Prot 35 g; Carbo 48 g; Fiber 6 g; T Fat 11 g; 24% Calories from Fat; Chol 85 mg; Sod 600 mg.

Betty Parker, Morgan County HFH, Fort Morgan, CO

Beef Stroganoff

Yield: 8 servings

1 pound lean steak,
    cubed
1 onion, chopped
2 cloves of garlic,
    finely chopped
3 tablespoons
    Worcestershire sauce

2 10-ounce cans cream
    of chicken soup
2 cups low-fat sour
    cream
4 tablespoons catsup
1 16-ounce package
    egg noodles, cooked

■ Brown steak in large skillet over medium heat. Add next 3 ingredients. Sauté until onion is tender; reduce heat to low. Stir in soup and sour cream. Add catsup 1 tablespoon at a time; stir after each addition. Simmer over low heat for 1 hour. Serve over cooked noodles.
Approx Per Serving: Cal 460; Prot 23 g; Carbo 52 g; Fiber 1 g; T Fat 18 g; 35% Calories from Fat; Chol 161 mg; Sod 752 mg.

Laurie Krones, HFH of Green County, Monroe, WI

French Beef Stew

Yield: 8 servings

1 5-pound beef chuck roast, fat trimmed, cubed
1/4 cup margarine
1/2 cup brandy
3 to 4 carrots, thickly sliced
2 large onions, sliced
1 to 2 cloves of garlic, crushed
2 tablespoons tomato paste

6 tablespoons flour
2 tablespoons beef extract
2 10-ounce cans beef consommé
2 cups red wine
3 to 4 potatoes, peeled, cubed
16 ounces mushrooms
1 cup frozen peas, thawed

■ Brown beef cubes on all sides in margarine in heavy skillet. Pour in brandy. Cook over high heat until liquid evaporates. Remove beef with slotted spoon to large casserole; add carrots. Sauté onions and garlic in pan drippings in skillet. Stir in tomato paste, flour and beef extract. Add consommé and 1 cup wine. Bring to a boil. Pour over beef and carrots. Stir in remaining wine. Add potatoes and mushrooms. Bake, covered, at 300 degrees for 3 hours. Add peas. Bake for 10 minutes longer. Garnish with parsley.
Approx Per Serving: Cal 657; Prot 61 g; Carbo 38 g; Fiber 5 g; T Fat 23 g; 31% Calories from Fat; Chol 159 mg; Sod 568 mg.

Karen Frutiger, Jubilee HFH, Jacksonville, IL

Swiss Bliss

Yield: 4 servings

1/4 cup mayonnaise
2 pounds sirloin tip, cut into strips
1 envelope onion soup mix
8 ounces mushrooms, sliced
1/2 green bell pepper, sliced

1 16-ounce can tomatoes
1/4 teaspoon salt
1/4 teaspoon pepper
1 tablespoon A-1 sauce
1 tablespoon cornstarch
1 tablespoon chopped parsley

■ Line 10x14-inch baking pan with heavy-duty foil; spread with mayonnaise. Layer sirloin strips, soup mix, mushrooms and green pepper in prepared pan. Drain tomatoes, reserving juice. Arrange tomatoes over top. Pour mixture of reserved juice and remaining ingredients over layers; cover with foil. Bake at 350 degrees for 2 1/2 hours.
Approx Per Serving: Cal 451; Prot 45 g; Carbo 12 g; Fiber 3 g; T Fat 25 g; 49% Calories from Fat; Chol 136 mg; Sod 624 mg.

Jane Adrian, HFH of Mercer County, Harrodsburg, KY

Teriyaki Roll-Ups

Yield: 4 servings

1 2-pound lean flank steak
1 tablespoon oil
1 teaspoon meat tenderizer
1 teaspoon dried minced garlic

2 teaspoons ground ginger
1/4 cup dry sherry
1/2 cup sugar
1 cup soy sauce
1 8-ounce can sliced pineapple, drained

■ Make 1/4-inch diagonal cuts on both sides of steak. Cut into 1/2-inch wide strips. Roll up; secure with wooden picks. Marinate in mixture of next 7 ingredients in bowl for 1 to 2 hours, turning twice. Drain, reserving marinade. Place on broiler pan. Marinate pineapple slices in reserved marinade for several minutes. Broil pinwheels for 7 minutes; turn. Broil for 5 minutes. Place pineapple slice on each portion. Broil for 2 minutes longer. May heat marinade and serve as sauce.
Approx Per Serving: Cal 507; Prot 46 g; Carbo 39 g; Fiber 1 g; T Fat 16 g; 30% Calories from Fat; Chol 128 mg; Sod 4628 mg.

Jane Carter, Mesilla Valley HFH, Las Cruces, NM

Easy Stroganoff

Yield: 6 servings

1/4 cup chopped green onions
1 clove of garlic, crushed
2 cups sliced mushrooms
2 tablespoons olive oil
1 pound ground beef
1 cup sour cream

1 10-ounce can cream of mushroom soup
1 cup white wine
1 tablespoon Worcestershire sauce
1 16-ounce package egg noodles, cooked

■ Sauté green onions, garlic and mushrooms in oil in large skillet. Add ground beef. Brown, stirring until crumbly; drain. Add mixture of next 4 ingredients. Simmer over low heat for 10 to 15 minutes, stirring occasionally. Serve over cooked noodles.
Approx Per Serving: Cal 652; Prot 27 g; Carbo 60 g; Fiber 1 g; T Fat 31 g; 44% Calories from Fat; Chol 200 mg; Sod 486 mg.

Jo Ellen Welborn, Ada HFH, Ada, OK

Busy-Day Burgers

Yield: 8 servings

1 pound ground beef
2 tablespoons flour

1 10-ounce can French
   onion soup

■ Brown ground beef in skillet, stirring until crumbly; drain. Stir in flour until dissolved. Add soup, stirring to mix. Simmer until mixture thickens. Serve on buns. May make ahead and freeze.

Approx Per Serving: Cal 139; Prot 12 g; Carbo 4 g; Fiber <1 g; T Fat 9 g; 55% Calories from Fat; Chol 37 mg; Sod 337 mg.

Marilyn Manley, Greater East Liverpool HFH
East Liverpool, OH

Dinner Burgers

Yield: 6 servings

1 pound ground beef
1 envelope onion soup
  mix
1 egg, beaten

¹/₄ to ¹/₂ cup dry bread
  crumbs
1 tablespoon oil

■ Combine ground beef, onion soup mix and egg in bowl; mix well. Add enough bread crumbs to hold mixture together. Shape into 6 patties. Brown in skillet in oil; drain. Add enough water to skillet to cover patties halfway. Simmer, covered, over low heat for 30 to 45 minutes. Remove patties with slotted spatula to serving plate. May use pan drippings for gravy to serve over mashed potatoes.

Approx Per Serving: Cal 222; Prot 16 g; Carbo 7 g; Fiber <1 g; T Fat 14 g; 58% Calories from Fat; Chol 85 mg; Sod 221 mg.

Eileen Hastings, Northern Kentucky HFH, Ft. Wright, KY

Cabbage Patch Stew with Dumplings

Yield: 6 servings

1 pound ground beef
2 onions, thinly sliced
1¹/₂ cups chopped
  cabbage
¹/₂ cup chopped celery
1 16-ounce can
  stewed tomatoes
1 15-ounce can
  kidney beans
2 to 3 cups water
1 teaspoon salt

¹/₂ teaspoon pepper
³/₄ teaspoon chili
  powder
1¹/₂ cups flour
2 teaspoons baking
  powder
³/₄ teaspoon salt
3 tablespoons
  shortening
³/₄ cup milk

■ Brown ground beef in skillet, stirring until crumbly; drain. Add onions, cabbage and celery. Cook until vegetables are light brown. Add undrained tomatoes, undrained beans, water, 1 teaspoon salt, pepper and chili powder; mix well. Bring to a boil; reduce heat. Simmer over low heat for several minutes. Combine flour, baking powder and salt in bowl. Cut in shortening until mixture is crumbly. Stir in milk. Drop by teaspoonfuls into simmering stew. Cook for 10 minutes; cover. Cook for 10 minutes longer.

Approx Per Serving: Cal 449; Prot 24 g; Carbo 47 g; Fiber 8 g; T Fat 19 g; 37% Calories from Fat; Chol 54 mg; Sod 1290 mg.

Betty J. Petron, Williston, ND

Campers' Stew

Yield: 4 servings

1 pound ground beef
Salt, pepper and garlic
  salt to taste

2 10-ounce cans
  vegetable soup

■ Brown ground beef in skillet, stirring until crumbly; drain. Stir in seasonings and soup. Simmer for 10 to 20 minutes, stirring occasionally.

Approx Per Serving: Cal 314; Prot 23 g; Carbo 14 g; Fiber 2 g; T Fat 18 g; 52% Calories from Fat; Chol 74 mg; Sod 1017 mg.

Marion Paquin, Highlands County HFH, Sebring, FL

Souper Casserole

Yield: 6 servings

1 pound ground round
1/2 cup chopped celery
1/2 cup chopped onion
1/2 cup chopped green
  bell pepper
3 to 4 tablespoons
  olive oil
1 10-ounce can cream
  of mushroom soup
1 10-ounce can
  chicken noodle soup
1 cup uncooked long
  grain rice

1/2 cup shredded sharp
  Cheddar cheese
1 tablespoon Kitchen
  Bouquet
1 teaspoon dried thyme
1 tablespoon red
  pepper flakes
Salt and black pepper
  to taste
1/2 to 1 cup Italian
  seasoned bread
  crumbs

■ Cook ground round, celery, onion and green pepper
in olive oil in large skillet for 3 to 4 minutes, stirring
until ground beef is crumbly; remove from heat. Stir
in mushroom soup, chicken noodle soup, rice, cheese,
Kitchen Bouquet, thyme, red pepper, salt and black
pepper; mix well. Spoon into 8x12-inch baking dish.
Top with bread crumbs. Bake, covered with foil, at 300
degrees for 1 1/2 hours.
Approx Per Serving: Cal 533; Prot 23 g; Carbo 46 g;
Fiber 2 g; T Fat 28 g; 48% Calories from Fat;
Chol 63 mg; Sod 975 mg.

Joseph E. Stockwell, Jr., Starkville HFH, Starkville, MS

Company Casserole

Yield: 8 servings

1/4 cup minced onion
1 tablespoon minced
  green bell pepper
3 tablespoons butter
1 1/2 pounds ground
  beef
2 8-ounce cans tomato
  sauce

1/2 teaspoon salt
1 teaspoon pepper
1 8-ounce package
  fine egg noodles
1/4 cup sour cream
1 cup cottage cheese
8 ounces cream cheese,
  softened

■ Sauté onion and green pepper in butter in large skillet
until tender. Add ground beef. Brown, stirring until
ground beef is crumbly; drain. Add tomato sauce, salt
and pepper. Simmer over low heat, stirring occasionally. Cook noodles using package directions;
drain. Mix with sour cream, cottage cheese and cream
cheese in large bowl. Stir in ground beef mixture. Pour
into greased 2-quart baking dish. Bake at 350 degrees
for 30 minutes.
Approx Per Serving: Cal 480; Prot 26 g; Carbo 26 g;
Fiber 1 g; T Fat 30 g; 57% Calories from Fat;
Chol 155 mg; Sod 760 mg.

Misty Northridge, Greenville Teen Chapter, Greenville, SC

Chili with Rice and Vegetables

Yield: 16 servings

1 pound ground beef
2 10-ounce cans
  tomato soup
2 soup cans water
1 quart canned
  tomatoes
1 16-ounce can chili
  beans, rinsed,
  drained

1 onion, chopped
2 carrots, chopped
1 potato, cubed
1 teaspoon celery seed
2 teaspoons chili
  powder
1/3 cup uncooked rice
8 to 10 drops of
  Tabasco sauce

■ Brown ground beef in skillet, stirring until crumbly;
drain. Spoon into slow cooker. Add tomato soup,
water, tomatoes, chili beans, onion, carrots, potato,
celery seed, chili powder, rice and Tabasco sauce; mix
well. Cook on Low for 7 to 8 hours or until vegetables
are tender. Cool completely. Chill overnight. Cook for
4 to 5 hours longer on Low or for 3 hours on High
before serving.
Approx Per Serving: Cal 146; Prot 8 g; Carbo 18 g;
Fiber 1 g; T Fat 5 g; 29% Calories from Fat;
Chol 19 mg; Sod 481 mg.

Evie Kooistra, HFH of Greater Sioux Falls, Sioux Falls, SD

Chili con Carne

Yield: 6 servings

1 pound ground beef
2 large onions,
  coarsely chopped
1 28-ounce can
  tomatoes, chopped

1 28-ounce can
  kidney beans
1 to 2 tablespoons chili
  powder
Salt to taste

■ Brown ground beef in skillet, stirring until crumbly;
drain. Add onions. Sauté until tender. Stir in undrained tomatoes, undrained kidney beans, chili
powder and salt. Simmer for 25 minutes, stirring frequently. Ladle into small bowls.
Approx Per Serving: Cal 313; Prot 23 g; Carbo 31 g;
Fiber 13 g; T Fat 12 g; 33% Calories from Fat;
Chol 49 mg; Sod 744 mg.

Eileen L. Oehler, Barry County HFH, Hastings, MI

Easy Chili

Yield: 6 servings

Chili lovers won't consider this to be real chili, but it is very tasty.

1/2 cup chopped onion
1 tablespoon bacon
  drippings
1 pound lean ground
  beef
1 10-ounce can
  tomato soup

1 28-ounce can dark
  red kidney beans,
  drained
1 teaspoon chili
  powder
1/4 teaspoon salt

■ Sauté onion in bacon drippings in large skillet. Add ground beef. Brown, stirring until ground beef is crumbly; drain. Stir in soup, beans, chili powder and salt. Simmer, covered, for 1 hour. May double recipe.
Approx Per Serving: Cal 319; Prot 22 g; Carbo 27 g; Fiber 10 g; T Fat 14 g; 40% Calories from Fat; Chol 63 mg; Sod 944 mg.

Sandy Beall, HFH of Southeastern Connecticut
Gales Ferry, CT

Slow-Cooker Chili

Yield: 8 servings

1 cup dried pinto or
  kidney beans
2 pounds coarsely
  ground chuck
2 16-ounce cans
  tomatoes, drained
1 large green bell
  pepper, coarsely
  chopped

2 onions, coarsely
  chopped
2 cloves of garlic,
  crushed
2 to 3 tablespoons chili
  powder
1 1/2 tablespoons salt
1 teaspoon pepper
1 teaspoon cumin

■ Parboil dried beans in small saucepan until tender; drain. Brown ground chuck in skillet, stirring until crumbly; drain. Combine beans, ground chuck, tomatoes, green pepper, chopped onions, garlic, chili powder, salt, pepper and cumin in slow cooker. Cook on Low for 10 to 12 hours or on High for 4 to 6 hours, stirring occasionally.
Approx Per Serving: Cal 355; Prot 28 g; Carbo 24 g; Fiber 8 g; T Fat 17 g; 42% Calories from Fat; Chol 74 mg; Sod 1484 mg.

Loretta Helmuth, Almost Heaven HFH, Harrisonburg, VA

Contanoodle

Yield: 6 servings

1 16-ounce package
  elbow macaroni
1 1/2 pounds ground
  beef
Salt, pepper and garlic
  powder to taste

1 large onion, sliced
1 10-ounce can
  tomato soup
1 soup can water
1/2 cup shredded
  Cheddar cheese

■ Cook macaroni using package directions; drain and set aside. Combine ground beef, salt, pepper and garlic powder in bowl; mix well. Layer macaroni, ground beef mixture and onion in casserole sprayed with nonstick cooking spray. Mix soup and water in small bowl. Pour over layers; top with cheese. Bake at 350 degrees for 1 to 1 1/2 hours or until bubbly.
Approx Per Serving: Cal 588; Prot 34 g; Carbo 65 g; Fiber 4 g; T Fat 21 g; 32% Calories from Fat; Chol 84 mg; Sod 454 mg.

Dorothy L. Edwards, Mid-Hudson Valley HFH
Poughkeepsie, NY

Burmese Curry

Yield: 8 servings

2 teaspoons butter
6 onions, sliced
2 pounds ground beef
3/4 teaspoon salt
3/4 teaspoon pepper
2 teaspoons curry
  powder

1 teaspoon ginger
2 28-ounce cans
  tomatoes
12 drops of Tabasco
  sauce
4 beef bouillon cubes
1/4 cup whipping cream

■ Melt butter in large electric skillet. Cover bottom of skillet with onions. Shape ground beef into small balls. Arrange over onions. Sprinkle with seasonings. Pour half the tomatoes over mixture. Cook, covered, at 375 degrees for 30 minutes. Add remaining tomatoes, Tabasco sauce and bouillon cubes; mix well. Cook, covered, at 350 degrees for 1 hour, stirring occasionally. Serve over rice, garnished with sliced bananas, coconut, peanuts or almonds and chutney.
Approx Per Serving: Cal 347; Prot 25 g; Carbo 18 g; Fiber 4 g; T Fat 21 g; 52% Calories from Fat; Chol 87 mg; Sod 1033 mg.

Ann L. Miller, Walker County HFH, Huntsville, TX

Beef Enchiladas

Yield: 5 servings

1 pound ground beef
1 onion, chopped
1   8-ounce can refried beans
8 ounces Cheddar cheese, shredded

10 flour tortillas
1   10-ounce can tomato soup
1   8-ounce jar enchilada sauce

- Brown ground beef and onion in skillet, stirring until ground beef is crumbly; drain. Stir in beans and half the cheese. Spoon equal amount of mixture in center of each tortilla; roll up. Place seam side down in 9x13-inch baking pan. Mix soup and enchilada sauce in small bowl; pour over tortillas. Sprinkle with remaining cheese. Bake at 350 degrees for 20 to 30 minutes. Garnish with sliced black olives.
Approx Per Serving: Cal 731; Prot 39 g; Carbo 67 g; Fiber 7 g; T Fat 37 g; 44% Calories from Fat; Chol 107 mg; Sod 1755 mg.

Nickie Van Stelten, HFH of South Central Minnesota
Good Thunder, MN

Hot Pot Ground Beef

Yield: 8 servings

1 1/2 pounds ground beef
1 onion, chopped
1 cup chopped celery
1   16-ounce can mixed vegetables
1   10-ounce can cream of mushroom soup

1   10-ounce can chicken and rice soup
1   8-ounce can mushroom pieces
1/4 cup soy sauce
2 cups chow mein noodles

- Brown ground beef, onion and celery in skillet, stirring until ground beef is crumbly; drain. Combine with undrained vegetables, soups, undrained mushrooms, soy sauce and chow mein noodles in bowl; mix well. Spoon into 2 1/2-quart casserole. Bake at 350 degrees for 1 hour.
Approx Per Serving: Cal 328; Prot 22 g; Carbo 21 g; Fiber 4 g; T Fat 18 g; 49% Calories from Fat; Chol 57 mg; Sod 1417 mg.

Wilma Carlsrud, Fergus Falls Area HFH
Fergus Falls, MN

Marzetti

Yield: 8 servings

1   6-ounce package noodles
1 1/4 pounds ground beef
1/3 cup chopped pimentos
1/3 cup condensed tomato soup
1   16-ounce can tomato sauce

1   8-ounce can mushroom pieces, drained
1 1/2 teaspoons Worcestershire sauce
2 tablespoons brown sugar
1 1/2 cups shredded American cheese

- Cook noodles using package directions; drain. Brown ground beef in skillet, stirring until crumbly. Drain and rinse ground beef with 1 quart hot water. Combine noodles, ground beef, pimentos, soup, tomato sauce, mushrooms, Worcestershire sauce, brown sugar and 1 cup cheese in bowl; mix well. Spoon into greased 2-quart casserole. Bake at 350 degrees for 25 minutes. Sprinkle with remaining cheese. Bake for 5 minutes longer.
Approx Per Serving: Cal 358; Prot 23 g; Carbo 26 g; Fiber 2 g; T Fat 19 g; 46% Calories from Fat; Chol 106 mg; Sod 722 mg.

Kay Wing, Southwest Iowa HFH, Farragut, IA

All-in-One Meatball Casserole

Yield: 6 servings

1 pound ground beef
1 potato, grated
1 carrot, grated
1/2 teaspoon seasoned salt
1 egg, beaten

1 small onion, chopped
2 tablespoons flour
1   10-ounce can cream of mushroom soup
1 soup can water

- Combine ground beef, potato, carrot, seasoned salt, egg, onion and flour in bowl; mix well. Shape into large balls. Brown lightly in skillet; drain. Place in 2-quart baking dish. Pour mixture of soup and water over meatballs. Bake, covered, at 325 degrees for 1 hour. Bake, uncovered, for 30 minutes longer. Serve with salad and bread.
Approx Per Serving: Cal 256; Prot 17 g; Carbo 13 g; Fiber 1 g; T Fat 15 g; 54% Calories from Fat; Chol 85 mg; Sod 551 mg.

Shirley Patterson, Eastside HFH, Carnation, WA

Cranberry Meatballs

Yield: 8 servings

2 pounds ground beef
1 envelope onion soup
  mix
1 cup bread crumbs
3 eggs, beaten
1 12-ounce bottle of
  chili sauce

12 ounces water
1 cup loosely packed
  brown sugar
1 16-ounce can
  sauerkraut, drained
1 16-ounce can whole
  cranberry sauce

■ Combine ground beef, onion soup mix, bread crumbs and eggs in bowl; mix well. Shape into balls. Place in 9x13-inch glass baking dish. Combine chili sauce, water, brown sugar, sauerkraut and cranberry sauce in saucepan; mix well. Cook over medium heat until mixture bubbles, stirring frequently. Pour over meatballs. Bake at 325 degrees for 2 hours. May reheat leftovers in slow cooker.

Approx Per Serving: Cal 580; Prot 27 g; Carbo 78 g; Fiber 3 g; T Fat 19 g; 29% Calories from Fat; Chol 155 mg; Sod 1237 mg.

Ruth Gossen, Morgan County HFH, Fort Morgan, CO

Meat and Vegetable Loaf

Yield: 8 servings

4 slices wheat bread,
  cubed
1 32-ounce can
  stewed tomatoes
2¹/₂ pounds lean
  ground beef
1 cup chopped onion
1 cup chopped green,
  red or yellow bell
  pepper

¹/₂ cup grated carrot
¹/₂ cup chopped celery
2 eggs, beaten
2 teaspoons mixed
  thyme, marjoram
  and oregano
2 teaspoons
  Worcestershire sauce
¹/₂ teaspoon pepper
Salt to taste

■ Soak bread in tomatoes in shallow bowl. Combine with ground beef, onion, bell pepper, carrot, celery, eggs, herbs, Worcestershire sauce, pepper and salt in large bowl; mix well. Pack into large loaf pan. Bake at 350 degrees for 1 hour.

Approx Per Serving: Cal 393; Prot 31 g; Carbo 19 g; Fiber 2 g; T Fat 22 g; 50% Calories from Fat; Chol 146 mg; Sod 575 mg.

Mary Kay Conroy, San Gabriel Valley HFH, Glendale, CA

Mexican Meat Loaf

Yield: 6 servings

1 egg, beaten
¹/₂ cup tomato sauce
1 4-ounce can
  chopped green
  chilies, drained
1 3-ounce can
  chopped
  mushrooms, drained
¹/₂ cup fine dry bread
  crumbs

1 teaspoon salt
Pepper to taste
1 teaspoon chili
  powder
1¹/₂ pounds lean
  ground beef
3 3-ounce slices
  Monterey Jack
  cheese, cut into
  quarters diagonally

■ Combine egg, tomato sauce, chilies, mushrooms, bread crumbs, salt, pepper and chili powder in large bowl; mix well. Stir in ground beef, mixing well. Invert a 2-inch glass in center of 8-inch microwave-safe bowl. Spread mixture around glass. Cover with waxed paper. Microwave on High for 14 minutes, turning 3 times. Remove glass; drain. Top with cheese slices. Microwave, uncovered, for 1 minute longer. Let stand for 8 minutes before slicing.

Approx Per Serving: Cal 450; Prot 34 g; Carbo 10 g; Fiber 1 g; T Fat 30 g; 61% Calories from Fat; Chol 149 mg; Sod 1043 mg.

Maggie Craig Chrisman, HFH International Board of Directors
Paradise Valley, AZ

Mediterranean Beef Skillet

Yield: 4 servings

1 pound ground beef
1 onion, chopped
1 clove of garlic,
  minced
1 small eggplant, cubed
1 potato, peeled, cubed
¹/₄ cup minced parsley
1 tablespoon lemon
  juice

¹/₂ cup water
¹/₂ teaspoon paprika
¹/₂ teaspoon ground
  allspice
1 green bell pepper,
  chopped
1 zucchini, sliced
1 tomato, cut into
  wedges

■ Brown ground beef, onion and garlic in skillet, stirring until ground beef is crumbly; drain. Add eggplant, potato, parsley, lemon juice, water, paprika and allspice. Bring to a boil; reduce heat. Simmer, covered, for 15 minutes, stirring occasionally. Add green pepper and zucchini. Cook for 15 minutes longer, stirring occasionally. Add tomato. Cook for 5 minutes longer or until vegetables are tender.

Approx Per Serving: Cal 312; Prot 24 g; Carbo 19 g; Fiber 5 g; T Fat 17 g; 47% Calories from Fat; Chol 74 mg; Sod 76 mg.

Claire Martindale, Habitat East, Bridgewater, VA

Mexican Cowboy Casserole

Yield: 6 servings

1 pound ground beef
1 16-ounce can
   Spanish rice
1 16-ounce can ranch-
   style beans

8 flour tortillas, torn
   into strips
8 ounces Longhorn
   cheese, shredded

■ Brown ground beef in skillet, stirring until crumbly; drain. Stir in rice and beans. Simmer for several minutes, stirring often. Line 9x9-inch baking dish with half the tortillas. Top with ground beef mixture, half the cheese and remaining tortillas. Sprinkle with remaining cheese. Bake at 350 degrees for 15 minutes or until cheese melts.
Approx Per Serving: Cal 573; Prot 32 g; Carbo 48 g; Fiber 1 g; T Fat 30 g; 45% Calories from Fat; Chol 89 mg; Sod 1148 mg.

Kathy Spann, Mt. Pleasant HFH, Mt. Pleasant, TX

Beef-Broccoli Pie

Yield: 6 servings

2 cups self-rising flour
2/3 cup milk
1/4 cup oil
1 pound very lean
   ground beef
1/4 cup chopped onion
2 teaspoons salt
1/2 teaspoon garlic
   powder
2 tablespoons flour
1 cup skim milk

3 ounces low-fat cream
   cheese
1 10-ounce package
   frozen chopped
   broccoli, cooked,
   drained
2 egg whites, beaten
4 ounces Monterey
   Jack cheese,
   shredded

■ Combine flour, milk and oil in bowl, stirring to form soft dough. Pat half the dough into 9-inch pie plate; reserve remaining dough. Brown ground beef and onion in skillet, stirring until ground beef is crumbly; drain. Add salt, garlic powder and flour. Cook on medium-low heat, stirring until flour is absorbed. Add skim milk and cream cheese. Cook, stirring until cheese is melted. Add broccoli. Remove from heat and cool. Add a small amount of mixture to beaten egg whites in bowl. Add egg whites to mixture, stirring constantly. Cook over low heat until thickened, stirring constantly. Pour into prepared pie plate. Top with Monterey Jack cheese. Cover with reserved dough. Bake at 350 degrees for 25 to 30 minutes or until brown. Let stand for 10 minutes before slicing.
Approx Per Serving: Cal 456; Prot 26 g; Carbo 41 g; Fiber 3 g; T Fat 21 g; 41% Calories from Fat; Chol 58 mg; Sod 1524 mg.

Elizabeth A. Copeland, Satilla HFH, Waycross, GA

Cheeseburger Pie

Yield: 4 servings

1 cup tomato sauce
1/2 cup chopped onion
1/2 green bell pepper,
   chopped
1 envelope beef broth
   mix
1 teaspoon artificial
   sweetener
1/2 teaspoon chili
   powder

1/4 teaspoon garlic
   powder
8 ounces cooked
   ground beef
2 cups cooked rice
4 ounces Cheddar
   cheese, shredded

■ Combine first 7 ingredients in saucepan; mix well. Simmer for 8 to 10 minutes, stirring often. Add ground beef, cooked rice and 2/3 of the cheese. Cook until cheese is melted, stirring constantly. Pour into 8x8-inch baking pan. Sprinkle with remaining cheese. Bake at 375 degrees for 30 minutes.
Approx Per Serving: Cal 373; Prot 21 g; Carbo 32 g; Fiber 2 g; T Fat 18 g; 43% Calories from Fat; Chol 67 mg; Sod 835 mg.

Tina Schlehuber, Northern Straits HFH, St. Ignace, MI

Habitat Widower's Dinner

Yield: 1 serving

1 frozen TV dinner

■ Go to freezer and choose frozen TV dinner. Remove from carton; read directions. Peel back foil from dessert compartment of dinner. Bake at 400 to 425 degrees using package directions. Remove from oven. Place on hot pad; peel off foil. Get a fork and a drink and enjoy your TV dinner.
Nutritional information for this recipe is not available.

Scott Mallinson, Greater Manchester HFH, Derry, NH

Pasta Pie

Yield: 4 servings

3 ounces spaghetti,
  cooked *al dente*
2 tablespoons grated
  Parmesan cheese
1 egg, beaten
1/2 teaspoon oregano
2/3 cup part-skim
  ricotta cheese
6 ounces very lean
  ground beef
2 cloves of garlic, minced
1/2 cup chopped onion

2 tablespoons olive oil
1/2 cup chopped red
  bell pepper
1/2 cup chopped green
  bell pepper
1/2 cup chopped carrot
1 8-ounce can no-salt-
  added whole tomatoes
2 teaspoons tomato
  paste
4 ounces mozzarella
  cheese, shredded

■ Pat mixture of first 4 ingredients into 9-inch deep-dish pie plate sprayed with PAM. Spread with ricotta cheese. Brown ground beef, garlic and onion in olive oil in skillet, stirring frequently. Add bell peppers and carrot. Cook for 2 minutes or until tender. Add tomatoes and tomato paste. Cook until bubbly, stirring often. Spoon over ricotta cheese. Sprinkle with mozzarella cheese. Bake at 350 degrees for 20 minutes or until brown. Let stand for 5 minutes.

Approx Per Serving: Cal 378; Prot 23 g; Carbo 28 g; Fiber 2 g; T Fat 20 g; 47% Calories from Fat; Chol 106 mg; Sod 308 mg.

Robert D. Bond, Hamilton HFH, Hamilton, NY

Pasta and Beef Casserole

Yield: 10 servings

12 ounces spaghetti,
  broken into 2-inch
  pieces, cooked
2 tablespoons butter
1/2 cup grated
  Parmesan cheese
1/2 teaspoon salt
1/4 teaspoon pepper
1 egg, beaten
16 ounces ricotta cheese
1 1/2 pounds ground
  chuck

1 onion, chopped
1 green bell pepper,
  chopped
2 cloves of garlic,
  minced
4 cups prepared
  spaghetti sauce
1 teaspoon sugar
1/2 teaspoon oregano
12 ounces mozzarella
  cheese, shredded

■ Mix first 6 ingredients in bowl. Spread in 9x13-inch casserole. Spoon ricotta cheese over spaghetti. Brown ground chuck, onion, green pepper and garlic in skillet, stirring frequently; drain. Stir in spaghetti sauce, sugar and oregano. Pour over ricotta layer. Bake at 350 degrees for 30 minutes. Sprinkle with mozzarella cheese. Bake for 10 minutes longer. Let stand for 10 to 15 minutes.

Approx Per Serving: Cal 604; Prot 33 g; Carbo 46 g; Fiber 3 g; T Fat 32 g; 47% Calories from Fat; Chol 124 mg; Sod 908 mg.

Anne Carroll, Omaha HFH, Omaha, NE

Italian Spaghetti with Meat Sauce

Yield: 6 servings

4 onions, chopped
1/4 cup olive oil
4 cloves of garlic,
  minced
2 pounds ground round
2 28-ounce cans
  Italian tomatoes
2 6-ounce cans Italian
  tomato paste
Salt and pepper to taste

1/2 teaspoon marjoram
1/2 teaspoon oregano
1/2 teaspoon thyme
1 bay leaf
2 pounds thin spaghetti
6 tablespoons melted
  butter
1 cup freshly grated
  Parmesan cheese

■ Sauté onions in olive oil in saucepan tender. Add garlic. Sauté until golden brown. Add ground beef. Cook, stirring until crumbly; drain. Add tomatoes, tomato paste, salt and pepper. Simmer over low heat for 3 hours or until thickened, stirring occasionally. Add seasonings. Simmer for 1 hour longer; discard bay leaf. Cook spaghetti using package directions; drain. Toss with butter and 1/4 cup Parmesan cheese. Serve with sauce and remaining Parmesan cheese.

Approx Per Serving: Cal 1007; Prot 37 g; Carbo 145 g; Fiber 13 g; T Fat 33 g; 29% Calories from Fat; Chol 63 mg; Sod 840 mg.

Vada Stanley, Westport, CT

A worker in Miami frames a window that will look out on a new vista of hope.

Spaghetti Pie

Yield: 8 servings

6 ounces spaghetti, cooked
2 tablespoons margarine
1/2 cup grated Parmesan cheese
2 eggs, beaten
1 cup cottage cheese
1 pound ground beef
1/2 cup chopped onion

1/4 cup chopped green bell pepper
1 8-ounce can tomatoes
1 6-ounce can tomato paste
1 teaspoon sugar
1 teaspoon garlic salt
1/2 cup shredded mozzarella cheese

■ Combine cooked spaghetti, margarine, Parmesan cheese and eggs in bowl; mix well. Spread in buttered 10-inch pie plate. Cover with cottage cheese. Brown ground beef, onion and green pepper in skillet, stirring until ground beef is crumbly; drain. Stir in undrained tomatoes, tomato paste, sugar and garlic salt. Cook until heated through, stirring occasionally. Spoon over cottage cheese. Bake at 350 degrees for 20 minutes. Sprinkle with mozzarella cheese. Bake for 5 minutes longer.
Approx Per Serving: Cal 339; Prot 23 g; Carbo 24 g; Fiber 2 g; T Fat 17 g; 45% Calories from Fat; Chol 104 mg; Sod 627 mg.

HelenSue L. Parrish, Starkville HFH, Starkville, MS

Baked Spaghetti

Yield: 8 servings

12 ounces spaghetti, cooked
1 egg, beaten
1 cup milk
2 cups shredded mozzarella cheese

Garlic salt to taste
1 32-ounce jar spaghetti sauce
8 ounces ground beef
4 ounces pepperoni, sliced

■ Combine cooked spaghetti, egg and milk in bowl; mix well. Spoon into 9x13-inch baking dish. Sprinkle with 1/2 cup mozzarella cheese and garlic salt. Pour in spaghetti sauce. Top with uncooked ground beef and remaining mozzarella cheese. Arrange pepperoni slices over cheese. Bake at 300 degrees for 1 hour. May add sliced mushrooms if desired.
Approx Per Serving: Cal 517; Prot 23 g; Carbo 53 g; Fiber 3 g; T Fat 24 g; 41% Calories from Fat; Chol 76 mg; Sod 996 mg.

Helen Hintz, Firelands HFH, Norwalk, OH

Spaghetti and Sauce

Yield: 6 servings

1 pound ground beef
1 onion, chopped
1 clove of garlic, minced
1 20-ounce can tomatoes
1 16-ounce can tomato sauce
1/2 cup water

1 teaspoon oregano
1/2 teaspoon thyme
2 tablespoons chopped parsley
1 tablespoon sugar
1 teaspoon salt
1 bay leaf
1 8-ounce package spaghetti

■ Brown ground beef, chopped onion and garlic in large saucepan, stirring until ground beef is crumbly; drain. Add tomatoes, tomato sauce, water, oregano, thyme, parsley, sugar, salt and bay leaf to saucepan. Cook over low heat for 1 to 4 hours, stirring occasionally. Remove bay leaf. Cook spaghetti using package directions; drain. Spoon sauce over spaghetti and serve.
Approx Per Serving: Cal 352; Prot 21 g; Carbo 42 g; Fiber 4 g; T Fat 12 g; 29% Calories from Fat; Chol 49 mg; Sod 1011 mg.

Linda Clinkenbeard, Knox County HFH, Vincennes, IN

Boy's Stew

Yield: 6 servings

1 pound lean ground beef
2 tablespoons chopped onion
3 large potatoes, cubed

3 carrots, coarsely chopped
1 1/2 cups water
1 10-ounce can cream of mushroom soup

■ Brown ground beef in large skillet, stirring until crumbly; drain. Add onion. Cook until onion is tender. Add potatoes, carrots and water. Simmer until vegetables are tender. Stir in soup. Simmer for 5 minutes, stirring occasionally.
Approx Per Serving: Cal 276; Prot 16 g; Carbo 21 g; Fiber 2 g; T Fat 14 g; 47% Calories from Fat; Chol 50 mg; Sod 442 mg.

Beth Weitzel, Marshall County HFH, Marshalltown, IA

As Christians we will agree on the use of the hammer as an instrument to manifest God's love.

Milliard Fuller (No More Shacks!)

Moss Stew

Yield: 6 servings

1 onion, chopped
3 tablespoons oil
1 pound ground beef
1 cup catsup

2 10-ounce cans
  vegetable soup
1 17-ounce can Shoe
  Peg corn, drained

- Sauté onion in oil in saucepan until tender. Add ground beef. Cook, stirring until brown and crumbly; drain. Add catsup, soup and corn. Simmer for 30 minutes, stirring often. Serve over hamburger buns.
Approx Per Serving: Cal 391; Prot 19 g; Carbo 38 g; Fiber 4 g; T Fat 20 g; 44% Calories from Fat; Chol 49 mg; Sod 1339 mg.

John S. Harris, Rapides HFH, Pineville, LA

Beef-Broccoli Strudel

Yield: 6 servings

1 pound ground beef
1 onion, chopped
1 10-ounce package
  frozen chopped
  broccoli, thawed,
  drained
4 ounces mozzarella
  cheese, shredded

1/2 cup sour cream
1/4 cup dry bread
  crumbs
8 ounces frozen phyllo
  dough, thawed
1/2 cup melted butter

- Brown ground beef and onion in skillet, stirring until ground beef is crumbly; drain. Mix in broccoli, cheese, sour cream and bread crumbs. Cook until heated through and cheese is melted. Place sheet of phyllo on waxed paper; brush with butter. Repeat with remaining dough, layering sheets. Spoon ground beef mixture evenly on half the dough. Roll up from ground beef side as for jelly roll. Place seam side down on baking sheet; brush with remaining butter. Bake at 350 degrees for 45 minutes or until golden brown. Remove to wire rack to cool for 15 minutes; slice.
Approx Per Serving: Cal 530; Prot 25 g; Carbo 33 g; Fiber 3 g; T Fat 34 g; 57% Calories from Fat; Chol 114 mg; Sod 431 mg.

Jerry and Kristin Howard-Crowley, Pemi-Valley Habitat
Ashland, NH

Tostado Casserole

Yield: 8 servings

1 pound ground beef
1 envelope taco
  seasoning mix
1 16-ounce can
  tomato sauce

2 1/2 cups corn chips
1 16-ounce can
  refried beans
1/2 cup shredded
  Cheddar cheese

- Brown ground beef in skillet, stirring until crumbly; drain. Add taco seasoning mix and 3/4 of the tomato sauce; mix well. Line 7x11-inch baking dish with 2 cups corn chips. Crush remaining chips. Spread ground beef mixture in prepared dish. Mix remaining tomato sauce and refried beans in small bowl. Spoon over ground beef layer. Bake at 350 degrees for 25 minutes. Sprinkle with Cheddar cheese and reserved crushed chips. Bake for 5 minutes longer or until cheese is melted.
Approx Per Serving: Cal 292; Prot 18 g; Carbo 24 g; Fiber 6 g; T Fat 14 g; 44% Calories from Fat; Chol 45 mg; Sod 1172 mg.

Sharon Meier, Southwest Iowa HFH, Shenandoah, IA

Ardy's Brunch Bake

Yield: 8 servings

2 cups plain croutons
1 cup chopped ham
2 tablespoons chopped
  onion
2 tablespoons chopped
  green bell pepper

1 cup shredded
  Cheddar cheese
6 eggs, beaten
2 cups milk
Salt and pepper to taste

- Layer croutons, ham, onion, green pepper and cheese in 9x13-inch baking dish. Beat eggs, milk, salt and pepper together in bowl. Pour over layers. Chill, covered with foil, overnight. Bake, covered, at 325 degrees for 45 minutes. Bake, uncovered, for 15 minutes longer. Serve immediately.
Approx Per Serving: Cal 210; Prot 16 g; Carbo 9 g; Fiber <1 g; T Fat 12 g; 53% Calories from Fat; Chol 192 mg; Sod 497 mg.

Gene Breitzman, HFH of Wausau, Wausau, WI

Banquet Ham Loaf

Yield: 8 servings

3 pounds ground ham
1 pound ground pork
4 eggs, beaten
1⅓ cups
   herb-seasoned bread
   crumbs
1 cup milk

Pepper to taste
½ cup packed brown
   sugar
¼ cup water
2 tablespoons vinegar
1 teaspoon prepared
   mustard

■ Mix ham, pork, eggs, bread crumbs, milk and pepper in bowl. Pack into 5x9-inch loaf pan. Bake at 375 degrees for 1 hour. Cook mixture of remaining ingredients over low heat until sugar dissolves, stirring constantly. Pour over ham loaf. Bake for 15 minutes.

Approx Per Serving: Cal 552; Prot 63 g; Carbo 31 g; Fiber 1 g; T Fat 19 g; 31% Calories from Fat; Chol 247 mg; Sod 2476 mg.

Donna Holter, Mercer County HFH, West Middlesex, PA

Cajun Red Beans with Ham and Sausage

Yield: 10 servings

2 pounds dried red
   beans
2 large bay leaves,
   crushed
2 cloves of garlic,
   crushed
2 large onions, chopped
1 pound ham, cubed

2 pounds Cajun
   sausage, cut into
   1-inch pieces
2 stalks celery, chopped
1 teaspoon cayenne
   pepper
2 to 3 tablespoons cumin
Salt to taste

■ Rinse beans; drain. Place in large saucepan with bay leaves, garlic and enough water to cover. Soak overnight. Add onions, ham, sausage, celery, cayenne pepper, cumin and salt. Cook over low heat for 10 to 12 hours, stirring often. Add more water for desired consistency. Serve over hot rice.

Approx Per Serving: Cal 551; Prot 42 g; Carbo 58 g; Fiber 21 g; T Fat 17 g; 28% Calories from Fat; Chol 60 mg; Sod 1186 mg.

Lucy Bugea, Trinity Presbyterian, Starkville, MS

Croissants with Ham and Mornay Sauce

Yield: 4 servings

4 croissants
8 thin slices ham
5½ tablespoons butter
3 tablespoons flour
2 cups milk

Salt, pepper and
   nutmeg to taste
4 ounces shredded
   Swiss cheese
Minced onion to taste

■ Split croissants. Place 2 slices ham in each croissant. Place in baking dish. Melt butter over medium heat in saucepan. Add flour. Cook for 30 to 45 seconds or until mixture is frothy, stirring frequently. Add milk. Cook until mixture begins to boil and thicken, beating constantly with whisk. Season with salt, pepper and nutmeg; reduce heat. Simmer for 3 to 4 minutes. Add cheese and onion. Bring to a boil, whisking constantly. Pour over and around croissants. Bake at 325 degrees for 30 to 40 minutes or until bubbly.

Approx Per Serving: Cal 667; Prot 32 g; Carbo 38 g; Fiber 1 g; T Fat 43 g; 58% Calories from Fat; Chol 129 mg; Sod 1463 mg.

Jeff Westbrook, Furman University Campus Chapter HFH
Greenville, SC

Ham and Sausage Jambalaya

Yield: 8 servings

2 cups sliced smoked
   sausage
1 cup finely chopped
   yellow onion
¾ cup chopped green
   bell pepper
1 large clove of garlic,
   chopped
2 cups chopped ham
½ cup dry white wine
1   16-ounce can
   tomatoes

1 teaspoon salt
½ teaspoon thyme
¼ teaspoon basil
¼ teaspoon marjoram
¼ teaspoon paprika
¼ teaspoon Tabasco
   sauce
2 tablespoons chopped
   fresh parsley
1 cup long grain
   converted rice

■ Sauté sausage in large saucepan for 10 minutes. Remove with slotted spoon to paper towels. Add onion, green pepper and garlic to pan drippings. Sauté for 5 minutes or until tender. Stir in sausage, ham, wine, undrained tomatoes, salt, thyme, basil, marjoram, paprika and Tabasco sauce. Bring to a boil; reduce heat. Add parsley and rice; mix well. Simmer, covered, for 25 minutes.

Approx Per Serving: Cal 296; Prot 18 g; Carbo 24 g; Fiber 1 g; T Fat 13 g; 40% Calories from Fat; Chol 41 mg; Sod 1314 mg.

Charlotte Rhoades, Habitat Gypsy, Middleville, MI

Baked Ham and Cheese Omelette

Yield: 6 servings

8 eggs
1/2 teaspoon salt
1 cup milk
1/2 cup chopped
  cooked ham

1 cup shredded
  Cheddar cheese
1 tablespoon minced
  onion flakes
1 teaspoon dried parsley

■ Beat eggs, salt and milk in mixer bowl at medium speed for 2 to 3 minutes. Stir in ham, cheese, onion flakes and parsley. Pour into buttered 9x9-inch pan. Bake at 325 degrees for 40 to 45 minutes or until set and golden brown.
Approx Per Serving: Cal 226; Prot 17 g; Carbo 3 g; Fiber <1 g; T Fat 16 g; 63% Calories from Fat; Chol 316 mg; Sod 558 mg.

Kathleen Schmidt, Black Hills Area HFH, Nemo, SD

Macaroni and Cheese Casserole with Ham

Yield: 6 servings

8 ounces elbow
  macaroni, cooked
16 ounces Cheddar
  cheese, shredded
1   4-ounce can
  mushroom pieces,
  drained
1   10-ounce can cream
  of mushroom soup

1 cup mayonnaise
1/2 cup milk
1/2 cup chopped onion
1 cup chopped cooked
  ham
15 butter crackers,
  crushed
1/4 cup melted butter

■ Combine macaroni, cheese, mushroom pieces, soup, mayonnaise, milk, onion and ham in bowl; mix well. Pour into greased baking dish. Top with crushed crackers; drizzle with butter. Bake at 350 degrees for 40 minutes.
Approx Per Serving: Cal 918; Prot 32 g; Carbo 42 g; Fiber 2 g; T Fat 70 g; 68% Calories from Fat; Chol 138 mg; Sod 1599 mg.

Alyssa DeLavan, Mercer University Campus Chapter HFH
Roswell, GA

Spinach and Ham Quiche

Yield: 8 servings

16 ounces ricotta cheese
8 ounces mozzarella
  cheese, shredded
4 ounces Parmesan
  cheese, grated
4 eggs, beaten
1 large onion, finely
  chopped

3 tablespoons olive oil
1   10-ounce package
  frozen chopped
  spinach
1 cup chopped cooked
  ham
2   9-inch all ready pie
  pastries

■ Combine first 3 ingredients in bowl; mix well. Stir in eggs. Sauté onion in oil in small skillet until tender. Stir into cheese mixture. Cook spinach using package directions; drain well. Stir spinach and ham into cheese mixture. Line 9-inch pie plate with 1 pie shell. Pour in cheese mixture. Cover with remaining pie shell. Flute edges and cut air vents. Bake at 375 degrees for 1 hour or until light brown.
Approx Per Serving: Cal 611; Prot 28 g; Carbo 31 g; Fiber 1 g; T Fat 41 g; 62% Calories from Fat; Chol 193 mg; Sod 995 mg.

Kimberly Ritchey, HFH International
Andover, OH

Roast Leg of Lamb

Yield: 8 servings

3 tablespoons flour
1 tablespoon dry
  mustard
1/2 teaspoon salt

Pepper to taste
1   4 to 6-pound leg of
  lamb, trimmed
3 to 4 slices bacon

I have always been a strong supporter and admirer of the outstanding work Habitat for Humanity is doing across America—and indeed around the world—to make the dream of homeownership a reality for people in need. But Habitat does more than build houses; it builds families, neighborhoods, and communities by bringing people together in a spirit of friendship and teamwork.

Jack Kemp, former Congressman, former Secretary of the Department of Housing and Urban Development; member of HFH International Board of Directors.

■ Combine flour, mustard, salt and pepper in small bowl. Add enough water to make smooth paste. Spread mixture over lamb. Place on rack in roasting pan. Cover with bacon; insert meat thermometer. Roast at 325 degrees for 45 minutes per pound or until meat thermometer registers 180 degrees.
Approx Per Serving: Cal 426; Prot 58 g; Carbo 3 g; Fiber <1 g; T Fat 19 g; 41% Calories from Fat; Chol 185 mg; Sod 323 mg.

Ellen J. Bromley, Pensacola HFH, Pensacola, FL

Utah Women's Strength

Yield: 4 servings

1 pound liver, cut into thin slices
1 tablespoon flour
1/2 teaspoon pepper
1/2 teaspoon paprika
1/2 teaspoon garlic salt
1 tablespoon oil

2 cups thinly sliced onions
1 1/2 cups beef broth
1/2 cup cold water
2 tablespoons cornstarch

■ Coat liver with mixture of next 4 ingredients. Sauté in oil in skillet for 1 minute on each side; remove to warm platter. Sauté onions in pan drippings until golden brown; remove from heat. Pour 3/4 cup beef broth in 9x12-inch baking dish. Layer half the onions, liver and remaining onions in prepared dish. Bake, covered, at 350 degrees for 45 minutes. Remove liver to warm platter. Pour onions and pan drippings into skillet. Add remaining broth. Add mixture of cold water and cornstarch. Simmer for 5 minutes or until thickened, stirring constantly. Pour over liver.
Approx Per Serving: Cal 187; Prot 19 g; Carbo 12 g; Fiber 1 g; T Fat 7 g; 35% Calories from Fat; Chol 265 mg; Sod 598 mg.

Cindy Lou McDonald, HFH of Castle Country, Helper, UT

Barbecued Spareribs

Yield: 4 servings

1 10-ounce can tomato soup
1/4 cup chopped onion
1/4 cup catsup
2 tablespoons vinegar
1 tablespoon prepared mustard

1 tablespoon Worcestershire sauce
1 teaspoon salt
1/8 teaspoon pepper
3/4 cup sugar
4 pounds spareribs

■ Combine first 9 ingredients in bowl; mix well. Place spareribs in baking pan. Bake at 450 degrees for 30 minutes. Reduce oven temperature to 350 degrees. Pour sauce over ribs. Bake for 30 minutes longer. May use sauce for pork chops.
Approx Per Serving: Cal 906; Prot 52 g; Carbo 53 g; Fiber 1 g; T Fat 54 g; 53% Calories from Fat; Chol 208 mg; Sod 1451 mg.

Denise Marcelt, Greater East Liverpool HFH, Lisbon, OH

Easy Brunswick Stew

Yield: 6 servings

1 20-ounce can Brunswick stew
1 10-ounce can barbecued pork
1 10-ounce can barbecued beef
1 11-ounce can whole kernel corn

1 17-ounce can lima beans, rinsed, drained
1/4 cup prepared barbecue sauce
1 teaspoon lemon juice

■ Combine all ingredients in 5-quart saucepan; mix well. Cook, covered, over medium heat for 20 minutes, stirring occasionally.
Approx Per Serving: Cal 187; Prot 12 g; Carbo 32 g; Fiber 10 g; T Fat 2 g; 10% Calories from Fat; Chol 13 mg; Sod 574 mg.
Nutritional information does not include barbecued pork and barbecued beef.

Louise V. Chisholm, Peach Area HFH, Ft. Valley, GA

Chalupas

Yield: 12 servings

1 3-pound pork loin roast
1 teaspoon salt
Pepper to taste
3 cloves of garlic, sliced
1 16-ounce package dried pinto beans
1 teaspoon oregano

1 teaspoon ground cumin
1 tablespoon chili powder
1 7-ounce can chopped green chilies, drained

■ Rub roast with salt and pepper. Cut small slits in roast; insert garlic slices. Place on rack in broiler pan. Broil for 15 minutes. Place roast in slow cooker. Rinse pinto beans; drain. Add to slow cooker. Add oregano, cumin, chili powder, green chilies and enough water to cover. Cook, covered, on Low for 9 hours, stirring occasionally. Cook, uncovered, for 1 hour longer. Skim off fat; discard bones. Serve on bed of corn chips with shredded cheese, chopped green onions, tomatoes, cucumbers, lettuce, avocado, salsa and sour cream.
Approx Per Serving: Cal 295; Prot 32 g; Carbo 24 g; Fiber 8 g; T Fat 8 g; 24% Calories from Fat; Chol 69 mg; Sod 365 mg.

Maggie Craig Chrisman, HFH International Board of Directors
Paradise Valley, AZ

Hmong Egg Rolls

Yield: 20 servings

8 ounces bean thread
noodles
2 pounds ground pork
2 carrots, grated
1 cup grated cabbage
1 large white onion,
finely chopped
1/4 cup sliced fresh
mushrooms

2 potatoes, grated
2 cloves of garlic,
grated
2 teaspoons fish sauce
2 teaspoons salt
1 teaspoon pepper
4 eggs
20 egg roll wrappers
Oil for deep frying

■ Soak bean thread noodles in a small amount of warm water until tender. Cut into small pieces. Combine with pork, carrots, cabbage, onion, mushrooms, potatoes, garlic, fish sauce, salt and pepper; mix well. Reserve 1 egg yolk. Stir remaining eggs into pork mixture. Spoon mixture evenly in center of egg roll wrappers. Roll up, sealing ends with reserved egg yolk. Deep-fry in hot oil until golden brown; drain.
Approx Per Serving: Cal 195; Prot 16 g; Carbo 21 g; Fiber 1 g; T Fat 5 g; 24% Calories from Fat; Chol 76 mg; Sod 396 mg.
Nutritional information does not include oil for deep frying and bean thread noodles.

Pang H. Thao, HFH of Wausau, Wausau, WI

No-Peek Pork Chops

Yield: 6 servings

1 cup uncooked long
grain rice
1/4 cup melted butter
1/3 cup milk
1 10-ounce can cream
of mushroom soup

1 10-ounce can cream
of celery soup
6 pork chops
1 envelope onion soup
mix

■ Sprinkle rice in 9x13-inch casserole. Mix butter and milk in small bowl; pour over rice. Mix mushroom and celery soups together. Pour over rice. Arrange pork chops on top. Sprinkle with onion soup mix. Bake, tightly covered, at 325 degrees for 2 1/2 hours.
Approx Per Serving: Cal 502; Prot 36 g; Carbo 33 g; Fiber 1 g; T Fat 24 g; 44% Calories from Fat; Chol 126 mg; Sod 993 mg.

Eva G. Reeves, Central Valley HFH, Bridgewater, VA

Pork Loin in Apple-Brandy Sauce

Yield: 8 servings

1 4-pound pork loin,
trimmed
Salt and pepper to taste
1/2 cup apple cider
vinegar
2/3 cup apple juice
1 small onion, chopped
1 clove of garlic,
crushed

2 tablespoons olive oil
8 slices Canadian
bacon
8 slices Gorgonzola
cheese
2 cups chicken stock
2 tablespoons brandy
1/3 cup whipping cream
2 tablespoons butter

■ Slice pork loin into eight 1-inch steaks; sprinkle with salt and pepper. Place in shallow dish. Cover with mixture of vinegar and apple juice. Marinate for 6 hours, turning occasionally; drain, reserving marinade. Pat dry and set aside. Sauté onion and garlic in olive oil in skillet until tender. Sear pork steaks in skillet; remove to roasting pan. Top with Canadian bacon. Bake at 400 degrees for 10 minutes. Place cheese on each pork steak. Bake for 5 minutes longer. Boil chicken stock in small saucepan until reduced to 1 cup; set aside. Boil reserved marinade in medium saucepan until reduced to 1/4 cup, skimming surface; set aside. Deglaze skillet with brandy, scraping up brown bits. Pour brandy into reduced marinade. Add reduced chicken stock and whipping cream. Bring to a boil. Cook until reduced by half. Whisk in butter. Cook until slightly thickened. Spoon onto serving plates. Top with steaks.
Approx Per Serving: Cal 603; Prot 60 g; Carbo 7 g; Fiber 1 g; T Fat 36 g; 54% Calories from Fat; Chol 199 mg; Sod 1204 mg.

Rev. Scott Hoezee, Newaygo County HFH
Fremont, MI

Habitat work sites are filled with smiles—and they're contagious!

Pork's Like Ham

Yield: 8 servings

1   4-pound pork picnic
3 cups water
1/2 cup packed brown
   sugar

3 tablespoons vinegar
1/2 teaspoon ground
   cloves
1 teaspoon dry mustard

■ Place pork picnic in large kettle with enough water to cover. Bring to a boil; reduce heat. Simmer over low heat for 1 hour; drain. Combine 3 cups water, brown sugar, vinegar, cloves and dry mustard in bowl; mix well. Pour over ham in kettle. Simmer for 1 hour longer, turning occasionally. Let stand in pan juices for several hours to overnight.

Approx Per Serving: Cal 391; Prot 45 g; Carbo 17 g; Fiber 0 g; T Fat 15 g; 35% Calories from Fat; Chol 139 mg; Sod 117 mg.

Ouida D. Simmons, Morgan County HFH, Ft. Morgan, CO

Scalloped Potatoes and Pork Chops

Yield: 6 servings

6 pork chops
4 cups thinly sliced
   potatoes
1/4 cup water

1   10-ounce can cream
   of mushroom soup
1/2 cup sour cream
Salt and pepper to taste

■ Brown pork chops on each side in skillet; drain on paper towels. Arrange potatoes in 9x12-inch casserole. Mix water, soup, and sour cream in small bowl; pour over potatoes. Arrange pork chops on top. Season with salt and pepper. Bake, covered, at 375 degrees for 1 1/4 hours.

Approx Per Serving: Cal 396; Prot 35 g; Carbo 22 g; Fiber 1 g; T Fat 18 g; 42% Calories from Fat; Chol 107 mg; Sod 475 mg.

Hilda Jakubec, Lorain County HFH, Lorain, OH

Baked Squash and Pork Chops

Yield: 4 servings

4 shoulder pork chops
2 tablespoons butter
1/2 cup water
2 acorn squash, peeled,
   seeded, sliced

2 apples, sliced
2 onion slices, chopped
1/4 cup packed brown
   sugar
Salt and pepper to taste

■ Brown pork chops in butter in skillet; remove to platter, reserving pan drippings. Stir water into pan drippings; set aside. Layer squash, apples and half the onion in medium casserole. Sprinkle with half the brown sugar. Arrange pork chops over layers; season with salt and pepper. Top with remaining onion and brown sugar. Pour pan drippings over layers. Bake, tightly covered, at 350 degrees for 1 1/2 hours. May substitute butternut squash for acorn squash.

Approx Per Serving: Cal 496; Prot 34 g; Carbo 56 g; Fiber 7 g; T Fat 17 g; 29% Calories from Fat; Chol 113 mg; Sod 142 mg.

Jeanne C. Gray, HFH of the Magic Valley, Hazelton, ID

Tasty Pork Roast

Yield: 4 servings

1   2 1/2-pound pork
   roast
1/3 cup water
1/4 cup Heinz 57 sauce

2 tablespoons soy sauce
2 1/4 teaspoons salt
1/4 teaspoon coarsely
   ground pepper

■ Brown roast in skillet on all sides; remove to roasting pan, reserving pan drippings. Add water, Heinz 57 sauce, soy sauce, salt and pepper to reserved pan drippings; mix well. Pour over roast. Roast at 375 degrees for 1 hour; baste with pan drippings. Reduce oven temperature to 300 degrees. Roast for 1 hour longer, basting occasionally with pan drippings.

Approx Per Serving: Cal 425; Prot 57 g; Carbo 3 g; Fiber <1 g; T Fat 18 g; 41% Calories from Fat; Chol 173 mg; Sod 1850 mg.

Dorothy B. Laboyeske, Our Savior's UCC-Ripon
Green Lake, WI

Dublin Coddle

Yield: 4 servings

An old Irish recipe

1 pound link sausage
4 to 6 slices bacon, chopped
3 onions, sliced

4 potatoes, peeled, sliced
Salt and pepper to taste

■ Place sausage and bacon in skillet; add enough water to cover. Bring to a boil; reduce heat. Cook, covered, for 10 minutes; drain, reserving liquid. Place in baking dish with onions and potatoes; season with salt and pepper. Pour in reserved liquid. Bake, covered, at 350 degrees for 30 minutes or until potatoes are tender. May cook in slow cooker.
Approx Per Serving: Cal 408; Prot 17 g; Carbo 36 g; Fiber 4 g; T Fat 22 g; 48% Calories from Fat; Chol 51 mg; Sod 850 mg.

Sheila Lee, Lorain County HFH, Lorain, OH

"Stuffed" Frankfurters

Yield: 10 servings

10 frankfurters
Mustard to taste
5 potatoes, boiled, mashed

Paprika to taste

■ Boil frankfurters in water in saucepan; drain. Split into halves lengthwise; place on baking sheet. Spread with mustard. Spoon potatoes on top; sprinkle with paprika. Broil until brown. May serve on bed of sauerkraut mixed with catsup.
Approx Per Serving: Cal 203; Prot 6 g; Carbo 15 g; Fiber 1 g; T Fat 13 g; 59% Calories from Fat; Chol 23 mg; Sod 507 mg.

Laura Rozeboom Hendel, HFH of South Central Minnesota
Nicollet, MN

Ramp Casserole

Yield: 4 servings

Ramps grow wild in the West Virginia mountains; they taste like wild onions.

1 pound pork sausage
2 potatoes, sliced
1 pint canned ramps or 30 fresh ramps, sliced
1 egg, beaten

2 cups milk
Salt to taste
2 cups shredded Cheddar cheese

■ Brown sausage in skillet, stirring until crumbly; drain. Layer potatoes, sausage and ramps in baking dish. Beat egg with milk in bowl. Pour over layers; season with salt. Top with cheese. Bake at 350 degrees for 30 to 45 minutes or until potatoes are tender.
Approx Per Serving: Cal 599; Prot 32 g; Carbo 25 g; Fiber 2 g; T Fat 41 g; 62% Calories from Fat; Chol 173 mg; Sod 1527 mg.

Ann Harris, Almost Heaven HFH, Cherry Grove, WV

Rice and Sausage Casserole

Yield: 15 servings

2 pounds pork sausage
2 envelopes chicken noodle soup mix
8 cups hot water
2 cups uncooked long grain rice

1½ cups chopped celery
2 large onions, finely chopped
½ cup slivered toasted almonds

■ Brown sausage in large skillet, stirring until crumbly; drain. Dissolve soup mix in hot water in 6-quart saucepan. Bring to a boil. Add rice, sausage and celery. Cook for 15 minutes over medium heat or until rice has absorbed liquid. Combine rice mixture with onions. Spread half the mixture in large baking dish; sprinkle with half the almonds. Top with remaining rice mixture and remaining almonds. Bake, covered with foil, at 325 degrees for 1 hour and 10 minutes; remove foil. Bake for 20 minutes longer.
Approx Per Serving: Cal 263; Prot 10 g; Carbo 28 g; Fiber 1 g; T Fat 12 g; 42% Calories from Fat; Chol 24 mg; Sod 1173 mg.

Joan Torgersen Magill, Boca-Delray HFH, Boca Raton, FL

Veal Marsala

Yield: 6 servings

6 slices veal
1 egg
3 tablespoons milk
1 1/4 cups bread crumbs
1/2 cup grated
    Parmesan cheese
1 teaspoon salt
1/2 teaspoon pepper
1 clove of garlic,
    minced

3 tablespoons butter
8 ounces mushrooms,
    sliced
1 cup water
2 teaspoons flour
1 chicken bouillon
    cube
1/2 cup Marsala wine
1/4 cup parsley

■ Pound veal until thin; slice into strips. Beat egg and milk in bowl. Combine bread crumbs and Parmesan cheese in shallow dish. Dip veal strips in egg mixture; coat with bread crumb mixture. Season with salt and pepper. Sauté veal and garlic in butter in skillet until brown. Add mushroom slices. Mix water, flour, bouillon cube and wine in bowl. Pour over veal; sprinkle with parsley. Simmer for 10 to 15 minutes.

Approx Per Serving: Cal 317; Prot 25 g; Carbo 21 g; Fiber 2 g; T Fat 13 g; 35% Calories from Fat; Chol 127 mg; Sod 936 mg.

Avalee Mowry, HFH of Northern Fox Valley, Barrington, IL

Bison Tamale Pie

Yield: 6 servings

Bison is low-fat and delicious.

1 small onion, chopped
1 red or green bell
    pepper, chopped
1 stalk celery, chopped
1 clove of garlic,
    chopped
1 tablespoon cumin
    seed
1 pound ground bison
Salt, pepper, paprika
    and oregano to taste
1/4 cup dry sherry
2 tablespoons tomato
    paste

1/2 cup low-fat cottage
    cheese
1 cup corn
1 egg
3/4 cup buttermilk
1 tablespoon honey
1 teaspoon baking
    powder
1 cup stone-ground
    corn flour
1   4-ounce can
    chopped green
    chilies, drained

■ Sauté onion, bell pepper, celery, garlic and cumin seed in nonstick skillet sprayed with nonstick cooking spray until vegetables are tender. Add bison, salt, pepper, paprika, oregano and sherry; mix well. Cook until bison is brown; do not overcook. Remove from heat. Stir in tomato paste, cottage cheese and corn. Spread in 9x13-inch casserole sprayed with nonstick cooking spray. Beat egg with buttermilk, honey and baking powder. Stir in corn flour and chilies. Spoon over bison mixture. Bake at 400 degrees for 20 minutes. Serve immediately.

Approx Per Serving: Cal 184; Prot 8 g; Carbo 30 g; Fiber 5 g; T Fat 3 g; 15% Calories from Fat; Chol 38 mg; Sod 326 mg.

Nutritional information does not include ground bison.

Jane Fonda, Turner Enterprises, Inc., Atlanta, GA

Jane Fonda

*H*abitat projects must build affordable houses. They do this through various partnerships—with individual volunteers, churches and synagogues, companies, high school and college groups, civic organizations and Habitat homeowners.

Bacon and Onion Frittata

Yield: 4 servings

5 eggs, slightly beaten
1/4 cup milk
1 cup shredded sharp
   Cheddar cheese
1 cup chopped cooked
   potatoes

1 cup chopped fried
   bacon
1 2-ounce can
   French-fried onions
2 tablespoons melted
   margarine

■ Combine first 5 ingredients and half the onions. Pour into pie plate brushed with melted margarine. Bake at 350 degrees for 20 minutes or until set. Top with remaining onions. Bake for 5 minutes longer.
Approx Per Serving: Cal 410; Prot 19 g; Carbo 17 g; Fiber 1 g; T Fat 30 g; 65% Calories from Fat; Chol 304 mg; Sod 610 mg.

Julie Richter, Sheboygan County HFH, Sheboygan, WI

Breakfast Casserole

Yield: 6 servings

4 slices bread,
   crumbled
1 pound sausage
6 eggs

1 1/2 cups milk
1 teaspoon dry mustard
2 cups shredded
   Cheddar cheese

■ Layer bread crumbs in greased 9x9-inch baking dish. Brown sausage in skillet, stirring until crumbly; drain. Sprinkle over bread. Beat eggs, milk and dry mustard in bowl. Pour over sausage layer. Top with cheese. Bake at 350 degrees for 30 minutes or until brown. Chill overnight if desired.
Approx Per Serving: Cal 452; Prot 26 g; Carbo 14 g; Fiber <1 g; T Fat 32 g; 64% Calories from Fat; Chol 290 mg; Sod 883 mg.

Sue Libak, Waco HFH, Waco, TX

Breakfast Cheese Strata

Yield: 6 servings

1 pound sausage
12 slices bread
8 ounces sharp
   Cheddar cheese,
   shredded
6 eggs
2 1/2 cups milk
3/4 teaspoon salt
1/8 teaspoon pepper

1/4 teaspoon dry
   mustard
1 teaspoon
   Worcestershire sauce
1 10-ounce can cream
   of mushroom soup
1 4-ounce can
   mushroom pieces,
   undrained

■ Brown sausage in skillet, stirring until crumbly; drain. Arrange half the bread in greased 9x13-inch baking dish. Top with sausage, cheese and remaining bread. Pour mixture of next 6 ingredients over layers. Chill for several hours. Bake at 350 degrees for 1 hour. Serve with heated mixture of soup and mushrooms.
Approx Per Serving: Cal 630; Prot 32 g; Carbo 38 g; Fiber 2 g; T Fat 39 g; 55% Calories from Fat; Chol 296 mg; Sod 1831 mg.

Phyllis M. Miller, Duluth HFH, Duluth, MN

Black-Eyed Pea Supper

Yield: 4 servings

8 ounces bulk sausage
1/2 cup chopped green
   bell pepper
1/2 cup chopped onion
1 clove of garlic,
   minced
2 cups canned tomatoes
1/4 teaspoon pepper

1/4 teaspoon oregano
1/4 teaspoon rosemary
1 16-ounce can
   black-eyed peas,
   undrained
1/2 to 1 cup shredded
   low-fat Swiss cheese

■ Brown sausage in skillet, stirring until crumbly; drain. Sauté green pepper, onion and garlic in skillet for 5 minutes. Add remaining ingredients. Simmer, covered, for 15 minutes. Serve sprinkled with cheese.
Approx Per Serving: Cal 328; Prot 20 g; Carbo 24 g; Fiber 10 g; T Fat 17 g; 47% Calories from Fat; Chol 48 mg; Sod 957 mg.

Reba L. Perkins, Hardy County HFH, Moorefield, WV

Don's Venison Delight

Yield: 4 servings

2 pounds venison, cut
   into 1/2-inch thick
   steaks
1/4 cup flour
2 tablespoons oil
1 10-ounce can cream
   of mushroom soup

1 10-ounce can cream
   of celery soup
1 4-ounce can
   mushroom pieces,
   drained
1/2 cup milk

■ Coat venison with flour. Brown in 1 tablespoon oil in skillet. Place in shallow baking dish coated with remaining oil. Pour mixture of remaining ingredients over steaks. Bake, covered, at 375 degrees for 1 hour. Let stand for 10 minutes.
Approx Per Serving: Cal 433; Prot 44 g; Carbo 19 g; Fiber 1 g; T Fat 20 g; 41% Calories from Fat; Chol 100 mg; Sod 1337 mg.

Donald J. Beal, Morgan County HFH, Fort Morgan, CO

POULTRY

"The Lord will guide you always; he will satisfy your needs in a sun-scorched land and will strengthen your frame."

Isaiah 58:11

Chicken Delight

Yield: 8 servings

2 3-pound chickens,
  cut up
1 cup flour
1 tablespoon salt
1 tablespoon paprika
1/8 teaspoon pepper
1/4 cup sesame seed

1 cup finely ground
  pecans
1 cup buttermilk
1 egg, slightly beaten
1/2 cup oil
1/3 cup pecan halves

■ Rinse chicken and pat dry. Combine next 6 ingredients in bowl. Dip chicken in mixture of buttermilk and egg; roll in flour mixture. Place chicken skin side up in oil in baking pan. Place pecan halves on each piece of chicken. Bake at 350 degrees for 1 1/4 hours or until chicken is tender.
Approx Per Serving: Cal 760; Prot 56 g; Carbo 20 g; Fiber 3 g; T Fat 51 g; 60% Calories from Fat; Chol 180 mg; Sod 988 mg.

Jane Anne Eairley, Highlands County HFH, Sebring, FL

Buttermilk Chicken

Yield: 6 servings

3 pounds chicken
  pieces
1/2 cup buttermilk
3/4 cup flour
1/2 teaspoon salt
1/4 teaspoon pepper

2 tablespoons melted
  margarine
1 cup buttermilk
1 10-ounce can cream
  of mushroom soup

■ Rinse chicken and pat dry. Dip in 1/2 cup buttermilk. Roll in mixture of flour, salt and pepper. Place in melted margarine in 9x13-inch baking pan. Bake at 400 degrees for 30 minutes. Turn chicken. Bake for 15 minutes. Turn chicken. Pour mixture of 1 cup buttermilk and soup over chicken. Bake for 15 minutes.
Approx Per Serving: Cal 379; Prot 37 g; Carbo 18 g; Fiber 1 g; T Fat 17 g; 40% Calories from Fat; Chol 104 mg; Sod 767 mg.

Sally Newton, Mt. Pleasant HFH, Mt. Pleasant, TX

Chicken with Capers

Yield: 4 servings

4 chicken breasts
3 tablespoons butter
3 tablespoons capers
3 tablespoons caper
  juice

1 teaspoon oregano
1 bay leaf
Salt and pepper to taste
1 cup whipping cream

■ Rinse chicken and pat dry. Brown in butter in skillet. Remove to baking pan. Add remaining ingredients to pan drippings. Cook over low heat to desired consistency, stirring constantly. Pour over chicken. Bake at 350 degrees for 1 hour. Remove bay leaf.
Approx Per Serving: Cal 422; Prot 28 g; Carbo 2 g; Fiber 0 g; T Fat 34 g; 72% Calories from Fat; Chol 177 mg; Sod 158 mg.
Nutritional information does not include capers and caper juice.

Marjorie Halliday, Southeast Volusia HFH
New Smyrna Beach, FL

Chicken Breasts Diavolo

Yield: 6 servings

*This was the 1991 $50,000 Grand Prize Winner in Newman's Own **Good Housekeeping** recipe contest.*

6 chicken breast filets
1/2 cup minced parsley
1 teaspoon lemon
  pepper
Salt to taste
Garlic powder to taste
3 tablespoons olive oil
3 6-ounce jars
  marinated artichoke
  hearts, drained
1 tablespoon lemon juice
1 26-ounce jar
  Newman's Own
  Diavolo Sauce

1/2 cup red wine
1 1/2 cups shredded
  mozzarella cheese
1 1/2 cups onion-garlic
  croutons
1 tablespoon olive oil
6 cups cooked pasta

■ Rinse chicken and pat dry. Flatten slightly between waxed paper. Sprinkle with next 4 ingredients. Roll to enclose seasonings; secure with wooden picks. Sauté chicken in 3 tablespoons olive oil in skillet until golden brown. Place in 9x13-inch baking dish. Remove wooden picks. Arrange artichokes sprinkled with lemon juice around chicken. Pour mixture of Diavolo Sauce and wine over all. Sprinkle with cheese. Top with croutons tossed with 1 tablespoon olive oil. Bake at 350 degrees for 30 to 40 minutes or until brown.
Approx Per Serving: Cal 718; Prot 42 g; Carbo 65 g; Fiber 9 g; T Fat 31 g; 39% Calories from Fat; Chol 94 mg; Sod 1468 mg.

Geraldine Kirkpatrick, Huntington Beach, CA

Chinese Chicken with Walnuts

Yield: 6 servings

1¹/₂ pounds chicken breast filets, cut into 1-inch pieces
3 tablespoons soy sauce
2 teaspoons cornstarch
2 tablespoons dry sherry
1 teaspoon grated gingerroot
¹/₂ teaspoon red pepper

1 teaspoon sugar
¹/₂ teaspoon salt
2 tablespoons oil
2 medium green bell peppers, cut into ³/₄-inch pieces
4 green onions, diagonally sliced into 1-inch lengths
¹/₂ cup walnut halves

■ Combine first 8 ingredients in bowl. Heat oil in wok over high heat. Stir-fry bell peppers and green onions for 2 minutes. Remove to warm dish. Add walnuts. Stir-fry for 1 to 2 minutes or until golden. Remove to warm dish. Stir-fry chicken¹/₂ at a time for 2 minutes. Return all chicken to wok. Stir in soy sauce mixture. Cook until bubbly, stirring constantly. Stir in vegetables and walnuts. Cook, covered, for 1 minute.
Approx Per Serving: Cal 259; Prot 28 g; Carbo 6 g; Fiber 1 g; T Fat 13 g; 46% Calories from Fat; Chol 72 mg; Sod 758 mg.

Tipper Gore, Wife of the Vice President of the United States
Washington, D.C.

Chicken à la Charles

Yield: 4 servings

1 3-pound chicken
¹/₄ cup butter, cut into pieces
2 carrots, sliced
3 unpeeled potatoes, sliced
1 cup chopped celery

3 onions, coarsely chopped
2 bulbs of garlic, separated
Tarragon, salt and pepper to taste

■ Rinse chicken and pat dry. Arrange butter in bottom of Dutch oven. Layer vegetables over butter. Place a portion of unpeeled garlic cloves in vegetables. Place the remaining cloves inside the cavity and under the skin of the chicken. Place chicken over vegetables. Sprinkle with seasonings. Bake, covered, at 400 degrees for 1 hour or until chicken is tender.
Approx Per Serving: Cal 599; Prot 54 g; Carbo 40 g; Fiber 5 g; T Fat 25 g; 37% Calories from Fat; Chol 183 mg; Sod 292 mg.

Marjorie Rowland, HFH of Grayson County, Denison, TX

Chicken and Dumplings

Yield: 8 servings

1 3-pound chicken
3 quarts water
1 10-ounce can cream of chicken soup
1 soup can water
6 chicken bouillon cubes
¹/₈ teaspoon celery seed
¹/₈ teaspoon sage
2 tablespoons onion soup mix
Parsley to taste
Lemon powder to taste
¹/₄ teaspoon pepper
16 flour tortillas, cut into eighths

■ Rinse chicken. Combine chicken and 3 quarts water in stockpot. Boil over high heat for 10 minutes. Cook, covered, on low heat for 1¹/₂ hours or until chicken is tender. Remove chicken from broth. Strain broth. Cool and bone chicken. Set aside. Bring strained broth, soup, 1 soup can water, bouillon cubes, celery seed, sage, soup mix, parsley, lemon powder and pepper to a boil in clean stockpot over high heat. Drop tortillas into boiling broth. Cook over high heat for 10 minutes, stirring to prevent sticking. Cook, covered, over low heat for 10 minutes. Stir in chicken. Heat through.
Approx Per Serving: Cal 443; Prot 33 g; Carbo 48 g; Fiber 2 g; T Fat 15 g; 29% Calories from Fat; Chol 80 mg; Sod 2471 mg.

Theresa Stewart, Las Vegas, New Mexico HFH
Henderson, NV

*H*abitat builds people, not just houses. I know of no organization that has created a deeper conviction that ordinary people can change the world. For me it is an extension of what the church is all about.

Dr. Tony Campolo, Habitat for Humanity International Advisory Board

Chicken Potpie

Yield: 6 servings

1 3-pound roasting
   chicken
1 cup flour
1 teaspoon salt
1 teaspoon baking
   powder
1 tablespoon
   shortening

1 egg, beaten
¹/₃ cup milk
1 10-ounce can
   chicken broth
2 carrots, sliced
3 potatoes, peeled,
   cubed
Parsley to taste

■ Rinse chicken. Combine chicken and enough water to cover in large saucepan. Bring to a boil; reduce heat. Simmer until chicken is tender. Drain; reserving broth. Strain broth. Chop chicken, discarding skin and bones. Combine sifted mixture of flour, salt and baking powder in bowl; mix well. Cut in shortening until crumbly. Stir in egg and milk to form dough . Roll ¹/₄ inch thick on floured surface. Cut into squares. Bring reserved strained broth, chicken, canned broth, carrots, potatoes and parsley to a boil in stockpot. Drop dough squares into boiling mixture. Cook, covered, over low heat for 20 to 25 minutes or until done to taste.

Approx Per Serving: Cal 408; Prot 39 g; Carbo 33 g; Fiber 2 g; T Fat 13 g; 28% Calories from Fat; Chol 139 mg; Sod 687 mg.

Joan M. McKee, Williamsport/Lycoming HFH
Montoursville, PA

Bob Hope's Favorite Chicken Hash

Yield: 2 servings

2 chicken breasts,
   broiled
2 slices crisp-fried
   bacon, crumbled
¹/₂ small onion,
   chopped
Salt and pepper to taste

¹/₂ teaspoon lemon
   juice
2 tablespoons butter
1 teaspoon dry sherry
2 tablespoons sour
   cream

■ Cut chicken into thin strips. Combine chicken, bacon, onion, salt, pepper, lemon juice and butter in skillet. Cook until onion is tender. Stir in sherry and sour cream. Cook just until heated. Serve immediately.

Approx Per Serving: Cal 323; Prot 29 g; Carbo 3 g; Fiber <1 g; T Fat 21 g; 59% Calories from Fat; Chol 115 mg; Sod 270 mg.

Bob Hope, Actor and Comedian, Palm Springs, CA

Bob Hope and Jimmy Carter at a work site in Charlotte, North Carolina

Arroz Con Pollo

Yield: 4 servings

1 3-pound chicken,
  cut up
1 14-ounce can
  stewed tomatoes

1 5-ounce package
  original-flavor
  Rice-A-Roni,
  prepared

■ Rinse chicken and pat dry. Combine undrained stewed tomatoes and rice in skillet. Arrange chicken on top. Cook, covered, for 35 to 45 minutes or until chicken is tender.
Approx Per Serving: Cal 478; Prot 52 g; Carbo 32 g; Fiber <1 g; T Fat 14 g; 28% Calories from Fat; Chol 152 mg; Sod 872 mg.

Carol Spangenberg, Wimberley Valley HFH, Wimberley, TX

Chicken Tangier

Yield: 4 servings

3 pounds mixed
  chicken legs, thighs
  and breast halves,
  skinned
1 tablespoon oil
1 tablespoon margarine
3/4 cup chopped onion
1 clove of garlic,
  minced
2 large tomatoes,
  chopped
1 16-ounce can
  tomato sauce

2 tablespoons chopped
  parsley
1 teaspoon salt
1/2 teaspoon cinnamon
1/4 teaspoon ginger
1/4 teaspoon cumin
Turmeric to taste
2 whole cloves
Hot sauce to taste
1 16-ounce can whole
  onions, drained
1/3 cup sliced almonds
1/3 cup golden raisins

■ Rinse chicken and pat dry. Heat oil and margarine in large heavy saucepan. Add chopped onion and garlic. Sauté for 5 minutes or until onion is tender. Stir in next 10 ingredients. Add chicken. Bring mixture to a boil. Reduce heat to low. Cook, covered, for 45 minutes. Cook, uncovered, for 15 minutes or until sauce is thickened and chicken is tender. Stir in whole onions. Cook for 5 minutes. Remove chicken to serving platter. Pour sauce over chicken. Sprinkle with almonds and raisins.
Approx Per Serving: Cal 546; Prot 55 g; Carbo 31 g; Fiber 7 g; T Fat 24 g; 38% Calories from Fat; Chol 152 mg; Sod 1828 mg.

Donna Ellison Ward, HFH of Gallatin Valley
Bozeman, MT

Greek Chicken Legs

Yield: 6 servings

12 chicken thighs
2 tablespoons olive oil
2 medium onions,
  coarsely chopped
1 cup coarsely chopped
  mushrooms
1 cup coarsely chopped
  zucchini
1 tablespoon Greek
  seasoning
1/2 teaspoon cinnamon

1 10-ounce can
  chicken broth
1 10 ounce can
  clam-tomato juice
1 tablespoon flour
4 ounces Feta cheese,
  crumbled
6 cups hot cooked
  noodles
3 tablespoons chopped
  black olives

■ Rinse chicken and pat dry. Cook chicken in olive oil in skillet for 10 minutes. Add onions, mushrooms and zucchini. Cook for 2 minutes, stirring constantly. Stir in Greek seasoning, cinnamon, broth and clam-tomato juice. Bring to a boil. Reduce heat to low. Cook, covered, for 40 minutes or until chicken is tender. Remove chicken to warm plate, reserving broth. Boil reserved broth for 5 minutes or until reduced by 1/2. Stir in flour and cheese until well mixed. Return chicken to pan. Simmer for 2 minutes. Place noodles on serving platter. Top with chicken and sauce. Sprinkle with olives.
Approx Per Serving: Cal 575; Prot 39 g; Carbo 50 g; Fiber 5 g; T Fat 24 g; 37% Calories from Fat; Chol 165 mg; Sod 688 mg.

John Hollon, Homestead HFH, Homestead, FL

Greek-Style Chicken and Potatoes

Yield: 4 servings

1 3-pound chicken,
  cut up
1/2 cup oil
1 teaspoon salt
1 tablespoon pepper
1 tablespoon oregano

Garlic to taste
1/2 cup lemon juice
5 potatoes, cut into
  halves
1/2 cup water

■ Rinse chicken and pat dry. Combine oil, salt, pepper, oregano, garlic and lemon juice in bowl; mix well. Coat chicken and potatoes with mixture. Place in non-stick baking pan. Pour water over top. Bake at 375 degrees for 1 hour or until chicken is tender.
Approx Per Serving: Cal 717; Prot 52 g; Carbo 36 g; Fiber 3 g; T Fat 40 g; 50% Calories from Fat; Chol 152 mg; Sod 688 mg.

Mary Kouchis, Boca-Delray HFH, Boca Raton, FL

Lemon-Garlic Chicken
Yield: 4 servings

1 3-pound chicken
2 lemons
1 clove of garlic
½ cup olive oil
Salt and black pepper
  to taste

White pepper to taste
Garlic powder and
  cayenne pepper to
  taste
½ cup water

■ Rinse chicken and pat dry. Pierce lemons; roll on hard surface until soft. Place lemons and garlic in chicken cavity; truss. Place breast side up in roasting pan. Drizzle with olive oil; sprinkle with seasonings. Pour water in pan. Bake at 375 degrees for 25 minutes. Turn chicken over. Sprinkle with seasonings. Bake for 25 minutes. Turn chicken over. Sprinkle with seasonings again. Bake for 25 minutes or until golden brown. Remove lemons and garlic before serving. Add your favorite herbs to the seasonings.

Approx Per Serving: Cal 573; Prot 50 g; Carbo 3 g; Fiber 1 g; T Fat 40 g; 63% Calories from Fat; Chol 152 mg; Sod 146 mg.

Teresa Reynolds, HFH of Chico, Chico, CA

Low-Cal Chicken
Yield: 8 servings

8 chicken breasts,
  skinned
1 8-ounce bottle of
  reduced-calorie
  Italian salad dressing

1 cup bread crumbs

■ Rinse chicken and pat dry. Combine with salad dressing in bowl. Marinate in refrigerator for 4 to 8 hours. Roll in bread crumbs. Place in baking pan. Bake at 350 degrees for 1 hour or until chicken is done.

Approx Per Serving: Cal 205; Prot 28 g; Carbo 11 g; Fiber 1 g; T Fat 5 g; 22% Calories from Fat; Chol 75 mg; Sod 378 mg.

Karen Stowers, Greater East Liverpool HFH
East Liverpool, OH

Roma Chicken
Yield: 6 servings

1 3-pound chicken,
  cut up, skinned
1 16-ounce bottle of
  Italian dressing

8 ounces Italian-style
  bread crumbs
1 cup grated Parmesan
  cheese

■ Rinse chicken and pat dry. Combine chicken and Italian dressing in bowl. Marinate in refrigerator for 4 hours or overnight. Roll chicken in mixture of bread crumbs and Parmesan cheese. Place in lightly greased baking pan. Bake at 325 degrees for 45 to 60 minutes or until chicken is tender.

Approx Per Serving: Cal 778; Prot 44 g; Carbo 36 g; Fiber 2 g; T Fat 60 g; 63% Calories from Fat; Chol 114 mg; Sod 997 mg.

Audrey Rebar, Benton HFH, Corvallis, OR

Mediterranean Chicken
Yield: 4 servings

2 pounds chicken
  pieces, skinned
1 14-ounce can
  tomatoes
¼ cup red wine
1 teaspoon sugar
1 teaspoon basil

1 clove of garlic, minced
4 ounces spaghetti,
  cooked
½ cup shredded
  Cheddar cheese
¼ cup sliced black
  olives

■ Rinse chicken and pat dry. Sauté chicken in skillet sprayed with nonstick cooking spray for 10 minutes or until brown. Add undrained chopped tomatoes, wine, sugar, basil and garlic; mix well. Bring to a boil. Reduce heat; simmer for 30 minutes. Serve chicken and sauce over spaghetti. Sprinkle with cheese and black olives.

Approx Per Serving: Cal 430; Prot 41 g; Carbo 28 g; Fiber 3 g; T Fat 16 g; 35% Calories from Fat; Chol 116 mg; Sod 428 mg.

Kandy Spade, Southeast Volusia HFH
Edgewater, FL

Sauerkraut and Chicken Skillet Supper

Yield: 8 servings

4 chicken legs
4 chicken thighs
4 pork chops
12 ounces smoked
  sausage
2 tablespoons oil

2 16-ounce jars
  sauerkraut
2 teaspoons caraway
  seed
1/2 cup white wine

■ Rinse chicken and pat dry. Brown chicken, pork chops and sausage in oil in heavy skillet. Add sauerkraut, caraway seed and white wine; mix well. Simmer, covered, for 1 to 1 1/2 hours or until chicken and meats are tender.
Approx Per Serving: Cal 345; Prot 35 g; Carbo 5 g; Fiber 2 g; T Fat 19 g; 52% Calories from Fat; Chol 111 mg; Sod 1139 mg.

Betty Edmondson, HFH of Northern Utah
Brigham City, UT

Sunday Chicken Supreme

Yield: 8 servings

1 3-pound chicken,
  cut up, skinned
1 cup uncooked rice
1 cup dry milk powder
1 10-ounce can cream
  of mushroom soup

1 10-ounce can cream
  of celery soup
2 soup cans water
2 tablespoons onion
  soup mix

■ Rinse chicken and pat dry. Combine uncooked rice and milk powder in bowl; mix well. Spoon into 9x13-inch baking pan. Stir in soups and water. Arrange chicken over mixture. Sprinkle with soup mix. Bake, covered, at 325 degrees for 2 1/2 hours or until chicken is tender.
Approx Per Serving: Cal 345; Prot 31 g; Carbo 30 g; Fiber 1 g; T Fat 11 g; 29% Calories from Fat; Chol 82 mg; Sod 923 mg.

Vicki J. Sprock, Northwest Nebraska HFH, Chadron, NE

Sweet and Pungent Chicken

Yield: 8 servings

2 3-pound chickens,
  cut up, skinned
1 15-ounce can
  pineapple tidbits
1/3 cup mustard
1/3 cup vinegar
1/3 cup molasses

1 teaspoon soy sauce
2 teaspoons cornstarch
1/2 teaspoon salt
1/4 teaspoon ginger
1 11-ounce can
  mandarin oranges,
  drained

■ Rinse chicken and pat dry. Arrange in 9x13-inch baking pan. Drain pineapple, reserving juice. Combine reserved pineapple juice, mustard, vinegar, molasses, soy sauce, cornstarch, salt and ginger in saucepan; mix well. Simmer for 5 minutes, stirring constantly. Brush both sides of chicken with sauce. Bake, covered, at 350 degrees for 30 minutes, basting frequently. Turn chicken. Bake, uncovered, for 30 minutes or until chicken is tender, basting frequently. Remove chicken to warm serving platter. Combine remaining sauce with pineapple and mandarin oranges. Cook over medium heat for 3 minutes or until bubbly. Pour over chicken. Garnish with parsley.
Approx Per Serving: Cal 429; Prot 50 g; Carbo 26 g; Fiber 1 g; T Fat 13 g; 28% Calories from Fat; Chol 152 mg; Sod 457 mg.

Robert R. Ward, HFH of Gallatin Valley, Bozeman, MT

Yogurt Chicken

Yield: 4 servings

8 boneless skinless
  chicken thighs
1 large clove of garlic,
  minced

1 tablespoon curry
  powder
1 cup plain yogurt

■ Rinse chicken and pat dry. Mix garlic, curry powder and yogurt in bowl. Coat chicken with mixture. Place in 9x9-inch baking pan. Bake at 375 degrees for 40 to 60 minutes or until chicken is tender.
Approx Per Serving: Cal 258; Prot 29 g; Carbo 4 g; Fiber 1 g; T Fat 13 g; 48% Calories from Fat; Chol 105 mg; Sod 119 mg.

Georgene Fabian, Pemi-Valley Habitat, Holderness, NH

Chicken Marinade

Yield: 2 cups

¹/₂ cup oil-free Italian dressing
¹/₂ cup soy sauce
¹/₂ cup vinegar
¹/₃ cup Worcestershire sauce

¹/₂ cup packed brown sugar
1 teaspoon garlic powder
2 tablespoons lime juice

■ Combine Italian dressing, soy sauce, vinegar, Worcestershire sauce, brown sugar, garlic powder and lime juice in bowl; mix well. Marinate chicken for 6 hours before baking.
Approx Per Cup: Cal 352; Prot 5 g; Carbo 89 g; Fiber <1 g; T Fat <1 g; 0% Calories from Fat; Chol 0 mg; Sod 5099 mg.

Mary Kay Tamlyn, Northern Straits HFH, St. Ignace, MI

Baked Chicken

Yield: 4 servings

4 chicken breasts
1 cup uncooked rice

1 10-ounce can cream of mushroom soup

■ Rinse chicken and pat dry. Spread rice in greased baking pan. Top with chicken. Pour soup over chicken. Bake, covered, at 350 degrees for 1 hour.
Approx Per Serving: Cal 381; Prot 31 g; Carbo 43 g; Fiber 1 g; T Fat 9 g; 21% Calories from Fat; Chol 73 mg; Sod 639 mg.

Michael Schlecht, Furman University Campus Chapter
Roswell, GA

Baked Mushroom Chicken

Yield: 2 servings

2 chicken breast filets
Salt and pepper to taste
4 slices bacon

2 thin slices corned beef
1 10-ounce can cream of mushroom soup

■ Rinse chicken and pat dry. Season with salt and pepper. Wrap chicken in bacon and corned beef. Place in baking pan. Spread soup over chicken. Bake at 350 degrees for 50 to 60 minutes or until chicken is tender.
Approx Per Serving: Cal 399; Prot 39 g; Carbo 12 g; Fiber <1 g; T Fat 22 g; 50% Calories from Fat; Chol 85 mg; Sod 1413 mg.

Anne Neil Chalker, Furman University Campus Chapter
Waynesboro, GA

Balsamic and Garlic Chicken Breasts

Yield: 8 servings

4 whole chicken breasts, split, boned
Salt and pepper to taste
2 tablespoons flour
2 tablespoons olive oil
12 ounces mushrooms, sliced
4 to 6 cloves of garlic, crushed

¹/₂ cup balsamic vinegar
¹/₂ cup chicken broth
1 bay leaf
¹/₄ teaspoon thyme
1 tablespoon flour
1 tablespoon butter

■ Rinse chicken and pat dry. Dredge in mixture of salt, pepper and 2 tablespoons flour. Brown chicken on 1 side in oil in skillet for 2 to 3 minutes. Turn chicken. Add mushrooms and garlic. Cook for 3 to 5 minutes or until chicken is brown. Stir in vinegar, broth, bay leaf and thyme. Cook, covered, over medium heat for 10 minutes or until chicken is tender. Remove chicken to serving platter. Stir in 1 tablespoon flour and butter. Cook for 7 minutes, stirring constantly. Discard bay leaf. Pour over chicken. Serve with wild rice.
Approx Per Serving: Cal 212; Prot 28 g; Carbo 6 g; Fiber 1 g; T Fat 8 g; 35% Calories from Fat; Chol 76 mg; Sod 126 mg.

Cathy Schatten, HFH of Boca-Delray, Boca Raton, FL

*E*very day they continued to meet together in the temple courts. They broke bread in their homes and ate together with glad and sincere hearts, praising God and enjoying the favor of all people.

Acts 2:46-47

Cheese-Stuffed Chicken Breasts

Yield: 4 servings

2 whole chicken
 breasts, split, boned
3 ounces chevre
2 tablespoons thinly
 sliced scallions with
 tops
1 tablespoon chopped
 mint

1 tablespoon lemon
 juice
1 teaspoon grated
 lemon rind
2 tablespoons melted
 unsalted butter

Rinse chicken and pat dry. Combine chevre, scallions, mint, lemon juice and lemon rind in bowl; mix well. Spoon cheese mixture under skin of each chicken breast. Tuck skin under; secure with wooden pick. Place in 1-quart baking pan. Drizzle with butter. Bake at 350 degrees for 40 to 45 minutes or until chicken is tender, basting 2 to 3 times.
Approx Per Serving: Cal 279; Prot 32 g; Carbo 1 g; Fiber <1 g; T Fat 16 g; 52% Calories from Fat; Chol 110 mg; Sod 196 mg.

James L. Hoyt, Lincoln HFH, Elmwood, NE

Chicken-Broccoli Casserole

Yield: 6 servings

4 chicken breasts,
 boned
2 tablespoons butter
1 cup water
2 10-ounce packages
 frozen broccoli
 spears

2 10-ounce cans
 cream of broccoli
 soup
1 cup shredded
 Cheddar cheese
1¹/₂ cups bread crumbs
1 tablespoon butter

Rinse chicken and pat dry. Cut each chicken breast into 3 or 4 pieces. Brown in 2 tablespoons butter in skillet. Pour water over chicken. Simmer, covered, for 20 minutes. Cook broccoli using package directions just until tender; drain. Arrange in 9x13-inch baking pan. Spoon mixture of chicken and soup over broccoli. Sprinkle with cheese. Top with bread crumbs and 1 tablespoon butter. Bake at 375 degrees for 20 minutes or until brown.
Approx Per Serving: Cal 411; Prot 29 g; Carbo 30 g; Fiber 4 g; T Fat 20 g; 42% Calories from Fat; Chol 89 mg; Sod 988 mg.

Marion Mitchell, Teen Campus Chapter, Greenville, SC

Chicken Casserole

Yield: 4 servings

4 chicken breast filets
4 slices Swiss cheese
1 10-ounce can
 chicken soup

¹/₃ cup water
³/₄ cup cracker crumbs
¹/₃ cup melted butter

Rinse chicken and pat dry. Arrange in 9x9-inch baking pan. Lay Swiss cheese over chicken. Spoon mixture of soup and water over cheese. Sprinkle with cracker crumbs. Drizzle with melted butter. Bake at 350 degrees for 1 hour.
Approx Per Serving: Cal 514; Prot 37 g; Carbo 18 g; Fiber <1 g; T Fat 32 g; 57% Calories from Fat; Chol 150 mg; Sod 1027 mg.

Jane Adrian, HFH of Mercer County, Harrodsburg, KY

Chicken Dish

Yield: 8 servings

8 chicken breast filets
4 eggs, beaten
1¹/₂ cups bread crumbs
1 10-ounce can
 chicken broth

1 cup sliced
 mushrooms
2 tablespoons butter
2 cups shredded
 Mozzarella cheese

Rinse chicken and pat dry. Combine chicken and eggs in bowl; mix well. Chill, covered, for 3 to 4 hours. Roll in bread crumbs. Place in 9x13-inch baking pan sprayed with nonstick cooking spray. Pour broth over chicken. Sauté mushrooms in butter until tender. Spoon over chicken. Sprinkle with cheese. Bake at 325 degrees for 45 to 60 minutes or until chicken is tender.
Approx Per Serving: Cal 366; Prot 38 g; Carbo 15 g; Fiber 1 g; T Fat 16 g; 40% Calories from Fat; Chol 210 mg; Sod 479 mg.

Margie K. Gettman, Morgan County HFH
Fort Morgan, CO

Chicken-Asparagus Divan

Yield: 4 servings

4 chicken breast filets
Chopped onion and
   celery tops to taste
Salt to taste
2 tablespoons chopped
   onion
1/2 cup grated
   Parmesan cheese

1 10-ounce can cream
   of chicken soup
1 pound asparagus,
   cooked tender-crisp
1/3 cup whipping cream
1/3 cup mayonnaise

■ Rinse chicken and pat dry. Combine chicken, onion and celery tops and salt in skillet. Add enough water to cover. Bring to a boil. Reduce heat; simmer until chicken is tender. Drain, discarding liquid. Combine 2 tablespoons onion, 1/3 cup cheese and soup in bowl; mix well. Spread 1/2 of the mixture in bottom of 9x13-inch baking pan. Arrange asparagus over prepared layer. Top with chicken. Spoon remaining soup mixture over chicken. Bake at 350 degrees for 25 minutes or until bubbly. Top with mixture of whipping cream and mayonnaise. Sprinkle with remaining cheese. Broil until brown. Serve immediately.
Approx Per Serving: Cal 479; Prot 37 g; Carbo 11 g; Fiber 2 g; T Fat 32 g; 60% Calories from Fat; Chol 124 mg; Sod 922 mg.

Jean Garrecht, AuSable Valley Habitat, Jay, NY

Chicken Divan

Yield: 6 servings

3 10-ounce packages
   frozen broccoli
4 chicken breasts,
   cooked
2 10-ounce cans
   cream of chicken
   soup

1 cup mayonnaise
1 teaspoon curry
   powder
2 tablespoons lemon
   juice
1/2 soup can water

■ Cook broccoli using package directions; drain. Place in greased 10x14-inch baking pan. Arrange chicken over broccoli. Spoon mixture of remaining ingredients over top. Bake at 350 degrees for 50 minutes.
Approx Per Serving: Cal 486; Prot 25 g; Carbo 16 g; Fiber 4 g; T Fat 37 g; 67% Calories from Fat; Chol 77 mg; Sod 1027 mg.

Daryl Lindholm, Westchester County HFH, Valhalla, NY

Chicken à la Maria

Yield: 12 servings

12 chicken breast filets
3/4 cup Italian bread
   crumbs
1/4 cup grated
   Parmesan cheese
1/2 cup sliced green
   onions
2 tablespoons butter

2 tablespoons flour
1 cup milk
1 10-ounce package
   frozen chopped
   spinach, thawed,
   drained
4 ounces boiled ham
   slices, diced

■ Rinse chicken and pat dry. Dip in mixture of bread crumbs and Parmesan cheese. Arrange in 9x13-inch baking pan. Reserve remaining crumb mixture. Sauté green onions in butter until tender. Add flour; mix well. Stir in milk. Cook until thickened, stirring constantly. Stir in spinach and ham. Spoon over chicken. Sprinkle with reserved crumb mixture. Bake at 350 degrees for 40 minutes or until chicken is tender.
Approx Per Serving: Cal 229; Prot 32 g; Carbo 8 g; Fiber 1 g; T Fat 7 g; 28% Calories from Fat; Chol 87 mg; Sod 311 mg.

Joyce Cameron, Cottage Grove HFH, Cottage Grove, OR

Chicken with Mozzarella

Yield: 4 servings

4 chicken breasts, boned
1 cup flour
Salt and pepper to taste
2 tablespoons butter
4 ounces prosciutto
2 cups shredded
   Mozzarella cheese

Oregano to taste
1/2 cup vermouth
1 chicken bouillon
   cube
3/4 cup hot water

■ Rinse chicken and pat dry. Flatten between waxed paper. Dredge chicken in mixture of flour, salt and pepper. Sauté in butter in skillet until tender. Arrange in baking pan. Top with prosciutto and cheese. Stir oregano and vermouth into pan drippings. Cook until liquid is reduced. Stir in mixture of bouillon cube and water. Pour sauce over cheese. Broil until cheese melts.
Approx Per Serving: Cal 547; Prot 48 g; Carbo 27 g; Fiber 1 g; T Fat 22 g; 36% Calories from Fat; Chol 147 mg; Sod 993 mg.

Kate Chasson, Macalester College Campus Chapter
St. Paul, MN

Chicken with Mustard Sauce

Yield: 3 servings

8 ounces chicken
  breast filets
1 tablespoon oil
2 leeks, sliced
1   6-ounce can lima
  beans
1/2 cup white wine

1/2 cup water
2 tablespoons coarse
  mustard
Salt and pepper to taste
1 tablespoon cornstarch
2 tablespoons water

■ Rinse chicken and pat dry. Cut into 1-inch pieces. Sauté in oil in skillet over medium heat until tender. Add leeks. Cook until tender. Stir in lima beans, wine and water. Add mustard, salt and pepper; mix well. Stir in mixture of cornstarch and water until thickened. Serve over rice or noodles.
Approx Per Serving: Cal 244; Prot 22 g; Carbo 17 g; Fiber 5 g; T Fat 7 g; 27% Calories from Fat; Chol 48 mg; Sod 372 mg.

P. C. Westcott, Freehold Area HFH, Jamesburg, NJ

Chicken in Nests

Yield: 4 servings

4 chicken breasts,
  boned
16 mushrooms, sliced
4 lemon slices

1/4 cup melted butter
4 teaspoons soy sauce
Salt and pepper to taste

■ Rinse chicken and pat dry. Form 4 large squares of foil into the shape of nests. Layer chicken, mushrooms and lemon slices in nests. Top with mixture of butter and soy sauce. Season with salt and pepper. Seal securely. Place in baking pan. Bake at 350 degrees for 30 minutes. Open tops of nests. Bake for 10 to 15 minutes or until chicken is tender and brown.
Approx Per Serving: Cal 266; Prot 28 g; Carbo 5 g; Fiber 2 g; T Fat 15 g; 50% Calories from Fat; Chol 103 mg; Sod 506 mg.

Doris Hartman, Pioneer Valley HFH, Amherst, MA

Chicken and Peppers

Yield: 4 servings

11/2 pounds chicken
  breast filets
1/2 teaspoon oil
2 teaspoons soy sauce
2 teaspoons cornstarch
2 teaspoons dry sherry
2 teaspoons water
Pepper to taste
1 clove of garlic,
  minced
2 tablespoons oil
11/2 cups sliced
  mushrooms

2 green bell peppers,
  cut into 1-inch pieces
1/2 cup sliced bamboo
  shoots
1/2 cup water
1 teaspoon dry sherry
1/4 teaspoon sugar
1 teaspoon sesame oil
1 tablespoon cornstarch
2 tablespoons soy sauce

■ Rinse chicken and pat dry. Cut into bite-sized pieces. Combine next 6 ingredients in bowl; mix well. Toss chicken in mixture. Let stand for 15 minutes. Stir-fry garlic and chicken in 1 tablespoon oil in wok for 3 minutes. Remove chicken. Add 1 tablespoon oil. Stir-fry mushrooms, green peppers and bamboo shoots for 1 minute, adding water if mixture appears too dry. Return chicken to wok. Stir in mixture of remaining ingredients until thickened and bubbly. Serve over rice or noodles.
Approx Per Serving: Cal 331; Prot 42 g; Carbo 9 g; Fiber 2 g; T Fat 13 g; 37% Calories from Fat; Chol 108 mg; Sod 784 mg.

Jennie Borland, HFH of Gallatin Valley, Bozeman, MT

Chicken Picante

Yield: 6 servings

6 chicken breast filets
1 cup chunky salsa
1/2 cup Dijon mustard
1/4 cup lime juice
2 tablespoons
  margarine

6 tablespoons low-fat
  plain yogurt
6 peeled lime slices
Cilantro to taste

■ Rinse chicken and pat dry. Marinate in mixture of salsa, mustard and lime juice in bowl for 30 minutes. Drain chicken, reserving marinade. Melt margarine in skillet until foamy. Add chicken. Cook on both sides for 10 minutes or until brown. Stir in marinade. Cook for 5 minutes or until chicken is tender and marinade is slightly reduced. Remove chicken to warm serving platter. Boil marinade for 1 minute. Pour over chicken. Top with yogurt, lime slices and cilantro.
Approx Per Serving: Cal 237; Prot 29 g; Carbo 7 g; Fiber <1 g; T Fat 10 g; 38% Calories from Fat; Chol 73 mg; Sod 888 mg.

Ellen Murphy, Benton HFH, Corvallis, OR

Chicken Stir-Fry

Yield: 4 servings

2 cups chopped cooked
  chicken
2 eggs, slightly beaten
1/4 teaspoon pepper
1 cup baking mix
1 tablespoon oil
3 carrots, sliced
1 green bell pepper,
  sliced

1 small onion, sliced
8 ounces snow peas
8 ounces mushrooms,
  sliced
2 tablespoons
  margarine
1   20-ounce can
  pineapple chunks,
  drained

■ Rinse chicken and pat dry. Dip chicken in eggs; coat with mixture of pepper and baking mix. Heat oil in skillet or wok over medium-high heat. Stir-fry carrots for 2 minutes. Add green pepper, onion and snow peas. Stir-fry for 2 minutes. Remove to warm platter. Stir-fry mushrooms in margarine in another skillet for 2 minutes. Remove to warm platter. Stir-fry chicken on both sides until brown. Add vegetables to skillet. Cook for 2 minutes. Stir in pineapple. Serve over rice.
Approx Per Serving: Cal 539; Prot 30 g; Carbo 56 g; Fiber 7 g; T Fat 22 g; 37% Calories from Fat; Chol 169 mg; Sod 584 mg.

Sharri L. Koslecki, Northern Straits HFH, Cedarville, MI

Chicken and Walnuts

Yield: 4 servings

1 pound chicken breast
  filets
1 egg white
1 tablespoon cornstarch
2 cups walnut halves
9 tablespoons oil
2 slices gingerroot

1 tablespoon white
  wine
1 teaspoon sugar
3 tablespoons soy sauce
1 teaspoon cornstarch
1 tablespoon water

■ Rinse chicken and pat dry. Cut into 1/2-inch pieces. Mix with unbeaten egg white and 1 tablespoon cornstarch. Fry walnuts in 3 tablespoons oil in skillet until light brown. Drain on paper towel. Heat 6 tablespoons oil in skillet. Add gingerroot and chicken. Cook until chicken is tender. Stir in wine, sugar and soy sauce until hot. Add mixture of 1 teaspoon cornstarch and water; mix well. Stir in walnuts. Cook until thickened and heated through.
Approx Per Serving: Cal 760; Prot 35 g; Carbo 14 g; Fiber 3 g; T Fat 65 g; 77% Calories from Fat; Chol 72 mg; Sod 853 mg.

Martin G. Benedict, Transylvania HFH, Pisgah Forest, NC

Curried Chicken

Yield: 5 servings

4 chicken breast filets
1/2 cup chopped
  almonds
4 cloves of garlic,
  finely chopped
1   2-inch piece of
  gingerroot, chopped
1   14-ounce can plum
  tomatoes, mashed
2 tablespoons olive oil
Sesame oil to taste

2 onions, chopped
1/4 cup (rounded) curry
  powder
1 teaspoon red pepper
1 teaspoon szechuan
  pepper
1/4 teaspoon nutmeg
1/4 teaspoon cinnamon
1 teaspoon cumin
1 teaspoon coriander
1 cup plain yogurt

■ Rinse chicken and pat dry. Cut into bite-sized pieces. Combine almonds, garlic, gingerroot and tomatoes in bowl; mix well. Set aside. Sauté chicken in olive oil and sesame oil in skillet until tender. Add onions and spices; mix well. Stir in tomato mixture. Add yogurt; mix well. Cook over medium-high heat until mixture is of desired consistency.
Approx Per Serving: Cal 322; Prot 28 g; Carbo 17 g; Fiber 5 g; T Fat 17 g; 46% Calories from Fat; Chol 64 mg; Sod 207 mg.

Jeffrey L. Davis, Warren County HFH, Inwood, WV

Easy Company Chicken

Yield: 6 servings

6 chicken breasts
1/2 cup melted butter
2 teaspoons mustard

1/2 cup mayonnaise
1 cup stuffing mix
3/4 cup water

■ Rinse chicken and pat dry. Dip in mixture of melted butter, mustard and mayonnaise. Roll in stuffing mix. Arrange chicken in foil-lined 9x13-inch baking pan. Add water. Bake, covered, at 325 degrees for 1 1/2 hours or until chicken is tender.
Approx Per Serving: Cal 452; Prot 28 g; Carbo 9 g; Fiber <1 g; T Fat 33 g; 67% Calories from Fat; Chol 124 mg; Sod 474 mg.

Peggy Wolverton, Starkville HFH, Starkville, MS

> *F or I was hungry and you gave me something to eat, I was thirsty and you gave me something to drink, I was a stranger and you invited me in.*
>
> **Matthew 25:35**

Elegant Chicken

Yield: 8 servings

8 chicken breasts,
  boned
8 slices bacon
1 4-ounce jar chipped
  beef

1 10-ounce can cream
  of mushroom soup
1 cup sour cream
Paprika to taste

■ Rinse chicken and pat dry. Wrap chicken with bacon. Line bottom of greased 9x9-inch baking pan with chipped beef. Arrange chicken in prepared pan. Spoon mixture of soup and sour cream over chicken. Sprinkle with paprika. Bake at 275 degrees for 3 hours or until chicken is tender.
Approx Per Serving: Cal 298; Prot 34 g; Carbo 4 g; Fiber <1 g; T Fat 15 g; 48% Calories from Fat; Chol 114 mg; Sod 958 mg.

Yvonne B. Fairchild, Santa Fe HFH, Santa Fe, NM

Greek Chicken

Yield: 4 servings

4 chicken breast filets
3 tablespoons olive oil
1/4 cup chopped onion
2 cloves of garlic,
  minced
2 tablespoons butter
2 tablespoons flour
1 cup milk
2 tablespoons Greek
  seasoning

1 teaspoon dry mustard
2 teaspoons black
  pepper
Red pepper to taste
1 16-ounce package
  frozen spinach,
  thawed, drained
2 cups shredded
  mozzarella cheese
3 cups cooked rice

■ Rinse chicken and pat dry. Brown in olive oil in skillet. Place in 9x13-inch baking pan. Sauté onion and garlic in skillet until tender. Melt butter in saucepan over low heat. Stir in flour until smooth. Add milk; mix well. Cook over medium heat until thickened. Add onion, garlic, Greek seasoning, dry mustard, black pepper and red pepper, stirring until well mixed. Add spinach. Cook for 3 minutes, stirring constantly. Pour sauce over chicken. Bake at 375 degrees for 20 minutes. Sprinkle with cheese. Bake for 5 minutes or until cheese melts. Serve over rice.
Approx Per Serving: Cal 701; Prot 47 g; Carbo 52 g; Fiber 4 g; T Fat 33 g; 43% Calories from Fat; Chol 140 mg; Sod 447 mg.
Nutritional information does not include Greek seasoning

Anne Selman Raybon, Huntington Area HFH
Huntington, WV

Honey-Baked Chicken

Yield: 4 servings

4 chicken breasts,
  skinned
1/3 cup melted
  margarine
1/3 cup honey

2 tablespoons mustard
1 teaspoon salt
1 teaspoon curry
  powder

■ Rinse chicken and pat dry. Arrange in baking pan sprayed with nonstick cooking spray. Spoon mixture of margarine, honey, mustard, salt and curry powder over chicken. Bake at 350 degrees for 1 1/4 hours, basting every 15 minutes.
Approx Per Serving: Cal 369; Prot 27 g; Carbo 24 g; Fiber <1 g; T Fat 19 g; 45% Calories from Fat; Chol 72 mg; Sod 874 mg.

Dee Reynolds, Laurel County HFH, London, KY

Honey-Dijon Chicken

Yield: 4 servings

4 chicken breast filets
Salt and pepper to taste
2 tablespoons oil
3/4 cup chicken broth
1/4 cup Dijon and
  honey barbecue
  sauce

1 medium onion, sliced
4 ounces sliced water
  chestnuts
1 green bell pepper,
  cut into strips
1 tablespoon cornstarch
2 tablespoons water

■ Rinse chicken and pat dry. Cut into strips. Season with salt and pepper. Cook in oil in electric skillet on both sides for 5 minutes or until brown. Stir in broth and barbecue sauce. Cook, covered, for 5 minutes. Add onion, water chestnuts and green pepper; mix well. Cook for 5 minutes. Stir in mixture of cornstarch and water until thickened. Serve immediately over rice.
Approx Per Serving: Cal 257; Prot 29 g; Carbo 11 g; Fiber 2 g; T Fat 11 g; 38% Calories from Fat; Chol 72 mg; Sod 340 mg.

Laura Mosena, Ottumwa HFH, Ottumwa, IA

Lemon-Garlic Chicken

Yield: 6 servings

6 chicken breast filets
1/2 cup melted butter
1 small clove of garlic,
  crushed
3/4 cup dry bread
  crumbs
1/2 cup grated
  Parmesan cheese

1 1/2 teaspoons minced
  parsley
1 teaspoon salt
Pepper to taste
2 tablespoons melted
  butter
Juice of 1 lemon
Paprika to taste

■ Rinse chicken and pat dry. Dip in mixture of 1/2 cup butter and garlic. Coat in mixture of bread crumbs, Parmesan cheese, parsley, salt and pepper. Roll tightly; secure with wooden picks. Arrange in nonstick baking pan. Drizzle with 2 tablespoons butter and lemon juice. Sprinkle with paprika. Bake at 325 degrees for 50 minutes or until chicken is tender.

Approx Per Serving: Cal 392; Prot 31 g; Carbo 10 g; Fiber 1 g; T Fat 25 g; 57% Calories from Fat; Chol 130 mg; Sod 798 mg.

Jennifer Harris, Furman University Campus Chapter
Durham, NC

Linguine with Chicken Scampi

Yield: 6 servings

1 pound chicken breast
  filets
1 egg, beaten
1 cup bread crumbs
1/2 teaspoon salt
1/4 teaspoon pepper
1/2 cup oil
1/4 cup low-calorie
  margarine
3 cloves of garlic,
  minced

1 tablespoon lemon
  juice
1/2 teaspoon salt
1/2 teaspoon pepper
1 1-pound package
  linguine, cooked
2 tablespoons
  low-calorie
  margarine
1/2 cup chopped parsley
Lemon wedges

■ Rinse chicken and pat dry. Cut into 1/2-inch pieces. Dip chicken in egg. Roll in mixture of bread crumbs, 1/2 teaspoon salt and 1/4 teaspoon pepper. Sauté chicken in oil in skillet until bread crumbs are golden brown. Remove chicken to warm platter. Wipe out skillet with paper towel. Melt margarine in skillet. Add garlic, lemon juice, 1/2 teaspoon salt and 1/2 teaspoon pepper; mix well. Toss chicken in sauce to coat. Spoon chicken and sauce over linguine that has been tossed with 2 tablespoons margarine. Sprinkle with parsley. Garnish with lemon wedges.

Approx Per Serving: Cal 665; Prot 31 g; Carbo 70 g; Fiber 4 g; T Fat 28 g; 39% Calories from Fat; Chol 85 mg; Sod 672 mg.

Linda Post, Endless Mountains HFH, Tunkhannock, PA

Marinated Chicken Breasts

Yield: 4 servings

4 chicken breast filets
2 tablespoons oil
2 tablespoons soy sauce
1 tablespoon lemon
  juice

1 tablespoon brown
  sugar
Garlic salt to taste
1/2 teaspoon basil

■ Rinse chicken and pat dry. Arrange in glass dish. Pour mixture of remaining ingredients over chicken. Marinate, covered, in refrigerator for 3 hours or longer. Grill over hot coals until tender. May broil in oven for 12 minutes or until chicken is tender, turning once.

Approx Per Serving: Cal 219; Prot 27 g; Carbo 4 g; Fiber <1 g; T Fat 10 g; 41% Calories from Fat; Chol 72 mg; Sod 579 mg.

Sharon Barnes, Freeborn/Mower HFH, Austin, MN

Pasta Primavera with Chicken

Yield: 4 servings

2 chicken breasts
1 clove of garlic, minced
2 tablespoons oil
1/2 cup chili sauce
1/2 cup chicken broth
1 teaspoon basil
1/2 teaspoon salt
1/8 teaspoon pepper
2 cups coarsely
  chopped broccoli
2 carrots, sliced

1 cup diagonally sliced
  celery
1/2 cup sliced red bell
  pepper
3 green onions, cut
  into 1/2-inch pieces
1 12-ounce package
  spaghetti, cooked
1/4 cup grated
  Parmesan cheese
2 tablespoons butter

■ Rinse chicken and pat dry. Cut into 1/4-inch strips. Sauté chicken and garlic in oil in skillet until chicken is brown. Stir in chili sauce, chicken broth, basil, salt, pepper, broccoli, carrots, celery, bell pepper and green onions. Cook, covered, over low heat for 8 to 10 minutes or until chicken is tender, stirring occasionally. Spoon over spaghetti which has been tossed with Parmesan cheese and butter.

Approx Per Serving: Cal 597; Prot 30 g; Carbo 81 g; Fiber 8 g; T Fat 17 g; 26% Calories from Fat; Chol 56 mg; Sod 1048 mg.

Susan Kilton, Sheboygan County HFH, Sheboygan, WI

Poppy Seed Chicken

Yield: 6 servings

5 chicken breasts, cooked, chopped
1 cup sour cream
1 10-ounce can cream of chicken soup
1/8 teaspoon curry powder

1/2 cup melted margarine
1 tablespoon poppy seed
1/3 1-pound package butter crackers, crushed

■ Arrange chicken in 1 1/2 quart baking dish. Spoon mixture of sour cream, soup and curry powder over chicken. Top with mixture of melted margarine, poppy seed and cracker crumbs. Bake at 350 degrees for 30 minutes.

Approx Per Serving: Cal 512; Prot 27 g; Carbo 23 g; Fiber <1 g; T Fat 37 g; 63% Calories from Fat; Chol 122 mg; Sod 826 mg.

Cheryl Seale, Hamblen County HFH, Morristown, TN

Texas White Chili

Yield: 4 servings

1 pound dried white beans
1 1/2 quarts chicken stock
1 1/2 medium onions, chopped
2 cloves of garlic, chopped
1 teaspoon salt
1 tablespoon corn oil
1 4-ounce can chopped green chilies

2 teaspoons cumin
2 teaspoons oregano
2 teaspoons coriander
Cloves and cayenne pepper to taste
4 chicken breast filets, cooked, chopped
1/2 cup shredded Monterey Jack cheese
4 green onions, sliced

■ Bring beans, chicken stock, half the onions, garlic and salt to a boil in stockpot. Reduce heat to low. Simmer for 1 1/2 hours or until beans are tender. Sauté remaining onions in oil in skillet for 5 minutes. Add chilies and spices; mix well. Cook for 20 minutes, stirring occasionally. Add to beans; mix well. Arrange chicken in 4 soup bowls. Ladle bean mixture over chicken. Sprinkle with cheese and green onions.

Approx Per Serving: Cal 476; Prot 49 g; Carbo 40 g; Fiber 11 g; T Fat 14 g; 26% Calories from Fat; Chol 87 mg; Sod 2041 mg.

Wanda L. Schulze, Walker County HFH, Huntsville, TX

Cashew Chicken

Yield: 6 servings

4 cups chopped cooked chicken
1 10-ounce can cream of chicken soup
1/2 cup dry minced onion

3/4 cup chopped celery
3/4 cup chicken broth
1 3-ounce can chow mein noodles
1 cup cashews

■ Combine chicken, soup, onion, chopped celery, chicken broth, 1/2 of the noodles and cashews in bowl; mix well. Spoon into nonstick 8x8-inch baking dish. Sprinkle with remaining noodles. Bake at 350 degrees for 30 minutes.

Approx Per Serving: Cal 437; Prot 35 g; Carbo 22 g; Fiber 3 g; T Fat 24 g; 48% Calories from Fat; Chol 89 mg; Sod 708 mg.

Gloria Holt, Benton HFH, Corvallis, OR

Chicken Casserole

Yield: 6 servings

1 3-pound chicken, cooked, skinned, chopped
1 cup chow mein noodles
1 10-ounce can cream of chicken soup
1 10-ounce can cream of mushroom soup

1 5-ounce can evaporated milk
1 cup crushed Special K cereal
3 tablespoons melted margarine

■ Arrange chicken in greased 8x8-inch baking pan. Sprinkle noodles over chicken. Spoon mixture of soups and evaporated milk over layers. Top with cereal. Drizzle with margarine. Bake at 325 degrees for 45 minutes.

Approx Per Serving: Cal 448; Prot 39 g; Carbo 18 g; Fiber <1 g; T Fat 24 g; 49% Calories from Fat; Chol 113 mg; Sod 1068 mg.

Mary C. Arkens, HFH of Wausau, Wausau, WI

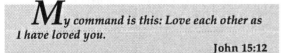

My command is this: Love each other as I have loved you.

John 15:12

Chicken-Rice Casserole

Yield: 6 servings

1 cup chopped cooked chicken
1 cup cooked rice
1/4 cup slivered almonds
1 small onion, diced
1/2 cup mayonnaise
2 hard-boiled eggs, chopped
1 teaspoon lemon juice
3/4 cup diagonally sliced celery
1   10-ounce can cream of mushroom soup
1 cup crushed potato chips

■ Combine chicken, rice, almonds, onion, mayonnaise, eggs, lemon juice, celery and soup in bowl; mix well. Spoon into buttered 6x10-inch baking pan. Top with potato chips. Bake at 350 degrees for 30 to 40 minutes or until brown.

Approx Per Serving: Cal 379; Prot 12 g; Carbo 21 g; Fiber 2 g; T Fat 28 g; 66% Calories from Fat; Chol 103 mg; Sod 587 mg.

Naomi West, Central Valley HFH, Bridgewater, VA

Chicken and Mushroom Casserole

Yield: 4 servings

1 cup rice
2 cups water
3 tablespoons butter
1   3-pound chicken, cooked, chopped
1   10-ounce can chicken broth
1   4-ounce can mushrooms
Salt and pepper to taste
1 teaspoon garlic salt
1 cup cracker crumbs

■ Combine rice, water and butter in saucepan. Cook for 5 minutes. Add chicken, broth, mushrooms, salt, pepper and garlic salt ; mix well. Spoon into nonstick baking pan. Top with cracker crumbs. Bake at 350 degrees for 45 minutes.

Approx Per Serving: Cal 674; Prot 55 g; Carbo 55 g; Fiber 2 g; T Fat 24 g; 33% Calories from Fat; Chol 182 mg; Sod 1350 mg.

Karen Hoffman, Firelands HFH, Milan, OH

Easy Chicken-Rice Casserole

Yield: 6 servings

1/2 cup chopped green bell pepper
1/2 cup chopped onion
1 cup sliced celery
1   2-ounce jar chopped pimento, drained
2 cups cooked rice
2 hard-boiled eggs, chopped
2 cups coarsely chopped cooked chicken
2 bouillon cubes, crushed
1/2 cup mayonnaise
Salt and pepper to taste
1/3 cup soft bread crumbs

■ Combine first 7 ingredients in bowl; mix well. Stir in mixture of bouillon cubes and mayonnaise. Season with salt and pepper. Top with bread crumbs. Bake at 350 degrees for 30 minutes.

Approx Per Serving: Cal 343; Prot 18 g; Carbo 22 g; Fiber 1 g; T Fat 20 g; 54% Calories from Fat; Chol 124 mg; Sod 581 mg.

Liane Luini, Prince George's County HFH
Landover Hills, MD

Quick Chicken Divan

Yield: 4 servings

1   10-ounce package frozen broccoli, cooked, drained
4 chicken breast filets, cooked, sliced
1   10-ounce can cream of chicken soup
1/3 cup milk
1/2 cup shredded Cheddar cheese

■ Layer broccoli in nonstick baking pan. Arrange chicken over broccoli. Top with mixture of soup and milk. Sprinkle with cheese. Broil for 8 minutes or until brown and bubbly.

Approx Per Serving: Cal 295; Prot 35 g; Carbo 10 g; Fiber 2 g; T Fat 13 g; 39% Calories from Fat; Chol 96 mg; Sod 733 mg.

Myrtle C. Patrice, Mid-Hudson Valley HFH
Poughkeepsie, NY

Escalloped Chicken Casserole

Yield: 10 servings

4 cups toasted bread cubes
1/4 cup chopped onion
1 cup chopped celery
1 teaspoon salt
1 teaspoon sage
1/3 cup melted butter
1   3-pound chicken, cooked, chopped
4 1/2 cups chicken broth
1 cup flour
1 teaspoon salt
1/4 teaspoon pepper
2 tablespoons butter

■ Combine bread cubes, onion, celery, 1 teaspoon salt, sage and 1/3 cup butter in bowl; mix well. Spoon into nonstick 9x13-inch baking pan. Arrange chicken over prepared layer. Add mixture of remaining ingredients. Bake at 350 degrees for 1 hour.

Approx Per Serving: Cal 314; Prot 25 g; Carbo 19 g; Fiber 1 g; T Fat 15 g; 43% Calories from Fat; Chol 84 mg; Sod 1075 mg.

Debbie Hillman, Council Bluffs HFH, Shenandoah, IA

Boneless Fried Chicken

Yield: 4 servings

1 cup flour
2 teaspoons baking
  powder
1 teaspoon sugar
1/4 teaspoon salt

1 egg, beaten
1 cup milk
1 3-pound chicken,
  cooked
Oil for deep frying

■ Sift flour, baking powder, sugar and salt in bowl; mix well. Stir in egg and milk. Debone chicken, leaving chicken in large pieces. Dip chicken in flour mixture. Fry in hot oil in skillet on both sides until golden brown. Drain on paper towels.

Approx Per Serving: Cal 501; Prot 56 g; Carbo 28 g; Fiber 1 g; T Fat 16 g; 30% Calories from Fat; Chol 213 mg; Sod 487 mg.
Nutritional information does not include oil for frying.

Irene A. Rouleau, Immokalee HFH, Marco Island, FL

Chicken Manicotti with Chive Cream Sauce

Yield: 6 servings

12 manicotti pasta shells
8 ounces whipped
  cream cheese with
  chives and onion
2/3 cup milk
1/4 cup grated Romano
  cheese
2 cups chopped cooked
  chicken

1 10-ounce package
  frozen chopped
  broccoli, thawed,
  drained
1 4-ounce jar chopped
  pimentos, drained
1/4 teaspoon pepper
Paprika to taste

■ Cook pasta shells using package directions. Rinse with cold water; drain. Stir cream cheese in saucepan over medium heat until melted. Add milk, stirring until blended. Stir in Romano cheese. Reserve 3/4 cup sauce. Combine reserved sauce, chicken, broccoli, pimentos and pepper in bowl; mix well. Stuff each pasta shell with 1/3 cup chicken mixture. Arrange in nonstick 9x13-inch baking pan. Spoon remaining sauce over pasta. Sprinkle with paprika. Bake, covered with foil, at 350 degrees for 25 to 30 minutes or until heated through.

Approx Per Serving: Cal 393; Prot 24 g; Carbo 31 g; Fiber 3 g; T Fat 20 g; 45% Calories from Fat; Chol 90 mg; Sod 225 mg.

Mayme Miracle, Mosinee, WI

Florida Pasta and Chicken

Yield: 4 servings

4 chicken breast filets
1/4 cup olive oil
1 tablespoon lime juice
1/8 teaspoon red pepper
  sauce
1 clove of garlic,
  crushed
1 tablespoon olive oil

1 16-ounce jar salsa
1 9-ounce package
  linguine, cooked
2 tablespoons melted
  margarine
1 tablespoon grated
  lime rind

■ Rinse chicken and pat dry. Combine chicken with 1/4 cup olive oil, lime juice and pepper sauce in bowl; mix well. Marinate in refrigerator for 20 minutes. Drain chicken. Grill over hot coals for 12 to 15 minutes or until tender. Slice; keep warm. Sauté garlic in 1 tablespoon olive oil in skillet until tender. Add salsa, stirring until heated. Arrange linguine tossed with margarine and lime rind on plate. Top with chicken. Spoon salsa over chicken. Garnish with lime wedges.

Approx Per Serving: Cal 619; Prot 35 g; Carbo 57 g; Fiber 3 g; T Fat 26 g; 39% Calories from Fat; Chol 72 mg; Sod 838 mg.

Judy McConnell, HFH of Boca-Delray, Delray Beach, FL

Chicken Spectacular

Yield: 8 servings

1 6-ounce package
  long grain and wild
  rice
3 cups chopped cooked
  chicken
1 10-ounce can cream
  of celery soup
1 medium onion,
  chopped
1 cup mayonnaise

1 2-ounce jar chopped
  pimento, drained
1 16-ounce can
  French-style green
  beans, drained
1 5-ounce can water
  chestnuts, drained,
  chopped
Salt and pepper to taste

■ Cook rice using package directions. Combine rice, chicken, soup, onion, mayonnaise, pimento, green beans, water chestnuts, salt and pepper in bowl; mix well. Spoon into nonstick 2-quart baking pan. Bake at 350 degrees for 45 minutes or until bubbly.

Approx Per Serving: Cal 426; Prot 19 g; Carbo 26 g; Fiber 2 g; T Fat 28 g; 58% Calories from Fat; Chol 67 mg; Sod 951 mg.

Mrs. Bill Howell, Starkville HFH, Starkville, MS

Chicken Potpie

Yield: 6 servings

1/3 cup margarine
1/3 cup flour
1/3 cup frozen chopped
  onion
1/2 teaspoon salt
1/4 teaspoon pepper
2 chicken bouillon
  cubes
1³/₄ cups hot water

2/3 cup milk
2 cups chopped cooked
  chicken
1   10-ounce package
  frozen mixed
  vegetables
1 package allready pie
  crusts

■ Melt margarine in skillet over low heat. Stir in flour, chopped onion, salt and pepper. Cook until smooth and bubbly, stirring constantly. Remove from heat. Stir in bouillon cubes dissolved in hot water. Add milk; mix well. Boil for 1 minute, stirring constantly. Fold in chicken and mixed vegetables. Spoon mixture into pastry-lined pie plate. Top with remaining pastry, sealing edge and cutting vents. Bake at 425 degrees for 30 to 35 minutes or until brown.
Approx Per Serving: Cal 575; Prot 18 g; Carbo 46 g; Fiber 2 g; T Fat 35 g; 55% Calories from Fat; Chol 66 mg; Sod 1122 mg.

Susan J. Batman, Warren County HFH, Stephens City, VA

Chicken Salad Casserole

Yield: 10 servings

3 cups chopped cooked
  chicken
2 cups diced celery
1   2-ounce jar pimento
1 cup sliced water
  chestnuts

1 cup mayonnaise
1¹/₂ cups cubed
  Velveeta cheese
1 cup crushed potato
  chips

■ Combine chicken, celery, pimento, water chestnuts and mayonnaise in bowl; mix well. Spoon into non-stick 6x9-inch baking dish. Arrange Velveeta cheese over mixture. Top with potato chips. Bake at 350 degrees for 30 to 45 minutes or until bubbly.
Approx Per Serving: Cal 327; Prot 16 g; Carbo 7 g; Fiber 1 g; T Fat 27 g; 73% Calories from Fat; Chol 63 mg; Sod 392 mg.

Wilma Canfield, Morgan County HFH, Fort Morgan, CO

Hot Chicken Salad

Yield: 6 servings

2 cups thinly sliced
  celery
2 cups chopped toasted
  almonds
1/2 teaspoon salt
2 teaspoons grated
  onion
1 cup mayonnaise

2 teaspoons lemon
  juice
2 cups chopped cooked
  chicken
1/2 cup shredded
  Cheddar cheese
1 cup crushed potato
  chips

■ Combine celery, almonds, salt, onion, mayonnaise, lemon juice and chicken in saucepan; mix well. Cook over low heat until heated through. Spoon into non-stick 5x7-inch baking pan. Sprinkle with cheese. Top with potato chips. Bake at 450 degrees for 15 minutes or until brown. Serve with apple slices.
Approx Per Serving: Cal 701; Prot 26 g; Carbo 17 g; Fiber 6 g; T Fat 62 g; 77% Calories from Fat; Chol 73 mg; Sod 569 mg.

Marion Boyum, St. John's Episcopal Church
Mankato, MN

Easy Chicken Salad

Yield: 6 servings

2 cups chopped cooked
  chicken
2 cups diced celery
1/2 cup slivered almonds
1/2 teaspoon MSG
2 tablespoons lemon
  juice

1/2 teaspoon salt
1 cup mayonnaise-type
  salad dressing
1/2 cup shredded
  Cheddar cheese
1 cup crushed potato
  chips

■ Combine chicken, celery, almonds, MSG, lemon juice, salt and salad dressing in bowl; mix well. Spoon into nonstick baking pan. Sprinkle with cheese; top with potato chips. Bake at 425 degrees for 20 minutes or until brown.
Approx Per Serving: Cal 402; Prot 19 g; Carbo 19 g; Fiber 2 g; T Fat 29 g; 63% Calories from Fat; Chol 62 mg; Sod 992 mg.

Carol Witteveen, Newaygo HFH, Fremont, MI

Chicken Stew Olé

Yield: 4 servings

1 cup sliced carrots
2 large potatoes, cubed
1¹/₂ quarts chicken
  broth
1 cup salsa
2 cups chopped cooked
  chicken
¹/₂ cup frozen corn
1   4-ounce can green
  chilies, drained

1 cup flour
¹/₂ cup cornmeal
2 teaspoons baking
  powder
¹/₂ teaspoon salt
1 egg
¹/₂ cup milk
2 tablespoons oil

■ Combine carrots, potatoes and chicken broth in stock-pot. Cook until vegetables are tender. Add salsa, chicken, corn and green chilies; mix well. Combine flour, cornmeal, baking powder, salt, egg, milk and oil in bowl; mix well. Drop dumpling batter in heaping tablespoonfuls on top of hot mixture. Cook, covered, for 18 minutes or until dumplings test done.
Approx Per Serving: Cal 579; Prot 38 g; Carbo 66 g; Fiber 5 g; T Fat 17 g; 27% Calories from Fat; Chol 121 mg; Sod 2253 mg.

Bernadine Meadows, Las Vegas, New Mexico HFH
Las Vegas, NM

Spicy Chicken Casserole

Yield: 6 servings

2 cups chopped cooked
  chicken
1 medium onion,
  finely chopped
1¹/₂   10-ounce cans
  chicken consommé
1   10-ounce can cream
  of chicken soup
1   10-ounce can cream
  of mushroom soup

1   10-ounce can Ro-Tel
  tomatoes and green
  chilies
12 corn tortillas, cut
  into quarters
1¹/₂ cups shredded
  Cheddar cheese

■ Combine chicken, onion, consommé, soups and tomatoes in bowl; mix well. Layer tortillas, chicken mixture and cheese ¹/₂ at a time in nonstick 9x9-inch baking pan. Let stand for 1 hour. Bake at 350 degrees for 30 minutes or until bubbly.
Approx Per Serving: Cal 458; Prot 30 g; Carbo 38 g; Fiber 6 g; T Fat 21 g; 41% Calories from Fat; Chol 76 mg; Sod 1530 mg.

Phyllis Caves, HFH of El Paso, El Paso, TX

Stuffed Cornish Hens

Yield: 4 servings

4   1-pound Cornish
  game hens
Salt to taste
1   6-ounce package
  long grain and wild
  rice
¹/₂ cup chopped celery

1   5-ounce can sliced
  water chestnuts,
  drained
1   3-ounce can chopped
  mushrooms, drained
¹/₄ cup melted butter
1 tablespoon soy sauce

■ Rinse Cornish hens and pat dry. Salt inside of cavities. Cook rice using package directions. Combine rice, celery, water chestnuts, mushrooms, butter and soy sauce in bowl; mix well. Stuff hens; truss. Place in baking pan. Bake at 375 degrees for 1³/₄ hours or until hens test done.
Approx Per Serving: Cal 710; Prot 71 g; Carbo 39 g; Fiber 1 g; T Fat 29 g; 37% Calories from Fat; Chol 234 mg; Sod 1330 mg.

Jerrine Brinker, HFH of Wausau, Schofield, WI

Turkey-Cornmeal Burgers with Salsa

Yield: 5 servings

1¹/₄ pounds ground
  turkey
2 tablespoons cornmeal
1 tablespoon lime juice
1 egg white
2 teaspoons cumin
2 teaspoons chili
  powder

¹/₂ teaspoon salt
¹/₄ teaspoon pepper
1 jalapeño pepper,
  seeded, chopped
1 tablespoon oil
1 cup frozen whole
  kernel corn
³/₄ cup salsa

■ Combine turkey, cornmeal, lime juice, egg white, cumin, chili powder, salt, pepper and jalapeño pepper in bowl; mix well. Shape into 5 patties. Fry in oil in skillet for 3 to 5 minutes on each side or to desired doneness. Combine whole kernel corn and salsa in saucepan; mix well. Cook until heated through. Serve with turkey burgers.
Approx Per Serving: Cal 284; Prot 24 g; Carbo 15 g; Fiber 2 g; T Fat 14 g; 45% Calories from Fat; Chol 72 mg; Sod 550 mg.

Ann K. Bennett, HFH of Wichita Falls, Wichita Falls, TX

Aztec Gold Chili

Yield: 8 servings

1 tablespoon oil
2 cloves of garlic, minced
2 large onions, coarsely chopped
3 to 6 tablespoons chili powder
1 teaspoon ground cumin
1 teaspoon oregano
1 teaspoon cinnamon
1/2 teaspoon black pepper

1/2 teaspoon cayenne pepper
1 teaspoon salt
2 pounds ground turkey
2 16-ounce cans tomatoes
2 16-ounce cans pinto beans
2 green bell peppers, coarsely chopped
1/2 ounce unsweetened chocolate, grated

■ Combine first 10 ingredients in microwave-safe dish; mix well. Microwave on High for 2½ minutes. Stir in 1 to 2 tablespoons water if mixture becomes too dry. Microwave on High for 2½ to 3 minutes or until onions are tender-crisp. Let stand for 3 minutes. Stir in turkey. Microwave on High for 10 to 13 minutes or until turkey is partially done, stirring once. Add undrained tomatoes, beans, bell peppers and chocolate; mix well. Microwave, covered, on Medium for 40 minutes, stirring 2 times. Serve with sour cream, grated cheese and tortilla chips.

Approx Per Serving: Cal 364; Prot 30 g; Carbo 29 g; Fiber 4 g; T Fat 16 g; 37% Calories from Fat; Chol 71 mg; Sod 1079 mg.

Lorraine Strahlmann, HFH of Greater Ocala, Ocala, FL

Crescent Turkey Squares

Yield: 4 servings

1 8-count can crescent rolls
3 ounces cream cheese, softened
2 tablespoons melted margarine
2 cups chopped cooked turkey
1/4 teaspoon salt
1/8 teaspoon pepper

2 tablespoons milk
1 tablespoon chopped onion
1 tablespoon chopped pimento
1 tablespoon melted margarine
3/4 cup seasoned croutons, crushed

■ Unroll crescent roll dough. Separate into 4 rectangles, pressing perforations together. Blend cream cheese and 2 tablespoons margarine in bowl until smooth. Add turkey, salt, pepper, milk, onion and pimento; mix well. Spoon 1/2 cup into center of each rectangle. Pull up 4 corners of dough, pinching to seal. Sprinkle with mixture of 1 tablespoon margarine and croutons. Place on ungreased baking sheet. Bake at 350 degrees for 25 minutes or until golden brown.

Approx Per Serving: Cal 497; Prot 26 g; Carbo 28 g; Fiber <1 g; T Fat 31 g; 56% Calories from Fat; Chol 78 mg; Sod 884 mg.

Wilma Weimer, Morgan County HFH, Fort Morgan, CO

Green Chili Enchiladas

Yield: 10 servings

12 corn tortillas
2 tablespoons oil
1/4 cup chopped onion
2 teaspoons oil
1 pound ground turkey
1 10-ounce can cream of chicken soup

1 10-ounce can cream of mushroom soup
1 cup water
1 4-ounce can green chilies
4 cups shredded Cheddar cheese

■ Dip tortillas in 2 tablespoons hot oil in small skillet. Drain on paper towels. Cook chopped onion in 2 teaspoons oil in large skillet until tender. Add turkey; mix well. Cook until of desired doneness; drain. Add soups, water and green chilies; mix well. Simmer for 5 minutes. Layer tortillas, turkey mixture and 3¾ cups cheese 1/2 at a time in nonstick baking dish. Top with remaining 1/4 cup cheese. Serve immediately.

Approx Per Serving: Cal 428; Prot 24 g; Carbo 21 g; Fiber 3 g; T Fat 28 g; 58% Calories from Fat; Chol 79 mg; Sod 854 mg.

*Fabiola E. Sanchez, Las Vegas, New Mexico HFH
Las Vegas, NM*

Bob's Favorite Meat Loaf

Yield: 4 servings

1½ pounds ground turkey
1 cup herb-seasoned stuffing mix
2 eggs, beaten
3 tablespoons chopped parsley

1/2 cup dry red wine
1 envelope onion soup mix
3 cloves of garlic, minced
Salt and pepper to taste

■ Combine all ingredients in bowl; mix well. Shape into loaf. Place in 5x9-inch nonstick loaf pan. Bake at 350 degrees for 1 hour or until meat loaf tests done. Cool slightly before slicing.

Approx Per Serving: Cal 422; Prot 39 g; Carbo 15 g; Fiber <1 g; T Fat 20 g; 46% Calories from Fat; Chol 214 mg; Sod 574 mg.

Robert Dessell, Pensacola HFH, Pensacola, FL

Hot Browns

Yield: 8 servings

1/4 cup margarine
1/2 cup flour
1/2 teaspoon salt
Pepper to taste
1 cup turkey broth
1/2 cup shredded
    Cheddar cheese

8 slices bread, toasted
8 slices cooked turkey
8 slices tomatoes
8 slices crisp-fried
    bacon
Paprika to taste

- Combine margarine, flour, salt, pepper and turkey broth in saucepan; mix well. Cook over medium heat until thickened, stirring constantly. Stir in cheese. Place bread on nonstick baking sheet. Arrange sliced turkey on bread. Spoon hot mixture over turkey. Top with tomatoes and bacon. Sprinkle with paprika. Bake at 400 degrees for 10 minutes.
Approx Per Serving: Cal 273; Prot 16 g; Carbo 20 g; Fiber 1 g; T Fat 14 g; 46% Calories from Fat; Chol 35 mg; Sod 607 mg.

Marilyn R. Munn, Ashland/Ironton Area HFH, Ashland, KY

Leftover Turkey Casserole

Yield: 4 servings

1   10-ounce can cream
    of chicken soup
1 cup milk
2 cups chopped cooked
    turkey
2 cups sliced cooked
    carrots

1/2 cup canned green
    beans
1 teaspoon garlic salt
3 1/2 cups cooked
    noodles
Salt and pepper to taste

- Combine soup, milk, turkey, carrots, green beans, garlic salt, cooked noodles, salt and pepper in saucepan in order listed; mix well. Cook over medium heat until heated through.
Approx Per Serving: Cal 437; Prot 31 g; Carbo 50 g; Fiber 6 g; T Fat 12 g; 24% Calories from Fat; Chol 111 mg; Sod 1242 mg.

Christy Storm, HFH of Wichita Falls, Wichita Falls, TX

Turkey Loaf

Yield: 5 servings

2 slices bread
1/2 cup hot milk
1 egg, beaten
1 pound ground turkey
1/4 cup minced onion

1/4 cup chopped parsley
1/2 teaspoon poultry
    seasoning
1/8 teaspoon pepper

- Soak bread in hot milk in bowl for several minutes. Stir in egg. Combine turkey, onion, parsley, poultry seasoning and pepper in bowl; mix well. Stir in milk mixture with fork until well mixed. Spoon into greased 5x9-inch loaf pan. Bake at 350 degrees for 1 hour or until brown.
Approx Per Serving: Cal 218; Prot 21 g; Carbo 8 g; Fiber 1 g; T Fat 11 g; 47% Calories from Fat; Chol 103 mg; Sod 161 mg.

Eleanor Tracy, HFH of Chico, Chico, CA

*L*ove the Lord your God with all your heart and with all your soul and with all your mind. This is the first and greatest commandment. And the second is like it: Love your neighbor as yourself.

Matthew 22:37

Turkey Potpie

Yield: 5 servings

2 10-ounce cans cream of broccoli soup
1 cup milk
1/4 teaspoon thyme
1/4 teaspoon pepper
1 cup chopped cooked broccoli
1 cup chopped cooked cauliflower

1 cup cooked sliced carrots
1 cup cooked diced potato
2 cups chopped cooked turkey
1 10-count can flaky biscuits, cut into quarters

- Combine soup, milk, thyme and pepper in 3-quart baking pan; mix well. Stir in vegetables and turkey. Bake at 400 degrees for 15 minutes or until bubbly. Stir; top with biscuits. Bake for 15 minutes or until biscuits are brown.

Approx Per Serving: Cal 389; Prot 24 g; Carbo 41 g; Fiber 4 g; T Fat 14 g; 32% Calories from Fat; Chol 56 mg; Sod 1273 mg.

Marilyn Thomas, Pilot Mountain Area HFH
Pilot Mountain, NC

New York Sidewalk Sandwich

Yield: 6 servings

This recipe won a $1,000 prize in the Land O' Lakes "Create the New York State Sandwich" contest.

6 large soft salted pretzels, toasted
12 slices cooked turkey
1 cup chopped sweet onion
1 cup chopped green pepper

1 cup chopped mushrooms
1/3 cup butter
6 slices American cheese
Red leaf lettuce

- Place pretzels on nonstick baking sheet. Arrange 2 slices turkey on each pretzel, covering hole. Sauté onion, green pepper and mushrooms in butter in skillet until tender. Spoon over turkey. Top with cheese. Bake at 350 degrees for 5 minutes or until cheese melts. Serve on plates lined with lettuce.

Approx Per Serving: Cal 478; Prot 30 g; Carbo 41 g; Fiber 1 g; T Fat 22 g; 41% Calories from Fat; Chol 98 mg; Sod 673 mg.

Jackie Howell, Cazenovia Area HFH, Chittenango, NY

Sunshine Turkey

Yield: 4 servings

1 2/3 cups thinly sliced carrots
1/4 cup canola oil
1/4 cup chopped onion
1 cup orange juice
1 cup water
2 tablespoons sugar

1 teaspoon salt
1 teaspoon grated orange rind
1/8 teaspoon pepper
1 1/2 cups chopped cooked turkey
1 1/3 cups minute rice

- Sauté carrots in oil in skillet over medium heat for 5 minutes or until tender-crisp, stirring frequently. Add onion, cooking until tender. Stir in orange juice, water, sugar, salt, orange rind and pepper. Bring to a boil. Add turkey and rice; mix well. Simmer, covered, for 8 minutes or until rice and carrots are tender.

Approx Per Serving: Cal 397; Prot 19 g; Carbo 43 g; Fiber 2 g; T Fat 17 g; 38% Calories from Fat; Chol 40 mg; Sod 582 mg.

Charlotte Goetsch, Sheboygan County HFH
Elkhart Lake, WI

Sweet-Sour Turkey Balls

Yield: 6 servings

1 pound ground turkey
1 egg, beaten
1 tablespoon cornstarch
1 teaspoon salt
2 tablespoons chopped onion
Pepper to taste
1 tablespoon oil
1 cup pineapple juice

3 tablespoons cornstarch
1 tablespoon soy sauce
3 tablespoons vinegar
6 tablespoons water
1/2 cup sugar
1 cup pineapple chunks
1 large green bell pepper, cut into strips

- Combine turkey, egg, 1 tablespoon cornstarch, salt, onion and pepper in bowl; mix well. Shape into 1-inch balls. Brown in oil in skillet. Drain, reserving 1 tablespoon pan drippings. Combine reserved pan drippings, pineapple juice, 3 tablespoons cornstarch, soy sauce, vinegar, water and sugar in skillet; mix well. Cook until thickened, stirring constantly. Stir in turkey balls, pineapple chunks and green pepper. Cook until heated through.

Approx Per Serving: Cal 287; Prot 16 g; Carbo 32 g; Fiber 1 g; T Fat 11 g; 34% Calories from Fat; Chol 83 mg; Sod 605 mg.

Miriam B. Buckwalter, Westside HFH, Chicago, IL

SEAFOOD
MEATLESS DISHES

"Your people will . . . raise up the age-old foundations; you will be called Repairer of Broken Walls, Restorer of Streets with Dwellings."

Isaiah 58:12

Baked Fish Supreme

Yield: 10 servings

1 tablespoon olive oil
3 pounds fresh
  whitefish filets
Salt and pepper to taste
4 cloves of garlic,
  minced
2 onions, thinly sliced
6 stalks celery, thinly
  sliced
4 to 5 potatoes, thinly
  sliced

4 to 6 carrots, thinly
  sliced
4 ripe tomatoes, thinly
  sliced
2 green bell peppers,
  sliced into thin rings
Juice of 1 lemon
Oregano to taste

■ Brush olive oil over bottom and side of electric roaster. Place fish filets in roaster, skin side down. Sprinkle with salt, pepper and half the garlic. Layer with onions, celery, potatoes, carrots, tomatoes and green peppers. Pour lemon juice over layers; sprinkle with salt, pepper and oregano. Roast, covered, at 300 degrees for 2 hours or until vegetables are tender.

Approx Per Serving: Cal 246; Prot 29 g; Carbo 25 g; Fiber 4 g; T Fat 3 g; 13% Calories from Fat; Chol 74 mg; Sod 159 mg.

Geraldine Kelly, Northern Straits HFH, St. Ignace, MI

Norwegian Fish Dish

Yield: 6 servings

This is a staple of Norwegian households. It is economical, if frozen fish is used, and delicious.

2 pounds red snapper
¼ cup butter
3 tablespoons flour
1½ cups milk

Salt and pepper to taste
3 eggs, beaten
1 tablespoon melted
  butter

■ Poach fish in simmering salted water for 15 to 20 minutes or until fish flakes easily; drain and cool. Flake fish, discarding skin and bones. Melt ¼ cup butter in saucepan. Stir in flour until blended. Add milk gradually. Cook over medium heat until thickened, stirring constantly; remove from heat. Season with salt and pepper. Beat small amount of mixture into beaten eggs. Add egg mixture to sauce, beating well. Stir in fish. Pour into buttered 1-quart baking dish. Cook at 350 degrees for 30 minutes; drizzle with 1 tablespoon melted butter. Bake for 10 minutes longer or until lightly browned.

Approx Per Serving: Cal 331; Prot 37 g; Carbo 6 g; Fiber <1 g; T Fat 17 g; 46% Calories from Fat; Chol 197 mg; Sod 210 mg.

Martha D. Linder, Lakeland HFH, Lakeland, FL

Millard's Grilled Grouper

Yield: 4 servings

Millard Fuller

½ cup chopped onion
½ cup oil
2 tablespoons
  margarine
1 tablespoon
  Worcestershire sauce

¼ cup lemon juice
1 tablespoon soy sauce
¼ teaspoon Tabasco
  sauce
2 pounds grouper filets

■ Sauté onion in oil and margarine in saucepan until tender. Remove from heat. Stir in Worcestershire sauce, lemon juice, soy sauce and Tabasco sauce. Cool slightly. Pat filets with paper towel; coat with sauce. Place on hot grill. Grill over medium heat for 10 to 15 minutes or until fish flakes, basting each time fish is turned. May substitute halibut or red snapper filets for grouper.

Approx Per Serving: Cal 521; Prot 46 g; Carbo 4 g; Fiber <1 g; T Fat 35 g; 62% Calories from Fat; Chol 85 mg; Sod 488 mg.

Millard Fuller, President HFH International, Americus, GA

Salmonette

Yield: 4 servings

1 14-ounce can salmon
1 egg, beaten
1/2 cup flour

1 teaspoon (heaping)
  baking powder
Oil for frying

- Drain and flake salmon, reserving 1/4 cup liquid. Combine salmon with egg and flour in bowl, mixing well. Stir baking powder into reserved liquid. Add to salmon mixture, stirring well. Drop by spoonfuls into hot oil in skillet. Fry until brown on each side.
Approx Per Serving: Cal 216; Prot 23 g; Carbo 12 g; Fiber <1 g; T Fat 8 g; 33% Calories from Fat; Chol 104 mg; Sod 649 mg.
Nutritional information does not include oil for frying.

Clara Hosier, Morgan County HFH, Fort Morgan, CO

Baked Salmon in the Dishwasher

Yield: 6 servings

An unusual way to get baked salmon that is tender and juicy. An old fisherman's trick!

1 3 to 4 pound whole
  salmon
Greek seasoning to
  taste

2 lemons, sliced 1/2
  inch thick

- Rinse salmon in cold water and pat dry. Sprinkle inside and outside with Greek seasoning. Place lemon slices in cavity, reserving 6 slices. Prepare foil boat with double thickness of aluminum foil. Place 3 lemon slices in center of foil. Arrange salmon over lemon slices; top with remaining slices. Fold up tightly to seal. Place on small cutting board on bottom rack of dishwasher. Run dishwasher through full cycle, turning salmon at start of drying cycle.
Approx Per Serving: Cal 528; Prot 66 g; Carbo 2 g; Fiber <1 g; T Fat 27 g; 47% Calories from Fat; Chol 211 mg; Sod 160 mg.

Lee Stevens, HFH-Colville Valley Partners, Colville, WA

Salmon Loaf

Yield: 6 servings

1 egg, beaten
1/4 cup water
1 1/3 cups bread crumbs
1/4 teaspoon salt
2 tablespoons chopped
  onion

1 15-ounce can
  salmon, drained,
  flaked
2 tablespoons chopped
  parsley

- Beat egg with water in bowl. Stir in bread crumbs, salt, onion, salmon and parsley. Pat mixture into greased 5x9-inch loaf pan. Bake at 350 degrees for 40 minutes. Let stand to cool before serving. May substitute 2 egg whites for 1 egg.
Approx Per Serving: Cal 200; Prot 18 g; Carbo 17 g; Fiber 1 g; T Fat 6 g; 29% Calories from Fat; Chol 73 mg; Sod 657 mg.

Fran Collier, HFH of Upper Keys, Key Largo, FL

Salmon Patties

Yield: 4 servings

3/4 cup crushed crackers
1 8-ounce can
  boneless pink
  salmon
1 or 2 eggs, beaten

1 teaspoon lemon juice
1/4 cup finely chopped
  onion
Oil for frying

- Combine cracker crumbs, salmon, egg, lemon juice and onion in bowl; mix well. Shape into patties. Fry each side in oil in skillet over medium heat until golden brown. Garnish with tartar sauce.
Approx Per Serving: Cal 188; Prot 15 g; Carbo 13 g; Fiber 1 g; T Fat 8 g; 39% Calories from Fat; Chol 140 mg; Sod 552 mg.
Nutritional information does not include oil for frying.

Kelly Moran, Northern Straits HFH, St. Ignace, MI

Salmon Tetrazzini

Yield: 6 servings

1/3 cup chopped onion
3 tablespoons olive oil
1/4 cup flour
1 1/4 teaspoons
   seasoned salt
1/8 teaspoon thyme
Pepper to taste
2 cups evaporated
   skim milk
6 ounces spaghetti,
   cooked, drained

1 1/2 tablespoons sherry
1 15-ounce can
   salmon, drained,
   flaked
1/2 cup sliced black
   olives
1/4 cup chopped green
   bell pepper
1/3 cup grated
   Parmesan cheese

■ Sauté onion in oil in saucepan for 5 minutes or until tender. Stir in flour, salt, thyme and pepper. Cook over low heat until mixture is smooth and bubbly; remove from heat. Stir in evaporated milk gradually. Cook over low heat until thickened and smooth, stirring constantly. Stir in spaghetti, sherry, salmon, olives and green pepper. Pour into 1 1/2-quart baking dish sprayed with nonstick cooking spray. Sprinkle with Parmesan cheese. Bake at 350 degrees for 20 to 25 minutes or until bubbly.
Approx Per Serving: Cal 401; Prot 27 g; Carbo 36 g; Fiber 2 g; T Fat 16 g; 37% Calories from Fat; Chol 43 mg; Sod 953 mg.

Nancy J. Berkheimer, Williamsport/Lycoming County HFH
Montoursville, PA

Sweet Onion-Crusted Snapper

Yield: 4 servings

3 tablespoons olive oil
1 pound sweet red
   onions, sliced
2 1/2 teaspoons
   Balsamic vinegar
4 teaspoons light
   brown sugar
Salt and pepper to taste
4 yellowtail snapper
   filets
1 cup Madeira wine

1 clove of garlic,
   chopped
1 shallot, chopped
1 teaspoon tomato
   paste
Juice of 1/2 lemon
2 teaspoons half and
   half
8 ounces butter, cut
   into 1/2-inch pieces

■ Heat 2 tablespoons olive oil in skillet. Add onions. Cook until browned but not crisp. Add vinegar, brown sugar, salt and pepper. Cook until mixture is caramelized and liquid has evaporated, stirring constantly. Spoon equal amount of onion mixture onto each filet, pressing down with fork. Heat 1 tablespoon olive oil in large skillet. Cook fish, onion side down, until browned and crisp. Remove with wide spatula; place onion side up on greased baking sheet. Bake at 375 degrees for 15 to 25 minutes or until fish flakes easily. Heat wine, garlic, shallot, tomato paste, lemon juice and half and half in saucepan over medium heat. Cook until mixture is reduced by 1/2, stirring frequently. Drop pieces of butter into mixture. Cook until thickened, beating with wire whisk. Season with salt and pepper. Ladle sauce onto individual serving plates; top with filets.
Approx Per Serving: Cal 731; Prot 27 g; Carbo 18 g; Fiber 2 g; T Fat 58 g; 74% Calories from Fat; Chol 168 mg; Sod 450 mg.

Judy McConnell, HFH of Boca-Delray, Delray Beach, FL

Baked Whole Stuffed Steelhead

Yield: 12 servings

1/4 cup chopped onion
1/4 cup chopped celery
1/4 cup butter
16 saltine crackers,
   crushed
1/2 teaspoon pepper
1/2 teaspoon poultry
   seasoning

1 tablespoon minced
   parsley
1 6-ounce can smoked
   oysters
1 15-pound whole
   steelhead
1/4 cup melted butter
Salt and pepper to taste

■ Sauté onion and celery in butter in skillet until tender. Combine with cracker crumbs, pepper, poultry seasoning and parsley in bowl. Drain oysters, reserving liquid. Stir in oysters. Add enough reserved liquid to moisten. Place fish on large foil sheet. Pack stuffing mixture into cavity. Brush with melted butter; sprinkle with salt and pepper. Fold up foil to enclose fish, sealing tightly. Bake at 350 degrees for 1 1/2 hours. Garnish with lemon slices and parsley.
Approx Per Serving: Cal 690; Prot 98 g; Carbo 4 g; Fiber <1 g; T Fat 31 g; 41% Calories from Fat; Chol 547 mg; Sod 438 mg.

Dot Fredericks, Benton HFH, Philomath, OR

Swordfish in Lemon and Capers

Yield: 4 servings

4 fresh swordfish
  steaks
1/2 cup bread crumbs
2 to 3 tablespoons
  fruity olive oil

Juice of 1 lemon
1/2 3-ounce jar capers,
  drained
1/2 cup dry white wine
1 lemon, sliced

■ Coat swordfish steaks with bread crumbs. Brown each side in olive oil in skillet over medium heat. Pierce each steak twice with fork. Drizzle with lemon juice; sprinkle with capers. Pour in wine. Cook over medium-low heat for 25 to 30 minutes or until fish flakes easily, shaking skillet from time to time to avoid sticking. Remove with slotted spatula to serving plates. Spoon liquid from skillet over steaks. Top with lemon slices and parsley.

Approx Per Serving: Cal 306; Prot 25 g; Carbo 12 g; Fiber 1 g; T Fat 16 g; 49% Calories from Fat; Chol 46 mg; Sod 198 mg.
Nutritional information does not include capers.

Diane Goodman, Allegheny College Campus Chapter HFH
Meadville, PA

Whitefish Au Gratin

Yield: 3 servings

1 cup chicken or fish
  broth
1 tablespoon flour
1 tablespoon butter,
  softened
1/2 teaspoon salt
1/4 teaspoon parsley
  flakes
1/4 teaspoon pepper
Ground thyme to taste

1/4 cup whipping cream
1 1/2 pounds white fish
  filets
3 tablespoons grated
  Parmesan cheese
2 tablespoons dry
  bread crumbs
1 tablespoon melted
  butter
1 teaspoon lemon juice

■ Bring broth to a boil in saucepan. Mix flour and butter in small bowl. Add to broth. Cook until thickened, stirring constantly; reduce heat. Stir in salt, parsley, pepper, thyme and cream. Cook until smooth and thickened, stirring constantly. Place fish in buttered baking pan. Pour sauce over fish. Bake at 375 degrees for 15 minutes. Combine Parmesan cheese, bread crumbs, melted butter and lemon juice in bowl; mix well. Sprinkle over fish. Bake for 15 minutes longer or until fish flakes easily.

Approx Per Serving: Cal 410; Prot 49 g; Carbo 6 g; Fiber <1 g; T Fat 20 g; 45% Calories from Fat; Chol 176 mg; Sod 1001 mg.

Daniel P. Moran, Northern Straits HFH, St. Ignace, MI

Crab Cakes, Baltimore Style

Yield: 4 servings

Most restaurants serving Baltimore crab cakes use too much bread stuffing and claw meat.
Use only fresh backfin meat and sauté in a little margarine—do not deep-fry!

2 slices white bread,
  cubed
2 tablespoons milk
1 egg, slightly beaten
1 tablespoon
  mayonnaise
1/2 teaspoon Old Bay
  seasoning
1 teaspoon chopped
  fresh parsley

1 teaspoon salt
1 tablespoon
  Worcestershire sauce
1 tablespoon baking
  powder
1 pound fresh backfin
  crab meat, flaked
1/2 cup cracker crumbs
3 tablespoons
  margarine

■ Dampen bread in milk in small bowl; do not soak. Combine with egg in large bowl. Add mayonnaise, Old Bay seasoning, parsley, salt, Worcestershire sauce and baking powder; mix well. Stir in crab meat. Shape into 4 patties; coat with cracker crumbs. Sauté each side in margarine in cast-iron skillet until light brown. Serve with potato salad and tomatoes.

Approx Per Serving: Cal 306; Prot 22 g; Carbo 17 g; Fiber 1 g; T Fat 16 g; 48% Calories from Fat; Chol 151 mg; Sod 1417 mg.

Lee Hoover, Southeast Volusia County HFH
New Smyrna Beach, FL

*F*uture Habitat homeowners are chosen locally based on need, willingness to work on their houses as well as the houses of others, and capability to pay for their houses. Religion and race are not factors in the selection of homeowner partners.

Hard-Shell Crabs and Linguine

Yield: 8 servings

3 tablespoons butter
5 tablespoons olive oil
2/3 cup chopped celery
2/3 cup chopped onion
4 large cloves of garlic,
   minced
2 tablespoons chopped
   parsley
1   32-ounce can
   crushed tomatoes in
   purée

5 cups water
1   15-ounce can
   tomato sauce
2 teaspoons tomato
   paste
1 teaspoon sweet basil
3 bay leaves
Salt, pepper and
   paprika to taste
8 large hard-shell crabs
1 1/2 pounds linguine

■ Heat butter and olive oil in 8-quart saucepan. Sauté celery and onion until tender. Add garlic. Sauté for 3 minutes; do not brown. Add parsley, tomatoes, water, tomato sauce, tomato paste, basil, bay leaves, salt, pepper and paprika; mix well. Simmer for 45 minutes or until sauce is reduced by 1/3. Steam crabs partially for 2 to 3 minutes; discard back shells. Add crabs to sauce. Simmer for 20 minutes longer; remove bay leaves before serving. Cook linguine using package directions; drain. Place in individual serving bowls with sauce; top each serving with crab. Garnish with grated Romano cheese and crushed red pepper. Serve with garlic bread, salad and red wine.

Approx Per Serving: Cal 563; Prot 30 g; Carbo 75 g; Fiber 6 g; T Fat 16 g; 25% Calories from Fat; Chol 98 mg; Sod 794 mg.

Tony Viola, Burlington County HFH, Mt. Laurel, NJ

Toasted-Cheese Crabbits

Yield: 6 servings

1 cup minced imitation
   crab meat
1/4 cup finely chopped
   celery
White portion of 3
   green onions,
   chopped
1/4 cup mayonnaise

1/2 teaspoon lemon
   juice
6 slices bread, toasted
6 slices crisp-fried
   bacon, broken into
   halves
6 slices Cheddar cheese

■ Mix crab meat, celery, green onions, mayonnaise and lemon juice in bowl. Spread equal amount over toasted bread. Top each slice with 2 halves bacon; cover with cheese. Place on baking sheet. Broil for 5 minutes or until cheese is melted.

Approx Per Serving: Cal 328; Prot 16 g; Carbo 18 g; Fiber 1 g; T Fat 21 g; 59% Calories from Fat; Chol 47 mg; Sod 758 mg.

Margaret B. Nelson, Lincoln HFH, Lincoln, NE

Corn-Oyster Pudding

Yield: 4 servings

1   20-ounce can
   cream-style corn
1 cup crushed unsalted
   crackers
1/2 cup milk
1/2 teaspoon salt

1/4 teaspoon pepper
1 teaspoon sugar
1/4 cup melted butter
1 cup small canned
   oysters, drained

■ Combine corn, cracker crumbs, milk, salt, pepper, sugar and butter in bowl; mix well. Fold in oysters. Pour into greased 2-quart baking dish. Bake at 375 degrees for 45 to 60 minutes or until firm.

Approx Per Serving: Cal 354; Prot 9 g; Carbo 45 g; Fiber 3 g; T Fat 17 g; 42% Calories from Fat; Chol 69 mg; Sod 1038 mg.

Mary L. Mangum, Central Valley HFH, Bridgewater, VA

Wayne's Scallops

Yield: 4 servings

1 tablespoon olive oil
1 clove of garlic,
   minced
1 large green bell
   pepper, sliced
1/2 bunch green onions,
   chopped

4 ounces snow peas
8 ounces fresh
   mushrooms
1 pound large scallops
1/4 cup white wine
1/2 cup milk

■ Heat oil in large skillet. Sauté garlic, green pepper and green onions until tender. Add snow peas and mushrooms. Sauté until tender-crisp. Add scallops. Cook for 4 minutes, stirring frequently. Add wine. Cook for 1 minute, stirring often. Stir in milk. Cook until heated through. Serve over hot cooked linguine.

Approx Per Serving: Cal 196; Prot 24 g; Carbo 11 g; Fiber 2 g; T Fat 6 g; 27% Calories from Fat; Chol 44 mg; Sod 197 mg.

Betty Putnam, York County HFH, Wells, ME

Barbecued Shrimp

Yield: 6 servings

1 cup butter
1/2 teaspoon Tabasco
  sauce
2 1/2 tablespoons
  Worcestershire sauce
2 cloves of garlic,
  minced

1/2 teaspoon ground
  rosemary
2 tablespoons pepper
2 pounds unpeeled
  shrimp
1 lemon, sliced

- Melt butter in microwave-safe dish. Add Tabasco sauce, Worcestershire sauce, garlic, rosemary and pepper; mix well. Add shrimp, tossing to coat. Arrange lemon slices over shrimp. Microwave, covered loosely with plastic wrap, on High for 5 minutes; stir. Microwave for 4 to 6 minutes longer or until shrimp are cooked through; stir. Serve with salad and French bread for dipping in sauce.
Approx Per Serving: Cal 388; Prot 23 g; Carbo 3 g; Fiber <1 g; T Fat 32 g; 74% Calories from Fat; Chol 293 mg; Sod 563 mg.

Belinda R. Mahon, Pensacola HFH, Pensacola, FL

Cajun Shrimp

Yield: 6 servings

2 to 3 tablespoons oil
2 cloves of garlic,
  minced
1 teaspoon minced
  ginger

2 pounds large shrimp,
  peeled, deveined
Cajun seasoning to
  taste

- Heat oil in large skillet over medium heat. Sauté garlic and ginger until lightly browned. Add shrimp, stirring to coat with oil. Cook until shrimp are pink, stirring frequently. Sprinkle with Cajun seasoning.
Approx Per Serving: Cal 169; Prot 23 g; Carbo <1 g; Fiber <1 g; T Fat 8 g; 44% Calories from Fat; Chol 211 mg; Sod 242 mg.

Dana Gaffney
University of Wisconsin-Stevens Point Campus Chapter
Stevens Point, WI

Shrimp and Pasta

Yield: 4 servings

4 ounces uncooked
  thin spaghetti
3 quarts water
1/4 cup butter
1/4 cup olive oil
4 large cloves of garlic,
  coarsely chopped
20 medium shrimp,
  peeled, deveined

1/4 teaspoon salt
1/2 teaspoon pepper
3 tablespoons minced
  fresh parsley
1/4 cup grated
  Parmesan cheese

- Cook spaghetti in boiling water in large saucepan for 8 to 10 minutes; drain. Heat butter and olive oil in large skillet. Sauté garlic until golden brown; discard. Add shrimp; sprinkle with salt, pepper and 2 tablespoons parsley. Cook for 1 to 3 minutes or until shrimp are pink; remove from heat. Stir in spaghetti and Parmesan cheese. Pour into warm serving bowl; top with remaining parsley.
Approx Per Serving: Cal 464; Prot 29 g; Carbo 23 g; Fiber 1 g; T Fat 28 g; 55% Calories from Fat; Chol 252 mg; Sod 575 mg.

Marian Kull, Highlands County HFH, Sebring, FL

Low Country Boil

Yield: Enough for 1 hungry person.

3 red potatoes
1 package shrimp and
  crab boil
1 teaspoon black
  pepper
1/2 teaspoon red pepper
1 lemon, sliced

2 pounds smoked
  sausage, sliced
1 onion
1 ear of corn
2 pounds peeled
  shrimp

- Bring potatoes, shrimp and crab boil, black pepper, red pepper, lemon and enough water to cover to a boil in stockpot. Cook for 5 minutes. Add sausage. Cook for 5 minutes. Add onion. Cook for 5 minutes. Add corn. Cook for 5 minutes or until all ingredients are tender. Add shrimp. Remove from heat. Let stand for 5 minutes; drain. Add ingredients in these amounts for each serving.
Nutritional information for this recipe is not available.

Chris and Dianne Fuller, Coastal Empire HFH
Savannah, GA

Shrimp Scampi

Yield: 6 servings

1/4 cup butter
2 cloves of garlic, minced
1/2 bunch green onions, chopped

1/4 cup dry sherry
2 pounds fresh shrimp, peeled, deveined
Juice of 1 lemon
Salt and pepper to taste

■ Melt butter in skillet over medium heat. Add garlic, green onions and sherry. Cook until garlic is tender. Add shrimp, tossing to coat with pan liquid. Cook for 10 minutes or until shrimp are pink. Remove to serving plate. Drizzle with lemon juice; season with salt and pepper. Serve with pasta or rice.
Approx Per Serving: Cal 192; Prot 23 g; Carbo 2 g; Fiber <1 g; T Fat 9 g; 42% Calories from Fat; Chol 231 mg; Sod 308 mg.

Neil Giordano, Duke University Community HFH
Durham, NC

Company Shrimp and Crab Meat Casserole

Yield: 14 servings

1/2 cup chopped green pepper
1/2 cup chopped onion
5 stalks celery, finely chopped
1/4 cup butter
3 pounds cooked shrimp, peeled

1 pound crab meat
2 1 1/2-ounce cans Chinese noodles
4 10-ounce cans cream of mushroom soup
1 2-ounce package slivered almonds

■ Sauté green pepper, onion and celery in butter in skillet until tender. Combine with shrimp, crab meat and Chinese noodles in large bowl; mix gently. Stir in soup, mixing well. Pour into 3-quart baking dish; top with almonds. Bake at 350 degrees for 45 minutes. Serve with oven-baked rice.
Approx Per Serving: Cal 300; Prot 30 g; Carbo 12 g; Fiber 1 g; T Fat 15 g; 44% Calories from Fat; Chol 232 mg; Sod 1065 mg.

Jo-Anne P. Scott, HFH of Gallatin Valley, Bozeman, MT

Crab and Shrimp Luncheon Dish

Yield: 8 servings

1 onion
6 to 8 whole cloves
1 salmon head
1 carrot, sliced
1 stalk celery with leaves, sliced
2 sprigs of parsley
1/4 cup butter
5 tablespoons flour
8 ounces Gruyère cheese, shredded
1 teaspoon thyme
1/4 teaspoon white pepper

1/4 teaspoon dillweed
1/2 cup dry sherry
1 pound medium shrimp, cooked, peeled
2 pounds imitation crab meat, cut into bite-sized pieces
2 tablespoons butter
8 English muffins, split
1/4 cup grated Parmesan cheese
Paprika to taste

■ Stud onion with whole cloves. Combine with salmon head, carrot, celery, parsley and enough water to cover in large saucepan. Bring to a boil; reduce heat. Simmer for 10 minutes. Strain, reserving broth. Melt 1/4 cup butter in saucepan. Stir in flour. Cook until lightly browned, stirring often. Add reserved broth gradually. Simmer until thickened, stirring constantly. Add Gruyère cheese, stirring until melted. Add next 6 ingredients; set aside. Spread remaining 2 tablespoons butter on muffins; toast lightly. Spoon equal amounts of shrimp mixture on muffin halves. Place on broiler pan. Sprinkle with Parmesan cheese and paprika. Broil for 2 minutes or until bubbly.
Approx Per Serving: Cal 548; Prot 37 g; Carbo 45 g; Fiber 2 g; T Fat 22 g; 37% Calories from Fat; Chol 158 mg; Sod 1647 mg.

Virginia Mattson, South Puget Sound HFH, Olympia, WA

Seafood Fettucini

Yield: 4 servings

2 tablespoons butter
4 teaspoons flour
1 3/4 cups half and half
1 teaspoon pepper
1/2 cup grated Parmesan cheese

1 8-ounce package imitation crab meat
6 ounces fettucini, cooked
1 tablespoon chopped fresh parsley

■ Melt butter in saucepan over medium heat. Blend in flour. Add half and half gradually. Cook over low heat until thickened, stirring constantly. Add pepper and cheese. Cook until cheese is melted, stirring often. Fold in crab meat. Cook for 3 minutes, stirring often. Serve over hot cooked fettucini; top with parsley.
Approx Per Serving: Cal 459; Prot 20 g; Carbo 45 g; Fiber 2 g; T Fat 22 g; 44% Calories from Fat; Chol 74 mg; Sod 758 mg.

Pauline M. Reeves, Grayson County HFH, Sherman, TX

Yield: 4 servings

Tortellini with Shrimp and Scallops

2 tablespoons butter
1 tablespoon olive oil
4 cloves of garlic, crushed
8 ounces shrimp, peeled, deveined
8 ounces scallops
1/8 teaspoon salt
1/4 teaspoon pepper
1/2 cup white wine
1/2 cup chicken broth
1 to 2 tablespoons lemon juice
16 ounces refrigerated cheese tortellini

- Heat butter and oil in large skillet. Add garlic, shrimp and scallops; sprinkle with salt and pepper. Cook over medium heat until seafood is pink; remove to warm bowl with slotted spoon. Add wine, broth and lemon juice to pan drippings. Bring to a boil; reduce heat. Add tortellini. Cook until tender. Return shrimp and scallops to skillet, stirring to coat. Serve over cooked tortellini. Garnish with parsley.

Approx Per Serving: Cal 554; Prot 37 g; Carbo 56 g; Fiber <1 g; T Fat 18 g; 31% Calories from Fat; Chol 169 mg; Sod 812 mg.

Deborah Vosburgh, Fergus Falls Area HFH, Fergus Falls, MN

Yield: 8 servings

Seafood Casserole

1 small green bell pepper, finely chopped
1 small onion, finely chopped
1 cup chopped celery
1 pound crab meat, flaked
1 pound peeled shrimp
1 teaspoon Worcestershire sauce
1 cup mayonnaise
1 cup bread crumbs
1 1/2 teaspoons Old Bay seasoning
Salt and pepper to taste

- Combine all ingredients in large bowl; mix well. Spoon mixture into greased baking dish. Bake at 350 degrees for 15 to 20 minutes or until heated through.

Approx Per Serving: Cal 358; Prot 23 g; Carbo 12 g; Fiber 1 g; T Fat 24 g; 61% Calories from Fat; Chol 162 mg; Sod 528 mg.

Chris Gaffney, Greenville County HFH, Greenville, SC

Yield: 10 servings

Seafood Stew

A superb blend of flavors that is a favorite of those who are venturesome

2 large green bell peppers, chopped
1 large yellow onion, chopped
4 cups chicken broth
2 bay leaves
2 teaspoons thyme
4 teaspoons Old Bay seasoning
4 teaspoons parsley
Salt and red pepper to taste
1 16-ounce package frozen whole kernel corn, thawed
1 16-ounce can Italian-style tomato sauce
2 pounds whitefish filets, cut into bite-sized pieces
2 pounds small shrimp, peeled, deveined

- Sauté green pepper and onion in nonstick saucepan until tender. Add chicken broth, bay leaves, thyme, Old Bay seasoning, parsley, salt and pepper. Stir in corn and tomato sauce. Bring to a boil; reduce heat. Simmer for 30 minutes, stirring occasionally. Add fish and shrimp. Simmer for 10 minutes, stirring often. Leftovers freeze well.

Approx Per Serving: Cal 226; Prot 35 g; Carbo 14 g; Fiber 3 g; T Fat 3 g; 13% Calories from Fat; Chol 176 mg; Sod 648 mg.

John Truby, Zanesville HFH, Zanesville, OH

Yield: 8 servings

Smoked 'Gator

1 3 to 5-pound alligator tail, jowl or backshap
1 envelope Italian salad dressing mix
1 cup oil

- Trim fat from meat; place in shallow dish. Mix salad dressing mix and oil in small bowl. Pour over meat. Add enough water to cover. Chill, covered, overnight. Smoke over cool, wet coals for 3 to 6 hours or until meat flakes easily. Cut into serving pieces.

Nutritional information for this recipe is not available.

Lindsey Hord, Okeechobee HFH, Okeechobee, FL

*H*abitat for Humanity International is one organization which would help us change the housing problems of the most needy people in our society. It is God's own project, I believe, which is why it cares for those people in our society who in the eyes of men are useless and hopeless. But, to God, they are precious and equal to the very important.

Uganda's First Lady Janet Museveni

Vegetarian Mushroom Burgers

Yield: 6 servings

2¹/₂ cups chopped mushrooms
1 cup plus 2 tablespoons seasoned dried bread crumbs
²/₃ cup low-fat cottage cheese
¹/₂ cup chopped onion
2 eggs, beaten
2 ounces mozzarella cheese, shredded
2 ounces chopped walnuts
1 teaspoon soy sauce
¹/₄ teaspoon garlic powder
Salt and pepper to taste
2 teaspoons oil

■ Combine mushrooms, bread crumbs, cottage cheese, onion, eggs, cheese, walnuts, soy sauce, garlic powder, salt and pepper in large bowl; mix thoroughly. Shape mixture into 6 patties. Spray large skillet with nonstick cooking spray. Add oil and heat over medium heat for 1 minute. Cook patties for 3 minutes on each side or until light brown. Place in nonstick baking pan. Bake at 325 degrees for 15 minutes. Serve with chili-yogurt sauce made with ¹/₈ teaspoon chili powder and 2 tablespoons low-fat yogurt.
Approx Per Serving: Cal 239; Prot 12 g; Carbo 19 g; Fiber 2 g; T Fat 13 g; 48% Calories from Fat; Chol 82 mg; Sod 362 mg.

Michelle Stopa, Bluffton College Campus Chapter
Brooklyn, OH

Almond Croquettes

Yield: 6 servings

This is a family favorite and guests never guess the main ingredient.

2 cups raw unblanched almonds, ground
¹/₂ cup wheat germ
¹/₂ cup raw sesame seed
1 small onion, finely chopped
1 clove of garlic, minced
8 ounces cottage cheese
2 eggs, beaten
1 teaspoon vegetable seasoning
¹/₄ teaspoon curry powder
¹/₂ teaspoon salt
1 tablespoon hot water
2 teaspoons olive oil

■ Combine ground almonds, wheat germ, sesame seed, onion, garlic, cottage cheese and eggs in bowl; mix well. Mix vegetable seasoning, curry powder and salt with hot water in small bowl. Stir into almond mixture. Shape mixture into 6 patties. Cook slowly in olive oil in skillet over low heat until outside is brown and crisp. Serve plain or with cheese, tomato or mushroom sauce.
Approx Per Serving: Cal 462; Prot 22 g; Carbo 17 g; Fiber 8 g; T Fat 37 g; 69% Calories from Fat; Chol 77 mg; Sod 364 mg.

Jean Spier, HFH of the Coachella Valley, Indio, CA

Vegetarian Chili

Yield: 6 servings

1 tablespoon olive oil
2 cloves of garlic, minced
1 onion, chopped
1   28-ounce can tomatoes
¹/₂ green bell pepper, cut into 1-inch pieces
1 cup chopped celery
1   16-ounce can kidney beans, drained
1   16-ounce can garbanzo beans, drained
Green chili peppers to taste
2 tablespoons vinegar
1 tablespoon chili powder
Salt and pepper to taste
¹/₂ teaspoon basil
¹/₂ teaspoon oregano
¹/₂ teaspoon cumin
¹/₄ teaspoon allspice
1 bay leaf
1¹/₂ cups beer
³/₄ cup shredded Cheddar cheese

■ Heat oil in large saucepan. Sauté garlic and onion for 4 minutes. Process undrained tomatoes, green pepper and celery in blender until smooth. Stir into onion mixture. Add kidney beans, garbanzo beans and chili peppers. Mix vinegar, chili powder, salt and pepper in small bowl. Add to tomato mixture with basil, oregano, cumin, allspice and bay leaf. Stir in beer. Simmer, covered, over low heat for 1¹/₄ hours, stirring occasionally and adding water for desired consistency. Remove bay leaf. Serve sprinkled with cheese.
Approx Per Serving: Cal 298; Prot 13 g; Carbo 41 g; Fiber 9 g; T Fat 9 g; 27% Calories from Fat; Chol 15 mg; Sod 826 mg.

Elaine B. Hartsell, Wythe County HFH, Max Meadows, VA

*E*ach one should use whatever gift he has received to serve others, faithfully administering God's grace in its various forms.

I Peter 4:10

Vegetable Curry

Yield: 5 servings

1 cup chopped onion
2 teaspoons oil
1½ tablespoons curry
  powder
1½ teaspoons ground
  coriander
¾ teaspoon ground
  cumin
½ teaspoon fennel
  seed

¼ teaspoon salt
2 cups cauliflowerets
2 cups sliced fresh
  green beans
1½ cups sliced carrots
1 16-ounce can Italian-
  style tomatoes,
  chopped
1½ cups vegetable
  bouillon

■ Sauté onion in oil in large saucepan until lightly browned. Add next 5 ingredients. Cook for 1 minute, stirring constantly. Add cauliflower, green beans, carrots, undrained tomatoes and bouillon. Simmer, covered, over low heat for 20 minutes or until vegetables are tender. Serve over brown rice.
Approx Per Serving: Cal 83; Prot 3 g; Carbo 14 g; Fiber 4 g; T Fat 3 g; 25% Calories from Fat; Chol <1 mg; Sod 715 mg.

Pat Stevens, Cayuga County HFH, Auburn, NY

Gas House Eggs

Yield: 4 servings

4 slices wheat bread
2 tablespoons
  margarine
4 eggs

Salt and pepper to taste
½ cup shredded
  Cheddar cheese

■ Cut out 1½-inch circle in center of each slice of bread. Melt margarine in nonstick skillet over medium-high heat. Add bread; break egg into center of each slice of bread. Cook until white is firm; turn over. Cook to desired degree of doneness. Place on baking sheet. Sprinkle with salt, pepper and cheese. Broil for 1 minute or until cheese is melted.
Approx Per Serving: Cal 257; Prot 13 g; Carbo 14 g; Fiber 2 g; T Fat 17 g; 60% Calories from Fat; Chol 228 mg; Sod 403 mg.

Buddy Greene, Singer/Songwriter, Nashville, TN

Green Enchiladas

Yield: 8 servings

⅓ cup margarine
⅓ cup chopped onion
½ teaspoon pepper
¼ teaspoon salt
½ teaspoon basil
½ teaspoon cumin
¼ teaspoon garlic salt
⅓ cup flour
1¾ cups water

⅔ cup milk
2 chicken bouillon
  cubes
½ cup puréed green
  chilies
12 corn tortillas
3½ cups shredded
  Colby cheese

■ Melt margarine in saucepan. Add next 6 ingredients. Stir in flour. Cook until bubbly, stirring constantly; remove from heat. Add water, milk and bouillon cubes. Bring to a boil. Boil for 1 minute, stirring constantly. Stir in green chilies. Pour scant 1 cup sauce into baking pan. Top with 3 tortillas and ¼ of the cheese. Repeat layers until all ingredients are used. Bake, covered, at 350 degrees for 1 hour.
Approx Per Serving: Cal 405; Prot 17 g; Carbo 28 g; Fiber 4 g; T Fat 26 g; 56% Calories from Fat; Chol 50 mg; Sod 818 mg.

Cheryl Lenhardt, Deming HFH, Deming, NM

Spinach Enchiladas

Yield: 6 servings

1 10-ounce package
  frozen chopped
  spinach, cooked
½ teaspoon garlic salt
Juice of 1 small lemon
1 small onion, chopped

1 tablespoon butter
1 cup sour cream
8 ounces Monterey
  Jack cheese,
  shredded
6 flour tortillas

■ Drain spinach, reserving a small amount of liquid. Combine liquid with garlic salt and lemon juice in bowl. Sauté onion in butter in skillet until tender. Add to spinach mixture. Stir in 3 to 4 tablespoons sour cream. Spoon equal amounts of mixture and ½ of the cheese onto tortillas; roll up to enclose filling. Place in greased baking pan. Drizzle with reserved liquid. Sprinkle with remaining cheese. Bake at 350 degrees for 15 to 20 minutes. Place on serving plate; top with remaining sour cream.
Approx Per Serving: Cal 367; Prot 15 g; Carbo 26 g; Fiber 3 g; T Fat 24 g; 57% Calories from Fat; Chol 57 mg; Sod 585 mg.

Janelle M. Garrett, Mount Pleasant HFH
Mount Pleasant, TX

Broccoli, Tomato and Basil Frittata
Yield: 3 servings

8 ounces egg substitute
3 tablespoons milk
3 tablespoons grated
  Parmesan cheese
Pepper to taste
1 onion, chopped
3 tablespoons olive oil

3 tomatoes, chopped
1 tablespoon fresh
  chopped basil
1/2 cup chopped
  broccoli
1/2 cup sliced
  mushrooms

■ Beat egg substitute, milk, Parmesan cheese and pepper in large bowl. Sauté onion in olive oil in skillet until tender. Add tomatoes and basil. Sauté for 10 minutes, stirring frequently. Add broccoli and mushrooms. Cook for 5 minutes longer. Stir vegetables into egg mixture. Pour into greased 8x8-inch baking dish. Bake at 325 degrees for 15 to 17 minutes or just until set. Do not overbake; serve immediately.
Approx Per Serving: Cal 264; Prot 14 g; Carbo 12 g; Fiber 3 g; T Fat 19 g; 62% Calories from Fat; Chol 7 mg; Sod 250 mg.

Lois E. Wolters, Habitat Gypsies, Columbus, NC

Lazy Day Lasagna
Yield: 8 servings

1   32-ounce jar
    meatless spaghetti
    sauce
1 cup water
15 ounces ricotta cheese
2 tablespoons chopped
    fresh chives
1/2 teaspoon oregano
    leaves

1 egg, beaten
8 ounces uncooked
    lasagna noodles
2 cups chopped
    steamed broccoli
16 ounces mozzarella
    cheese, sliced
2 tablespoons grated
    Parmesan cheese

■ Mix spaghetti sauce and water in medium bowl; set aside. Combine ricotta cheese, chives, oregano leaves and egg in small bowl; mix well. Spread 1½ cups spaghetti sauce into 9x13-inch baking pan. Layer uncooked noodles, ricotta cheese mixture, broccoli and mozzarella cheese ½ at a time in prepared dish. Pour remaining spaghetti sauce over layers. Sprinkle with Parmesan cheese. Chill, covered, overnight. Bake, uncovered, at 350 degrees for 1 hour. Let stand for 15 minutes before serving.
Approx Per Serving: Cal 510; Prot 26 g; Carbo 44 g; Fiber 3 g; T Fat 26 g; 45% Calories from Fat; Chol 98 mg; Sod 857 mg.

Janet Cornell, Westchester County HFH, Valhalla, NY

Mushroom-Zucchini Lasagna
Yield: 6 servings

2 cups sliced fresh
    mushrooms
1 cup light ricotta
    cheese
2 eggs, beaten
2 cups coarsely
    shredded carrots

2 cups coarsely
    shredded zucchini
9 lasagna noodles,
    cooked
3 cups spaghetti sauce
1 cup shredded
    mozzarella cheese

■ Spray skillet with nonstick cooking spray. Heat over medium heat. Add mushrooms. Cook, covered, for 5 minutes. Cook, uncovered, until liquid evaporates. Mix ricotta cheese and beaten eggs in bowl. Mix half the mixture with shredded carrots and half the mixture with zucchini in small bowls. Spray 9x13-inch baking pan with nonstick cooking spray. Layer 3 noodles, carrot mixture and 1/3 of the spaghetti sauce in pan. Top with layers of 3 noodles, zucchini mixture, 1/3 of the spaghetti sauce, 3 noodles, mushrooms and 1/3 of the spaghetti sauce. Sprinkle with mozzarella cheese. Bake at 375 degrees for 25 to 30 minutes or until bubbly.
Approx Per Serving: Cal 466; Prot 20 g; Carbo 62 g; Fiber 4 g; T Fat 16 g; 31% Calories from Fat; Chol 98 mg; Sod 781 mg.

Linda DeMaine, Merrimack, NH

*H*abitat for Humanity seeks to build lives as we build houses. Through the houses we build, hope is restored and lives are changed as the cycle of need is broken.

Low-Fat Spinach Lasagna

Yield: 12 servings

30 ounces no-fat ricotta cheese
1   10-ounce package frozen chopped spinach, thawed, drained
8 ounces no-fat mozzarella cheese, shredded
1/2 cup grated no-fat Parmesan cheese
1/4 cup egg substitute

2 tablespoons parsley
1 teaspoon garlic powder
1/2 teaspoon basil
1/2 teaspoon oregano
1/2 teaspoon nutmeg
1/2 teaspoon salt
1/4 teaspoon pepper
1   32-ounce jar chunky spaghetti sauce
12 no-boil lasagna noodles

■ Combine ricotta cheese, spinach, half the mozzarella cheese, 1/4 cup Parmesan cheese, egg substitute, parsley, garlic powder, basil, oregano, nutmeg, salt and pepper in bowl; mix well. Pour 1 cup spaghetti sauce into 9x13-inch baking dish. Layer 3 noodles, 1 cup spaghetti sauce and 1/3 of the ricotta-spinach mixture in prepared dish. Repeat layers twice. Top with remaining noodles, remaining sauce, remaining mozzarella cheese and remaining Parmesan cheese. Bake, covered with foil, at 350 degrees for 25 minutes; remove foil. Bake for 5 to 10 minutes longer or until cheese is light brown.
Approx Per Serving: Cal 270; Prot 20 g; Carbo 36 g; Fiber 2 g; T Fat 6 g; 18% Calories from Fat; Chol 3 mg; Sod 839 mg.

Sandra Oudheusden, Westchester County HFH, Valhalla, NY

Make-Ahead Lasagna

Yield: 8 servings

1   32-ounce jar spaghetti sauce
1/2 cup water
3/4 cup low-fat ricotta cheese
3/4 cup low-fat cottage cheese

1/2 cup grated Parmesan cheese
2 cups shredded mozzarella cheese
1 egg, beaten
1/2 teaspoon nutmeg
8 lasagna noodles

■ Combine spaghetti sauce and water in bowl; mix well. Combine ricotta cheese, cottage cheese, Parmesan cheese, mozzarella cheese, egg and nutmeg in bowl; mix well. Spoon 1/2 cup of spaghetti sauce mixture in nonstick 9x13-inch baking pan. Layer 1/2 of the uncooked noodles, 1/2 of the cheese mixture and 1/2 of the remaining sauce in prepared pan. Repeat layers with remaining ingredients, ending with sauce. Chill, covered, for 24 hours. Bake at 350 degrees for 1 hour.
Approx Per Serving: Cal 394; Prot 20 g; Carbo 42 g; Fiber 1 g; T Fat 16 g; 37% Calories from Fat; Chol 61 mg; Sod 888 mg.

Loretta Troyer, HFH International, Middlebury, IN

Vegetable Lasagna

Yield: 12 servings

1/4 cup margarine
1/2 cup flour
1/2 teaspoon garlic powder
1/2 teaspoon Italian seasoning
1/2 teaspoon salt
2 cups chicken broth
1 cup evaporated skim milk
12 ounces low-fat cottage cheese
1/2 cup grated Parmesan cheese
3/4 cup chopped onion

1   10-ounce package frozen chopped spinach, thawed, drained
3/4 cup shredded carrot
8 ounces zucchini, shredded
1 green bell pepper, chopped
1 tomato chopped
8 ounces lasagna noodles
4 ounces Monterey Jack cheese, shredded

■ Melt margarine in saucepan over medium heat. Stir in flour, garlic powder, Italian seasoning and salt. Cook until bubbly, stirring frequently. Add chicken broth and evaporated milk. Cook until smooth and thickened, stirring constantly; set aside. Combine cottage cheese and Parmesan cheese in large bowl. Add onion, spinach, carrot, zucchini, green pepper and tomato; mix well. Spray 8x10-inch baking dish with nonstick cooking spray. Spread a small amount of white sauce in pan. Layer with noodles, spinach mixture and sauce 1/3 at a time. Sprinkle with Monterey Jack cheese; cover with foil. Bake at 375 degrees for 50 minutes; remove foil. Bake for 10 minutes longer. Let stand for several minutes before serving. May top with additional Parmesan cheese.
Approx Per Serving: Cal 243; Prot 15 g; Carbo 26 g; Fiber 2 g; T Fat 9 g; 34% Calories from Fat; Chol 15 mg; Sod 541 mg.

Jolene Baldwin, Longview HFH, Longview, TX

Greek-Style Linguine and Spinach
Yield: 6 servings

1 8-ounce package
   linguine
1 10-ounce package
   frozen chopped
   spinach
1 16-ounce can
   garbanzo beans,
   drained

8 ounces feta cheese,
   crumbled
1/2 cup chopped onion
2 to 3 teaspoons
   sesame oil
Garlic powder and
   cayenne pepper to
   taste

■ Cook linguine using package directions; drain. Cook spinach using package directions; drain well. Combine linguine, spinach, garbanzo beans, feta cheese and onion in large bowl; mix gently. Add sesame oil, garlic powder and cayenne pepper, tossing to coat.
Approx Per Serving: Cal 367; Prot 16 g; Carbo 51 g; Fiber 3 g; T Fat 12 g; 29% Calories from Fat; Chol 33 mg; Sod 688 mg.

Patty Trowbridge, Williamsport/Lycoming HFH
Cogan Station, PA

Spinach Manicotti
Yield: 6 servings

6 tablespoons
   margarine
1/4 cup flour
2 cups half and half
1 14-ounce can
   chicken bouillon
1/4 teaspoon basil
1/4 teaspoon mace
1 10-ounce package
   frozen chopped
   spinach, thawed,
   drained

2 cups cottage cheese
1 4-ounce can sliced
   mushrooms, drained
1/4 cup chopped green
   onions
12 uncooked manicotti
   noodles
8 ounces sharp
   Cheddar cheese,
   shredded
1/2 to 3/4 cup grated
   Parmesan cheese

■ Melt margarine in large saucepan over medium heat. Add flour, stirring to form paste. Add half and half slowly. Cook until thickened, stirring constantly. Stir in chicken bouillon, basil and mace. Cook until thickened, stirring frequently; set aside. Combine spinach, cottage cheese, mushrooms and green onions in bowl; mix well. Fill manicotti shells with mixture. Spoon half the sauce into 9x13-inch baking dish. Place shells in sauce. Cover with remaining sauce; top with Cheddar and Parmesan cheeses. Bake, covered, at 325 degrees for 1 hour.
Approx Per Serving: Cal 645; Prot 33 g; Carbo 39 g; Fiber 3 g; T Fat 40 g; 56% Calories from Fat; Chol 88 mg; Sod 1205 mg.

Caitlin Morrell, HFH of Green County, Madison, WI

Mexican Pepper Casserole
Yield: 6 servings

4 eggs, beaten
1 1/2 cups sour cream
1 1/2 cups thinly sliced
   onions
3 cloves of garlic,
   crushed
1 teaspoon salt
1 teaspoon cumin
1 teaspoon coriander
1/2 teaspoon dry
   mustard
1/4 teaspoon black
   pepper

1/4 teaspoon red pepper
2 tablespoons butter
2 tablespoons olive oil
3 red bell peppers, cut
   into julienne strips
3 green bell peppers,
   cut into julienne
   strips
2 tablespoons flour
8 ounces sharp
   Cheddar cheese,
   thinly sliced
Paprika to taste

■ Beat eggs and sour cream together in bowl; set aside. Sauté onions, garlic, salt, cumin, coriander, mustard and black and red peppers in butter and olive oil in large skillet until onions are tender. Add red and green bell peppers. Sauté over low heat for 10 minutes. Sprinkle with flour. Cook until liquid evaporates, stirring frequently. Layer vegetable mixture and Cheddar cheese 1/2 at a time in buttered round baking dish. Pour sour cream mixture over layers. Sprinkle with paprika. Bake, covered, at 375 degrees for 30 minutes. Bake, uncovered, for 15 minutes longer.
Approx Per Serving: Cal 442; Prot 17 g; Carbo 12 g; Fiber 2 g; T Fat 37 g; 74% Calories from Fat; Chol 218 mg; Sod 702 mg.

Mark Forrester, HFH of Montgomery County, Clarksville, TN

The righteous cry out, and the Lord hears them; he delivers them from all their troubles. The Lord is close to the brokenhearted and saves those who are crushed in spirit.

Psalms 34:17-18

Meal-in-a-Pouf

Yield: 4 servings

3 eggs, beaten
1 cup milk
3 slices bread, cubed
1 cup chopped cooked broccoli
1/2 cup sliced mushrooms

1 teaspoon Worcestershire sauce
1 teaspoon dry mustard
Tabasco sauce to taste
1/8 teaspoon onion powder
1/2 teaspoon salt

■ Beat eggs with milk in bowl. Stir in remaining ingredients. Pour into buttered 9-inch pie plate. Chill for 6 hours to overnight. Bake at 350 degrees for 35 minutes or until golden brown.
Approx Per Serving: Cal 171; Prot 10 g; Carbo 17 g; Fiber 2 g; T Fat 7 g; 39% Calories from Fat; Chol 168 mg; Sod 468 mg.

Renata Sittler, HFH of Wausau, Wausau, WI

Hot and Quick Black Beans and Rice

Yield: 2 servings

It's a challenge for vegetarians to get enough protein, but this combination does it.

1 cup quick-cooking brown rice
1 1/4 cups water
2 teaspoons margarine
3 cloves of garlic, minced
1 teaspoon salt
1 tablespoon Tennessee Sunshine hot sauce
1/2 cup salsa

1 1/2 cups canned black beans, drained
1/2 cup shredded Monterey Jack cheese
1/2 white onion, chopped
1 cup salsa

■ Combine rice, water, margarine, garlic, salt, hot sauce and 1/2 cup salsa in microwave-safe container. Microwave, covered, on High for 4 to 5 minutes or until rice is tender; stir. Add black beans to mixture. Microwave for 2 to 3 minutes, stirring once. Pour into individual serving dishes. Top with Monterey Jack cheese, remaining 1 cup salsa and chopped onion.
Approx Per Serving: Cal 716; Prot 26 g; Carbo 118 g; Fiber 4 g; T Fat 15 g; 19% Calories from Fat; Chol 26 mg; Sod 3060 mg.

Margaret Becker, Margaret Becker Productions, Nashville, TN

Pilau

Yield: 6 servings

1 cup uncooked lentils
1 quart water
1 teaspoon salt
2 tablespoons ground fresh ginger
1/4 teaspoon turmeric
2 teaspoons crushed cardamom seed
1/2 teaspoon cayenne pepper

1/2 teaspoon crushed dried red pepper
1/2 teaspoon curry powder
2 tablespoons chopped fresh cilantro
Juice of 1/2 lemon

■ Combine lentils, water and salt in saucepan. Bring to a boil; reduce heat. Simmer for 1 hour or until lentils are tender, skimming surface. Add ginger, turmeric, cardamom and cayenne pepper. Simmer for 20 minutes or until liquid evaporates and mixture thickens, stirring frequently. Add red pepper, curry, cilantro and lemon juice. Cook for 10 minutes longer.
Approx Per Serving: Cal 116; Prot 9 g; Carbo 20 g; Fiber 4 g; T Fat <1 g; 3% Calories from Fat; Chol 0 mg; Sod 360 mg.

Aaron Spevacck, Macalester College Campus Chapter
St. Paul, MN

Pesto Pizza

Yield: 4 servings

3/4 cup whole wheat flour
1 tablespoon olive oil
1 tablespoon butter, softened
2 to 4 tablespoons water
4 cups basil leaves
4 cloves of garlic

6 tablespoons butter
1/4 cup sunflower seed
1 cup olive oil
1 cup grated Parmesan cheese
4 ounces fresh mushrooms, sliced
6 ounces Fontina cheese, sliced

■ Combine flour, 1 tablespoon olive oil, 1 tablespoon butter and water in bowl, stirring to form soft dough. Roll out on floured surface to 12-inch circle. Line pizza pan with dough. Bake at 375 degrees for 15 minutes. Process basil, garlic, 6 tablespoons butter and sunflower seed in blender until smooth. Add 1 cup olive oil and Parmesan cheese, processing constantly. Spread half the pesto over prepared crust. Top with mushrooms and Fontina cheese. Bake for 10 to 15 minutes longer or until cheese is bubbly. Serve remaining pesto over spaghetti or freeze.
Approx Per Serving: Cal 1138; Prot 29 g; Carbo 36 g; Fiber 8 g; T Fat 103 g; 78% Calories from Fat; Chol 119 mg; Sod 560 mg.

Betty Neville Michelozzi, HFH-Santa Cruz County
Corralitos, CA

Broccoli Quiche
Yield: 6 servings

1 10-ounce package
frozen chopped
broccoli, thawed,
drained
1½ cups shredded
Cheddar cheese

1 unbaked 9-inch pie
shell
3 eggs, beaten
1½ cups half and half
½ teaspoon dried basil
⅛ teaspoon pepper

■ Combine broccoli and cheese in bowl; toss gently.
Spoon into pie shell. Beat eggs and half and half in
bowl. Stir in basil and pepper. Pour over broccoli mixture. Bake at 375 degrees for 40 to 45 minutes or until
golden brown. Let stand for 10 minutes before serving. May add chopped Canadian bacon.
Approx Per Serving: Cal 395; Prot 15 g; Carbo 19 g;
Fiber 2 g; T Fat 29 g; 66% Calories from Fat;
Chol 158 mg; Sod 429 mg.

Kim Marzilli, Rehoboth, MA

Zucchini Quiche
Yield: 8 servings

4 small unpeeled
zucchini, thinly
sliced or grated
1 cup baking mix
½ cup finely chopped
onion
½ cup grated
Parmesan cheese
2 tablespoons minced
parsley
½ teaspoon salt

½ teaspoon seasoned
salt
½ teaspoon dried
oregano
½ teaspoon dried
marjoram
Pepper to taste
1 clove of garlic,
minced
⅓ cup olive oil
4 eggs, beaten

■ Combine zucchini, baking mix, onion, Parmesan
cheese, parsley, salt, seasoned salt, oregano, marjoram, pepper, garlic and olive oil in bowl, tossing
well. Stir in beaten eggs. Pour into greased 9x13-inch
baking pan. Bake at 350 degrees for 25 minutes. May
substitute egg whites or egg substitute for eggs.
Approx Per Serving: Cal 229; Prot 8 g; Carbo 15 g;
Fiber 1 g; T Fat 16 g; 61% Calories from Fat;
Chol 110 mg; Sod 545 mg.

Elaine B. Hartsell, Wythe County HFH, Max Meadows, VA

Cheese Dream Soufflé
Yield: 8 servings

12 slices bread, crusts
trimmed
3 cups shredded sharp
Cheddar cheese
7 eggs, beaten
3 cups milk

1½ teaspoons dry
mustard
1 teaspoon salt
1 cup crushed
cornflakes
½ cup melted butter

■ Arrange bread in 12x16-inch baking pan. Cover with
Cheddar cheese. Beat eggs with milk, dry mustard
and salt. Pour over cheese layer. Chill, covered, overnight. Remove from refrigerator and let stand until at
room temperature. Sprinkle with crushed cornflakes;
drizzle with butter. Bake at 300 degrees for 1½ hours
or until brown and puffed. Let stand for 15 minutes
before slicing.
Approx Per Serving: Cal 868; Prot 23 g; Carbo 27 g;
Fiber 1 g; T Fat 75 g; 77% Calories from Fat;
Chol 383 mg; Sod 1320 mg.

Ruth Athay, Dungeness Valley HFH, Sequim, WA

Pasta-Veggie Stir-Fry
Yield: 6 servings

1 cup sliced carrots
1 cup broccoli flowerets
1 cup sliced zucchini
2 tablespoons oil
1½ teaspoons Mrs.
Dash seasoning

1 16-ounce package
pasta twists, cooked
Caesar salad dressing
to taste

■ Stir-fry carrots, broccoli and zucchini in hot oil in wok
until tender-crisp. Season with Mrs. Dash seasoning.
Toss with hot cooked pasta and salad dressing to taste.
Serve with garlic bread.
Approx Per Serving: Cal 331; Prot 10 g; Carbo 60 g;
Fiber 4 g; T Fat 6 g; 15% Calories from Fat;
Chol 0 mg; Sod 10 mg.

Di Buzzoni, Loudoun HFH, Bluemont, VA

VEGETABLES SIDE DISHES

"And it will be said: Build up, build up, prepare the road! Remove the obstacles out of the way of my people."

Isaiah 57:14

Stuffed Artichokes Italian-Style

Yield: 6 servings

6 fresh artichokes
3 cups plain bread
  crumbs
6 cloves of garlic,
  finely chopped

1 cup grated Romano
  cheese
1/4 teaspoon pepper
1/2 teaspoon salt
1 to 2 teaspoons oil

▪ Cut bottoms off artichokes; pull off bottom row of leaves. Snip top of each leaf close to the core, pulling apart gently. Stuff mixture of next 5 ingredients between leaves. Place in large saucepan filled with 1 inch of water; drizzle artichokes with small amount of oil. Simmer gently for 1 hour or until tender, adding water if necessary.

Approx Per Serving: Cal 327; Prot 15 g; Carbo 51 g; Fiber 12 g; T Fat 8 g; 23% Calories from Fat; Chol 18 mg; Sod 813 mg.

Sandie DePianta, Lakeland HFH, Lakeland, FL

Artichoke and Spinach Casserole

Yield: 8 servings

2 10-ounce packages
  frozen chopped
  spinach, cooked,
  drained
1 16-ounce can
  artichokes, drained,
  chopped
1/2 cup margarine

16 ounces cream
  cheese, softened
1/2 large onion,
  chopped
Garlic powder to taste
1/2 cup bread crumbs
1 tablespoon margarine

▪ Combine first 6 ingredients in bowl; mix well. Spoon into greased baking dish. Sprinkle with bread crumbs; dot with 1 tablespoon margarine. Bake at 350 degrees for 20 minutes.

Approx Per Serving: Cal 380; Prot 9 g; Carbo 14 g; Fiber 2 g; T Fat 33 g; 77% Calories from Fat; Chol 62 mg; Sod 567 mg.

Nancy H. Ross, Bay County HFH, Panama City, FL

Sweet 'n Sour Beans

Yield: 20 servings

4 onions, sliced,
  separated into rings
1/2 to 1 cup packed
  brown sugar
1 teaspoon dry mustard
1 teaspoon salt
1/2 cup vinegar
2 15-ounce cans tiny
  lima beans, drained

1 16-ounce can green
  lima beans, drained
1 16-ounce can red
  kidney beans, drained
1 27-ounce can New
  England-style baked
  beans
8 slices bacon, crisp-
  fried, crumbled

▪ Cook onions with brown sugar, mustard, salt and vinegar in covered saucepan for 20 minutes. Combine with lima beans, kidney beans and baked beans in bowl; mix well. Stir in bacon. Spoon into 3-quart baking dish. Bake at 350 degrees for 1 hour.

Approx Per Serving: Cal 195; Prot 8 g; Carbo 39 g; Fiber 9 g; T Fat 2 g; 8% Calories from Fat; Chol 2 mg; Sod 539 mg.

Kathleen K. Coffman, Central Valley HFH, Dayton, VA

Aunt Anna's Baked Beans

Yield: 8 servings

1 16-ounce package
  dried lima beans
Salt to taste
12 ounces bacon,
  chopped
1 cup chopped onion
1 16-ounce can
  tomatoes

1 8-ounce can tomato
  sauce
1 cup dark corn syrup
1/4 cup packed dark
  brown sugar
Pepper to taste

▪ Cook lima beans in boiling salted water until tender; drain. Fry bacon and onion in skillet until bacon is crisp and onion is tender; drain. Stir in remaining ingredients. Pour over beans in baking dish. Bake at 350 degrees for 1 1/2 hours.

Approx Per Serving: Cal 441; Prot 17 g; Carbo 81 g; Fiber 19 g; T Fat 7 g; 14% Calories from Fat; Chol 11 mg; Sod 509 mg.

Edith Coles, Crawford County HFH, English, IN

Mock Boston Baked Beans

Yield: 10 servings

2 21-ounce cans pork
  and beans
1/2 cup packed brown
  sugar

1 teaspoon dry mustard
1/2 cup catsup
6 slices bacon, cut up

▪ Layer beans, mixture of next 3 ingredients and bacon 1/2 at a time in 2-quart baking dish. Bake at 300 degrees for 3 hours.

Approx Per Serving: Cal 222; Prot 8 g; Carbo 42 g; Fiber 7 g; T Fat 4 g; 15% Calories from Fat; Chol 11 mg; Sod 608 mg.

Grace J. Bushouse, Lakeshore HFH, Holland, MI

Cowboy Beans

Yield: 15 servings

8 ounces ground beef
4 ounces bacon, chopped
1 onion, chopped
1 28-ounce can pork and beans
1/2 cup packed brown sugar

1 cup catsup
1 16-ounce can each lima beans and kidney beans, drained
2 tablespoons prepared mustard
2 tablespoons vinegar
Salt and pepper to taste

■ Brown first 3 ingredients in skillet, stirring until ground beef is crumbly; drain. Combine with remaining ingredients in large bowl; mix well. Spoon into 2-quart baking dish. Bake at 300 degrees for 1 hour.
Approx Per Serving: Cal 215; Prot 10 g; Carbo 36 g; Fiber 8 g; T Fat 4 g; 18% Calories from Fat; Chol 15 mg; Sod 619 mg.

Steve Miller, Yakima Valley Partners HFH, Selah, WA

Green Bean Casserole

Yield: 6 servings

2 10-ounce packages frozen green beans
1 10-ounce can cream of mushroom soup
1/2 cup milk

1 teaspoon soy sauce
Seasonings to taste
1 3-ounce can French-fried onions

■ Cook green beans using package directions; drain. Combine soup, milk, soy sauce and seasonings in bowl; mix well. Stir in beans and half the onions, mixing well. Spoon into 1 1/2-quart baking dish. Bake at 350 degrees for 25 minutes. Sprinkle remaining onions on top. Bake for 5 minutes longer.
Approx Per Serving: Cal 174; Prot 4 g; Carbo 16 g; Fiber 3 g; T Fat 11 g; 56% Calories from Fat; Chol 3 mg; Sod 553 mg.

June Leach, Rabun County HFH, Sky Valley, GA
Priscilla Allen, Pemi-Valley Habitat, Plymouth, NH

Kansas Beans

Yield: 12 servings

1 16-ounce can red kidney beans, drained
1 16-ounce can butter beans, drained
1 10-ounce can lima beans, drained
1 32-ounce can pork and beans

1 pound bacon, crisp-fried, chopped
4 onions, chopped
1/2 teaspoon dry mustard
3/4 cup packed brown sugar
1/2 cup vinegar

■ Combine first 4 ingredients in 9x10-inch baking dish. Mix remaining ingredients in bowl. Pour over beans and stir. Bake at 350 degrees for 1 hour.
Approx Per Serving: Cal 314; Prot 13 g; Carbo 52 g; Fiber 10 g; T Fat 7 g; 20% Calories from Fat; Chol 15 mg; Sod 756 mg.

Catherine Swanson, Singing River HFH, Ocean Springs, MS

Black "Eyes of Texas" Casserole

Yield: 8 servings

1 1/2 pounds lean ground beef
1 large onion, chopped
2 cloves of garlic, minced
1 16-ounce can black-eyed peas with jalapeño peppers
1 10-ounce can tomatoes with green chilies

1 10-ounce can cream of chicken soup
1 10-ounce can cream of mushroom soup
1 10-ounce can enchilada sauce
6 corn tortillas, cut into eighths
2 cups shredded sharp Cheddar cheese

■ Brown first 3 ingredients in large skillet, stirring frequently; drain. Add black-eyed peas, tomatoes, soups and enchilada sauce; mix well. Layer ground beef mixture and tortillas 1/2 at a time in greased 9x13-inch baking pan. Sprinkle with Cheddar cheese. Bake at 350 degrees for 35 minutes or until bubbly.
Approx Per Serving: Cal 505; Prot 30 g; Carbo 33 g; Fiber 7 g; T Fat 29 g; 51% Calories from Fat; Chol 89 mg; Sod 1545 mg.

Brenda C. Taylor Coleman, HFH–Abilene, Abilene, TX

Cheesy Broccoli Casserole

Yield: 6 servings

2 10-ounce packages frozen broccoli flowerets, cooked
8 ounces Velveeta cheese, sliced

4 ounces butter crackers, crushed
1/2 cup melted margarine

■ Alternate layers of broccoli and Velveeta cheese in 2-quart baking dish. Top with cracker crumbs; drizzle with margarine. Bake at 350 degrees for 30 minutes.
Approx Per Serving: Cal 398; Prot 13 g; Carbo 19 g; Fiber 3 g; T Fat 33 g; 70% Calories from Fat; Chol 36 mg; Sod 930 mg.

Angela G. Ray, HFH of Oshkosh, Oshkosh, WI

Broccoli with Almonds
Yield: 6 servings

2 10-ounce packages
  frozen broccoli,
  cooked, drained
1/2 cup mayonnaise
1 tablespoon lemon
  juice
1/2 cup shredded sharp
  Cheddar cheese

1 cup canned cream of
  mushroom soup
1 cup crushed cheese
  crackers
1 2-ounce jar chopped
  pimento, drained
1/4 cup slivered
  almonds

■ Place broccoli in buttered baking dish. Combine mayonnaise, lemon juice, cheese and soup in bowl; mix well. Pour over broccoli. Top with cracker crumbs, pimento and almonds. Bake at 350 degrees for 20 minutes or until heated through and bubbly.
Approx Per Serving: Cal 298; Prot 8 g; Carbo 13 g; Fiber 4 g; T Fat 25 g; 73% Calories from Fat; Chol 24 mg; Sod 577 mg.

Isabell Freeman, Peach Area HFH, Fort Valley, GA

Broccoli-Rice Casserole
Yield: 6 servings

1/2 cup chopped onion
1/4 cup butter
2 10-ounce cans
  cream of chicken
  soup
1 8-ounce jar Cheez
  Whiz

1/2 cup milk
2 10-ounce packages
  frozen broccoli,
  cooked, drained
2 cups quick-cooking
  rice

■ Sauté onion in butter in skillet until tender. Combine with soup, Cheez Whiz and milk in bowl; mix well. Stir in broccoli and uncooked rice. Spoon into 9x9-inch baking dish. Bake at 350 degrees for 40 minutes.
Approx Per Serving: Cal 441; Prot 16 g; Carbo 43 g; Fiber 4 g; T Fat 23 g; 47% Calories from Fat; Chol 55 mg; Sod 1288 mg.

Sandy Bosrock, Battle Creek Area HFH, Battle Creek, MI

Celery-Sauced Broccoli-Rice Casserole
Yield: 6 servings

2 cups frozen chopped
  broccoli
1 cup cooked quick-
  cooking rice
1/2 cup chopped onion

1/2 cup chopped celery
1 10-ounce can cream
  of celery soup
2/3 8-ounce jar Cheez
  Whiz

■ Cook broccoli in boiling water for 2 minutes; drain. Combine with rice, onion, celery and soup in bowl; mix well. Place Cheez Whiz in microwave-safe bowl. Microwave on Medium for 2 1/2 minutes. Stir into broccoli mixture; spoon into 1 1/2-quart baking dish. Bake at 350 degrees for 30 minutes.
Approx Per Serving: Cal 170; Prot 8 g; Carbo 16 g; Fiber 3 g; T Fat 8 g; 43% Calories from Fat; Chol 21 mg; Sod 680 mg.

Nancy C. Hall, Warren County HFH, Stephens City, VA

Chicken-Sauced Broccoli-Rice Casserole
Yield: 12 servings

1 cup rice
2 10-ounce packages
  frozen chopped
  broccoli, thawed
2 10-ounce cans cream
  of chicken soup

1/2 cup melted butter
8 ounces Velveeta
  cheese, shredded
1 onion, chopped
3/4 cup water

■ Cook rice using package directions. Combine with broccoli, soup, butter, Velveeta cheese, onion and water in bowl; mix well. Spoon into baking dish. Bake, covered, at 350 degrees for 40 minutes; uncover. Bake for 20 minutes longer. May also add a small can of drained mushrooms.
Approx Per Serving: Cal 256; Prot 8 g; Carbo 20 g; Fiber 2 g; T Fat 17 g; 57% Calories from Fat; Chol 42 mg; Sod 718 mg.

Nadine Noxon, Morgan County HFH, Fort Morgan, CO

*H*e told them another parable: "The kingdom of heaven is like a mustard seed, which a man took and planted in his field. Though it is the smallest of all your seeds, yet when it grows, it is the largest of garden plants and becomes a tree, so that the birds of the air come and perch in its branches."

Matthew 13:31-32

Creamed Broccoli

Yield: 8 servings

2   10-ounce packages
frozen broccoli
2 eggs, beaten
1   10-ounce can cream
of mushroom soup
1 cup shredded sharp
Cheddar cheese

1 tablespoon minced
onion
1 cup mayonnaise
1¼ cups stuffing mix
2 tablespoons melted
margarine

- Cook broccoli using package directions; drain. Mix eggs, soup, cheese, onion and mayonnaise in bowl. Stir in broccoli. Spoon into 2-quart baking dish. Cover with stuffing mix; drizzle with margarine. Bake at 375 degrees for 30 minutes.
Approx Per Serving: Cal 396; Prot 10 g; Carbo 16 g; Fiber 2 g; T Fat 34 g; 75% Calories from Fat; Chol 85 mg; Sod 744 mg.

Mrs. A.G. Bennett, Sr., Starkville HFH, Starkville, MS

Broccoli Custard Casserole

Yield: 8 servings

¼ cup minced onion
¼ cup margarine
2 tablespoons flour
½ cup water
1   8-ounce jar cheese
spread

2   10-ounce packages
frozen chopped
broccoli, thawed
3 eggs, beaten
½ cup cracker crumbs

- Sauté onion in margarine in saucepan until tender. Stir in flour. Add water. Cook over low heat until mixture thickens and begins to boil, stirring constantly. Add cheese spread, stirring until melted. Add broccoli, stirring to coat. Mix in eggs. Pour into 1½-quart greased baking dish. Sprinkle with cracker crumbs. Bake at 325 degrees for 30 minutes.
Approx Per Serving: Cal 213; Prot 10 g; Carbo 12 g; Fiber 2 g; T Fat 14 g; 59% Calories from Fat; Chol 98 mg; Sod 558 mg.

Ruth Harris, Rapides HFH, Pineville, LA

Broccoli and Corn Bake

Yield: 8 servings

1   10-ounce package
frozen chopped
broccoli
2 eggs, beaten
1   16-ounce can
cream-style corn
2 cups herb-seasoned
stuffing mix

1½ teaspoons dried
minced onion
Salt and pepper to taste
3 tablespoons melted
margarine

- Cook broccoli using package directions; drain. Combine with beaten eggs, corn, stuffing mix, onion, salt, pepper and melted margarine in bowl; mix well. Spoon into 1½-quart baking dish. Bake at 350 degrees for 40 minutes.
Approx Per Serving: Cal 175; Prot 6 g; Carbo 25 g; Fiber 2 g; T Fat 7 g; 32% Calories from Fat; Chol 53 mg; Sod 471 mg.

Sally Matts, HFH of St. Joseph County, Notre Dame, IN

Broccoli Casserole Everyone Loves

Yield: 10 servings

My family would never eat broccoli until I tried this—it's been a favorite for years.

4   10-ounce packages
frozen chopped
broccoli
½ cup frozen chopped
onion
2 eggs, beaten

2   10-ounce cans
cream of mushroom
soup
1 cup light mayonnaise
2 cups shredded
Cheddar cheese

- Cook broccoli using package directions; drain. Combine with onion, eggs, soup and mayonnaise; mix well. Stir in cheese. Spoon into 2½-quart baking dish. Bake at 350 degrees for 45 minutes or until golden brown on top.
Approx Per Serving: Cal 255; Prot 11 g; Carbo 15 g; Fiber 4 g; T Fat 18 g; 61% Calories from Fat; Chol 74 mg; Sod 760 mg.

Jean Stanton, Pensacola HFH, Pensacola, FL

I couldn't come to Atlanta without taking note of ... a part-time carpenter and his wife who have provided shelter for so many in this very city. Of course, I'm talking about the former President Jimmy Carter and Rosalynn Carter. They deserve our thanks, as do all the people behind Habitat for Humanity.

**Former President George Bush, speech to the 1990 convention of the
National Association of Home Builders**

Broccoli with Water Chestnuts and Rice   *Yield: 8 servings*

½ cup chopped onion
½ cup chopped celery
6 tablespoons butter
1 cup cooked rice
1   10-ounce can cream
of mushroom soup
1   8-ounce can water
chestnuts, chopped

1   16-ounce package
frozen broccoli,
thawed
1   8-ounce jar Cheez
Whiz

■ Sauté onion and celery in butter in saucepan until tender. Stir in rice, soup, water chestnuts, broccoli and cheese; mix well. Spoon into baking dish. Bake at 325 degrees for 1 hour. May also add 1 cup chopped cooked chicken.
Approx Per Serving: Cal 268; Prot 9 g; Carbo 19 g; Fiber 3 g; T Fat 18 g; 60% Calories from Fat; Chol 18 mg; Sod 746 mg.

Mildred Quinn, Starkville HFH, Starkville, MS

Amma's Cabbage Pugadh   *Yield: 4 servings*

½ head cabbage
3 tablespoons oil
1½ teaspoons black
mustard seed
1½ teaspoons Dhal

1 small onion, chopped
2 teaspoons crushed
red pepper
Turmeric, cumin and
curry powder to taste

■ Slice cabbage into 1x3-inch long strips. Heat oil in skillet for 5 to 8 minutes. Add mustard seed and Dhal. Cook until mustard seed begin to pop. Add chopped onion and red pepper; reduce heat to medium. Cook for 2 to 3 minutes. Add cabbage, turmeric, cumin and curry powder. Simmer for several minutes or until heated through. May substitute spinach or green beans for cabbage. Dhal may be purchased at any Indian food store.
Approx Per Serving: Cal 108; Prot 1 g; Carbo 4 g; Fiber 1 g; T Fat 10 g; 83% Calories from Fat; Chol 0 mg; Sod 7 mg.

Ranjit Souri, HFH International, Barnesville, OH

Baked Kraut   *Yield: 6 servings*

4 slices bacon, cut into
small pieces
1 onion, chopped
1   36-ounce can
sauerkraut, drained

1   32-ounce can
chopped tomatoes,
drained
1 cup packed brown
sugar

■ Fry bacon and onion in skillet until bacon is crisp; drain. Combine bacon, onion, sauerkraut, tomatoes and brown sugar in bowl; mix well. Spoon into baking dish. Bake at 350 degrees for 1 hour.
Approx Per Serving: Cal 265; Prot 5 g; Carbo 60 g; Fiber 5 g; T Fat 3 g; 9% Calories from Fat; Chol 4 mg; Sod 1459 mg.

Berniece Roth, Wayland, IA

Carrot Soufflé   *Yield: 6 servings*

1 pound cooked carrots
3 eggs
⅓ cup sugar
3 tablespoons flour
1 teaspoon vanilla
extract
½ cup melted butter

Nutmeg to taste
¼ to ½ cup crushed
cornflakes
3 tablespoons brown
sugar
2 teaspoons butter,
softened

■ Process carrots and eggs in blender until puréed. Add sugar, flour, vanilla, melted butter and nutmeg. Process until smooth. Pour into greased 1½-quart soufflé dish. Bake at 350 degrees for 40 minutes. Top with mixture of cornflake crumbs, brown sugar and 2 teaspoons butter. Bake for 5 to 10 minutes longer.
Approx Per Serving: Cal 325; Prot 5 g; Carbo 34 g; Fiber 3 g; T Fat 20 g; 53% Calories from Fat; Chol 151 mg; Sod 298 mg.

Phyllis George, Lexington, KY

Honey-Glazed Carrots

Yield: 8 servings

2 pounds carrots,
   thinly sliced
1/2 cup water
3 tablespoons honey

3 tablespoons brown
   sugar
2 tablespoons
   margarine

■ Place carrots with water in saucepan. Bring to a boil; reduce heat. Simmer, covered, for 8 minutes or until carrots are tender-crisp; drain. Stir in honey, brown sugar and margarine. Cook over low heat until brown sugar is dissolved, stirring constantly.
Approx Per Serving: Cal 118; Prot 1 g; Carbo 23 g; Fiber 4 g; T Fat 3 g; 22% Calories from Fat; Chol 0 mg; Sod 76 mg.

Charlene Cook, Starkville HFH, Starkville, MS

Stuffed Carrots

Yield: 6 servings

12 carrots, tips and
   tops trimmed
1/2 cup cooked rice
1/2 cup dry Italian
   bread crumbs
1/3 cup shredded
   Cheddar cheese
1/2 teaspoon salt

2 tablespoons finely
   chopped onion
2 tablespoons finely
   chopped green bell
   pepper
1/4 cup melted
   margarine

■ Cook carrots in water in saucepan for 20 minutes or until tender but firm. Scoop out centers of carrots, leaving shells. Mix remaining ingredients in small bowl. Stuff carrots with mixture. Place in 9x13-inch baking dish; cover with foil. Chill overnight. Let stand at room temperature for 30 minutes. Bake at 350 degrees for 15 minutes or until heated through
Approx Per Serving: Cal 208; Prot 5 g; Carbo 25 g; Fiber 5 g; T Fat 10 g; 44% Calories from Fat; Chol 7 mg; Sod 417 mg.

R.R. Johnston, Jr., Thermal Belt HFH, Columbus, NC

Baked Corn Supper

Yield: 10 servings

1 16-ounce can whole
   kernel corn,
   undrained
1 16-ounce can
   cream-style corn
1/2 cup margarine,
   softened

2 eggs, beaten
1 tablespoon sugar
1 cup sour cream
1 7-ounce package
   corn muffin mix

■ Combine all ingredients in bowl; mix well. Spoon into 8x12-inch baking dish. Bake at 350 degrees for 45 minutes or until light brown.
Approx Per Serving: Cal 251; Prot 4 g; Carbo 25 g; Fiber 2 g; T Fat 17 g; 57% Calories from Fat; Chol 53 mg; Sod 466 mg.

*C. Sue Pensinger-Jones, Cass County Indiana HFH
Logansport, IN*

Corn Pudding

Yield: 6 servings

2 tablespoons butter
1/2 cup sugar
2 eggs, beaten
1 cup milk
1 tablespoon cornstarch

1 16-ounce can whole
   kernel corn, drained
1 teaspoon salt
1 tablespoon lemon or
   vanilla extract

■ Melt butter in 1 1/2-quart baking dish in 400-degree oven. Combine remaining ingredients in bowl; mix well. Spoon into prepared baking dish. Bake for 40 to 55 minutes or until firm.
Approx Per Serving: Cal 222; Prot 5 g; Carbo 35 g; Fiber 1 g; T Fat 8 g; 31% Calories from Fat; Chol 87 mg; Sod 603 mg.

Pat Anderson, South Central HFH, Petersburg, VA

Jalapeño Scalloped Corn

Yield: 8 servings

1 4-ounce can chopped
   jalapeño peppers
1/4 cup chopped green
   bell pepper
1/2 cup chopped onion
1/4 cup margarine
3 eggs, beaten

1 7-ounce package
   corn muffin mix
1 cup sour cream
2 16-ounce cans
   cream-style corn
1 cup shredded
   Cheddar cheese

■ Sauté jalapeño peppers, green pepper and onion in margarine in skillet until tender. Combine with next 4 ingredients in large bowl; mix well. Spoon into 11x13-inch baking dish; top with cheese. Bake at 375 degrees for 30 to 45 minutes or until light brown.
Approx Per Serving: Cal 338; Prot 9 g; Carbo 33 g; Fiber 3 g; T Fat 20 g; 52% Calories from Fat; Chol 107 mg; Sod 838 mg.

Eunice Bourquin, Morgan County HFH, Fort Morgan, CO

Shoe Peg Corn Mix-Up

Yield: 6 servings

1/2 cup margarine
8 ounces cream cheese
2 11-ounce cans Shoe Peg corn, drained

2 4-ounce cans chopped green chilies, drained

- Melt margarine and cream cheese in saucepan, stirring frequently. Stir in corn and chilies, mixing well. Pour into greased 1-quart baking dish. Bake at 350 degrees for 35 to 40 minutes or until light brown.
  Approx Per Serving: Cal 361; Prot 6 g; Carbo 23 g; Fiber 1 g; T Fat 29 g; 70% Calories from Fat; Chol 41 mg; Sod 799 mg.

Shirley H. Carley, Starkville HFH, Starkville, MS

Swiss Corn Bake

Yield: 6 servings

1 16-ounce can whole kernel corn, drained
1 5-ounce can evaporated milk
1 cup shredded process Swiss cheese
2 eggs, beaten

2 tablespoons chopped onion
Pepper to taste
1 cup soft bread crumbs
2 tablespoons melted butter

- Combine corn, evaporated milk, 3/4 of the cheese, eggs, onion and pepper in bowl; mix well. Spoon into 1-quart baking dish. Toss bread crumbs with butter to coat. Arrange over corn mixture; top with remaining cheese. Bake at 350 degrees for 25 to 30 minutes or until light brown.
  Approx Per Serving: Cal 245; Prot 12 g; Carbo 21 g; Fiber 1 g; T Fat 14 g; 49% Calories from Fat; Chol 106 mg; Sod 343 mg.

Bev Kembel, Morgan County HFH, Fort Morgan, CO

Frozen Cucumbers

Yield: 16 servings

2 quarts sliced cucumbers
2 tablespoons salt
1 large onion, thinly sliced

1 1/2 cups sugar
1/2 cup vinegar
1 teaspoon dillseed

- Combine cucumbers, salt and onion in covered container. Chill overnight; drain. Stir in mixture of remaining ingredients. Chill, covered, overnight. Serve chilled or store in freezer.
  Approx Per Serving: Cal 83; Prot <1 g; Carbo 21 g; Fiber 1 g; T Fat <1 g; 1% Calories from Fat; Chol 0 mg; Sod 801 mg.

LaVone J. Walters, Presque Isle Maine HFH, Presque Isle, ME

Sweet and Sour Lentils

Yield: 2 servings

2 cups beef bouillon
2 ounces dried lentils, cooked
1 bay leaf
1 clove of garlic, minced

1/8 teaspoon ground cloves
1/8 teaspoon nutmeg
3 tablespoons cider vinegar
3 tablespoons honey

- Combine bouillon, cooked lentils, bay leaf and garlic in saucepan. Cook over low heat for 5 minutes, stirring often. Add cloves, nutmeg, vinegar and honey. Cook for 5 minutes longer, stirring frequently. Discard bay leaf.
  Approx Per Serving: Cal 213; Prot 11 g; Carbo 44 g; Fiber 3 g; T Fat 1 g; 3% Calories from Fat; Chol 1 mg; Sod 787 mg.

Jack Byron Abrams, Venice Area HFH, Venice, FL

Easy Vidalia Onion Casserole

Yield: 8 servings

6 to 7 Vidalia onions, sliced, separated into rings
1/2 cup margarine

1/2 cup grated Parmesan cheese
4 ounces butter crackers, crushed

- Sauté onions in margarine in skillet until tender. Alternate layers of onions, cheese and cracker crumbs 1/2 at a time in 1 1/2-quart baking dish. Bake at 350 degrees for 30 minutes or until brown.
  Approx Per Serving: Cal 243; Prot 5 g; Carbo 21 g; Fiber 2 g; T Fat 18 g; 61% Calories from Fat; Chol 4 mg; Sod 373 mg.

R.R. Johnston, Jr., Thermal Belt HFH, Columbus, NC

Cottage Potatoes

Yield: 10 servings

10 potatoes, cooked, peeled, cubed
16 ounces Velveeta cheese, cubed
1 slice bread, torn into small pieces
1/2 cup melted margarine

1/2 cup chopped green bell pepper
1 1/2 teaspoons Italian seasoning
1/2 to 3/4 cup milk

■ Combine potatoes, Velveeta cheese, bread, margarine, green pepper, Italian seasoning and milk in bowl; mix well. Spoon into greased 2-quart baking dish. Bake at 350 degrees for 1 hour or until bubbly.
Approx Per Serving: Cal 387; Prot 13 g; Carbo 30 g; Fiber 2 g; T Fat 24 g; 55% Calories from Fat; Chol 46 mg; Sod 785 mg.

Jane Q. Patterson, Central Valley HFH, Bridgewater, VA

Lemon Twist-Potato Casserole

Yield: 10 servings

1 2-pound package frozen hashed brown potatoes, thawed
1/2 cup melted butter
1/2 cup chopped onion
1 10-ounce can cream of chicken soup

1 cup sour cream
1 cup shredded Cheddar cheese
2 cups cornflakes, crushed
1/4 cup melted butter
1/2 lemon, thinly sliced

■ Combine potatoes, 1/2 cup melted butter, onion, soup, sour cream and cheese in bowl; mix well. Spoon into greased 2 1/2-quart baking dish. Toss crushed cornflakes with 1/4 cup melted butter; spread over potatoes. Bake at 350 degrees for 50 minutes. Top with twisted lemon slices. Garnish with parsley
Approx Per Serving: Cal 497; Prot 9 g; Carbo 41 g; Fiber 2 g; T Fat 35 g; 61% Calories from Fat; Chol 62 mg; Sod 621 mg.

Becky Meriwether, Mt. Pleasant HFH, Mt. Pleasant, TX

Luscious Potato Casserole

Yield: 12 servings

2 cups cream-style cottage cheese
1 cup sour cream
1/3 cup sliced green onions
1 clove of garlic, minced

2 teaspoons salt
5 cups chopped cooked potatoes
1/2 cup shredded sharp Cheddar cheese
Paprika to taste

■ Combine first 5 ingredients in large bowl; mix well. Fold in potatoes. Pour into greased shallow 1 1/2-quart baking dish. Top with cheese; sprinkle with paprika. Bake at 350 degrees for 40 minutes.
Approx Per Serving: Cal 145; Prot 7 g; Carbo 13 g; Fiber 1 g; T Fat 7 g; 44% Calories from Fat; Chol 19 mg; Sod 540 mg.

Emilie Thompson, Starkville HFH, Mississippi State, MS

Polly's Potatoes

Yield: 12 servings

1 2-pound package frozen hashed brown potatoes, thawed
2 cups sour cream
1 10-ounce can cream of chicken soup
1 cup milk

8 ounces Cheddar cheese, shredded
1 teaspoon salt
1 6-ounce package stuffing mix
1/2 cup margarine, softened

■ Combine first 6 ingredients in bowl; mix well. Spoon into greased 9x13-inch baking dish. Toss stuffing mix with margarine. Spread over potato mixture. Bake at 350 degrees for 1 hour.
Approx Per Serving: Cal 478; Prot 12 g; Carbo 36 g; Fiber 2 g; T Fat 33 g; 61% Calories from Fat; Chol 42 mg; Sod 813 mg.

Virginia Godfrey, Rabun County IIFII, Clayton, GA

Potato Breakfast Casserole

Yield: 8 servings

1 6-ounce package hashed brown potato mix with onions
4 cups hot water
5 eggs, beaten
1/2 cup cottage cheese
1 cup shredded Swiss cheese

1 green onion, chopped
1 teaspoon salt
1/8 teaspoon pepper
4 drops of hot pepper sauce
6 slices bacon, crisp-fried, crumbled
Paprika to taste

■ Cover potato mix with hot water in bowl. Let stand for 10 minutes; drain. Combine potato mix with next 7 ingredients; mix well. Spoon into buttered 10-inch pie plate. Sprinkle with bacon and paprika. Chill, covered, overnight. Place, uncovered, in cold oven. Bake at 350 degrees for 35 minutes or until potatoes are tender.
Approx Per Serving: Cal 227; Prot 12 g; Carbo 20 g; Fiber <1 g; T Fat 11 g; 43% Calories from Fat; Chol 152 mg; Sod 495 mg.

David L. Long, New River HFH, Beckley, WV

Sesame Seed Potatoes

Yield: 12 servings

1   2-pound package
   frozen hashed
   brown potatoes,
   thawed
6 tablespoons melted
   butter
1 cup chopped onion
8 ounces Cheddar
   cheese, shredded
1 teaspoon salt
1/2 teaspoon garlic salt

2   10-ounce cans
   cream of chicken
   soup
2 cups sour cream
2 cups crushed
   cornflakes
6 tablespoons melted
   butter
1   3-ounce package
   sesame seed

■ Combine potatoes, 6 tablespoons melted butter, onion, cheese, salt, garlic salt, soup and sour cream in large bowl; mix well. Spoon into 9x13-inch baking pan. Toss cornflakes with 6 tablespoons melted butter. Spread over top of potato mixture; sprinkle with sesame seed. Bake, covered with foil, at 350 degrees for 1 1/2 hours.
Approx Per Serving: Cal 559; Prot 13 g; Carbo 38 g; Fiber 3 g; T Fat 41 g; 65% Calories from Fat; Chol 72 mg; Sod 1038 mg.

Jeffrey Jones, Eau Claire Area HFH, Eau Claire, WI

Yummy Potatoes

Yield: 8 servings

1   2-pound package
   frozen hashed
   brown potatoes,
   thawed
1 cup chopped onion
1 cup cream of chicken
   soup
1 cup sour cream

1/2 cup melted
   margarine
8 ounces shredded
   Monterey Jack
   cheese
Salt and pepper to taste
1 cup buttered bread
   crumbs

■ Combine first 6 ingredients and salt and pepper in bowl; mix well. Spoon into greased 2-quart baking dish. Bake at 375 degrees for 1 1/4 hours. Top with buttered bread crumbs.
Approx Per Serving: Cal 601; Prot 14 g; Carbo 46 g; Fiber 3 g; T Fat 42 g; 61% Calories from Fat; Chol 42 mg; Sod 678 mg.

Edith Harford, Highlands County HFH, Sebring, FL

Joel's Potatoes

Yield: 6 servings

12 baking potatoes,
   peeled, cut into
   quarters
6 onions, cut into
   quarters

1 whole clove of garlic
1/2 to 3/4 cup olive oil
Salt and coarsely
   ground pepper to
   taste

■ Combine all ingredients in large bowl, tossing to coat. Spoon into 9x11-inch glass baking dish. Bake at 350 degrees for 1 1/2 hours, stirring 3 times during baking.
Approx Per Serving: Cal 586; Prot 8 g; Carbo 79 g; Fiber 7 g; T Fat 28 g; 42% Calories from Fat; Chol 0 mg; Sod 19 mg.

W. Keith Wentworth, Solano County HFH, Vacaville, CA

Aunt Elsie's Three-Cheese Potatoes

Yield: 10 servings

2 pounds peeled
   cooked potatoes
2 tablespoons butter
3 ounces cream cheese,
   softened
1/4 cup grated
   Parmesan cheese
1 egg
1 egg yolk
Salt and pepper to taste

2 tablespoons milk
1 to 2 tablespoons
   chopped green bell
   pepper
2 green onions, finely
   chopped
1 tablespoon chopped
   pimento
2 ounces Cheddar
   cheese, shredded

■ Mash potatoes with butter, cream cheese, Parmesan cheese, egg and egg yolk in bowl. Season with salt and pepper. Add milk, beating well. Stir in green pepper, green onions and pimento. Spoon into buttered 2-quart baking dish. Sprinkle with Cheddar cheese. Bake at 350 degrees for 30 minutes
Approx Per Serving: Cal 177; Prot 6 g; Carbo 19 g; Fiber 1 g; T Fat 9 g; 45% Calories from Fat; Chol 66 mg; Sod 131 mg.

Kathy Magnuson, HFH of Wausau, Wausau, WI

Cheesy Potatoes

Yield: 12 servings

1   2-pound package
   frozen hashed brown
   potatoes, thawed
1/2 cup margarine,
   softened
1 teaspoon salt
1/2 teaspoon pepper
2 cups sour cream
1/2 cup chopped onion

1 cup shredded sharp
   Cheddar cheese
1   10-ounce can cream
   of chicken soup
2 cups crushed
   cornflakes
1/4 cup melted
   margarine

■ Combine first 8 ingredients in greased 9x13-inch baking dish. Top with mixture of cornflake crumbs and melted margarine. Bake at 350 degrees for 50 to 60 minutes or until browned.
Approx Per Serving: Cal 455; Prot 8 g; Carbo 35 g; Fiber 2 g; T Fat 33 g; 63% Calories from Fat; Chol 29 mg; Sod 742 mg.

Marilynn Martin, HFH of Butler County, Slippery Rock, PA

Tasty Cheddar-Potato Casserole

Yield: 12 servings

8 to 10 large potatoes,
cooked, peeled
1/4 cup hot milk
6 ounces cream cheese,
softened
2 tablespoons butter,
softened

1 cup sour cream
1 cup shredded
Cheddar cheese
Salt and pepper to taste
1 tablespoon butter

■ Mash potatoes with hot milk until fluffy. Add cream cheese, 2 tablespoons butter and sour cream, stirring well. Spoon into buttered 2-quart baking dish. Sprinkle with cheese, salt and pepper; dot with remaining 1 tablespoon butter. Bake, covered with foil, at 325 degrees for 30 minutes; remove foil. Bake for 10 minutes longer.
Approx Per Serving: Cal 256; Prot 6 g; Carbo 24 g; Fiber 2 g; T Fat 15 g; 53% Calories from Fat; Chol 42 mg; Sod 142 mg.

Jimmy and Ginger Dancy, Rutherford County HFH
Rutherfordton, NC

Mashed Potato Casserole

Yield: 12 servings

12 potatoes, peeled,
cooked
8 ounces cream cheese,
softened
1/4 cup butter, softened
1 cup sour cream

2 eggs, lightly beaten
1/2 cup milk
1/4 cup finely chopped
onion
1 teaspoon salt
Pepper to taste

■ Mash potatoes in bowl until fluffy. Add cream cheese and butter, beating well. Stir in sour cream. Beat eggs with milk, onion, salt and pepper in small bowl. Add to potato mixture, beating until light and fluffy. Spoon into 9-inch round baking dish. Bake at 350 degrees for 45 minutes. May make ahead and chill, bringing to room temperature before baking.
Approx Per Serving: Cal 280; Prot 6 g; Carbo 30 g; Fiber 2 g; T Fat 16 g; 50% Calories from Fat; Chol 76 mg; Sod 298 mg.

Nancy Warner, Firelands HFH, Norwalk, OH

Spinach and Mashed Potatoes

Yield: 6 servings

6 to 8 large potatoes,
cooked, peeled
3/4 cup sour cream
1/2 cup butter, softened
1 tablespoon sugar
2 teaspoons chopped
chives

1 teaspoon dillweed
2 teaspoons salt
1 teaspoon pepper
1 10-ounce package
frozen chopped
spinach, thawed,
drained

■ Mash potatoes with sour cream and butter until light and fluffy. Stir in sugar, chives, dillweed, salt and pepper. Fold in spinach. Pour into 3-quart baking dish. Bake at 425 degrees for 20 minutes. May top with shredded cheese.
Approx Per Serving: Cal 377; Prot 6 g; Carbo 42 g; Fiber 4 g; T Fat 22 g; 50% Calories from Fat; Chol 54 mg; Sod 904 mg.

Beth Funderburg, Northern Straits HFH, Moran, MI

Pizza Potatoes

Yield: 4 servings

1 5-ounce package
scalloped potato mix
1 16-ounce can
tomatoes
1 1/2 cups water

1/4 teaspoon oregano
1 6-ounce package
sliced pepperoni
4 ounces mozzarella
cheese, shredded

■ Arrange potato slices in 2-quart casserole; sprinkle with seasoning packet. Combine undrained tomatoes, water and oregano in saucepan. Bring to a boil, stirring frequently. Pour over potatoes. Layer with pepperoni; sprinkle with cheese. Bake at 400 degrees for 30 to 35 minutes or until potatoes are tender. May substitute 8 ounces cooked ground beef or 8 ounces cooked pork sausage for pepperoni.
Approx Per Serving: Cal 333; Prot 16 g; Carbo 11 g; Fiber 1 g; T Fat 25 g; 68% Calories from Fat; Chol 37 mg; Sod 1273 mg.

Deanna Risser, Bluffton College Campus Chapter
Middlebury, IN

T here will always be poor people in the land. Therefore I command you to be openhanded toward your brothers and toward the poor and needy in your land.

Deuteronomy 15:11

Potato Pancakes

Yield: 8 servings

4 pounds potatoes,
    peeled
2 large onions, grated
1 egg, beaten
2 teaspoons baking
    powder

1½ cups flour
1 teaspoon lemon juice
1 teaspoon salt
Nutmeg to taste
Oil for frying

■ Grate potatoes into colander; let stand to drain. Mix with onions and egg in bowl. Combine next 5 ingredients in bowl. Stir into potato mixture. Drop small amount of mixture into hot oil in skillet. Fry for 5 minutes on each side or until golden brown; drain.
Approx Per Serving: Cal 305; Prot 8 g; Carbo 67 g; Fiber 5 g; T Fat 1 g; 4% Calories from Fat; Chol 27 mg; Sod 370 mg.
Nutritional analysis does not include oil for frying.

John J. Kostecki, Sr., Northern Straits HFH, Cedarville, MI

Scalloped Potatoes

Yield: 6 servings

6 potatoes
1 small onion, cut into
    quarters
3 tablespoons flour

¼ teaspoon pepper
1 teaspoon salt
¼ cup butter
2 cups milk

■ Slice potatoes very thinly in food processor. Arrange in greased 2-quart baking dish. Process onion in food processor for 3 seconds or until chopped. Add flour, pepper and salt. Process for 5 seconds longer. Add butter. Process for 10 seconds. Add milk slowly, continuing to process. Pour mixture over potatoes. Bake, covered, at 350 degrees for 30 minutes. Bake, uncovered, for 1 to 1½ hours longer or until potatoes are tender. Let stand 5 to 10 minutes before serving.
Approx Per Serving: Cal 284; Prot 6 g; Carbo 42 g; Fiber 3 g; T Fat 11 g; 33% Calories from Fat; Chol 32 mg; Sod 462 mg.

*Cynthia Oliver, Michigan State University Campus Chapter
St. Ignace, MI*

Scalloped Potatoes Supreme

Yield: 8 servings

8 potatoes, peeled,
    sliced
¼ cup chopped green
    bell pepper
¼ cup minced onion
2 teaspoons salt

Pepper to taste
1   10-ounce can cream
    of mushroom soup
1 cup milk
½ cup shredded
    Cheddar cheese

■ Alternate layers of potatoes, green pepper and onion in greased 2-quart baking dish, sprinkling each layer with salt and pepper. Mix soup with milk in small bowl until smooth. Pour over layers. Sprinkle with cheese. Bake, covered, at 350 degrees for 1½ hours.
Approx Per Serving: Cal 231; Prot 6 g; Carbo 38 g; Fiber 3 g; T Fat 6 g; 24% Calories from Fat; Chol 12 mg; Sod 885 mg.

*Freddye Mae Smith, Three Trails Neighbors HFH
Independence, MO*

Spicy Scalloped Potatoes

Yield: 8 servings

8 unpeeled potatoes,
    sliced
12 cups water
2 teaspoons salt
1 cup cubed cooked
    ham
½ cup shredded
    American cheese
½ cup shredded Swiss
    cheese

½ cup butter
½ cup flour
1 teaspoon salt
½ teaspoon white
    pepper
2 teaspoons bacon bits
1 teaspoon crushed red
    pepper
¼ teaspoon paprika

■ Boil potatoes in water seasoned with 2 teaspoons salt in large saucepan until potatoes are partially cooked. Drain, reserving cooking liquid. Arrange potatoes in 8x11-inch baking dish. Layer with ham and cheeses. Melt butter in saucepan over low heat. Add flour gradually, stirring until smooth. Add reserved cooking liquid 1 cup at a time until of desired consistency. Stir in 1 teaspoon salt, white pepper, bacon bits, red pepper and paprika. Pour over layers. Bake at 350 degrees for 20 minutes.
Approx Per Serving: Cal 327; Prot 11 g; Carbo 33 g; Fiber 2 g; T Fat 17 g; 46% Calories from Fat; Chol 54 mg; Sod 1259 mg.

Michael Galvin, Homestead HFH, Homestead, FL

Yield: 8 servings

Twenty Dollar Potatoes

A friend of mine tasted these potatoes at a party and asked for the recipe. She was told she could have it by paying $20 to join a recipe club. She did, and discovered that this was the simplest recipe imaginable. To this day they've been called "Twenty Dollar Potatoes."

6 to 7 potatoes, boiled, peeled
1/4 cup butter
1 10-ounce can cream of mushroom soup
3 tablespoons minced onion
2 cups sour cream

1 1/2 cups shredded Cheddar cheese
1 teaspoon salt
1/2 teaspoon pepper
1/2 cup cornflakes
2 tablespoons melted butter

■ Grate cooled cooked potatoes into bowl; set aside. Heat butter and soup in saucepan, stirring until smooth. Stir in onion, sour cream, cheese, salt and pepper. Add to potatoes, mixing well. Spoon into greased baking dish. Top with mixture of cornflakes and melted butter. Chill in refrigerator overnight. Bake at 350 degrees for 1 hour.
Approx Per Serving: Cal 432; Prot 10 g; Carbo 31 g; Fiber 2 g; T Fat 31 g; 63% Calories from Fat; Chol 72 mg; Sod 811 mg.

Mike Field, Chesapeake HFH, Baltimore, MD

Yield: 10 servings

Potatoes and Ramps

2 gallons ramps, cleaned, sliced
10 potatoes, peeled, cubed

Oil for frying
6 to 10 eggs, beaten
Salt and pepper to taste

■ Cook ramps in boiling water to cover until tender; drain. Fry potatoes in oil in skillet until browned and tender; drain. Combine potatoes, ramps, eggs, salt and pepper. Cook in large skillet until eggs are set.
Approx Per Serving: Cal 368; Prot 14 g; Carbo 65 g; Fiber 10 g; T Fat 7 g; 17% Calories from Fat; Chol 213 mg; Sod 86 mg.
Nutritional information does not include oil for frying.

Ann Nelson, Almost Heaven HFH, Circleville, WV

Yield: 6 servings

Spinach with Cream Cheese

2 10-ounce packages frozen chopped spinach
8 ounces cream cheese, softened
1 teaspoon salt

1 teaspoon pepper
1 cup cracker crumbs
1/2 cup butter
2 cups seasoned croutons

■ Cook spinach using package directions; drain well. Combine with cream cheese, salt, pepper and cracker crumbs in bowl; mix well. Spoon into 8x8-inch baking dish. Melt butter in saucepan; add croutons. Toss until butter is absorbed. Spread over spinach mixture. Bake at 350 degrees for 30 minutes.
Approx Per Serving: Cal 389; Prot 8 g; Carbo 24 g; Fiber 3 g; T Fat 30 g; 69% Calories from Fat; Chol 87 mg; Sod 991 mg.

Cindy Riess, First Congregational Church, HFH of Oshkosh
Oshkosh, WI

Yield: 8 servings

Sweet and Sour Spinach

I like to take this "dressed up" vegetable to potlucks when it is cool outside.

2 slices bacon
1 cup minced onion
1 tablespoon flour
3/4 cup spinach cooking liquid
1/4 cup vinegar

2 tablespoons sugar
1 teaspoon salt
1/4 teaspoon pepper
2 cups cooked spinach
Slivered almonds, optional

■ Brown bacon in Dutch oven until crisp. Cook minced onion in bacon drippings until yellow. Stir in flour. Add spinach liquid, vinegar, sugar, salt and pepper. Bring to a boil, stirring constantly. Stir in cooked spinach and almonds. Pour into 2-quart baking dish. Bake at 275 degrees for 1 hour or until heated through. Sprinkle with crumbled bacon.
Approx Per Serving: Cal 65; Prot 2 g; Carbo 7 g; Fiber 1 g; T Fat 3 g; 45% Calories from Fat; Chol 16 mg; Sod 349 mg.

Sharon J. Andrews, HFH of Green County
South Wayne, WI

Turkish Spinach and Rice

Yield: 4 servings

1 onion, chopped
¼ cup olive oil
⅓ cup uncooked rice
1 bunch fresh spinach,
    torn into bite-sized
    pieces

1 to 2 tablespoons
    tomato paste
Salt and pepper to taste
½ cup water
1 clove of garlic, minced
1½ cups plain yogurt

■ Sauté onion in olive oil in saucepan until tender. Add rice. Sauté for several minutes or until light brown. Add spinach. Cook for 5 minutes. Add tomato paste, salt, pepper and water. Cook over medium heat for 15 minutes or until rice is tender and liquid has evaporated. Serve hot or cold with sauce of garlic mixed with yogurt.

Approx Per Serving: Cal 261; Prot 6 g; Carbo 23 g; Fiber 3 g; T Fat 17 g; 56% Calories from Fat; Chol 11 mg; Sod 90 mg.

Cheryl Dorsey, Montgomery HFH, Wetumpka, AL

Yellow Squash Casserole

Yield: 12 servings

1 7-ounce package
    corn bread mix
¼ cup melted
    margarine
2 pounds yellow
    squash, sliced
1 onion, chopped

1 cup sour cream
1 10-ounce can cream
    of chicken soup
Salt and pepper to taste
1½ cups shredded
    Cheddar cheese

■ Prepare and bake corn bread using package directions; cool and crumble. Toss with melted margarine; set aside. Cook squash and onion in boiling water until tender; drain. Combine with corn bread crumbs, sour cream, soup, salt, pepper and 1 cup cheese in bowl; mix well. Spoon into 3-quart baking dish. Top with remaining cheese. Bake at 350 degrees for 30 minutes.

Approx Per Serving: Cal 248; Prot 7 g; Carbo 19 g; Fiber 1 g; T Fat 17 g; 59% Calories from Fat; Chol 34 mg; Sod 441 mg.

Cordella Faye Rice, Americus-Sumter County HFH
Wildwood, FL

Orange Sweet Potatoes

Yield: 8 servings

1 32-ounce can sweet
    potatoes
½ cup chopped pecans
½ cup raisins
1 tablespoon grated
    orange rind

1 cup orange juice
¼ teaspoon salt
2 tablespoons
    cornstarch
½ cup sugar
2 tablespoons butter

■ Arrange sweet potatoes in 1½-quart baking dish; sprinkle with chopped pecans and raisins. Combine orange rind, orange juice, salt, cornstarch, sugar and butter in saucepan. Cook over medium heat until thickened, stirring frequently. Pour over sweet potato mixture. Bake at 350 degrees for 30 to 40 minutes or until bubbly.

Approx Per Serving: Cal 290; Prot 3 g; Carbo 53 g; Fiber 4 g; T Fat 8 g; 25% Calories from Fat; Chol 8 mg; Sod 177 mg.

Ethel Wilson, Mississippi State University Campus Chapter
Mississippi State, MS

Sunday Sweet Potatoes

Yield: 6 servings

3 cups mashed sweet
    potatoes
1 cup sugar
⅓ cup melted butter
2 eggs, beaten
1 teaspoon vanilla
    extract

1 cup flaked coconut
1 cup chopped pecans
1 cup packed brown
    sugar
⅓ cup flour
⅓ cup melted butter

■ Beat sweet potatoes with sugar, ⅓ cup melted butter, eggs and vanilla in bowl until fluffy. Spoon into 2½-quart baking dish. Combine coconut, pecans, brown sugar and flour in small bowl. Add ⅓ cup melted butter, mixing well. Sprinkle over sweet potato mixture. Bake at 325 degrees for 20 to 30 minutes or until golden brown.

Approx Per Serving: Cal 892; Prot 8 g; Carbo 131 g; Fiber 4 g; T Fat 40 g; 39% Calories from Fat; Chol 126 mg; Sod 240 mg.

Jeanette Dollar, Peach Area HFH, Fort Valley ,GA

Sweet Potato Hash

Yield: 10 servings

3¹/₄ pounds sweet
  potatoes, peeled, cut
  into 1-inch cubes
3 quarts water
1 teaspoon salt

2 tablespoons butter
2 tablespoons oil
3 cups chopped onion
¹/₂ teaspoon white
  pepper

■ Combine potatoes, water and salt in large saucepan. Bring to a boil. Cook, covered, for 3 minutes; drain. Cover potatoes with cold water. Pour into colander; let stand for 15 minutes to drain. Heat butter and oil in large deep skillet over medium heat. Sauté onion until tender. Add potatoes and pepper. Cook for 5 to 8 minutes or until heated through, stirring often.
Approx Per Serving: Cal 217; Prot 3 g; Carbo 40 g; Fiber 5 g; T Fat 6 g; 23% Calories from Fat; Chol 6 mg; Sod 253 mg.

Louise V. Chisholm, Peach Area HFH, Fort Valley, GA

Sweet Potatoes with Pineapple

Yield: 6 servings

¹/₃ cup honey
¹/₄ cup water
6 small sweet potatoes,
  cooked, peeled, sliced

¹/₂ 8-ounce can sliced
  pineapple, drained

■ Combine honey and water in bowl, mixing well. Pour enough of mixture into baking dish to coat bottom of dish. Arrange sweet potatoes in prepared baking dish. Top with pineapple slices. Pour remaining honey mixture over top. Bake at 400 degrees for 10 minutes.
Approx Per Serving: Cal 187; Prot 2 g; Carbo 46 g; Fiber 4 g; T Fat <1 g; 2% Calories from Fat; Chol 0 mg; Sod 16 mg.

Mrs. Robert Hancock, Mid-Hudson Valley HFH
Poughkeepsie, NY

Tomatoes Columbia

Yield: variable

■ Slice 1 tomato per serving into halves. Place in broiler pan. Dot with butter. Season with salt and pepper. Bake at 400 degrees for 20 to 30 minutes or until soft. Add 1 teaspoon brown sugar to each tomato half; broil until brown. Slice ¹/₂ peeled tomato; dredge with flour. Sauté in 1 tablespoon butter in skillet, stirring to scramble. Add ¹/₂ cup light cream and 1 tablespoon brown sugar. Cook until thickened, stirring constantly. Serve over tomato halves.

Patty and James W. Rouse, Columbia, MD
The Enterprise Foundation

Ruffled Yams

Yield: 8 servings

5 yams, peeled, cooked
1 cup sugar
6 tablespoons butter
3 eggs
1 5-ounce can
  evaporated milk
1 teaspoon vanilla
  extract

¹/₂ teaspoon nutmeg
¹/₂ cup packed brown
  sugar
2 tablespoons butter
1 cup pecan pieces
¹/₂ cup shredded
  coconut

■ Mash yams with sugar and butter in bowl until fluffy. Beat eggs with evaporated milk in small bowl. Add to yams, stirring well. Stir in vanilla and nutmeg. Pour into baking dish. Spread mixture of remaining ingredients over yams. Bake at 350 degrees for 35 minutes.
Approx Per Serving: Cal 554; Prot 6 g; Carbo 75 g; Fiber 4 g; T Fat 27 g; 43% Calories from Fat; Chol 116 mg; Sod 174 mg.

Frances P. Mitchell, Peach Area HFH, Fort Valley, GA

Yam Casserole

Yield: 6 servings

2 16-ounce cans yams,
  drained
3 eggs
¹/₂ cup packed dark
  brown sugar

¹/₂ cup melted butter
1 teaspoon salt
12 whole pecans, cut
  into halves

■ Beat yams in mixer bowl at medium speed until fluffy. Beat in eggs and brown sugar. Stir in butter and salt. Pour into 1-quart baking dish sprayed with nonstick cooking spray. Arrange pecan halves on top. Bake at 375 degrees for 25 to 30 minutes
Approx Per Serving: Cal 460; Prot 7 g; Carbo 59 g; Fiber 4 g; T Fat 23 g; 44% Calories from Fat; Chol 148 mg; Sod 641 mg.

Marjorie A. Pearsall, Cumberland, VA

Baked Zucchini Casserole
Yield: 6 servings

4 to 5 cups sliced
  zucchini
1 4-ounce can
  chopped green
  chilies, drained
1 cup shredded
  Cheddar cheese

2 eggs, beaten
3/4 cup buttermilk
  baking mix
1 1/2 cups milk
1 4-ounce package
  chipped beef,
  crumbled

■ Parboil zucchini until tender-crisp; drain. Layer zucchini, chilies and cheese 1/2 at a time in greased 1 1/2-quart baking dish. Combine eggs, baking mix and milk in bowl, mixing well. Stir in crumbled chipped beef. Pour over layers. Bake, covered, at 350 degrees for 30 minutes. Bake, uncovered, for 30 minutes longer or until crusty and browned.
Approx Per Serving: Cal 260; Prot 17 g; Carbo 18 g; Fiber 1 g; T Fat 13 g; 46% Calories from Fat; Chol 130 mg; Sod 1155 mg.

Ruth Hazelton, Las Vegas, New Mexico HFH, Las Vegas, NM

Creamy Zucchini Casserole
Yield: 6 servings

1 small zucchini,
  thinly sliced
1 8-ounce package
  herb-flavored
  stuffing mix

1 cup sour cream
1/4 cup chopped onion
1 10-ounce can cream
  of mushroom soup
1 cup shredded carrots

■ Combine zucchini, stuffing mix, sour cream, onion, soup and carrots in bowl; mix well. Spoon into greased 2-quart baking dish. Bake at 350 degrees for 30 minutes or until zucchini is tender.
Approx Per Serving: Cal 290; Prot 8 g; Carbo 36 g; Fiber 1 g; T Fat 13 g; 40% Calories from Fat; Chol 18 mg; Sod 1060 mg.

*Sue Widmann, Williamsport/Lycoming HFH
Williamsport, PA*

Zucchini and Rice
Yield: 8 servings

3 tablespoons butter
2 pounds zucchini,
  shredded
1 onion, chopped
1 7-ounce package
  herb and butter-
  flavored rice and
  pasta mix

1 10-ounce can cream
  of mushroom soup
1/3 cup water
1/2 cup shredded
  Monterey Jack
  cheese

■ Melt butter in large skillet. Add zucchini, onion and rice and pasta mix, reserving seasoning packet. Sauté for 3 minutes; remove from heat. Mix soup and water in small bowl. Stir into zucchini mixture. Add reserved seasoning packet and half the cheese, stirring well. Spoon into 2-quart baking dish. Sprinkle with remaining cheese. Bake at 425 degrees for 25 minutes or until golden brown and bubbly. Let stand for 5 minutes before serving.
Approx Per Serving: Cal 224; Prot 6 g; Carbo 27 g; Fiber 2 g; T Fat 11 g; 43% Calories from Fat; Chol 19 mg; Sod 738 mg.

Cynthia E. Lopez, HFH of Wichita Falls, Wichita Falls, TX

Hot Vegetable Casserole
Yield: 12 servings

1 10-ounce package
  frozen lima beans
1 16-ounce can
  French-style green
  beans
1 8-ounce can small
  green peas
1 cup mayonnaise

1 onion, grated
1 teaspoon prepared
  mustard
1 teaspoon
  Worcestershire sauce
Tabasco sauce to taste
3 hard-boiled eggs,
  chopped

■ Cook lima beans using package directions. Add green beans and peas. Simmer for 15 minutes; drain. Spoon into serving bowl. Mix mayonnaise, onion, mustard, Worcestershire sauce, Tabasco sauce and eggs in bowl. Spoon over vegetables.
Approx Per Serving: Cal 201; Prot 5 g; Carbo 10 g; Fiber 4 g; T Fat 16 g; 71% Calories from Fat; Chol 64 mg; Sod 273 mg.

Elaine W. Thomas, HFH in Mobile County, Mobile, AL

Apple Marmalade

Yield: 64 servings

1 orange, peeled
1¹/₂ cups water
5 cups sugar
2 tablespoons lemon
  juice

8 cups thinly sliced
  peeled tart apples

■ Purée orange and ¹/₂ cup water in blender . Heat 1 cup water and sugar in saucepan, stirring until sugar is dissolved. Add lemon juice, orange and apples. Boil until mixture thickens and apples are tender, stirring often; remove from heat. Skim mixture; stir for 5 minutes. Ladle into hot sterilized jars leaving ¹/₂ inch headspace; seal with 2-piece lids.
Approx Per Serving: Cal 70; Prot <1 g; Carbo 18 g; Fiber <1 g; T Fat <1 g; 1% Calories from Fat; Chol 0 mg; Sod <1 mg.

Ruth Hubbard, Northern Straits HFH, St. Ignace, MI

Almond-Cranberry Sauce

Yield: 16 servings

2 cups sugar
1 cup water
1 pound fresh
  cranberries
Juice of 2 lemons

7 tablespoons apricot
  jam
36 almonds, blanched,
  peeled

■ Boil sugar and water in saucepan for 5 minutes; do not stir. Add cranberries. Cook for 5 minutes; remove from heat. Stir in lemon juice and jam. Pour into serving bowl; top with almonds. Chill until serving time.
Approx Per Serving: Cal 151; Prot 1 g; Carbo 36 g; Fiber 2 g; T Fat 1 g; 8% Calories from Fat; Chol 0 mg; Sod 2 mg.

Donna J. Bond, Battle Creek Area HFH, Battle Creek, MI

Cranberry Relish

Yield: 20 servings

2 16-ounce packages
   frozen cranberries,
   partially thawed,
   ground
1 cup packed light
  brown sugar

1 cup sugar
Grated rind of 1¹/₂
  oranges
1¹/₂ cups orange juice
¹/₄ teaspoon cinnamon

■ Bring all ingredients to a boil in saucepan, stirring constantly. Boil for 4 to 5 minutes or until of desired consistency, stirring frequently. Chill, covered, until serving time.
Approx Per Serving: Cal 126; Prot <1 g; Carbo 33 g; Fiber 1 g; T Fat <1 g; <1% Calories from Fat; Chol 0 mg; Sod 7 mg.

Linda Fuller, HFH International, Americus, GA

Baked Pineapple Dressing

Yield: 6 servings

¹/₂ cup butter, softened
1 20-ounce can
   crushed pineapple,
   drained
3 eggs, beaten

6 slices whole wheat
  bread, torn into
  small pieces
1 cup sugar

■ Combine all ingredients in 1¹/₂-quart baking dish; mix well. Bake, covered, at 350 degrees for 40 minutes. Bake, uncovered, for 5 minutes longer.
Approx Per Serving: Cal 422; Prot 7 g; Carbo 59 g; Fiber 3 g; T Fat 20 g; 40% Calories from Fat; Chol 148 mg; Sod 345 mg.

Delores E. Johnson, Highlands County HFH, Avon Park, FL

Catsup

Yield: 48 (1-ounce) servings

1 peck ripe tomatoes,
  peeled
2 cups vinegar
3 cups sugar

3 tablespoons salt
¹/₄ teaspoon catsup
  spices

■ Cook tomatoes in saucepan until tender. Drain in cotton or cheesecloth bag for 6 to 8 hours. Press pulp through sieve into saucepan. Stir in vinegar, sugar, salt and spices. Boil for 10 minutes, stirring frequently. Pour into hot sterilized jars, leaving ¹/₂ inch headspace; seal with 2-piece lids.
Approx Per Serving: Cal 65; Prot 1 g; Carbo 17 g; Fiber 1 g; T Fat <1 g; 2% Calories from Fat; Chol 0 mg; Sod 407 mg.

Lois Harsh, Highlands County HFH, Lorida, FL

Tennessee Sausage Bread Stuffing

Yield: 10 servings

1 pound country
   sausage
1 onion, chopped
³/4 cup chopped celery
1 teaspoon salt
¹/2 teaspoon pepper
1 teaspoon dried basil

¹/2 teaspoon dried
   oregano
10 cups dry bread
   cubes
2 tablespoons minced
   fresh parsley
1 to 2 cups chicken broth

■ Brown sausage in large skillet, stirring until crumbly. Drain all but ¹/2 cup pan drippings. Add onion and celery to sausage in skillet. Sauté until tender. Stir in salt, pepper, basil and oregano. Combine mixture with bread cubes and parsley in large bowl. Add enough chicken broth to moisten; mix well. Spoon into baking dish. Bake at 350 degrees for 30 minutes. May use to stuff 12 to 14-pound turkey.

Approx Per Serving: Cal 306; Prot 9 g; Carbo 24 g; Fiber 1 g; T Fat 19 g; 57% Calories from Fat; Chol 85 mg; Sod 1164 mg.

Rhomalda Malone, HFH of the Kokomo Community
Kokomo, IN

Cornmeal Squares with Salsa

Yield: 15 servings

1 cup yellow cornmeal
1 teaspoon chili
   powder
4 cups water
1 teaspoon salt
1   4-ounce can
   chopped green
   chilies, drained,
   patted dry

1 cup shredded
   Monterey Jack
   cheese
¹/4 cup chopped cilantro
6 tablespoons oil
1   11-ounce jar
   Newman's Own All
   Natural Salsa

■ Mix cornmeal and chili powder in bowl. Bring water and salt to a boil in saucepan over medium heat. Sprinkle with cornmeal mixture ¹/4 cup at a time, whisking constantly. Cook for 10 minutes or until thickened, stirring constantly. Stir in green chilies, cheese and cilantro. Spread in oiled 10x15-inch baking pan. Chill in refrigerator. Cut into 15 squares. Cook 5 squares at a time on both sides in 2 tablespoons oil in large nonstick skillet over medium-high heat for 8 to 10 minutes or until golden brown. Serve with salsa.

Approx Per Serving: Cal 119; Prot 3 g; Carbo 9 g; Fiber 1 g; T Fat 8 g; 60% Calories from Fat; Chol 7 mg; Sod 366 mg.

Paul Newman, Newman's Own, Inc., Westport, CT

Paul Newman (front, center) is joined by Millard Fuller
(second from right, second row) and a crew of volunteers during
the break at a building site in Lexington, Kentucky.

Habitat does not build houses FOR people in need, but WITH people in need. They are equal partners and Habitat projects aspire to empower them and assist them in developing their self-sufficiency.

Dumplings That Cannot Fail

Yield: 6 servings

I've had this recipe since I was married almost 56 years ago.

1½ cups flour
1 teaspoon (heaping) baking powder
1 teaspoon salt

1 tablespoon butter
1 egg, beaten
½ cup milk

■ Sift flour, baking powder and salt in bowl. Cut in butter. Add beaten egg and milk, stirring until soft dough forms. Bring saucepan of water to a boil; remove from heat. Drop mixture by tablespoonfuls into water. Cook, covered, over medium heat for 20 minutes.
Approx Per Serving: Cal 157; Prot 5 g; Carbo 25 g; Fiber 1 g; T Fat 4 g; 22% Calories from Fat; Chol 43 mg; Sod 447 mg.

Zella M. Rease, North Bradley Church of God, Coleman, MI

Tomato-Cheese Dumplings

Yield: 8 servings

2 cups flour
4 teaspoons baking powder
¾ teaspoon salt
3 tablespoons margarine
1 teaspoon dried basil
1 cup milk

5 cups canned tomatoes
1 teaspoon salt
¼ teaspoon pepper
1 teaspoon brown sugar
1 cup shredded Cheddar cheese
¼ teaspoon salt

■ Combine flour, baking powder and ¾ teaspoon salt in bowl; cut in margarine. Add basil. Stir in milk. Combine tomatoes, 1 teaspoon salt, pepper and brown sugar in large saucepan. Bring to a boil. Drop dough by tablespoonfuls on top of tomatoes. Cook for 5 minutes; cover. Cook for 10 minutes longer. Sprinkle with shredded cheese and ¼ teaspoon salt. Cook, covered, for 2 minutes.
Approx Per Serving: Cal 262; Prot 9 g; Carbo 33 g; Fiber 2 g; T Fat 11 g; 36% Calories from Fat; Chol 19 mg; Sod 1093 mg.

Mary Dale Seaton Kamerrer, Oregon Trail HFH Hermiston, OR

Garlic Noodles

Yield: 12 servings

1 10-ounce package noodles
2 cups cottage cheese
2 cups sour cream
Salt to taste

2 white onions, chopped
2 cloves of garlic, minced
2 tablespoons Worcestershire sauce

■ Boil noodles in salted water in saucepan for 6 to 10 minutes or to desired degree of doneness; drain. Add remaining ingredients to noodles; mix well. Spoon into buttered 3-quart baking dish. Bake at 350 degrees for 45 minutes.
Approx Per Serving: Cal 221; Prot 9 g; Carbo 22 g; Fiber <1 g; T Fat 11 g; 44% Calories from Fat; Chol 64 mg; Sod 191 mg.

Carol Freeland, HFH International Board of Directors Richardson, TX

Chili Grits

Yield: 8 servings

Best served hot but also delicious cold.

1 cup grits
3 cups water
1 teaspoon salt
½ cup margarine
1 12-ounce can evaporated milk

2 eggs, beaten
8 ounces Cheddar cheese, shredded
1 4-ounce can chopped green chilies, drained

■ Cook grits in boiling water and salt using package directions; remove from heat. Stir in margarine until melted; cool. Add evaporated milk, eggs, cheese and chilies, mixing well. Pour into 8x12-inch baking dish. Bake at 350 degrees for 50 minutes.
Approx Per Serving: Cal 369; Prot 13 g; Carbo 21 g; Fiber 2 g; T Fat 26 g; 63% Calories from Fat; Chol 96 mg; Sod 739 mg.

Ed Verploegh, Mesilla Valley HFH, Mesilla Park, NM

Baked Rice
Yield: 6 servings

1 to 2 cloves of garlic, minced
1 onion, chopped
2/3 cup butter

2 cups brown Basmati rice
1 teaspoon salt
4 cups boiling water

■ Sauté garlic and onion in butter in skillet until tender. Add rice and salt. Sauté until light brown. Spoon into 2-quart baking dish; stir in boiling water. Bake, tightly covered, at 325 degrees for 1¼ hours.
Approx Per Serving: Cal 433; Prot 7 g; Carbo 53 g; Fiber 3 g; T Fat 21 g; 44% Calories from Fat; Chol 55 mg; Sod 528 mg.

Lila Creager, Cottage Grove Area HFH, Cottage Grove, OR

Pulao (Indian-Style Rice)
Yield: 6 servings

1/4 cup margarine
1/2 cup uncooked rice
1 small onion, chopped
1/4 teaspoon cumin
1/4 teaspoon pepper
1 bay leaf
1/2 stick cinnamon

1/8 teaspoon ground cloves
1/2 teaspoon salt
1¼ cups water
8 ounces fresh green peas

■ Melt margarine in skillet over medium heat. Add rice. Cook for 5 minutes or until rice is light brown, stirring often. Add next 7 ingredients. Cook until onion is tender, stirring frequently. Add water. Bring to a boil. Simmer for 5 minutes. Add peas. Cook, covered, for 10 minutes or until rice is tender. Remove bay leaf. May add raisins and cashews 3 minutes before serving.
Approx Per Serving: Cal 161; Prot 3 g; Carbo 19 g; Fiber 2 g; T Fat 8 g; 44% Calories from Fat; Chol 0 mg; Sod 270 mg.

Linda Simonson, Habitat South Central Region, Wilmore, KY

Herbed Tomato Sauce
Yield: 5 servings

2 tablespoons olive oil
1 onion, finely chopped
4 cloves of garlic, crushed
1   28-ounce can tomatoes
1   6-ounce can tomato paste

3 tablespoons sugar
1/8 teaspoon pepper
1 tablespoon Italian seasoning
1 bunch fresh basil, chopped

■ Heat olive oil in skillet. Sauté onion until tender. Add garlic. Sauté until tender but not browned. Add next 5 ingredients. Cook over low heat for 30 minutes, stirring often. Stir in basil.
Approx Per Serving: Cal 151; Prot 3 g; Carbo 24 g; Fiber 4 g; T Fat 6 g; 34% Calories from Fat; Chol 0 mg; Sod 281 mg.

Linda and Richard Dove, MSU Campus Chapter
Starkville, MS

Wheat Delight
Yield: 6 servings

6 cups water
1 teaspoon mace

2 cups coarsely ground wheat

■ Combine water, mace and wheat in saucepan. Bring to a rolling boil, stirring constantly; reduce heat. Simmer for 5 to 10 minutes or until of desired consistency.
Approx Per Serving: Cal 200; Prot 6 g; Carbo 43 g; Fiber 10 g; T Fat 1 g; 4% Calories from Fat; Chol 0 mg; Sod 2 mg.

Robert B. Herchenroeder, HFH of the Kokomo Community
Kokomo, IN

Ditalini and Broccoli
Yield: 6 servings

1 bunch broccoli, cut up
1 clove of garlic, minced
2 tablespoons butter

2 tablespoons olive oil
1 cup ditalini, cooked
Pepper to taste
1 cup grated Romano cheese

■ Cook broccoli in boiling water in saucepan until tender-crisp; drain. Sauté garlic in butter and oil in large skillet. Add broccoli and cooked ditalini. Cook until heated through, stirring often. Add pepper and cheese, stirring to mix.
Approx Per Serving: Cal 177; Prot 8 g; Carbo 9 g; Fiber 2 g; T Fat 13 g; 63% Calories from Fat; Chol 26 mg; Sod 237 mg.

Ann DiLorenzo, Orleans County HFH, Lyndonville, NY

BREADS

"Unless the Lord builds the house, its builders labor in vain."

Psalm 127:1

Angel Flake Biscuits

Yield: 36 servings

1½ envelopes dry yeast
3 tablespoons
   lukewarm water
5 cups flour
1 teaspoon baking soda
1 teaspoon salt

1 tablespoon baking
   powder
3 tablespoons sugar
¾ cup cold butter
2 cups buttermilk

■ Dissolve yeast in lukewarm water. Sift flour, baking soda, salt, baking powder and sugar in bowl; mix well. Cut in butter until crumbly. Add buttermilk and yeast; mix well. Chill for 12 hours to overnight. Pat on lightly floured surface. Do not knead. Cut with biscuit cutter. Place on nonstick baking sheet. Bake at 400 degrees for 12 to 15 minutes or until light brown.
Approx Per Serving: Cal 108; Prot 2 g; Carbo 15 g; Fiber 1 g; T Fat 4 g; 35% Calories from Fat; Chol 11 mg; Sod 157 mg.

Eva G. Reeves, Central Valley HFH, Bridgewater, VA

Carrot-Flecked Biscuits

Yield: 5 servings

The addition of carrots is colorful and adds beta carrotene.

2 cups sifted flour
1 tablespoon baking
   powder
¼ teaspoon salt

¼ cup shortening
¼ cup finely chopped
   carrot
⅔ cup milk

■ Sift flour, baking powder and salt together in bowl; mix well. Cut in shortening and carrot until crumbly. Stir in milk until ingredients are moistened. Pat dough ½ inch thick on lightly floured surface. Cut with biscuit cutter. Place on ungreased baking sheet. Bake at 450 degrees for 15 to 16 minutes or until brown.
Approx Per Serving: Cal 297; Prot 6 g; Carbo 41 g; Fiber 1 g; T Fat 12 g; 36% Calories from Fat; Chol 4 mg; Sod 320 mg.

Jacqueline V. Lone, Mountain Country HFH, Branson, MO

Cloud Biscuits

Yield: 12 servings

2 cups flour
½ teaspoon salt
4 teaspoons baking
   powder

1 tablespoon sugar
½ cup shortening
⅔ cup milk
1 egg, beaten

■ Sift flour, salt, baking powder and sugar in bowl; mix well. Cut in shortening until crumbly. Stir in milk and egg. Knead on lightly floured surface for 3 minutes. Pat dough ½ inch thick; cut with biscuit cutter. Place on nonstick baking sheet. Bake at 450 degrees for 10 to 14 minutes or until golden brown.
Approx Per Serving: Cal 172; Prot 3 g; Carbo 18 g; Fiber 1 g; T Fat 10 g; 51% Calories from Fat; Chol 20 mg; Sod 210 mg.

Stephanie Lenhardt, Deming HFH, Deming, NM

Apricot-Prune Coffee Cake

Yield: 12 servings

½ cup packed brown
   sugar
2 tablespoons butter,
   softened
2 tablespoons flour
1 teaspoon sugar
¾ cup butter, softened
1½ cups sugar
4 eggs
1½ teaspoons vanilla
   extract
1½ teaspoons baking
   powder

3 cups flour
¾ teaspoon baking
   soda
¼ teaspoon salt
1 cup sour cream
¾ cup coarsely
   chopped dried
   apricots
¾ cup coarsely
   chopped dried prunes
3 tablespoons
   confectioners' sugar

■ Combine first 4 ingredients in bowl until crumbly. Beat ¾ cup butter in mixer bowl until light and fluffy. Add sugar; mix well. Beat in eggs 1 at a time. Stir in vanilla. Beat in mixture of baking powder, 3 cups flour, baking soda and salt ⅓ at a time alternately with sour cream. Beat at medium speed for 1 minute. Fold in apricots and prunes. Layer batter and crumb mixture ⅓ at a time in nonstick 12-inch bundt pan. Bake at 350 degrees for 1 hour or until coffee cake tests done. Cool in pan for 20 minutes. Invert onto serving plate. Sprinkle with confectioners' sugar.
Approx Per Serving: Cal 542; Prot 7 g; Carbo 87 g; Fiber 4 g; T Fat 20 g; 32% Calories from Fat; Chol 116 mg; Sod 291 mg.

Nancy MacLeod, HFH of Green County, Monroe, WI

Cherry Coffee Cake

Yield: 12 servings

2 8-count cans crescent rolls
8 ounces cream cheese, softened
1/3 cup confectioners' sugar
1 egg yolk
1/2 teaspoon vanilla extract
1 cup cherry pie filling
1 egg white, slightly beaten
1 recipe confectioners' sugar icing

- Divide crescent roll dough into triangles. Press 12 triangles into round baking pan, leaving 3 inch area in center of pan uncovered. Beat cream cheese, confectioners' sugar, egg yolk and vanilla in mixer bowl until light and fluffy. Spread over prepared layer. Drizzle with pie filling. Cut remaining 4 dough triangles into halves. Place over pie filling to resemble spokes on a wheel. Brush dough with egg white. Bake at 350 degrees for 25 to 30 minutes or until light brown. Drizzle with confectioners' sugar icing.
Approx Per Serving: Cal 276; Prot 4 g; Carbo 33 g; Fiber <1 g; T Fat 14 g; 47% Calories from Fat; Chol 39 mg; Sod 376 mg.

Janet Ostrowski, HFH of Wausau, Wausau, WI

Polish Babka

Yield: 5 servings

My husband's mother made this coffee cake for him when he was a child in pre-war Poland.

1 cup butter, softened
1 cup sugar
5 eggs
1 cup milk
4 cups flour
2 tablespoons baking powder
1/2 cup raisins
2 tablespoons vanilla extract
2 tablespoons confectioners' sugar

- Cream butter and sugar in mixer bowl until light and fluffy. Add mixture of eggs and milk alternately with mixture of flour and baking powder, mixing well after each addition. Fold in raisins with last addition of flour mixture. Stir in vanilla. Spoon into greased and floured tube pan. Bake at 350 degrees for 1 hour or until golden brown. Cool in pan for 10 minutes. Sprinkle with confectioners' sugar when completely cooled.
Approx Per Serving: Cal 345; Prot 6 g; Carbo 46 g; Fiber 1 g; T Fat 15 g; 39% Calories from Fat; Chol 106 mg; Sod 266 mg.

Nora Swierczynski, Greater Springfield, VT Area HFH

Povitica

Yield: 16 servings

2 cakes yeast
1/2 teaspoon sugar
1/2 cup lukewarm water
1/2 cup sugar
1 cup melted butter
6 egg yolks
2/3 cup lukewarm half and half
2/3 cup lukewarm milk
5 cups flour
1 teaspoon salt
1 1/2 pounds ground walnuts
1/2 cup melted butter
1 1/2 cups evaporated milk
1 1/2 cups packed brown sugar
1/2 cup honey
4 egg whites, stiffly beaten
Grated rind of 1/2 lemon
1/2 teaspoon lemon juice
1 teaspoon vanilla extract
1/4 teaspoon cinnamon
3 tablespoons brandy
1 tablespoon cinnamon
1 15-ounce package golden raisins
1 egg, slightly beaten

- Dissolve yeast and 1/2 teaspoon sugar in lukewarm water. Cream 1/2 cup sugar, 1 cup melted butter and egg yolks in mixer bowl until light. Add lukewarm half and half, lukewarm milk and yeast mixture; mix well. Stir in sifted mixture of flour and salt. Knead on lightly floured surface until smooth and elastic. Place in buttered bowl, turning to coat surface. Let rise, covered, in warm place for 2 hours or until doubled in bulk. Cook walnuts, 1/2 cup melted butter, evaporated milk, brown sugar and honey in saucepan over medium heat until of desired consistency. Stir in egg whites, lemon rind, lemon juice, vanilla, 1/4 teaspoon cinnamon and brandy. Roll dough into very thin rectangle on lightly floured surface. Spread filling over entire surface of dough. Sprinkle with 1 tablespoon cinnamon and raisins. Roll as for jelly roll. Place in large baking pan. Let rise for 1 hour or until doubled in bulk. Brush top with egg. Bake at 325 degrees for 1 1/2 hours.
Approx Per Serving: Cal 893; Prot 16 g; Carbo 103 g; Fiber 6 g; T Fat 50 g; 48% Calories from Fat; Chol 152 mg; Sod 352 mg.

Sister Teri Wall, HFH International, Great Bend, KS

Easy Coffee Cake
Yield: 12 servings

½ cup packed brown
  sugar
2 teaspoons cinnamon
2 tablespoons flour
2 tablespoons oil
½ cup chopped pecans
2 eggs, beaten

1 cup sugar
2 cups flour
4 teaspoons baking
  powder
1 teaspoon salt
1 cup milk
¼ cup oil

■ Combine brown sugar, cinnamon, 2 tablespoons flour, 2 tablespoons oil and pecans in bowl; mix well. Set aside. Beat eggs and sugar in mixer bowl until smooth. Add mixture of flour, baking powder and salt alternately with milk, mixing well after each addition. Add ¼ cup oil; mix well. Spoon into greased 9x13-inch baking pan. Sprinkle with brown sugar mixture. Bake at 375 degrees for 20 to 25 minutes or until coffee cake tests done.

Approx Per Serving: Cal 308; Prot 4 g; Carbo 47 g; Fiber 1 g; T Fat 12 g; 35% Calories from Fat; Chol 38 mg; Sod 313 mg.

John McNabb, Cornell University Campus Chapter
Ithaca, NY

Norwegian Kringlar
Yield: 18 servings

1 cup flour
½ cup butter, softened
1 cup plus 2
  tablespoons water
½ cup butter
1 cup flour
3 eggs
½ teaspoon almond
  extract

1 cup confectioners'
  sugar
1 tablespoon half and
  half
1 tablespoon butter,
  softened
1 teaspoon almond
  extract
½ cup sliced almonds

■ Mix 1 cup flour, ½ cup butter and 2 tablespoons water in bowl until crumbly. Pat into two 3x10-inch strips on nonstick 10x15-inch baking sheet. Bring 1 cup water and ½ cup butter to a rolling boil in saucepan. Remove from heat. Stir in 1 cup flour until smooth. Add eggs 1 at a time, mixing well after each addition. Stir in ½ teaspoon almond flavoring. Spread mixture over entire surface of dough strips. Bake at 375 degrees for 45 minutes or until golden brown. Frost cooled bread with mixture of confectioners' sugar, half and half, 1 tablespoon butter, 1 teaspoon almond flavoring and almonds. Chill until firm. Store, lightly covered, at room temperature.

Approx Per Serving: Cal 202; Prot 3 g; Carbo 18 g; Fiber 1 g; T Fat 13 g; 59% Calories from Fat; Chol 65 mg; Sod 104 mg.

Marlene Tobias, Black Hills Area HFH, Rapid City, SD

Holiday Nut Rolls
Yield: 36 servings

½ cake yeast
½ teaspoon sugar
¼ cup lukewarm water
3 eggs
½ cup sugar
1 teaspoon salt
1 teaspoon vanilla
  extract
5 cups flour
¾ cup melted
  margarine, cooled

1 cup warm milk
6 cups ground pecans
1 cup honey
½ cup sugar
1 teaspoon vanilla
  extract
1 to 2 tablespoons
  orange juice
1 egg, beaten
2 tablespoons water

■ Dissolve yeast and ½ teaspoon sugar in lukewarm water. Combine 3 eggs, ½ cup sugar, salt and 1 teaspoon vanilla in mixer bowl, beating until blended. Add flour, margarine and warm milk; mix well. Stir in yeast mixture. Knead on lightly floured surface until smooth and elastic. Place in greased bowl, turning to coat surface. Let rise for 1½ hours or until doubled in bulk. Divide into 6 portions. Roll into 6 rectangles. Combine pecans, honey, ½ cup sugar and 1 teaspoon vanilla in bowl; mix well. Add enough orange juice to make of spreading consistency. Spread over dough. Roll each portion as for jelly roll, sealing edge and ends. Place on greased baking sheet. Brush with mixture of egg and water. Let rise for 40 minutes. Bake at 350 degrees for 30 minutes. Remove to wire rack to cool completely.

Approx Per Serving: Cal 401; Prot 6 g; Carbo 34 g; Fiber 3 g; T Fat 29 g; 63% Calories from Fat; Chol 25 mg; Sod 116 mg.

Alice Skander, HFH of Butler County, Mars, PA

Rhubarb Coffee Cake

Yield: 12 servings

2 cups flour
1 teaspoon baking soda
1 teaspoon cinnamon
Salt to taste
1/2 cup shortening
1 1/2 cups packed
  brown sugar
1 egg

1 cup sour milk
1 teaspoon vanilla
  extract
1 1/2 cups finely
  chopped rhubarb
1/2 cup sugar
1 teaspoon cinnamon
1/2 cup chopped walnuts

- Sift flour, baking soda, 1 teaspoon cinnamon and salt together. Cream shortening and brown sugar in mixer bowl until light and fluffy. Add egg; mix well. Add dry ingredients alternately with sour milk, mixing well after each addition. Stir in vanilla. Fold in rhubarb. Spoon into greased 9x13-inch baking pan. Sprinkle with mixture of sugar, 1 teaspoon cinnamon and walnuts. Bake at 350 degrees for 40 minutes or until coffee cake tests done.

Approx Per Serving: Cal 366; Prot 4 g; Carbo 60 g; Fiber 1 g; T Fat 13 g; 31% Calories from Fat; Chol 21 mg; Sod 100 mg.

Marian E. Smith, Dixon HFH, Dixon, IL

Sour Cream Coffee Cake

Yield: 24 servings

Do not bake on a humid day.

3 tablespoons
  margarine, softened
1/3 cup chopped pecans
1/2 cup packed brown
  sugar
1 teaspoon vanilla
  extract
3/4 cup sugar

1/2 cup oil
3 eggs, beaten
2 cups flour
1 teaspoon baking
  powder
1 teaspoon baking soda
1/4 teaspoon salt
1 cup sour cream

- Stir margarine, pecans and brown sugar in bowl until crumbly. Set aside. Beat vanilla, sugar, oil and eggs in mixer bowl until smooth. Add mixture of flour, baking powder, baking soda and salt alternately with sour cream, mixing well after each addition. Layer batter and crumb mixture 1/2 at a time in greased tube pan. Bake at 350 degrees for 50 minutes or until coffee cake tests done.

Approx Per Serving: Cal 178; Prot 2 g; Carbo 21 g; Fiber <1 g; T Fat 10 g; 49% Calories from Fat; Chol 31 mg; Sod 103 mg.

HelenSue L. Parrish, Starkville HFH, Starkville, MS

Swedish Coffee Cake

Yield: 10 servings

1/2 cup water
1/2 cup margarine
1 1/3 cups sugar
2 eggs
1 teaspoon baking
  powder
1 1/3 cups flour

1/2 to 1 teaspoon
  almond extract
1/4 cup margarine
1/4 cup sugar
1 tablespoon flour
1 tablespoon water
1/2 cup sliced almonds

- Bring 1/2 cup water and 1/2 cup margarine to a boil in saucepan; mix well. Remove from heat. Beat 1 1/3 cups sugar and eggs in mixer bowl until blended. Add margarine mixture; mix well. Stir in mixture of baking powder and flour. Add almond extract; mix well. Spoon into greased and floured 9-inch bundt pan. Bake at 350 degrees for 30 minutes or until coffee cake tests done. Cool in pan for several minutes. Invert onto ovenproof plate. Melt 1/4 cup margarine in saucepan. Add 1/4 cup sugar and mixture of 1 tablespoon flour and 1 tablespoon water. Bring to a boil. Boil for 3 to 5 minutes, stirring constantly. Pour over warm coffee cake; sprinkle with almonds. Broil until brown.

Approx Per Serving: Cal 352; Prot 4 g; Carbo 46 g; Fiber 1 g; T Fat 17 g; 44% Calories from Fat; Chol 43 mg; Sod 209 mg.

Patritia Kiley, Greater Lawrence HFH, Andover, MA

*H*ow we build is just as important as what we build. Habitat houses are built with a contribution of hundreds of hours of "sweat equity" labor on the part of the homeowners. By investing themselves in the building process, homeowners gain self-reliance, self-esteem and new skills.

Walnut Wonder Cake

Yield: 15 servings

1/3 cup packed brown
  sugar
1/2 cup sugar
1 teaspoon cinnamon
1 cup chopped walnuts
1 cup margarine,
  softened
1 cup sugar

2 eggs
1 teaspoon vanilla
  extract
1 cup sour cream
2 cups flour
1 teaspoon baking
  powder
1/2 teaspoon salt

- Combine brown sugar, 1/2 cup sugar, cinnamon and walnuts in bowl; mix well. Cream margarine and 1 cup sugar in mixer bowl until light and fluffy. Add eggs and vanilla; mix well. Add sour cream alternately with sifted mixture of flour, baking powder and salt, mixing well after each addition. Layer batter and brown sugar mixture 1/2 at a time in nonstick 9x13-inch baking pan. Bake at 350 degrees for 35 minutes.
Approx Per Serving: Cal 364; Prot 4 g; Carbo 41 g; Fiber 1 g; T Fat 21 g; 51% Calories from Fat; Chol 35 mg; Sod 257 mg.

Mary Ann Hubbs, HFH of Metro Louisville, Louisville, KY

Grandma's Doughnuts

Yield: 12 servings

3 cups flour
4 teaspoons baking
  powder
1 teaspoon nutmeg
1/2 teaspoon mace
3/4 teaspoon salt
1 1/2 tablespoons butter,
  softened

1 1/2 tablespoons
  margarine, softened
2/3 cup sugar
1 egg, beaten
2/3 cup milk
1 teaspoon vanilla
  extract
Oil for deep frying

- Sift flour, baking powder, nutmeg, mace and salt together. Cream butter, margarine and sugar in mixer bowl until light and fluffy. Add egg, milk and vanilla; mix well. Add dry ingredients; mix well. Roll dough 1/4 inch thick on lightly floured surface. Cut with doughnut cutter. Deep-fry in 375-degree oil, turning once to brown on both sides. Drain on paper towels.
Approx Per Serving: Cal 199; Prot 4 g; Carbo 36 g; Fiber 1 g; T Fat 4 g; 19% Calories from Fat; Chol 24 mg; Sod 284 mg.
Nutritional information does not include oil for deep frying.

Lois M. Faler, Benton HFH, Corvallis, OR

Sour Cream Doughnuts

Yield: 36 servings

2 teaspoons baking
  powder
1 teaspoon baking soda
1/2 teaspoon nutmeg
1 teaspoon salt
3 cups flour
3 eggs, beaten

1 cup sugar
1 teaspoon vanilla
  extract
3/4 cup sour cream
1/2 cup skim milk
Oil for deep frying

- Mix baking powder,, baking soda, nutmeg, salt and flour together. Beat eggs, sugar and vanilla in mixer bowl until blended. Add sour cream and skim milk; mix well. Stir in dry ingredients. Spoon into doughnut maker. Deep-fry in 375-degree oil, turning to brown on both sides. Drain on paper towels.
Approx Per Serving: Cal 78; Prot 2 g; Carbo 14 g; Fiber <1 g; T Fat 2 g; 18% Calories from Fat; Chol 20 mg; Sod 111 mg.
Nutritional information does not include oil for deep frying.

Wilma Carlsrud, Fergus Falls Area HFH, Fergus Falls, MN

Cinnamon-Crunch French Toast

Yield: 8 servings

6 eggs, beaten
1 teaspoon vanilla
  extract
8 thick slices round
  sourdough bread,
  cut into halves

4 cups crushed
  cornflakes
2 teaspoons cinnamon
2 tablespoons
  confectioners' sugar

- Combine eggs and vanilla in bowl; mix well. Dip bread slices in egg mixture. Coat with mixture of cornflakes and cinnamon. Bake on lightly buttered griddle until brown on both sides, turning once. Sprinkle with confectioners' sugar. Serve with warm maple syrup.
Approx Per Serving: Cal 293; Prot 11 g; Carbo 49 g; Fiber 1 g; T Fat 6 g; 17% Calories from Fat; Chol 160 mg; Sod 688 mg.

Cindy Schultz, South Puget Sound HFH, Olympia, WA

Apricot Loaf

Yield: 12 servings

1 cup dried apricots
1 egg
1 cup sugar
2 tablespoons shortening
1/4 cup water
1/2 cup orange juice

2 cups sifted flour
2 teaspoons baking powder
1/4 teaspoon baking soda
1 teaspoon salt
1 cup chopped walnuts

■ Soak apricots in enough water to cover in bowl for several minutes; drain. Cut apricots into quarters with scissors. Combine egg, sugar and shortening in mixer bowl until blended. Add 1/4 cup water and orange juice; mix well. Stir in sifted mixture of flour, baking powder, baking soda and salt. Fold in walnuts and apricots. Spoon into greased and floured 5x9-inch loaf pan. Bake at 350 degrees for 55 to 65 minutes or until loaf tests done. Remove to wire rack to cool.
Approx Per Serving: Cal 255; Prot 4 g; Carbo 41 g; Fiber 2 g; T Fat 9 g; 31% Calories from Fat; Chol 18 mg; Sod 258 mg.

Catherine Kooistra, Lakeshore HFH, Holland, MI

Banana-Chocolate-Nut Bread

Yield: 12 servings

4 large bananas, mashed
1/4 cup oil
1 teaspoon vanilla extract
1/2 cup sugar
1/2 teaspoon nutmeg
2 tablespoons milk
2 eggs, beaten

1 cup all-purpose flour
3/4 cup whole wheat flour
1 1/4 teaspoons baking powder
1/2 teaspoon baking soda
1/2 cup chopped pecans
1 cup chocolate chips

■ Combine bananas, oil, vanilla, sugar and nutmeg in bowl; mix well. Blend in milk and eggs. Add flours, baking powder and baking soda; mix well. Fold in pecans and chocolate chips. Spoon into lightly greased 5x9-inch loaf pan. Bake at 350 degrees for 1 hour Remove to wire rack to cool.
Approx Per Serving: Cal 290; Prot 5 g; Carbo 40 g; Fiber 3 g; T Fat 14 g; 42% Calories from Fat; Chol 36 mg; Sod 84 mg.

Barbara Schultz, HFH of Chico, Paradise, CA

Banana-Nut Bread

Yield: 12 servings

1 2/3 cups sugar
2/3 cup oil
2 eggs
1/3 cup buttermilk
1 1/2 teaspoons baking soda
1 1/2 teaspoons baking powder

2 1/2 cups flour
1/2 teaspoon salt
1 1/2 cups mashed bananas
2 cups chopped walnuts

■ Cream sugar, oil and eggs in mixer bowl until light and fluffy. Add mixture of buttermilk and baking soda; mix well. Add baking powder, flour and salt; mix well. Fold in bananas and walnuts. Spoon into greased and floured 5x9-inch loaf pan. Bake at 300 degrees for 1 hour or until loaf tests done. Remove to wire rack to cool.
Approx Per Serving: Cal 480; Prot 7 g; Carbo 58 g; Fiber 2 g; T Fat 26 g; 47% Calories from Fat; Chol 36 mg; Sod 255 mg.

Neva Hagemeier, Knox County HFH, Freelandville, IN

Best-Ever Banana Bread

Yield: 24 servings

2 cups sugar
2 1/2 cups cake flour
2 teaspoons baking soda

1 teaspoon salt
1 cup butter, softened
6 ripe bananas, mashed
4 eggs, beaten

■ Sift sugar, cake flour and baking soda together 3 times. Cream salt and butter in mixer bowl until light and fluffy. Add bananas and eggs; mix well. Stir in sugar mixture just until moistened. Spoon into 2 greased and floured 5x9-inch loaf pans. Bake at 350 degrees for 45 to 60 minutes or until loaves test done. Cool in pans for 10 minutes. Remove to wire rack to cool completely.
Approx Per Serving: Cal 213; Prot 2 g; Carbo 32 g; Fiber 1 g; T Fat 9 g; 37% Calories from Fat; Chol 56 mg; Sod 234 mg.

Jeanette Dollar, Peach Area HFH, Fort Valley, GA

Blu'Bana Bread
Yield: 24 servings

1 cup butter, softened
2 cups sugar
4 eggs
2 teaspoons vanilla
  extract
5 bananas, mashed
4 cups sifted kflour
2 cups fresh or frozen
  blueberries, drained

2 teaspoons baking
  soda
1 teaspoon baking
  powder
1 tablespoon allspice
1/2 teaspoon salt

■ Cream butter and sugar in mixer bowl until light and fluffy. Beat in eggs and vanilla. Fold in bananas and 2 cups flour; mix well. Toss blueberries with 2 tablespoons of the remaining flour in bowl. Sift remaining flour, baking soda, baking powder, allspice and salt together. Fold sifted mixture and blueberries into batter. Spoon into 2 greased and floured loaf pans. Bake at 325 degrees for 50 minutes or until bread tests done. Remove to wire rack to cool.
Approx Per Serving: Cal 250; Prot 4 g; Carbo 40 g; Fiber 1 g; T Fat 9 g; 32% Calories from Fat; Chol 56 mg; Sod 204 mg.

Gerald and Betty Ford, Former President and First Lady
Rancho Mirage, CA

Cream Cheese-Banana Bread
Yield: 12 servings

1 cup sugar
8 ounces cream cheese,
  softened
1 cup mashed bananas

2 eggs
2 cups buttermilk
  baking mix
1/2 cup chopped pecans

■ Cream sugar and cream cheese in mixer bowl until light and fluffy. Add bananas and eggs; mix well. Stir in baking mix and pecans just until moistened. Spoon into greased 5x9-inch loaf pan. Bake at 350 degrees for 45 minutes. Cover with foil. Bake for 15 minutes longer or until loaf tests done. Remove to wire rack to cool completely.
Approx Per Serving: Cal 284; Prot 5 g; Carbo 37 g; Fiber 1 g; T Fat 14 g; 43% Calories from Fat; Chol 56 mg; Sod 333 mg.

Paula Krivchenia, Ashland-Ironton HFH, Ashland, KY

Coconut Bread
Yield: 24 servings

2 envelopes dry yeast
1/2 cup lukewarm water
1 14-ounce can
   coconut milk

1/2 cup sugar
1 teaspoon salt
1/2 cup oil
4 to 6 cups flour

■ Dissolve yeast in lukewarm water. Combine coconut milk, sugar, salt and oil in bowl; mix well. Stir in yeast. Add 2 cups flour, beating until smooth and elastic. Knead in remaining flour 1/2 cup at a time until dough is no longer sticky. Let rise in warm place until doubled in bulk. Shape into 2 loaves. Place on greased baking sheet. Let rise until doubled in bulk. Bake at 350 degrees for 30 minutes or until golden brown. Remove to wire rack to cool.
Approx Per Serving: Cal 204; Prot 4 g; Carbo 29 g; Fiber 1 g; T Fat 8 g; 37% Calories from Fat; Chol 0 mg; Sod 92 mg.

Alene Campbell, HFH of Butler County, Chicora, PA

Grandma Josie's Date Loaf
Yield: 12 servings

1 pound dates, chopped
1 pound whole pecans
1 cup flour
2 teaspoons baking
  powder

1/2 teaspoon salt
1 cup sugar
4 eggs, beaten
1 teaspoon vanilla
  extract

■ Combine dates, pecans, flour, baking powder, salt and sugar in bowl; mix well. Add eggs and vanilla, stirring just until moistened. Spoon into nonstick 5x9-inch loaf pan. Bake at 325 degrees for 2 hours or until loaf tests done. Remove to wire rack to cool.
Approx Per Serving: Cal 485; Prot 7 g; Carbo 60 g; Fiber 6 g; T Fat 28 g; 48% Calories from Fat; Chol 71 mg; Sod 169 mg.

Heath Kostecki, Northern Straits HFH, Cedarville, MI

Food Processor French Bread

Yield: 36 servings

French bread pans are available in kitchen specialty shops.

6 cups bread flour
1 tablespoon sugar
1 tablespoon (scant) salt

2 tablespoons RapidRise yeast
2¹/₂ cups water

- Combine bread flour, sugar, salt and yeast in food processor container. Add water, processing constantly until dough is smooth and elastic. Let rise, covered, until doubled in bulk. Punch dough down. Let rise, covered, until doubled in bulk. Divide into 3 portions. Let rest for 10 minutes. Shape into 3 long loaves. Place on greased baking sheet or in 3 French bread pans. Let rise until doubled in bulk. Bake at 400 degrees for 30 minutes or until bread sounds hollow when tapped. Remove to wire rack to cool.

Approx Per Serving: Cal 78; Prot 2 g; Carbo 16 g; Fiber 1 g; T Fat <1 g; 3% Calories from Fat; Chol 0 mg; Sod 178 mg.

Liz Hoff, Fergus Falls Area HFH, Fergus Falls, MN

Natural Fruit Bread

Yield: 12 servings

1 cup rye flour
¹/₂ cup whole wheat flour
¹/₂ cup barley flour
¹/₄ cup oats
2 teaspoons baking powder
¹/₂ teaspoon cinnamon
¹/₈ teaspoon each nutmeg, cloves and ginger
¹/₄ teaspoon salt
2 tablespoons walnut halves

2 tablespoons filbert halves
2 tablespoons each whole dried apricots, figs and pitted prunes
2 tablespoons raisins
¹/₄ cup oil
¹/₃ cup water
¹/₄ cup frozen apple juice concentrate
1 teaspoon vanilla extract

- Combine flours, oats, baking powder, spices and salt in large bowl; mix well. Stir in walnuts, filberts and fruit. Add mixture of oil, water, apple juice concentrate and vanilla; mix well. Spoon into nonstick 5x9-inch loaf pan. Bake at 350 degrees for 35 to 45 minutes or until loaf tests done. Remove to wire rack to cool.

Approx Per Serving: Cal 168; Prot 3 g; Carbo 24 g; Fiber 4 g; T Fat 7 g; 38% Calories from Fat; Chol 0 mg; Sod 102 mg.

Lonnie and SueAnn Belknap, Benton HFH-Partner Family
Corvallis, OR

No-Knead Cheese Bread

Yield: 24 servings

We love it warm or toasted.

1 envelope dry yeast
¹/₄ cup lukewarm water
1¹/₄ cups milk, scalded
1³/₄ teaspoons salt
5 tablespoons sugar

¹/₄ cup melted butter
2 eggs, beaten
4¹/₂ cups flour
5 ounces Cheddar cheese, shredded

- Dissolve yeast in lukewarm water. Combine hot milk, salt and sugar in bowl; mix well. Stir in butter and eggs. Cool to lukewarm. Stir in yeast. Beat in flour until smooth. Let rise, covered, in warm place until doubled in bulk. Stir batter down. Add cheese; mix well. Spoon into 2 greased 5x9-inch loaf pans. Let rise until doubled in bulk. Bake at 350 degrees for 30 minutes. Remove to wire rack to cool.

Approx Per Serving: Cal 151; Prot 5 g; Carbo 21 g; Fiber 1 g; T Fat 5 g; 30% Calories from Fat; Chol 31 mg; Sod 220 mg.

Cheryl Sneller, Newaygo HFH, Fremont, MI

Scooping up freshly-made stucco from a wheelbarrow, two volunteers work side-by-side with a Tijuana homeowner family finishing the walls of their new home.

Herb-Parmesan Casserole Bread
Yield: 24 servings

2 envelopes dry yeast
2 cups 105 to
　115-degree water
2 teaspoons sugar
2 teaspoons salt
2 tablespoons butter,
　softened

1/2 cup grated
　Parmesan cheese
1 1/2 tablespoons
　oregano
4 1/4 cups sifted flour
1 tablespoon grated
　Parmesan cheese

■ Sprinkle yeast over lukewarm water in mixer bowl. Let stand for a few minutes; stir to dissolve. Add sugar, salt, butter, 1/2 cup Parmesan cheese, oregano and 3 cups flour. Beat at low speed until smooth. Beat at high speed for 2 minutes. Beat in remaining flour gradually with wooden spoon. Let rise, covered with waxed paper and towel, in warm place for 45 minutes or until doubled in bulk. Stir batter down. Beat vigorously for 30 seconds or for 25 strokes. Spoon into greased 1 1/2 to 2-quart baking dish. Sprinkle with 1 tablespoon Parmesan cheese. Bake at 375 degrees for 55 minutes or until golden brown. Remove to wire rack to cool.
Approx Per Serving: Cal 95; Prot 3 g; Carbo 16 g; Fiber 1 g; T Fat 2 g; 17% Calories from Fat; Chol 4 mg; Sod 222 mg.

Marilyn Boron, HFH of San Fernando/Santa Clarita Valleys
Santa Clarita, CA

Old-Fashioned Honey-Wheat Bread
Yield: 24 servings

2 envelopes dry yeast
1 cup lukewarm water
1 teaspoon salt
1/2 cup honey
2 tablespoons
　shortening

1 cup milk, scalded
3 cups whole wheat
　flour
3 cups all-purpose
　flour

■ Dissolve yeast in lukewarm water. Combine salt, honey, shortening and milk in bowl; mix well. Cool to lukewarm. Stir in yeast. Add flours, stirring until a stiff dough forms. Knead on lightly floured surface until smooth and elastic. Place in greased bowl, turning to coat surface. Let rise, covered, until doubled in bulk. Shape into 2 loaves. Place in 2 greased 5x9-inch loaf pans. Let rise until doubled in bulk. Bake at 350 degrees for 50 to 60 minutes or until golden brown. Remove to wire rack to cool.
Approx Per Serving: Cal 146; Prot 4 g; Carbo 29 g; Fiber 2 g; T Fat 2 g; 11% Calories from Fat; Chol 1 mg; Sod 95 mg.

Mary Fleming, Pensacola HFH, Pensacola, FL

Irish Soda Bread
Yield: 12 servings

In Ireland, they do not use caraway seed or egg in this bread.

2 cups raisins
2 tablespoons caraway
　seed
5 cups sifted flour
1 teaspoon baking soda
1 1/2 tablespoons
　baking powder
1 1/2 teaspoons salt

1 cup sugar
3 tablespoons butter,
　softened
2 1/2 cups buttermilk
1 egg, slightly beaten
2 tablespoons melted
　butter
1 tablespoon sugar

■ Coat raisins and caraway seed with 1/4 cup flour in small bowl. Combine remaining flour, baking soda, baking powder, salt and 1 cup sugar in large bowl. Cut in 3 tablespoons butter until crumbly. Stir in raisins and caraway seed. Add mixture of buttermilk and egg; mix well. Knead on lightly floured surface until smooth and elastic. Divide into 2 portions. Shape into 2 round loaves. Place on greased baking sheet or in two 8-inch round baking pans. Make a cross in top of each loaf. Brush with 2 tablespoons butter; sprinkle with 1 tablespoon sugar. Bake at 350 degrees for 1 hour. Remove to wire rack to cool. This is best if you toast it.
Approx Per Serving: Cal 400; Prot 8 g; Carbo 79 g; Fiber 3 g; T Fat 6 g; 14% Calories from Fat; Chol 33 mg; Sod 563 mg.

Mary Clare Freeman, HFH of Wausau, Wausau, WI

Jim's Lefse

Yield: 24 servings

5 pounds red potatoes,
  cooked, peeled,
  mashed
1/4 cup sugar

1 teaspoon salt
1 cup butter
4 cups flour

- Combine potatoes, sugar, salt, butter and flour in bowl, stirring until mixture forms a ball. Chill in refrigerator. Roll into 6 to 8-inch circles 1/8 inch thick on lightly floured surface. Bake on 450-degree non-stick griddle for 20 seconds on each side or until light brown. Remove to plate; cover with towel.

Approx Per Serving: Cal 234; Prot 4 g; Carbo 37 g; Fiber 2 g; T Fat 8 g; 30% Calories from Fat; Chol 21 mg; Sod 158 mg.

Jim and Karen Hoiness, Rogue Valley HFH, Ashland, OR

Oatmeal Bread

Yield: 12 servings

1 1/2 cups boiling water
1 cup quick-cooking
  oats
1/2 cup margarine,
  softened
1 cup sugar
1 cup packed brown
  sugar

2 eggs
1 teaspoon vanilla
  extract
1 3/4 cups flour
1 teaspoon baking soda
1/2 teaspoon salt
1 teaspoon cinnamon

- Pour boiling water over oats in bowl; set aside. Cream margarine, sugar and brown sugar in mixer bowl until light and fluffy. Beat in eggs 1 at a time. Add vanilla; mix well. Add mixture of flour, baking soda, salt and cinnamon; mix well. Stir in oats. Spoon into greased and floured 5x9-inch loaf pan. Bake at 350 degrees for 1 hour or until loaf tests done. Cool in pan for 10 minutes. Remove to wire rack to cool completely.

Approx Per Serving: Cal 323; Prot 4 g; Carbo 57 g; Fiber 1 g; T Fat 9 g; 25% Calories from Fat; Chol 36 mg; Sod 269 mg.

Nancy Moldin, Greenville/Pitt HFH, Greenville, NC

Onion-Dill Bread

Yield: 12 servings

1 1/2 cups flour
1 envelope dry yeast
1 1/4 cups milk
2 tablespoons sugar
1 teaspoon salt
2 tablespoons
  margarine

2 teaspoons dillseed
2 teaspoons dried
  minced onion
1 egg
1 1/2 cups flour

- Combine 1 1/2 cups flour and yeast in mixer bowl; mix well. Heat milk, sugar, salt, margarine, dillseed and onion in saucepan until margarine melts, stirring constantly. Add to flour mixture; mix well. Add egg. Beat at low speed for 30 seconds. Beat at high speed for 2 minutes. Stir in 1 1/2 cups flour by hand. Let rise, covered, for 20 minutes. Punch dough down. Spread in greased 5x9-inch loaf pan. Let rise for 30 minutes. Bake at 375 degrees for 35 to 40 minutes or until golden brown. Remove to wire rack to cool.

Approx Per Serving: Cal 163; Prot 5 g; Carbo 28 g; Fiber 1 g; T Fat 4 g; 20% Calories from Fat; Chol 21 mg; Sod 217 mg.

Joyce P. Fuller, Central Valley HFH, Bridgewater, VA

Easy Poppy Seed Bread

Yield: 24 servings

1 2-layer package
  yellow cake mix
1 4-ounce package
  lemon instant
  pudding mix

1/2 cup oil
1/4 cup poppy seed
1 cup hot water
4 eggs

- Combine cake mix, pudding mix, oil, poppy seed, hot water and eggs in mixer bowl; mix well. Beat at high speed for 4 minutes. Spoon into 2 greased and floured 5x9-inch loaf pans. Bake at 350 degrees for 30 minutes or until loaves test done. Remove to wire rack to cool.

Approx Per Serving: Cal 170; Prot 2 g; Carbo 23 g; Fiber <1 g; T Fat 8 g; 42% Calories from Fat; Chol 36 mg; Sod 174 mg.

Jayne Gibbon
Univ. of Wisconsin-Stevens Point Campus Chapter
Montfort, WI

Poppy Seed Holiday Bread

Yield: 24 servings

3 cups flour
1¹/₂ teaspoons salt
1¹/₂ teaspoons baking
   powder
2¹/₂ cups sugar
2 tablespoons poppy
   seed
1¹/₂ teaspoons almond
   extract
1¹/₂ teaspoons vanilla
   extract

3 eggs
1¹/₂ cups milk
1¹/₃ cups oil
6 tablespoons sugar
¹/₄ teaspoon almond
   extract
2 tablespoons orange
   juice
2 tablespoons melted
   margarine

■ Combine flour, salt, baking powder, 2¹/₂ cups sugar, poppy seed, flavorings, eggs, milk and oil in mixer bowl. Beat at medium speed until mixed. Spoon into 2 greased and floured 5x9-inch loaf pans. Bake at 350 degrees for 1¹/₄ hours or until loaves test done. Brush hot loaves with mixture of 6 tablespoons sugar, ¹/₄ teaspoon almond extract, orange juice and margarine.
Approx Per Serving: Cal 289; Prot 3 g; Carbo 37 g; Fiber <1 g; T Fat 15 g; 45% Calories from Fat; Chol 29 mg; Sod 181 mg.

Martha Monroe, First Presbyterian Church, Jefferson, IA

Holiday Pumpkin Bread

Yield: 12 servings

1²/₃ cups flour
1¹/₄ cups sugar
1 teaspoon baking soda
¹/₂ teaspoon cinnamon
¹/₂ teaspoon nutmeg
¹/₄ teaspoon salt

¹/₂ cup oil
2 eggs
1 cup canned pumpkin
¹/₂ cup chopped
   candied cherries
¹/₂ cup chopped pecans

■ Sift flour, sugar, baking soda, cinnamon, nutmeg and salt together. Combine oil, eggs and pumpkin; mix well. Stir in dry ingredients. Fold in cherries and pecans. Spoon into greased 5x9-inch loaf pan. Bake at 350 degrees for 1 hour or until loaf tests done. Remove to wire rack to cool.
Approx Per Serving: Cal 307; Prot 4 g; Carbo 44 g; Fiber 1 g; T Fat 14 g; 39% Calories from Fat; Chol 36 mg; Sod 126 mg.

Carol Brenneman, Highlands County HFH, Sebring, FL

Pumpkin Bread

Yield: 12 servings

3¹/₃ cups flour
3 cups sugar
2 teaspoons baking
   soda
1¹/₂ teaspoons salt
1¹/₂ tablespoons
   cinnamon

1 16-ounce can
   pumpkin
1 cup oil
²/₃ cup water
4 eggs, slightly beaten

■ Combine flour, sugar, baking soda, salt and cinnamon in mixer bowl; mix well. Add pumpkin, oil, water and eggs. Beat at medium speed for 2 minutes. Spoon into nonstick 5x9-inch loaf pan. Bake at 350 degrees for 1 hour. Cover with foil. Bake for 45 minutes longer or until loaf tests done. Cool in pan for 10 minutes. Remove to wire rack to cool completely.
Approx Per Serving: Cal 519; Prot 6 g; Carbo 79 g; Fiber 2 g; T Fat 21 g; 35% Calories from Fat; Chol 71 mg; Sod 430 mg.

Cherie Holcombe, Mountain Country HFH, Branson, MO

"Home for the Holidays" takes on new meaning for the Habitat homeowner.

Pumpkin Pie Bread

Yield: 36 servings

3¹/₂ cups flour
¹/₂ teaspoon baking powder
1 teaspoon salt
¹/₄ teaspoon nutmeg
¹/₄ teaspoon allspice
¹/₂ teaspoon cinnamon
1 teaspoon baking soda
2³/₄ cups sugar
1 cup shortening
3 eggs
2 cups mashed pumpkin
³/₄ cup chopped pecans

■ Combine first 7 ingredients. Cream sugar, shortening and eggs in mixer bowl. Add pumpkin; mix well. Stir in flour mixture. Fold in pecans. Spoon into 3 nonstick 5x9-inch loaf pans. Bake at 315 degrees for 1¹/₄ hours or until loaves test done. Remove to wire rack to cool.
Approx Per Serving: Cal 181; Prot 2 g; Carbo 26 g; Fiber 1 g; T Fat 8 g; 39% Calories from Fat; Chol 18 mg; Sod 94 mg.

Charlene McArthur, Odessa HFH, Mayview, MO

Quick Pumpkin Bread

Yield: 36 servings

1 21-ounce can pumpkin pie filling
2 16-ounce packages pound cake mix
4 eggs
²/₃ cup milk
1 teaspoon nutmeg
1 teaspoon cinnamon
1 cup chopped pecans

■ Combine first 6 ingredients in mixer bowl. Beat at low speed until moistened. Beat at medium speed for 3 minutes. Stir in pecans. Spoon into 3 greased and floured 5x9-inch loaf pans. Bake at 325 degrees for 1 to 1¹/₄ hours. Cool in pans for 20 minutes. Remove to wire rack to cool completely.
Approx Per Serving: Cal 205; Prot 3 g; Carbo 32 g; Fiber <1 g; T Fat 7 g; 31% Calories from Fat; Chol 24 mg; Sod 210 mg.

John D. Lawther, Morgan County HFH, Brush, CO

Swedish Limpe Bread

Yield: 24 servings

1 envelope dry yeast
1 tablespoon lukewarm water
2 cups water
¹/₂ cup packed brown sugar
2 teaspoons caraway seed
2 tablespoons shortening
1 teaspoon aniseed
4 cups all-purpose flour
2 teaspoons salt
2 cups rye flour

■ Dissolve yeast in 1 tablespoon water. Bring next 5 ingredients to a boil in saucepan. Cool. Stir in yeast. Add enough all-purpose flour to make consistency of muffin batter, beating until smooth. Stir in remaining all-purpose flour, salt and rye flour until dough pulls from side of bowl. Knead until smooth. Let rise until doubled. Punch down. Let rise until doubled. Punch down. Shape into 2 loaves. Place in 2 greased 5x9-inch loaf pans. Let rise again. Slash tops diagonally. Bake at 400 degrees for 20 minutes; turn. Bake for 5 minutes.
Approx Per Serving: Cal 140; Prot 3 g; Carbo 29 g; Fiber 2 g; T Fat 1 g; 9% Calories from Fat; Chol 0 mg; Sod 181 mg.

Ruth Dettinger, HFH of Wausau, Wausau, WI

Swedish Rye Bread

Yield: 24 servings

2 cups water
¹/₂ cup packed brown sugar
1 teaspoon salt
1 teaspoon caraway seed
1 teaspoon anise
1 tablespoon shortening
1 ounce yeast
3¹/₂ cups all-purpose flour
2 cups rye flour

■ Combine first 6 ingredients in saucepan; mix well. Cook for 3 minutes, stirring constantly. Cool to lukewarm. Add yeast; mix well. Stir in all-purpose flour. Let rise for 1¹/₂ hours. Stir in rye flour. Knead lightly. Place in greased bowl, turning to coat surface. Let rise, covered with damp cloth until doubled. Knead lightly. Divide into 2 portions. Let rise, covered, for 10 to 15 minutes. Place in 2 greased 5x9-inch loaf pans. Let rise, covered, until doubled. Bake at 375 degrees for 35 minutes or until loaves test done.
Approx Per Serving: Cal 128; Prot 3 g; Carbo 27 g; Fiber 2 g; T Fat 1 g; 6% Calories from Fat; Chol 0 mg; Sod 93 mg.

Alice C. Hadley, HFH of South Central Minnesota
North Mankato, MN

Three-in-One Bread

Yield: 12 servings

1 egg, beaten
1 cup sugar
1 cup sour milk
1 teaspoon baking soda
1 teaspoon salt

1 cup quick-cooking
  oats
1 cup All-Bran cereal
1 cup flour

■ Beat egg and sugar in mixer bowl until blended. Add mixture of sour milk and baking soda; mix well. Stir in salt, oats, cereal and flour. Spoon into greased and floured 5x9-inch loaf pan. Bake at 350 degrees for 45 to 50 minutes or until loaf tests done. May add plumped raisins to batter.

Approx Per Serving: Cal 165; Prot 4 g; Carbo 35 g; Fiber 3 g; T Fat 2 g; 9% Calories from Fat; Chol 21 mg; Sod 342 mg.

Mary Burkle, Newaygo HFH, Fremont, MI

Francis Johnson's Wheat Bread

Yield: 24 servings

3 cups lukewarm water
2 envelopes dry yeast
3 tablespoons honey
2 tablespoons oil
5¹/₂ cups wheat flour
1 cup gluten flour

1 cup all-purpose flour
1 cup oatbran
1 cup raw sunflower
  seed
1 teaspoon salt

■ Combine lukewarm water, yeast and honey in bowl; mix well. Let stand until bubbles form. Stir in oil. Combine with mixture of flours, oatbran, sunflower seed and salt in large bowl; mix well. Knead 10 to 15 times. Let rise until doubled in bulk. Punch dough down. Let rest for 7 to 10 minutes. Knead 15 times. Divide into 2 portions. Shape into loaves. Place in 2 large nonstick loaf pans. Let rise until doubled in bulk. Bake at 375 degrees for 30 minutes. Remove to wire rack to cool.

Approx Per Serving: Cal 196; Prot 9 g; Carbo 32 g; Fiber 5 g; T Fat 5 g; 21% Calories from Fat; Chol 0 mg; Sod 91 mg.

Francis Johnson, Benton HFH, Corvallis, OR

Vermont Special

Yield: 48 servings

¹/₂ cup lukewarm water
¹/₈ teaspoon sugar
1 tablespoon plus 1
  teaspoon dry yeast
1¹/₃ cups instant dry
  milk
4 cups hot water
¹/₃ cup canola oil

1 tablespoon plus 1
  teaspoon salt
¹/₂ cup honey
2 cups oats
5 to 5¹/₂ cups
  all-purpose flour
4 cups whole wheat
  flour

■ Combine lukewarm water, sugar and yeast; mix well. Let stand until bubbly. Combine milk powder and hot water in bowl; mix well. Stir in oil, salt, honey and oats. Cool to lukewarm. Add yeast mixture; mix well. Beat in 2¹/₂ cups all-purpose flour until well mixed. Add remaining all-purpose flour and whole wheat flour gradually, stirring until dough can be easily handled. Knead on lightly floured surface until smooth and elastic. Place in greased bowl, turning to coat surface. Let rise, covered, in warm place until doubled in bulk. Knead on lightly floured surface until smooth and elastic. Place in bowl. Let rise until doubled in bulk. Knead on lightly floured surface until smooth and elastic. Divide into 4 portions. Shape into loaves. Place in 4 greased 5x9-inch loaf pans. Let rise until doubled in bulk. Bake at 350 degrees for 45 minutes or until loaves test done. Remove to wire rack to cool.

Approx Per Serving: Cal 130; Prot 4 g; Carbo 24 g; Fiber 2 g; T Fat 2 g; 14% Calories from Fat; Chol <1 mg; Sod 189 mg.

Barbara K. Bull, Green Mountain HFH
South Burlington, VT

If there is a poor man among your brothers in any of the towns of the land that the Lord your God is giving you, do not be hardhearted or tightfisted toward your poor brother. Rather be openhanded and freely lend him whatever he needs. Give generously to him and do so without a grudging heart; then because of this the Lord your God will bless you in all your work and in everything you put your hand to.

Deuteronomy 15:7-8, 10

Yield: 24 servings

Zucchini Bread

My grandmother's recipe. I am the parent for the first Coos Bay Area Habitat for Humanity House.

4 cups flour
1 teaspoon salt
1 teaspoon baking soda
1/2 teaspoon baking
   powder
2 teaspoons cinnamon
1/2 teaspoon nutmeg
1/4 teaspoon cloves

3 eggs, beaten
1 cup oil
2 cups packed brown
   sugar
3 teaspoons vanilla
   extract
3 cups grated zucchini
1 cup chopped pecans

■ Mix flour, salt, baking soda, baking powder and spices in bowl with fork. Stir mixture of eggs, oil, brown sugar, vanilla and zucchini into dry ingredients just until moistened. Fold in pecans. Spoon into 2 nonstick 5x9-inch loaf pans. Bake at 350 degrees for 1 hour.
Approx Per Serving: Cal 291; Prot 4 g; Carbo 40 g; Fiber 1 g; T Fat 13 g; 41% Calories from Fat; Chol 27 mg; Sod 150 mg.

Suzie Gibbs, Coos Bay Area HFH, Coos Bay, OR

Yield: 60 servings

Alaskan Six-Week Muffins

2 teaspoons baking
   soda
4 cups buttermilk
4 eggs, beaten
3 cups sugar

1 cup oil
5 cups flour
2 teaspoons salt
1 16-ounce package
   Raisin Bran cereal

■ Mix baking soda and buttermilk together in bowl. Add eggs, sugar, oil, flour and salt; mix well. Stir in cereal. Spoon into nonstick muffin cups. Bake at 425 degrees for 20 to 25 minutes or until muffins test done. Store remaining batter in airtight container in refrigerator. May substitute bran flakes or Mueslix for Raisin Bran.
Approx Per Serving: Cal 145; Prot 3 g; Carbo 25 g; Fiber 1 g; T Fat 4 g; 26% Calories from Fat; Chol 15 mg; Sod 166 mg.

Patricia L. Becker, Painesville Area HFH, Painesville, OH

Yield: 12 servings

Blueberry-Corn Muffins

3/4 cup cornmeal
1/4 cup sugar
1/2 teaspoon salt
1/2 cup blueberries
2/3 cup flour

2 teaspoons baking
   powder
1 egg, slightly beaten
1/3 cup oil
3/4 cup milk

■ Combine cornmeal, sugar, salt, blueberries, flour and baking powder in bowl; mix well. Stir in mixture of egg, oil and milk just until moistened. Spoon into microwave-safe muffin cups. Microwave on High for 3 1/2 to 6 minutes or until muffins test done, turning once. Let stand in muffin cups for 10 minutes.
Approx Per Serving: Cal 146; Prot 2 g; Carbo 18 g; Fiber 1 g; T Fat 7 g; 44% Calories from Fat; Chol 20 mg; Sod 156 mg.

Chere Anderson, HFH of Northern Fox Valley
Sleepy Hollow, IL

Yield: 12 servings

Lemon-Blueberry Muffins

1 1/2 cups unbleached
   all-purpose flour
1 1/2 cups whole wheat
   pastry flour
1 teaspoon baking soda
2 teaspoons baking
   powder
1 teaspoon salt

2 teaspoons grated
   lemon rind
2/3 cup honey
1/2 cup applesauce
2/3 cup buttermilk
2 eggs, beaten
1/4 cup lemon juice
3 cups blueberries

■ Sift flours, baking soda, baking powder, salt and lemon rind together in bowl. Make well in center of flour mixture. Pour mixture of honey, applesauce, buttermilk, eggs and lemon juice into well, stirring just until moistened. Fold in blueberries. Fill muffin cups 2/3 full. Bake at 350 degrees for 20 to 30 minutes or until muffins test done. Cool in pan for 5 minutes. Remove to wire rack to cool completely.
Approx Per Serving: Cal 207; Prot 5 g; Carbo 45 g; Fiber 3 g; T Fat 2 g; 7% Calories from Fat; Chol 36 mg; Sod 331 mg.

Mary Anne Landis, HFH of the Mendocino Coast, Ukiah, CA

Fruity Bran Muffins

Yield: 36 servings

1 cup boiling water
1 cup 100% bran cereal
1¹/₂ cups sugar
¹/₂ cup shortening
2 eggs
2 cups buttermilk
2¹/₂ cups flour

2¹/₂ teaspoons baking
   soda
2 teaspoons salt
2 cups All-Bran cereal
1¹/₂ cups chopped
   walnuts
1 cup raisins

■ Pour boiling water over 100% bran cereal in bowl; mix well. Let stand 10 minutes. Cream sugar and shortening in mixer bowl until light and fluffy. Add eggs and buttermilk; mix well. Stir in sifted mixture of flour, baking soda and salt. Add 100% bran cereal mixture; mix well. Add All-Bran, stirring until well mixed. Fold in walnuts and raisins. Spoon into nonstick muffin cups. Bake at 400 degrees for 18 to 20 minutes or until muffins test done.

Approx Per Serving: Cal 161; Prot 3 g; Carbo 25 g; Fiber 3 g; T Fat 7 g; 34% Calories from Fat; Chol 12 mg; Sod 262 mg.

Jane Armstrong, Washington County HFH
West Lafayette, IN

Bran Muffins

Yield: 36 servings

1 cup boiling water
3 cups All-Bran cereal
2¹/₂ cups flour
2¹/₂ teaspoons baking
   soda

1 cup sugar
1 teaspoon salt
2 eggs, beaten
2 cups buttermilk
¹/₂ cup oil

■ Pour boiling water over cereal in bowl; mix well. Let stand for several minutes. Combine flour, baking soda, sugar and salt in large bowl; mix well. Add eggs and buttermilk; mix well. Fold in cereal mixture. Pour in oil; mix well. Fill nonstick muffin cups ¹/₂ to ³/₄ full. Bake at 400 degrees for 15 to 20 minutes or until muffins test done.

Approx Per Serving: Cal 107; Prot 3 g; Carbo 18 g; Fiber 2 g; T Fat 4 g; 28% Calories from Fat; Chol 12 mg; Sod 215 mg.

Connie Schingle, Morgan County HFH, Fort Morgan, CO

Morning Glory Muffins

Yield: 15 servings

1 cup sugar
2 cups flour
2 teaspoons baking
   soda
2 teaspoons cinnamon
¹/₄ teaspoon cloves
¹/₂ teaspoon salt
3 eggs, beaten
²/₃ cup oil

2 tablespoons vanilla
   extract
2 cups grated carrots
1 large apple, grated
¹/₂ cup flaked coconut
¹/₂ cup raisins
¹/₂ cup chopped
   walnuts

■ Sift sugar, flour, baking soda, cinnamon, cloves and salt together. Combine eggs, oil and vanilla in bowl; mix well. Stir in carrots, apple, coconut, raisins and walnuts. Add dry ingredients; mix well. Spoon into nonstick muffin cups. Bake at 350 degrees for 22 to 27 minutes or until muffins test done.

Approx Per Serving: Cal 287; Prot 4 g; Carbo 36 g; Fiber 2 g; T Fat 14 g; 44% Calories from Fat; Chol 43 mg; Sod 202 mg.

Esther Brouwer, Lakeshore HFH, Holland, MI

Thanksgiving Muffins

Yield: 15 servings

2 cups flour
1 cup plus 2
   tablespoons sugar
1 teaspoon salt
¹/₂ teaspoon baking
   soda
1³/₄ teaspoons baking
   powder
1 egg, beaten

2 cups cranberries, cut
   into halves
¹/₂ cup chopped walnuts
1 teaspoon grated
   orange rind
¹/₃ cup orange juice
¹/₄ cup water
2 tablespoons melted
   butter

■ Sift flour, sugar, salt, baking soda and baking powder together in bowl; mix well. Stir in egg, cranberries, walnuts, orange rind, orange juice, water and butter. Fill muffin cups sprayed with nonstick cooking spray ²/₃ full. Bake at 350 degrees for 20 to 30 minutes or until muffins test done.

Approx Per Serving: Cal 172; Prot 3 g; Carbo 31 g; Fiber 1 g; T Fat 5 g; 24% Calories from Fat; Chol 18 mg; Sod 227 mg.

Diane W. Kirkpatrick, HFH of Metro Louisville
Louisville, KY

French Puffs

Yield: 24 servings

1 1/2 cups sifted flour
1 1/2 teaspoons baking
  powder
1/2 teaspoon salt
1/4 teaspoon nutmeg
1/3 cup shortening,
  softened

1/2 cup sugar
1 egg
1/2 cup milk
6 tablespoons melted
  margarine
1/2 cup sugar
1 teaspoon cinnamon

■ Sift flour, baking powder, salt and nutmeg together. Cream shortening, 1/2 cup sugar and egg in mixer bowl until light and fluffy. Add dry ingredients alternately with milk, mixing well after each addition. Fill greased miniature muffin cups 2/3 full. Bake at 350 degrees for 20 to 25 minutes or until golden brown. Dip hot puffs in margarine; roll in mixture of 1/2 cup sugar and cinnamon.
Approx Per Serving: Cal 116; Prot 1 g; Carbo 14 g; Fiber <1 g; T Fat 6 g; 47% Calories from Fat; Chol 10 mg; Sod 104 mg.

Marilyn Burns, Greater Springfield HFH, Wilbraham, MA

Æbleskiver

Yield: 20 servings

1 cake yeast
1/4 cup lukewarm water
1 tablespoon sugar
1/2 teaspoon salt
1 cup milk
1 cup light cream

2 cups sifted flour
4 eggs
1 teaspoon nutmeg
1/3 cup butter
1/4 cup confectioners'
  sugar

■ Dissolve yeast in lukewarm water in small bowl; mix well. Stir in sugar and salt. Heat milk and cream in saucepan until lukewarm. Add flour and yeast; mix well. Beat in eggs 1 at a time. Stir in nutmeg. Let rise, lightly covered, in warm place for 2 hours or overnight. Brush each cup of heated æbleskiver pan with butter. Spoon 1 tablespoon batter into each cup. Bake in pan on top of stove for 3 minutes, turning to brown both sides. Roll in confectioners' sugar.
Approx Per Serving: Cal 117; Prot 3 g; Carbo 12 g; Fiber <1 g; T Fat 6 g; 47% Calories from Fat; Chol 57 mg; Sod 103 mg.

Elaine I. Clarke, Grants Pass Area HFH, Grants Pass, OR

Gingerbread Pancakes

Yield: 12 servings

3 eggs
1/4 cup packed brown
  sugar
1/2 cup buttermilk
1/2 cup milk
1/4 cup coffee
2 1/2 cups flour
1 teaspoon baking
  powder

1/2 teaspoon salt
1 1/2 teaspoons baking
  soda
1 teaspoon ground
  cloves
1 tablespoon cinnamon
1 tablespoon ginger
1 tablespoon nutmeg
1/4 cup melted butter

■ Cream eggs and brown sugar in bowl until light and fluffy. Add buttermilk, milk and coffee; mix well. Stir in sifted mixture of flour, baking powder, salt, baking soda and spices. Add butter; mix well. Bake on hot griddle using manufacturer's instructions.
Approx Per Serving: Cal 181; Prot 5 g; Carbo 27 g; Fiber 1 g; T Fat 6 g; 30% Calories from Fat; Chol 65 mg; Sod 286 mg.

Kathy Watkins, Warren County HFH, Front Royal, VA

Strawberry Pancakes

Yield: 6 servings

4 cups strawberries,
  slightly mashed
1 cup sugar
1 cup water
1 envelope strawberry
  instant drink mix
1/3 cup cornstarch
1/2 cup water

2 cups buttermilk
2 teaspoons baking
  soda
2 tablespoons oil
2 eggs
2 tablespoons sugar
2 cups flour

■ Bring strawberries, 1 cup sugar, 1 cup water and drink mix to a boil in saucepan. Stir in mixture of cornstarch and 1/2 cup water until thickened. Set aside. Beat buttermilk, baking soda, oil, eggs and 2 tablespoons sugar in mixer bowl until blended. Add flour 1/2 cup at a time, mixing well after each addition. Drop batter by spoonfuls onto hot griddle. Bake until bubbles appear on surface and underside is golden brown. Turn pancakes over. Serve pancakes with warm or cooled strawberry sauce.
Approx Per Serving: Cal 473; Prot 11 g; Carbo 90 g; Fiber 4 g; T Fat 8 g; 15% Calories from Fat; Chol 74 mg; Sod 992 mg.

Janet Hennemann, Vining, MN

Yeast Pancakes

Yield: 4 servings

My very own recipe—as I could not find any recipe for yeast pancakes in any cookbook.

1 egg, at room
  temperature
1/2 teaspoon salt
1 1/2 tablespoons sugar
3/4 teaspoon dry yeast
1/2 cup 90 to 100-degree
  water

1/2 cup 90 to 100-degree
  milk
1 to 1 1/2 cups flour
2 tablespoons
  shortening

- Beat egg, salt and sugar in mixer bowl until blended. Add yeast, warm water and warm milk; mix well. Add flour. Beat at low speed until a stiff batter forms. Let rise, covered, in warm place for 30 to 45 minutes or until mixture is full of bubbles. Stir batter down. Let rise for 10 to 20 minutes. Stir in shortening. Spoon batter onto hot griddle. Bake for 4 to 5 minutes or until brown on both sides, turning once. May store batter in refrigerator for 2 to 3 days.

Approx Per Serving: Cal 285; Prot 8 g; Carbo 42 g; Fiber 1 g; T Fat 9 g; 30% Calories from Fat; Chol 57 mg; Sod 298 mg.

Howard Nichols, HFH-Mercer County, Harrodsburg, KY

Pita or Arabic Pocket Bread

Yield: 12 servings

*Pita bread is the staple food of the Arabic world. Before the advent of ovens,
Arabs baked their bread on heated stones.*

1 tablespoon dry yeast
1 teaspoon sugar
1 1/4 cups lukewarm
  water

1 tablespoon oil
3 cups flour
1 1/2 teaspoons salt

- Dissolve yeast and sugar in lukewarm water in bowl. Stir in oil, flour and salt. Knead on lightly floured surface until smooth. Divide into 6 portions. Knead until smooth and elastic. Roll each portion into a 1/4-inch thick circle. Place on greased baking sheet. Let rise, covered, for 45 minutes. Bake at 450 degrees for 15 minutes or until puffed and brown. Remove to wire racks to cool; store in covered container.

Approx Per Serving: Cal 127; Prot 4 g; Carbo 24 g; Fiber 1 g; T Fat 1 g; 11% Calories from Fat; Chol 0 mg; Sod 267 mg.

Margaret Humphrey, Prescott Area HFH, Prescott, AZ

Pushover Popovers

Yield: 8 servings

1 cup Wondra flour
1 teaspoon salt

2 eggs, slightly beaten
1 cup milk

- Combine flour, salt, eggs and milk in bowl just until moistened. Fill buttered muffins cups 3/4 full. Bake at 450 degrees for 25 minutes. Reduce temperature to 350 degrees. Bake for 15 minutes or until golden brown. Remove from pan immediately.

Approx Per Serving: Cal 89; Prot 4 g; Carbo 12 g; Fiber 0 g; T Fat 3 g; 26% Calories from Fat; Chol 57 mg; Sod 296 mg.

Sigrid Goetsch, HFH of Wausau, Wausau, WI

Pretzels

Yield: 11 servings

1 envelope dry yeast
1 1/3 cups lukewarm
  water
1 tablespoon sugar
1/2 teaspoon salt

3 1/2 cups flour
1 egg, beaten
1 tablespoon water
1 tablespoon salt

- Dissolve yeast in lukewarm water in bowl. Stir in sugar, 1/2 teaspoon salt and flour. Knead on lightly floured surface for 5 minutes. Mold into pretzel shapes. Place on greased baking sheet. Brush with mixture of egg and water. Sprinkle with 1 tablespoon salt. Bake at 425 degrees for 15 minutes.

Approx Per Serving: Cal 158; Prot 5 g; Carbo 32 g; Fiber 1 g; T Fat 1 g; 5% Calories from Fat; Chol 19 mg; Sod 731 mg.

John J. Kostecki, Jr., Northern Straits HFH, Cedarville, MI

Butterhorn Dinner Rolls

Yield: 48 servings

This recipe has been a holiday favorite of our family for the past 25 years when we gather for holiday companionship. The word companion means "with bread."

1 envelope dry yeast
1 teaspoon sugar
1/4 cup lukewarm water
1 cup milk, scalded
4 cups sifted flour
1 teaspoon salt

1/4 cup sugar
Grated rind of 1 lemon
1/2 cup butter, softened
1/2 cup shortening
3 egg yolks, beaten
1/2 cup melted butter

■ Dissolve yeast and sugar in lukewarm water in bowl. Stir in scalded milk. Combine flour, salt, sugar and lemon rind in large bowl; mix well. Cut in 1/2 cup butter and shortening until crumbly. Stir in yeast mixture and egg yolks. Store, covered, in refrigerator overnight. Divide into 3 portions. Roll each into circle on lightly floured surface. Brush with butter. Cut into wedges. Roll up from wide end. Shape into horns on nonstick baking sheet. Let rise for 2 to 3 hours or until doubled in bulk. Bake at 400 degrees for 10 minutes.
Approx Per Serving: Cal 100; Prot 1 g; Carbo 9 g; Fiber <1 g; T Fat 7 g; 59% Calories from Fat; Chol 24 mg; Sod 80 mg.

Sandra L. Struve-Seberger, Black Hills Area HFH
Rapid City, SD

My Favorite Rolls

Yield: 24 servings

2 envelopes dry yeast
1 cup lukewarm water
1 cup sugar
1 cup shortening

1 1/2 teaspoons salt
1 cup boiling water
2 eggs, beaten
6 cups flour

■ Dissolve yeast in lukewarm water. Mix sugar, shortening and salt in bowl. Add boiling water; mix well. Let stand to cool. Stir in eggs and yeast. Add flour; mix well. Shape into 1-inch balls. Arrange 3 balls in each nonstick muffin cup. Let rise 4 hours or until doubled in bulk. Bake at 400 degrees until brown. May store dough in refrigerator for 4 days.
Approx Per Serving: Cal 230; Prot 4 g; Carbo 32 g; Fiber 1 g; T Fat 9 g; 37% Calories from Fat; Chol 18 mg; Sod 140 mg.

Kay Reynolds, Starkville HFH, Starkville, MS

Sticky Icebox Rolls

Yield: 36 servings

1 envelope dry yeast
1/4 cup lukewarm water
2/3 cup shortening
1/2 cup sugar
1 cup milk
2 eggs, beaten
2 teaspoons salt
1 cup mashed potatoes
5 to 6 cups bread flour
1/2 cup margarine, softened
3 cups packed brown sugar

1/2 cup butter, softened
1 1/2 cups honey
1 1/2 cups light corn syrup
1/4 cup dark corn syrup
1/4 cup water
1 teaspoon vanilla
1/2 cup melted butter
1/2 cup packed brown sugar
2 teaspoons cinnamon
1 cup chopped pecans

■ Dissolve yeast in lukewarm water. Bring shortening, sugar and milk to a boil in saucepan, stirring constantly. Let stand to cool. Add yeast, eggs, salt, potatoes and flour; mix well. Knead on lightly floured surface until smooth and elastic. Place in greased bowl, turning to coat surface. Let rise until doubled in bulk. Combine next 8 ingredients in mixer bowl. Beat at medium speed until blended. Spread in bottom of 9x13-inch baking pan. Roll dough into rectangle on lightly floured surface. Spread with 1/2 cup melted butter; sprinkle with 1/2 cup brown sugar and cinnamon. Roll as for jelly roll. Cut into slices. Arrange in prepared pan. Let rise in warm place until doubled in bulk. Bake at 375 degrees for 12 to 15 minutes or until brown. Cool in pan for 5 minutes. Invert onto serving platter. Top with pecans. May store dough in refrigerator for 5 days.
Approx Per Serving: Cal 407; Prot 3 g; Carbo 68 g; Fiber 1 g; T Fat 15 g; 33% Calories from Fat; Chol 27 mg; Sod 241 mg.

Vera Kuhns, Almost Heaven HFH, Harrisonburg, VA

Kringlas

Yield: 10 servings

1 cup sugar
1/2 cup shortening
1 egg
1 teaspoon vanilla
  extract
1 teaspoon baking soda

1/2 teaspoon salt
1 cup buttermilk
2 1/2 cups flour
1 teaspoon baking
  powder
1/4 cup butter

■ Cream sugar and shortening in mixer bowl. Blend in egg and vanilla. Add mixture of baking soda, salt and buttermilk; mix well. Stir in mixture of flour and baking powder until soft dough forms. Chill dough for several hours. Form into figure 8 shapes. Place on nonstick baking sheet. Bake at 400 degrees for 15 minutes. Spread bottoms of kringlas with butter.
Approx Per Serving: Cal 340; Prot 5 g; Carbo 45 g; Fiber 1 g; T Fat 16 g; 42% Calories from Fat; Chol 35 mg; Sod 294 mg.

Karen Hovey, Des Moines HFH, Des Moines, IA

Lowell Inn Rolls

Yield: 24 servings

2 envelopes dry yeast
1/4 cup lukewarm water
3/4 cup milk, scalded,
  cooled
1/2 cup sugar

3/4 teaspoon salt
1/2 cup shortening
2 eggs, beaten
4 cups flour

■ Dissolve yeast in lukewarm water. Combine milk, sugar, salt, shortening and eggs in bowl; mix well. Stir in yeast. Add flour; mix well. Knead on floured surface until smooth and elastic. Place in greased bowl, turning to coat surface. Let rise until doubled in bulk. Roll into circle on floured surface. Cut into wedges. Roll up from wide end. Place on nonstick baking sheet. Let rise until doubled in bulk. Bake at 350 degrees for 12 minutes or until golden brown.
Approx Per Serving: Cal 143; Prot 3 g; Carbo 21 g; Fiber 1 g; T Fat 5 g; 33% Calories from Fat; Chol 19 mg; Sod 76 mg.

Sara E. Mentink
Univ. of Wisconsin-Stevens Point Campus Chapter
Stevens Point, WI

Multi-Grain Rolls

Yield: 24 servings

2 2/3 cups 140-degree
  water
1/3 cup oil
1 cup packed dark
  brown sugar
1/4 cup yeast
2 eggs, beaten
2 teaspoons salt

2 cups cracked wheat
  flour
2 cups seven-grain
  cereal
2 tablespoons millet
  seed
3 to 4 cups all-purpose
  flour

■ Mix first 4 ingredients in bowl. Let stand for 15 minutes. Add eggs and salt; mix well. Blend in wheat flour, cereal and millet seed. Stir in enough all-purpose flour to make stiff dough. Knead on floured surface until smooth and elastic. Shape into rolls. Place on nonstick baking sheet. Let rise in warm place for 5 minutes. Bake at 425 degrees for 10 minutes.
Approx Per Serving: Cal 248; Prot 6 g; Carbo 45 g; Fiber 4 g; T Fat 4 g; 16% Calories from Fat; Chol 18 mg; Sod 190 mg.

Virginia Butler, Mesilla Valley HFH, Las Cruces, NM

Gail's Sticky Buns

Yield: 10 servings

18 frozen dinner
  rolls
1 cup packed brown
  sugar
1/2 cup butter
1 teaspoon cinnamon

1 4-ounce package
  butterscotch
  pudding and pie
  filling mix
1/2 cup chopped pecans

■ Arrange rolls in greased tube pan. Combine brown sugar and butter in saucepan. Heat until sugar is dissolved, stirring constantly. Drizzle over rolls. Sprinkle with pudding mix, cinnamon and pecans. Let rise, covered, overnight. Bake at 350 degrees for 30 minutes. Invert onto serving platter. Serve.
Approx Per Serving: Cal 409; Prot 4 g; Carbo 61 g; Fiber 2 g; T Fat 17 g; 37% Calories from Fat; Chol 25 mg; Sod 425 mg.

Judy Marine, Highlands County HFH, Sebring, FL

Oatmeal Buns

Yield: 48 servings

2 envelopes dry yeast
1/2 cup lukewarm water
2 cups rolled oats
1/2 cup packed brown
  sugar

1 tablespoon salt
1/2 cup shortening
4 cups boiling water
8 to 10 cups flour

■ Dissolve yeast in lukewarm water. Mix oats, brown sugar, salt and shortening in bowl. Pour boiling water over mixture; mix well. Cool to lukewarm. Stir in yeast and flour. Knead on lightly floured surface until dough is easily handled. Place in greased bowl, turning to coat surface. Let rise, covered, until doubled in bulk. Shape into buns. Place on nonstick baking sheet. Let rise until doubled in bulk. Bake at 350 degrees for 15 to 20 minutes or until golden brown.
Approx Per Serving: Cal 135; Prot 3 g; Carbo 24 g; Fiber 1 g; T Fat 3 g; 18% Calories from Fat; Chol 0 mg; Sod 134 mg.

Vera Christensen, Morgan County HFH, Fort Morgan, CO

Oatmeal Rolls

Yield: 24 servings

2 cups boiling water
1 cup rolled oats
3 tablespoons oil
1 envelope dry yeast
1/3 cup lukewarm water

2/3 cup packed brown
  sugar
2 teaspoons salt
5 to 51/2 cups flour

■ Combine boiling water, oats and oil in bowl; mix well. Cool to lukewarm. Dissolve yeast in lukewarm water in bowl. Stir in brown sugar and salt. Add to oat mixture; mix well. Stir in flour. Let rise in warm place until doubled in bulk. Punch dough down. Let rise until doubled in bulk. Shape into rolls. Place on nonstick baking sheet. Let rise until doubled in bulk. Bake at 350 degrees for 20 minutes.
Approx Per Serving: Cal 162; Prot 4 g; Carbo 32 g; Fiber 1 g; T Fat 2 g; 12% Calories from Fat; Chol 0 mg; Sod 182 mg.

Faye L. Adolf, Morgan County HFH, Brush, CO

Welsh Bake Stones

Yield: 18 servings

31/2 cups flour
1 cup sugar
11/2 teaspoons baking
  powder
1/2 teaspoon baking
  soda

1 teaspoon salt
1 cup shortening
1 egg, beaten
3/4 cup milk
11/4 cups raisins

■ Mix flour, sugar, baking powder, baking soda and salt in bowl. Cut in shortening until crumbly. Stir in egg, milk and raisins mixing until stiff dough forms. Pat 1/4 inch thick on lightly floured surface. Cut into 2-inch rounds. Bake on hot lightly greased griddle until brown on both sides, turning once.
Approx Per Serving: Cal 277; Prot 4 g; Carbo 39 g; Fiber 1 g; T Fat 12 g; 39% Calories from Fat; Chol 13 mg; Sod 179 mg.

Janeth Coray, Lakeshore HFH, Holland, MI

Yeast Rolls

Yield: 24 servings

1 envelope dry yeast
1 tablespoon sugar
1/4 cup lukewarm milk
3/4 cup milk, scalded
1/2 cup margarine

1/3 cup sugar
1/2 teaspoon salt
3 eggs, beaten
4 cups flour

■ Dissolve yeast and 1 tablespoon sugar in lukewarm milk. Combine milk, margarine, 1/3 cup sugar and salt in bowl; mix well. Let stand to cool. Stir in eggs and yeast mixture. Add flour gradually; mix well. Place in greased bowl, turning to coat surface. Let rise until doubled in bulk. Shape into rolls. Place on nonstick baking sheet. Let rise until doubled in bulk. Bake at 375 degrees for 15 minutes.
Approx Per Serving: Cal 137; Prot 3 g; Carbo 19 g; Fiber 1 g; T Fat 5 g; 33% Calories from Fat; Chol 28 mg; Sod 103 mg.

Barbara Specht, Livingston County HFH, Howell, MI

Cinnamon Rolls

Yield: 36 servings

2 envelopes dry yeast
1 tablespoon sugar
Salt to taste
2¹/₂ cups lukewarm
    water
¹/₂ cup sugar
2 teaspoons salt
3 eggs, beaten
8 cups flour
2 cups cooked raisins
¹/₂ cup shortening
¹/₄ cup butter

1 cup plus 2
    tablespoons packed
    brown sugar
2 teaspoons cinnamon
1 cup whipping cream,
    whipped
¹/₂ teaspoon vanilla
    extract
¹/₃ cup packed brown
    sugar
1 recipe confectioners'
    sugar icing

■ Dissolve yeast, 1 tablespoon sugar and salt to taste in ¹/₂ cup lukewarm water in bowl. Let stand for several minutes. Add 2 cups lukewarm water, ¹/₂ cup sugar, 2 teaspoons salt, eggs and 3 cups flour; mix well. Let stand until bubbly. Stir in raisins, shortening and enough remaining flour to make a soft dough. Let rise until doubled. Roll dough into a rectangle on floured surface. Spread with butter; sprinkle with 1 cup plus 2 tablespoons brown sugar and cinnamon. Roll up. Cut into slices. Place in nonstick 9x13-inch baking pan. Let rise until doubled. Top with mixture of whipped cream, vanilla and ¹/₃ cup brown sugar. Bake at 350 degrees for 25 minutes or until brown. Frost.
Approx Per Serving: Cal 257; Prot 4 g; Carbo 45 g; Fiber 1 g; T Fat 7 g; 25% Calories from Fat; Chol 30 mg; Sod 144 mg.

Lary K. Dodge, Morgan County HFH, Fort Morgan, CO

Cinnamon Rounds

Yield: 12 servings

2 cups flour
1 tablespoon baking
    powder
1 teaspoon salt
¹/₄ cup butter, softened

¹/₂ cup milk
¹/₄ cup melted butter
1¹/₂ teaspoons
    cinnamon
3 tablespoons sugar

■ Sift flour, baking powder and salt in bowl; mix well. Cut in ¹/₄ cup butter until crumbly. Add milk, stirring until dough forms a ball. Knead on lightly floured surface until smooth and elastic. Roll into rectangle. Brush with ¹/₄ cup melted butter; sprinkle with mixture of cinnamon and sugar. Roll as for jelly roll. Cut into ¹/₂-inch slices. Place on greased baking sheet. Bake at 425 degrees for 10 minutes.
Approx Per Serving: Cal 163; Prot 3 g; Carbo 20 g; Fiber 1 g; T Fat 8 g; 45% Calories from Fat; Chol 22 mg; Sod 329 mg.

Christina Lamb, Eckerd College Campus Chapter
St. Petersburg, FL

Quick and Easy Caramel Rolls

Yield: 16 servings

¹/₂ cup chopped pecans
18 frozen dinner rolls
1 4-ounce package
    butterscotch
    pudding and pie
    filling mix

¹/₄ teaspoon cinnamon
¹/₂ cup packed brown
    sugar
6 tablespoons melted
    butter

■ Sprinkle pecans in bottom of lightly greased bundt pan. Arrange dinner rolls over pecans. Sprinkle with next 3 ingredients. Drizzle with melted butter. Let stand at room temperature overnight. Place in cold oven. Bake at 350 degrees for 30 minutes or until brown. Invert onto serving platter. Serve warm.
Approx Per Serving: Cal 211; Prot 3 g; Carbo 30 g; Fiber 1 g; T Fat 9 g; 39% Calories from Fat; Chol 12 mg; Sod 250 mg.

Wilma, Mandy and Mindy Cochran, Morgan County HFH
Fort Morgan, CO

Country Butter

Yield: 16 servings

1 pound margarine,
    softened

³/₄ cup oil
1 cup buttermilk

■ Beat softened margarine in mixer bowl until smooth. Add oil and buttermilk; beat until light. Store, covered, in refrigerator.
Approx Per Serving: Cal 300; Prot 1 g; Carbo 1 g; Fiber 0 g; T Fat 33 g; 98% Calories from Fat; Chol 1 mg; Sod 283 mg.

Virginia Murray, North Bradley Church of God, Coleman, MI

DESSERTS

"For we are God's fellow workers; you are God's field, God's building."

I Corinthians 3:9

Yankee Doodle Apple Dessert

Yield: 6 servings

½ cup sifted flour
¾ cup packed brown
  sugar
1 teaspoon baking
  powder
¼ teaspoon salt
Mace to taste

Cinnamon to taste
1 egg
½ teaspoon vanilla
  extract
1 cup chopped tart
  apple
½ cup chopped pecans

■ Sift first 6 ingredients into bowl. Stir in egg and vanilla. Fold in apple and pecans. Spoon into greased 8-inch round baking pan. Bake at 350 degrees for 25 to 30 minutes or until bubbly. Serve with ice cream or whipped topping.
Approx Per Serving: Cal 255; Prot 3 g; Carbo 46 g; Fiber 1 g; T Fat 8 g; 27% Calories from Fat; Chol 36 mg; Sod 171 mg.

Eileen Fyock, Highlands County HFH, Lorida, FL

Delicious Apple Slump

Yield: 6 servings

4 cups sliced tart
  apples
¼ cup sugar
½ teaspoon cinnamon
1 cup sifted flour
1½ teaspoons baking
  powder

½ teaspoon salt
2 teaspoons sugar
2 tablespoons butter,
  softened
¾ cup milk
2 tablespoons butter

■ Combine apples, ¼ cup sugar and cinnamon in bowl; mix well. Arrange in nonstick 8x8-inch baking pan. Sift flour, baking powder, salt and 2 teaspoons sugar in bowl; mix well. Cut in butter until crumbly. Stir in milk. Spread over apples. Dot with 2 tablespoons butter. Bake at 400 degrees for 30 minutes or until apples are tender.
Approx Per Serving: Cal 238; Prot 3 g; Carbo 37 g; Fiber 2 g; T Fat 9 g; 34% Calories from Fat; Chol 25 mg; Sod 338 mg.

Violet E. Merberger, Greater Johnstown HFH, Johnstown, PA

Frozen Banana Split

Yield: 24 servings

¾ cup melted
  margarine
1½ cups flour
½ cup finely chopped
  pecans
3 bananas, thinly sliced
8 ounces neopolitan
  ice cream, softened
1 cup chopped pecans
1 cup chocolate chips
½ cup margarine

2 cups confectioners'
  sugar
1 12-ounce can
  evaporated milk
1 teaspoon vanilla
  extract
2 envelopes whipped
  topping mix,
  prepared
1 cup graham cracker
  crumbs

■ Pat mixture of first 3 ingredients into nonstick 9x13-inch baking pan. Bake at 350 degrees for 20 minutes. Cover baked layer with bananas. Top with ice cream. Sprinkle with 1 cup pecans. Freeze until firm. Combine chocolate chips and ½ cup margarine in double boiler. Cook over boiling water until smooth, stirring constantly. Add confectioners' sugar and evaporated milk; mix well. Cook for 20 minutes or until slightly thickened, stirring constantly. Cool; stir in vanilla. Spread over frozen layer. Spread with whipped topping. Sprinkle with crumbs. Store in freezer.
Approx Per Serving: Cal 333; Prot 4 g; Carbo 35 g; Fiber 1 g; T Fat 23 g; 62% Calories from Fat; Chol 10 mg; Sod 79 mg.

Sally Newton, Mt. Pleasant HFH, Mt. Pleasant, TX

Banana Split Fantasy

Yield: 18 servings

2 cups graham cracker
  crumbs
½ cup melted
  margarine
2 eggs
1 cup margarine,
  softened
2 cups confectioners'
  sugar
1 teaspoon vanilla
  extract

1 20-ounce can
  pineapple, drained
3 cups sliced fresh
  strawberries
4 bananas, sliced
16 ounces whipped
  topping
½ cup chopped pecans

■ Combine graham cracker crumbs and ½ cup melted margarine in bowl; mix well. Pat into nonstick 9x13-inch baking pan. Chill until firm. Beat eggs, 1 cup margarine, confectioners' sugar and vanilla in mixer bowl for 20 minutes. Spread over chilled layer. Chill until set. Layer pineapple, strawberries and bananas over top. Spread with whipped topping; sprinkle with pecans. Store in refrigerator.
Approx Per Serving: Cal 410; Prot 3 g; Carbo 44 g; Fiber 3 g; T Fat 26 g; 56% Calories from Fat; Chol 24 mg; Sod 276 mg.

Lori Rath, University of Iowa Campus Chapter, Iowa City, IA

Mama's Easy Berry Cobbler

Yield: 8 servings

1/4 cup margarine
3/4 cup milk
1 cup sugar
1 cup flour

1 1/2 teaspoons baking powder
2 cups fresh blueberries
1/4 cup sugar

■ Melt margarine in 8-inch round baking pan. Combine milk, 1 cup sugar, flour and baking powder in bowl; mix well. Pour into prepared pan. Do not stir. Top with blueberries. Do not stir. Sprinkle 1/4 cup sugar over berries. Bake at 350 degrees for 30 minutes. May use any canned or frozen fruit.

Approx Per Serving: Cal 264; Prot 3 g; Carbo 49 g; Fiber 1 g; T Fat 7 g; 23% Calories from Fat; Chol 3 mg; Sod 141 mg.

Diane Ramey, Rockingham HFH, Dry Fork, VA

Lillian's Blueberry Buckle

Yield: 15 servings

2 16-ounce packages vanilla wafers, crushed

1 1/4 cups melted butter
5 cups fresh blueberries
1/4 cup sugar

■ Combine wafer crumbs and butter in bowl; mix well. Press 2/3 of crumb mixture into bottom of nonstick 9x13-inch baking pan. Spread with mixture of blueberries and sugar. Pat remaining crumb mixture over blueberries. Bake at 350 degrees for 35 minutes or until bubbly.

Approx Per Serving: Cal 455; Prot 4 g; Carbo 54 g; Fiber 2 g; T Fat 26 g; 51% Calories from Fat; Chol 79 mg; Sod 359 mg.

Shannon Hakala
Univ. of Wisconsin-Stevens Point Campus Chapter
Stevens Point, WI

Blueberry Dump Cake

Yield: 18 servings

2 1/2 cups crushed pineapple
3 cups blueberries
3/4 cup sugar

1 2-layer package yellow cake mix
1/2 cup melted butter
1 cup chopped pecans

■ Layer undrained pineapple, blueberries, sugar and cake mix in buttered 9x13-inch baking pan. Do not stir. Drizzle with butter; sprinkle with pecans. Bake at 350 degrees for 45 minutes.

Approx Per Serving: Cal 289; Prot 2 g; Carbo 44 g; Fiber 1 g; T Fat 12 g; 37% Calories from Fat; Chol 15 mg; Sod 249 mg.

Faye S. Curtis, Starkville HFH, Starkville, MS

Crown Jewel Dessert

Yield: 12 servings

1 1/2 cups graham cracker crumbs
1/3 cup sugar
1/2 cup melted margarine
1 3-ounce package strawberry gelatin
1 cup boiling water
1/2 cup cold water
1 3-ounce package black cherry gelatin
1 cup boiling water
1/2 cup cold water

1 3-ounce package lemon gelatin
1/4 cup sugar
1 cup boiling water
1 cup crushed pineapple
1/2 cup cold water
3 tablespoons lemon juice
1/8 teaspoon salt
1 1/2 cups whipping cream, whipped

■ Mix graham cracker crumbs, 1/3 cup sugar and margarine in bowl. Press into bottom of springform pan. Chill completely. Dissolve strawberry gelatin in 1 cup boiling water in bowl. Add 1/2 cup cold water. Pour into 8x8-inch dish. Chill until set. Cut into 1/2-inch cubes. Dissolve black cherry gelatin in 1 cup boiling water in bowl. Add 1/2 cup cold water. Pour into 8x8-inch dish. Chill until set. Cut into 1/2-inch cubes. Dissolve lemon gelatin with 1/4 cup sugar in 1 cup boiling water in bowl. Add crushed pineapple and 1/2 cup cold water, lemon juice and salt. Chill until partially set. Whip until fluffy. Fold in gelatin cubes and whipped cream. Spoon into prepared springform pan. Garnish with chopped walnuts.

Approx Per Serving: Cal 369; Prot 4 g; Carbo 46 g; Fiber 1 g; T Fat 20 g; 48% Calories from Fat; Chol 41 mg; Sod 283 mg.

Norma Thaler, Barry County HFH, Freeport, MI

Better-Than-Anything Dessert

Yield: 15 servings

1 2-layer package devil's food cake mix
1 14-ounce can sweetened condensed milk
1 6-ounce jar caramel ice cream topping
8 ounces whipped topping
3 toffee candy bars, crushed

■ Prepare and bake cake using package directions for 9x13-inch cake pan. Pierce with fork. Pour condensed milk and caramel topping over cake. Chill, covered, overnight. Top with whipped topping and candy.
Approx Per Serving: Cal 439; Prot 6 g; Carbo 55 g; Fiber <1 g; T Fat 22 g; 45% Calories from Fat; Chol 53 mg; Sod 374 mg.

Janice Craig, Mercer University Campus Chapter
Macon, GA

Cherry-Berry in a Cloud

Yield: 15 servings

7 egg whites
1/2 teaspoon cream of tartar
1/4 teaspoon salt
1/2 cup sugar
2 10-ounce packages frozen strawberries, thawed, drained
1 21-ounce can cherry pie filling
1 teaspoon lemon juice
8 ounces cream cheese, softened
1 cup sugar
1 teaspoon vanilla extract
2 cups whipping cream, whipped
2 cups marshmallows

■ Beat egg whites in mixer bowl until foamy. Add cream of tartar and salt; beat until soft peaks form. Add 1/2 cup sugar, beating constantly until stiff peaks form. Spoon into 9x13-inch baking pan. Bake at 275 degrees for 1 hour. Turn off oven. Let stand in closed oven overnight. Combine strawberries, pie filling and lemon juice in bowl; mix well. Spread over baked layer. Beat cream cheese, 1 cup sugar and vanilla in mixer bowl until smooth. Add mixture of whipping cream and marshmallows; mix well. Spoon over berry layer. Chill until set. Store in refrigerator.
Approx Per Serving: Cal 323; Prot 4 g; Carbo 41 g; Fiber 2 g; T Fat 17 g; 46% Calories from Fat; Chol 60 mg; Sod 135 mg.

Paul Rozeboom, HFH of South Central Minnesota
Mankato, MN

Frozen Cherry Dessert

Yield: 6 servings

2 egg whites, at room temperature
2 tablespoons sugar
1 cup whipped cream
1/2 cup Grape Nuts
1/2 teaspoon vanilla extract
1/4 cup confectioners' sugar
1/4 cup maraschino cherries, cut into quarters
1 tablespoon maraschino cherry juice

■ Beat egg whites in mixer bowl until stiff. Add sugar; mix well. Fold in whipped cream, Grape Nuts, vanilla, confectioners' sugar, maraschino cherries and maraschino cherry juice. Spoon into glass dish. Freeze until set. Serve with hot fudge sauce.
Approx Per Serving: Cal 154; Prot 3 g; Carbo 20 g; Fiber 1 g; T Fat 7 g; 42% Calories from Fat; Chol 27 mg; Sod 90 mg.

Carla Groenenboom, Newago HFH, Grand Rapids, MI

Easy Cheesecake

Yield: 10 servings

1 1/4 cups graham cracker crumbs
1/4 cup sugar
1/4 cup melted butter
16 ounces cream cheese, softened
3 eggs
1 cup sugar
1 teaspoon vanilla extract
1 cup sour cream

■ Combine graham cracker crumbs, 1/4 cup sugar and butter in bowl; mix well. Press in bottom of foil-lined 9 or 10-inch springform pan. Bake at 375 degrees for 5 minutes. Mix cream cheese, eggs, 1 cup sugar, vanilla and sour cream in mixer bowl in order listed. Beat at medium speed until smooth. Spoon into cooled baked layer. Bake for 20 minutes. Turn off oven. Let stand in closed oven for 1 hour. Chill until serving time. Remove side of pan.
Approx Per Serving: Cal 432; Prot 7 g; Carbo 39 g; Fiber <1 g; T Fat 29 g; 58% Calories from Fat; Chol 136 mg; Sod 299 mg.

Gloria J. Welch, Durham County HFH, Durham, NC

Cheesecake

Yield: 10 servings

24 graham crackers, crushed
6 tablespoons butter, softened
2 tablespoons sugar
16 ounces cream cheese, softened
1/2 cup sugar

2 eggs
1/2 teaspoon salt
3 tablespoons lemon juice
2 cups sour cream
1/4 cup sugar
1/2 teaspoon vanilla extract

- Press mixture of graham cracker crumbs, butter and 2 tablespoons sugar over bottom and side of springform pan. Beat cream cheese, 1/2 cup sugar, eggs, salt and lemon juice in mixer bowl until smooth. Spoon into prepared pan. Bake at 375 degrees for 20 minutes. Top with mixture of remaining ingredients. Bake at 400 degrees for 5 minutes. Cool in pan. Chill for 12 hours before serving.

Approx Per Serving: Cal 474; Prot 7 g; Carbo 34 g; Fiber <1 g; T Fat 35 g; 66% Calories from Fat; Chol 131 mg; Sod 441 mg.

Betty Johnson, Benton HFH, Corvallis, OR

Chocolate Cheesecake

Yield: 12 servings

8 ounces chocolate wafers, crushed
1/2 cup melted butter
1/4 teaspoon cinnamon
32 ounces cream cheese, softened
2 cups sugar
4 eggs

2 cups chocolate chips, melted
1 tablespoon baking cocoa
2 teaspoons vanilla extract
2 cups sour cream

- Press mixture of wafer crumbs, butter and cinnamon over bottom and side of 10-inch springform pan. Chill. Process cream cheese, 2 cups sugar and eggs in food processor with steel blade until smooth. Add chocolate chips. Process until blended. Add baking cocoa and vanilla; mix well. Stir in sour cream. Spoon into prepared pan. Bake at 350 degrees for 1 1/4 hours. Cool. Chill for 5 hours.

Approx Per Serving: Cal 800; Prot 12 g; Carbo 68 g; Fiber 1 g; T Fat 57 g; 62% Calories from Fat; Chol 191 mg; Sod 472 mg.

Elaine Wade, HFH of Wausau, Wausau, WI

Chocolate-Amaretto Cheesecake

Yield: 12 servings

8 ounces chocolate wafers, crushed
1/2 cup melted butter
3/4 cup sugar
24 ounces cream cheese, softened
4 eggs
1 cup chocolate chips, melted, cooled

1 cup sour cream
1/2 cup Amaretto
1/4 cup melted butter
1 teaspoon vanilla extract
1 cup sour cream
2 tablespoons Amaretto
1 cup toasted sliced almonds

- Press mixture of wafer crumbs and 1/2 cup butter over bottom and 2 inches up side of 9-inch springform pan. Chill. Cream sugar and cream cheese in mixer bowl. Add eggs 1 at a time, beating after each addition. Add chocolate chips, 1 cup sour cream, 1/2 cup Amaretto, 1/4 cup butter and vanilla; mix well. Spoon into prepared pan. Bake at 350 degrees for 65 minutes or until set. Top with mixture of 1 cup sour cream and 2 tablespoons Amaretto. Bake for 3 minutes. Cool in pan. Chill, covered, until serving time. Sprinkle with toasted almonds.

Approx Per Serving: Cal 713; Prot 11 g; Carbo 45 g; Fiber 1 g; T Fat 53 g; 68% Calories from Fat; Chol 181 mg; Sod 447 mg.

Brenda Davis, HFH of Wausau, Wausau, WI

Easy Lemon Cheesecake

Yield: 8 servings

1/2 cup sugar
16 ounces cream cheese, softened
1/2 teaspoon vanilla extract
2 eggs

1 tablespoon fresh lemon juice
1/2 teaspoon grated lemon rind
1 9-inch graham cracker shell

- Cream first 3 ingredients at medium speed in mixer bowl until light. Beat in eggs. Stir in lemon juice and rind. Spoon into pie shell. Bake at 350 degrees for 40 minutes or until center is nearly set. Cool on wire rack. Chill for 3 hours or longer.

Approx Per Serving: Cal 379; Prot 7 g; Carbo 24 g; Fiber <1 g; T Fat 29 g; 67% Calories from Fat; Chol 115 mg; Sod 323 mg.

Ellen Carver, George School Campus Chapter, Newtown, PA

Family Celebration Cheesecake

Yield: 18 servings

6 tablespoons butter, softened
1 cup flour
¼ cup sugar
1 egg yolk, beaten
½ teaspoon vanilla extract
40 ounces cream cheese, softened
1¾ cups sugar
3 tablespoons flour

1 teaspoon vanilla extract
5 eggs, at room temperature
2 egg yolks, at room temperature
¼ cup whipping cream
2 cups sliced strawberries
2 tablespoons sugar

■ Combine butter, 1 cup flour, ¼ cup sugar, 1 egg yolk and ½ teaspoon vanilla in bowl; mix well. Press evenly over bottom and side of parchment-lined 9-inch springform pan. Combine cream cheese and 1¾ cups sugar in mixer bowl just until blended. Add 3 tablespoons flour; mix well. Stir in 1 teaspoon vanilla. Add eggs 1 at a time, mixing just until blended. Stir in 2 egg yolks 1 at a time. Blend in cream. Spoon into prepared pan. Bake at 475 degrees for 12 minutes. Reduce oven temperature to 250 degrees. Bake for 1½ hours. Turn off oven. Let stand in closed oven for 1 hour. Cool; store in refrigerator or freezer. Top with strawberries sprinkled with 2 tablespoons sugar.
Approx Per Serving: Cal 428; Prot 8 g; Carbo 34 g; Fiber 1 g; T Fat 30 g; 61% Calories from Fat; Chol 178 mg; Sod 242 mg.

Peter Flick, Freeborn/Mower HFH, Albert Lea, MN

Lenore's Bullfrog Cheesecake

Yield: 16 servings

2 cups sour cream
¼ cup sugar
1 teaspoon vanilla extract
¾ cup coarsely ground walnuts
¾ cup graham cracker crumbs
3 tablespoons melted unsalted butter

32 ounces cream cheese, softened
4 eggs
1¼ cups sugar
1 tablespoon lemon juice
2 teaspoons vanilla extract
1 21-ounce can cherry pie filling

■ Combine sour cream, ¼ cup sugar and 1 teaspoon vanilla in bowl; mix well. Chill, covered, in refrigerator. Combine walnuts, graham cracker crumbs and butter in bowl; mix well. Press evenly over bottom and side of lightly buttered 10-inch springform pan. Beat cream cheese in mixer bowl until light and fluffy. Add eggs, 1¼ cups sugar, lemon juice and 2 teaspoons vanilla; mix well. Spoon into prepared pan. Bake at 350 degrees for 40 to 45 minutes or until set. Let stand for 15 minutes. Spread chilled sour cream mixture to within ½ inch of edge. Bake for 15 minutes. Remove to wire rack to cool. Chill for 1 to 3 days. Top with pie filling before serving.
Approx Per Serving: Cal 492; Prot 9 g; Carbo 37 g; Fiber 1 g; T Fat 36 g; 64% Calories from Fat; Chol 134 mg; Sod 248 mg.

Jo Anne Krolak, Chemung County HFH, Elmira, NY

Quick Cheesecake

Yield: 12 servings

2½ cups graham cracker crumbs
6 tablespoons sugar
½ cup butter
1 teaspoon cinnamon
24 ounces cream cheese, softened
1½ cups sugar

4 egg yolks, at room temperature
1 cup sour cream, at room temperature
1 teaspoon vanilla extract
4 egg whites, stiffly beaten

■ Mix graham cracker crumbs, 6 tablespoons sugar, butter and cinnamon in bowl. Press into springform pan. Place in freezer while preparing filling. Beat cream cheese in mixer bowl until light. Add 1½ cups sugar, beating until fluffy. Beat in egg yolks 1 at a time. Fold in sour cream, vanilla and egg whites. Spoon into prepared pan. Bake at 300 degrees for 1 hour or until set and golden brown. Cool on wire rack. Garnish with confectioners' sugar. Serve immediately or chill until serving time.
Approx Per Serving: Cal 560; Prot 9 g; Carbo 53 g; Fiber 1 g; T Fat 36 g; 57% Calories from Fat; Chol 162 mg; Sod 416 mg.

Lynda Johnson Robb
Wife of Charles Robb, U.S. Senator, Virginia, McLean, VA

Best Cheesecake

Yield: 12 servings

1 1/2 cups graham
    cracker crumbs
2 tablespoons sugar
1 teaspoon cinnamon
6 tablespoons melted
    butter
1 cup sugar
24 ounces cream
    cheese, softened

4 eggs
2 teaspoons vanilla
    extract
2 cups sour cream
2 tablespoons sugar
1 teaspoon vanilla
    extract

■ Press mixture of graham cracker crumbs, 2 tablespoons sugar, cinnamon and butter over bottom and 3/4 inch up side of buttered 9-inch springform pan. Chill in freezer. Cream 1 cup sugar and cream cheese in mixer bowl. Beat in eggs 1 at a time. Beat in 2 teaspoons vanilla. Spoon into prepared pan. Bake at 350 degrees for 40 minutes. Cool on wire rack. Spread mixture of remaining ingredients over cheesecake. Bake at 500 degrees for 5 minutes. Cool on wire rack. Chill for 2 hours or longer.

Approx Per Serving: Cal 501; Prot 9 g; Carbo 36 g; Fiber <1 g; T Fat 37 g; 65% Calories from Fat; Chol 165 mg; Sod 352 mg.

Margaret Golden, Pensacola HFH, Milton, FL

Poppy Seed Cheesecake

Yield: 12 servings

2 cups fine Zwieback
    crumbs
1/2 cup sugar
1 1/2 tablespoons poppy
    seed
1/2 cup margarine,
    softened
1 cup sugar

4 eggs
24 ounces cottage
    cheese
1 cup light cream
2 tablespoons lemon
    juice
1/4 cup flour
1/4 teaspoon salt

■ Combine Zwieback crumbs, 1/2 cup sugar and poppy seed in bowl. Add margarine; mix well. Reserve 3/4 cup crumb mixture for topping. Press remaining crumb mixture over bottom and sides of 8x10-inch baking dish. Beat remaining 1 cup sugar into eggs. Process cottage cheese in blender until smooth. Add to egg mixture with remaining ingredients; beat until smooth. Spoon into prepared dish; sprinkle with reserved crumbs. Bake at 350 degrees for 1 1/4 hours or until center is set. Turn off oven. Let stand in oven for 1 hour. Cool on wire rack. Chill until serving time.

Approx Per Serving: Cal 360; Prot 12 g; Carbo 42 g; Fiber <1 g; T Fat 16 g; 40% Calories from Fat; Chol 87 mg; Sod 437 mg.

Peggy Ann Kress, Sheboygan County HFH, Sheboygan, WI

My Kind of Cheesecake

Yield: 12 servings

1/2 cup butter
1 cup sifted flour
1/4 cup sugar
1 teaspoon grated
    lemon rind
1 egg yolk
1/4 teaspoon vanilla
    extract
40 ounces cream
    cheese, softened
1/4 teaspoon vanilla
    extract
3/4 teaspoon grated
    lemon rind

1 3/4 cups sugar
3 tablespoons flour
1/4 teaspoon salt
4 or 5 eggs
2 egg yolks
1/4 cup whipping cream
3 tablespoons sugar
1 tablespoon cornstarch
1 cup unsweetened
    pineapple juice
1/4 teaspoon grated
    lemon rind
6 pineapple slices, cut
    into halves

■ Cut butter into mixture of next 3 ingredients in bowl. Add 1 egg yolk and 1/4 teaspoon vanilla; mix well. Remove side of springform pan. Press 1/3 of the mixture over bottom of pan. Bake at 400 degrees for 8 minutes. Replace side of pan. Press remaining mixture 1 3/4 inches up side of pan. Beat cream cheese with 1/4 teaspoon vanilla and 3/4 teaspoon lemon rind. Blend in 1 3/4 cups sugar, 3 tablespoons flour and salt. Beat in eggs and 2 egg yolks 1 at a time. Stir in cream. Spoon into prepared pan. Bake at 450 degrees for 12 minutes. Bake at 300 degrees for 55 minutes. Cool on wire rack for 30 minutes. Loosen from side of pan with knife. Cool for 30 minutes. Place on serving plate; remove side of pan. Cool for 2 hours. Mix 3 tablespoons sugar and cornstarch in saucepan. Stir in pineapple juice and 1/4 teaspoon lemon rind. Cook until thickened, stirring constantly. Cool. Arrange pineapple on cheesecake. Spoon glaze over top. Chill overnight.

Approx Per Serving: Cal 677; Prot 12 g; Carbo 56 g; Fiber 1 g; T Fat 46 g; 61% Calories from Fat; Chol 273 mg; Sod 423 mg.

Vicki Katsikis, Coos Bay Area HFH, Coos Bay, OR

Chocolate Cream Squares
Yield: 48 servings

2 16-ounce rolls refrigerator chocolate chip cookie dough
16 ounces cream cheese, softened

2 eggs
1 cup sugar
2 teaspoons vanilla extract

■ Slice cookie dough. Arrange half the slices in 9x13-inch greased baking dish. Combine cream cheese, eggs, sugar and vanilla in mixer bowl; beat until smooth. Spread in prepared dish; top with remaining cookie dough slices. Bake at 350 degrees for 40 minutes. Cool on wire rack. Cut into squares.
Approx Per Serving: Cal 138; Prot 2 g; Carbo 15 g; Fiber 0 g; T Fat 7 g; 48% Calories from Fat; Chol 25 mg; Sod 98 mg.

Denise Turcotte, Pinellas HFH, St. Petersburg, FL

Chocolate Dessert
Yield: 12 servings

2 cups graham cracker crumbs
3/4 cup melted butter
12 ounces whipped topping
1 cup sugar
8 ounces cream cheese, softened

1 3-ounce package vanilla instant pudding mix
1 3-ounce package chocolate instant pudding mix
3 cups very cold milk
1 cup chopped pecans

■ Combine graham cracker crumbs and butter in bowl. Press into bottom of 9x13-inch dish. Beat half the whipped topping, sugar and cream cheese in bowl until smooth. Spread in prepared dish. Beat pudding mixes and milk in mixer bowl until thickened. Spread over top layer. Spread with remaining whipped topping; sprinkle with pecans.
Approx Per Serving: Cal 564; Prot 6 g; Carbo 57 g; Fiber 1 g; T Fat 36 g; 56% Calories from Fat; Chol 60 mg; Sod 404 mg.

Ruth Mullenax, Almost Heaven HFH, Cherry Grove, WV

Chocolate Eclair Dessert
Yield: 12 servings

2 3-ounce packages French vanilla instant pudding mix
2²/₃ cups milk
1 envelope unflavored gelatin
8 ounces whipped topping
1 16-ounce package cinnamon graham crackers

5 tablespoons margarine, softened
6 tablespoons baking cocoa
2 teaspoons light corn syrup
1 teaspoon vanilla extract
3/4 cup confectioners' sugar
3 tablespoons milk

■ Beat pudding mix, 2²/₃ cups milk and unflavored gelatin in mixer bowl until thickened. Fold in whipped topping gently. Line 9x13-inch dish with whole graham crackers. Spread with half the pudding. Repeat layers. Cover with graham crackers. Beat margarine, baking cocoa, corn syrup, vanilla, confectioners' sugar and remaining milk in bowl until smooth. Spread over top layer. Chill overnight.
Approx Per Serving: Cal 421; Prot 6 g; Carbo 60 g; Fiber 1 g; T Fat 18 g; 37% Calories from Fat; Chol 8 mg; Sod 411 mg.

Judy Early, Central Valley HFH, Broadway, VA

Chocolate Eclair Delight
Yield: 20 servings

1 16-ounce package graham crackers
2 3-ounce packages French vanilla instant pudding mix
3¹/₂ cups milk
8 ounces whipped topping
2 ounces unsweetened chocolate, melted

2 teaspoons light corn syrup
2 teaspoons vanilla extract
2 tablespoons butter, softened
1¹/₂ cups confectioners' sugar
3 tablespoons milk

■ Line bottom of buttered 9x13-inch dish with graham crackers. Combine pudding mix and 3¹/₂ cups milk in mixer bowl. Beat at medium speed for 2 minutes. Fold in whipped topping gently. Spread half the mixture in prepared dish. Alternate layers of graham crackers, remaining pudding mixture and graham crackers. Chill for 2 hours. Combine chocolate, corn syrup, vanilla, butter, confectioners' sugar and remaining 3 tablespoons milk in bowl. Beat until smooth. Spread over top layer. Chill for 24 hours. Cut into squares. Store in refrigerator.
Approx Per Serving: Cal 254; Prot 4 g; Carbo 40 g; Fiber 1 g; T Fat 9 g; 33% Calories from Fat; Chol 9 mg; Sod 228 mg.

Loretta Smith, Genesee Valley HFH, Alfred, NY

Chocolate Eclair Pie

Yield: 12 servings

1 16-ounce package
  graham crackers
2 3-ounce packages
  vanilla instant
  pudding mix
3 cups cold milk

8 ounces whipped
  topping
1 16-ounce can
  ready-spread
  chocolate frosting

■ Line 9x13-inch dish with whole graham crackers. Beat pudding mix and milk in mixer bowl until thickened. Fold in whipped topping gently. Spread half the mixture in prepared dish. Alternate layers of remaining graham crackers and remaining pudding mixture over top. Microwave chocolate frosting in glass dish on High for 25 seconds or until softened. Spread over graham cracker layer. Chill overnight.
Approx Per Serving: Cal 467; Prot 6 g; Carbo 73 g; Fiber 1 g; T Fat 17 g; 33% Calories from Fat; Chol 8 mg; Sod 439 mg.

Marietta Payne, North Webster HFH, Springhill, LA

Giant Cream Puff

Yield: 24 servings

1 cup water
1/2 cup margarine
1 cup flour
4 eggs
2 3-ounce packages
  vanilla instant
  pudding mix

2 1/2 cups milk
8 ounces cream cheese,
  softened
8 ounces whipped
  topping
1 8-ounce can
  chocolate syrup

■ Prepare first 4 ingredients as above. Spread on greased baking sheet. Bake at 400 degrees for 25 to 35 minutes or until golden brown. Cool. Beat pudding mix and milk in mixer bowl for 2 minutes. Add cream cheese; mix well. Spread over baked layer. Top with whipped topping. Drizzle with chocolate syrup.
Approx Per Serving: Cal 192; Prot 4 g; Carbo 20 g; Fiber <1 g; T Fat 12 g; 52% Calories from Fat; Chol 49 mg; Sod 152 mg.

Gertrude Potter, Newaygo HFH, Fremont, MI

Cream Puffs

Yield: 36 servings

1 cup water
1/2 cup butter
1 cup flour
4 eggs
3/4 cup sugar

1/3 cup flour
2 cups milk
2 eggs, beaten
1 teaspoon vanilla
  extract

■ Bring water and butter to a boil in saucepan. Add 1 cup flour, beating until mixture thickens and forms a ball. Remove from heat. Cool slightly. Add 4 eggs 1 at a time, beating well after each addition. Drop by spoonfuls onto baking sheet. Bake at 400 degrees for 35 to 40 minutes or until golden brown; split. Mix sugar and 1/3 cup flour in saucepan. Stir in milk, 2 eggs and vanilla. Cook over medium heat until thickened, stirring constantly. Cool. Fill puffs. Chill.
Approx Per Serving: Cal 77; Prot 2 g; Carbo 8 g; Fiber <1 g; T Fat 4 g; 46% Calories from Fat; Chol 44 mg; Sod 39 mg.

Sister Francine Schwarzenberger, HFH International
Great Bend, KS

Cream Puff Squares

Yield: 8 servings

1/2 cup butter
1 cup flour
1 cup water
1/4 teaspoon salt
4 eggs
8 ounces cream cheese,
  softened
1 6-ounce package
  vanilla instant
  pudding mix,
  prepared

8 ounces whipped
  topping
1 8-ounce can
  chocolate syrup

■ Melt butter in large saucepan over low heat. Stir in flour and water. Cook until mixture begins to form ball. Beat in salt and eggs. Spread in 9x13-inch baking dish. Bake at 425 degrees for 20 minutes. Let stand until cool. Beat cream cheese in bowl until smooth. Add pudding; mix well. Spread over cooled baked layer. Top with whipped topping. Drizzle with chocolate syrup. Chill for 1 hour. Cut into squares
Approx Per Serving: Cal 564; Prot 11 g; Carbo 56 g; Fiber 1 g; T Fat 35 g; 54% Calories from Fat; Chol 180 mg; Sod 594 mg.

Laura VanDeKrol, Caldwell County HFH, Lenoir, NC

Mini Puffs

Yield: 48 servings

1 cup water
1/2 cup shortening
1/8 teaspoon salt
1 cup flour
4 eggs
1 cup sugar
1/4 cup cornstarch
3 cups milk
4 egg yolks, slightly
  beaten
8 teaspoons margarine

2 teaspoons vanilla
  extract
1/2 teaspoon almond
  extract
2 ounces unsweetened
  chocolate
1/4 cup margarine,
  softened
4 cups confectioners'
  sugar

■ Bring water to a boil in saucepan. Add shortening and 1/8 teaspoon salt. Return to a boil. Stir in flour with a wooden spoon. Cook until mixture forms a ball. Remove from heat. Add eggs 1 at a time, beating well after each addition. Beat until mixture is thick and shiny. Drop by teaspoonfuls 2 inches apart onto ungreased baking sheet. Bake at 450 degrees for 10 to 12 minutes. Reduce heat to 350 degrees and bake for 10 to 12 minutes longer. Combine sugar and cornstarch in saucepan. Add 2 2/3 cups milk gradually, stirring constantly. Cook over medium heat until thickened, stirring constantly. Cook for 2 minutes longer. Stir a small amount of hot mixture into 4 beaten egg yolks; stir egg yolks into hot mixture. Cook for 2 minutes longer, stirring constantly. Remove from heat. Stir in 8 teaspoons margarine, 1 teaspoon vanilla and almond flavoring. Let stand until cool. Melt chocolate in small saucepan. Let stand until cool. Cream 1/4 cup margarine with 2 cups confectioners' sugar in mixer bowl until light and fluffy. Add remaining 1 teaspoon vanilla and 2 tablespoons of the remaining milk; mix well. Add chocolate, beating constantly. Add remaining 2 cups confectioners' sugar and remaining milk gradually, beating constantly until of desired consistency. Split cream puffs. Fill with cooled custard. Spread chocolate frosting over tops.
Approx Per Serving: Cal 127; Prot 2 g; Carbo 18 g; Fiber <1 g; T Fat 6 g; 40% Calories from Fat; Chol 38 mg; Sod 37 mg.

Nola Morrell, HFH of Green County, Monroe, WI

Women doing "housework" in Minnesota

Dirt Cake

Yield: 10 servings

1 10-ounce package
  Oreo cookies,crushed
8-ounces cream cheese,
  softened
1 cup confectioners'
  sugar
1/4 cup margarine,
  softened

2 4-ounce packages
  vanilla instant
  pudding mix
3 1/2 cups milk
10 ounces whipped
  topping

■ Line bottom of bowl with 1/3 of the crushed cookies. Beat cream cheese, confectioners' sugar and margarine in mixer bowl until light and fluffy. Combine pudding mixes, milk and whipped topping in bowl; mix well. Spoon 1/2 of the cream cheese mixture over cookies in prepared bowl. Top with 1/2 of the pudding mixture. Sprinkle with 1/3 of the cookies. Repeat layers, ending with cookies.
Approx Per Serving: Cal 531; Prot 6 g; Carbo 65 g; Fiber 1 g; T Fat 28 g; 47% Calories from Fat; Chol 36 mg; Sod 449 mg.

Jeanette Ross, Bahama, NC

Dirt Pie

Yield: 10 servings

1/2 cup butter
1 16-ounce package
  Oreo cookies,
  crushed
8 ounces cream cheese,
  softened

2 6-ounce packages
  vanilla instant
  pudding mix
12 ounces whipped
  topping

■ Melt butter in baking pan. Press crushed cookies over butter. Prepare pudding mixes using package directions. Combine cream cheese and pudding in blender container. Process for 2 minutes. Spoon into prepared pan. Chill until set. Top with whipped topping.
Approx Per Serving: Cal 670; Prot 9 g; Carbo 74 g; Fiber <1 g; T Fat 40 g; 52% Calories from Fat; Chol 68 mg; Sod 817 mg.

Damon Malone, HFH of the Kokomo Community, Kokomo, IN

Dirt Pudding Dessert

Yield: 15 servings

1 20-ounce package
  Oreo cookies
1/4 cup margarine,
  softened
8 ounces cream cheese,
  softened
1 cup confectioners'
  sugar

31/2 cups milk
2 3-ounce packages
  vanilla instant
  pudding mix
12 ounces whipped
  topping
1 20-ounce can cherry
  pie filling

■ Process cookies in food processor until crushed. Cream next 3 ingredients in mixer bowl until smooth. Mix milk and pudding mix in bowl. Fold in whipped topping gently. Stir into cream cheese mixture. Place 1/3 of the cookies crumbs in clean 8-inch flowerpot. Layer pudding mixture, pie filling and remaining cookies crumbs 1/2 at a time in flowerpot. Chill for 8 hours to overnight. Decorate with artificial flowers. Serve with garden trowel. May add a few gummy worms between layers and as garnish for top.
Approx Per Serving: Cal 480; Prot 5 g; Carbo 64 g; Fiber 1 g; T Fat 24 g; 43% Calories from Fat; Chol 24 mg; Sod 376 mg.

James C. Picard, HFH-Anchorage, Anchorage, AK

Pennsylvania Dutch Apple Dumplings

Yield: 5 servings

2 cups flour
1 teaspoon salt
2/3 cup shortening
1/4 to 1/2 cup water
5 apples, cored, peeled
5 teaspoons sugar

Cinnamon to taste
5 teaspoons margarine
11/2 cups sugar
11/2 cups water
1/4 teaspoon cinnamon
1/4 cup margarine

■ Mix flour, salt and shortening in bowl. Add 1/4 to 1/2 cup water gradually, stirring until mixture forms ball. Roll into five 8-inch circles on lightly floured surface. Place 1 apple in center of each circle. Fill each apple with 1 teaspoon sugar, cinnamon and 1 teaspoon margarine. Fold pastry over apples, pressing edges to seal. Place in baking pan. Boil remaining ingredients in saucepan for 5 minutes, stirring constantly. Spoon around apples. Bake at 425 degrees for 40 minutes or until brown.
Approx Per Serving: Cal 858; Prot 6 g; Carbo 121 g; Fiber 4 g; T Fat 41 g; 42% Calories from Fat; Chol 0 mg; Sod 581 mg.

Jeanne Jacoby Smith
McPherson College Campus Chapter
McPherson, KS

Fungie or Blueberry Dumplings

Yield: 4 servings

3/4 cup flour
2 teaspoons baking
  powder
1/8 teaspoon salt
1/2 cup milk
2 cups blueberries

1/4 cup sugar
1/2 teaspoon cinnamon
1/4 teaspoon nutmeg
1 teaspoon grated
  lemon rind
1 teaspoon lemon juice

■ Mix flour, baking powder, salt and milk in bowl. Cook remaining ingredients in saucepan over low heat until thickened, stirring constantly. Drop flour mixture by teaspoonfuls on top. Cook for 10 minutes or until dumplings test done.
Approx Per Serving: Cal 196; Prot 4 g; Carbo 43 g; Fiber 3 g; T Fat 2 g; 7% Calories from Fat; Chol 4 mg; Sod 249 mg.

Lynn Hopper, Benton HFH, Corvallis, OR

Flan

Yield: 6 servings

²/₃ cup sugar
5 eggs
2 egg yolks
4 cups half and half
¹/₄ teaspoon salt

1 cup sugar
1 tablespoon vanilla
   extract
1 cup sugar
1 cup water

▪ Sprinkle ²/₃ cup sugar in heavy skillet. Heat over medium heat for 5 minutes or until sugar melts and turns golden brown, stirring constantly. Pour into baking dish, coating sides and bottom. Set aside to cool. Beat eggs, egg yolks and half and half in bowl until smooth. Blend in salt and 1 cup sugar. Add vanilla; mix well. Strain; pour into prepared dish. Place in pan of hot water. Bake, covered, at 325 degrees for 1¹/₂ hours or until flan tests done. Cool slightly. Invert onto serving platter. Cool completely before serving. Sprinkle 1 cup sugar in heavy skillet. Heat over medium heat until sugar melts and turns golden brown, stirring constantly. Add 1 cup water; mix well. Boil until sugar dissolves, stirring constantly. Serve flan with cooled sugar mixture.

Approx Per Serving: Cal 646; Prot 11 g; Carbo 97 g; Fiber 0 g; T Fat 25 g; 34% Calories from Fat; Chol 308 mg; Sod 217 mg.

Kenneth P. Blinn, HFH of Butler County, Slippery Rock, PA

Grape Nuts Custard

Yield: 6 servings

¹/₃ cup sugar
3 eggs
1 teaspoon vanilla
   extract
2 cups half and half

6 teaspoons Grape
   Nuts
1 tablespoon
   cinnamon sugar

▪ Combine sugar, eggs, and vanilla in blender container. Process on High for 30 seconds. Heat half and half in saucepan just to the boiling point. Pour into egg mixture. Process on Medium for 30 seconds. Spoon into 6 buttered ramekins. Sprinkle with cereal and cinnamon sugar. Place in 9x13-inch baking pan. Add enough hot water to pan to come halfway up sides of ramekins. Bake at 350 degrees for 30 minutes or until set.

Approx Per Serving: Cal 204; Prot 6 g; Carbo 19 g; Fiber <1 g; T Fat 12 g; 53% Calories from Fat; Chol 136 mg; Sod 84 mg.

Dana's by the Gorge Restaurant, for Upper Valley HFH
Quechee, VT

Coconut-Pecan Praline Ice Cream Bars

Yield: 36 servings

¹/₂ cup packed brown
   sugar
2 cups flour
¹/₂ cup quick-cooking
   oats
1 cup chopped pecans
1 cup melted margarine

1 cup shredded
   coconut, toasted
1 16-ounce jar
   caramel ice cream
   topping
¹/₂ gallon vanilla ice
   cream, sliced

▪ Combine brown sugar, flour, oats, pecans and margarine in bowl; mix well. Pat into nonstick 9x13-inch baking pan. Bake at 350 degrees for 15 minutes. Stir with fork. Reserve ¹/₂ of the crumb mixture. Press remaining mixture into nonstick 9x13-inch baking pan. Sprinkle with ¹/₂ of the coconut. Drizzle with ¹/₂ of the ice cream topping. Arrange sliced ice cream over prepared layers. Sprinkle with reserved crumbs. Top with remaining coconut and ice cream topping. Freeze until firm.

Approx Per Serving: Cal 223; Prot 3 g; Carbo 29 g; Fiber 1 g; T Fat 12 g; 46% Calories from Fat; Chol 13 mg; Sod 132 mg.

Adrienne M. Stevens
University of Kentucky Campus Chapter, Lexington, KY

T his is how we know what love is: Jesus Christ laid down his life for us. And we ought to lay down our lives for our brothers. If anyone has material possessions and sees his brother in need but has no pity on him, how can the love of God be in him? Dear children, let us not love with words or tongue but with actions and in truth.

I John 3:16-18

Lemon Velvet Ice Cream

Yield: 16 servings

5¹/₃ cups whipping cream
5¹/₃ cups milk
Juice of 8 lemons
4 cups sugar

2 teaspoons lemon extract
1 tablespoon grated lemon rind

- Combine all ingredients in bowl; mix well. Pour into ice cream freezer container. Freeze using manufacturer's instructions.
Approx Per Serving: Cal 522; Prot 4 g; Carbo 58 g; Fiber <1 g; T Fat 32 g; 54% Calories from Fat; Chol 120 mg; Sod 65 mg.

Alice H. Cummings, Southeast Volusia HFH
New Smyrna Beach, FL

Kid's Dessert

Yield: 6 servings

3 English muffins, split, toasted
3 teaspoons butter

6 tablespoons vanilla ice cream, softened

- Spread toasted muffin halves with butter. Top each with 1 tablespoon ice cream. Serve immediately. May substitute any flavor ice cream.
Approx Per Serving: Cal 104; Prot 3 g; Carbo 15 g; Fiber 1 g; T Fat 3 g; 30% Calories from Fat; Chol 9 mg; Sod 212 mg.

Anita Domenichini, HFH of Chico, Durham, CA

Oreo Cookie-Ice Cream Dessert

Yield: 24 servings

27 oreo cookies, crushed
¹/₃ cup melted butter
¹/₂ gallon coffee ice cream, softened

1 16-ounce jar fudge ice cream topping
16 ounces whipped topping
3 oreo cookies, crushed

- Combine 27 crushed cookies with butter in bowl; mix well. Pat into nonstick 9x13-inch dish. Freeze, covered, for 20 minutes. Spoon ice cream over frozen layer. Drizzle with fudge topping. Freeze, covered, for 20 minutes. Spread with whipped topping. Sprinkle with 3 crushed cookies. Freeze, covered, overnight. Cut into squares.
Approx Per Serving: Cal 298; Prot 3 g; Carbo 34 g; Fiber 1 g; T Fat 17 g; 51% Calories from Fat; Chol 27 mg; Sod 145 mg.

Sarah K. Rutter, Homestead HFH, Homestead, FL

Lemon Meringue Delight

Yield: 18 servings

55 butter crackers, crushed
³/₄ cup melted margarine
4 egg whites

1 cup sugar
2 21-ounce cans lemon pie filling
12 ounces whipped topping

- Combine cracker crumbs and margarine in bowl; mix well. Pat evenly into 9x13-inch baking pan. Beat egg whites in mixer bowl until soft peaks form. Add sugar gradually, beating until stiff peaks form. Spread over crumb layer. Bake at 350 degrees for 15 minutes. Spread pie filling over cooled meringue. Top with whipped topping. Store in refrigerator.
Approx Per Serving: Cal 283; Prot 2 g; Carbo 39 g; Fiber 1 g; T Fat 15 g; 46% Calories from Fat; Chol 0 mg; Sod 217 mg.

Karen Bentz, HFH of Wausau, Wausau, WI

Mango Pango

Yield: 6 servings

1 large mango, peeled, chopped
1 large banana, thinly sliced

2 tablespoons chocolate syrup

- Combine mango, banana and chocolate syrup in bowl; mix well. Spoon into Popsicle molds. Freeze until firm. May substitute crushed pineapple or chopped strawberries for chocolate.
Approx Per Serving: Cal 54; Prot 1 g; Carbo 14 g; Fiber 2 g; T Fat <1 g; 4% Calories from Fat; Chol 0 mg; Sod 6 mg.

Bob Graham, Homestead HFH, Naples, FL

Poof

Yield: 5 servings

1 tablespoon
  unflavored gelatin
1/2 cup water
2 egg whites
3 tablespoons cold
  water
1/3 cup sugar
3/4 teaspoon vanilla
  extract

1/2 cup chopped pecans
1 tablespoon sugar
1 tablespoon baking
  cocoa
1 cup whipping cream,
  whipped

■ Soften gelatin in 1/2 cup water in saucepan. Cook over medium heat until gelatin dissolves, stirring constantly. Beat egg whites in mixer bowl until soft peaks form. Add 3 tablespoons cold water while beating. Add 1/3 cup sugar gradually, beating until stiff peaks form. Stir in cooled gelatin, vanilla and pecans. Reserve 1/2 of the mixture. Add 1 tablespoon sugar and baking cocoa to remaining mixture; mix well. Spoon into nonstick 3-cup mold. Top with reserved gelatin mixture. Chill until set. Top with whipped cream.
Approx Per Serving: Cal 319; Prot 5 g; Carbo 20 g; Fiber 1 g; T Fat 26 g; 70% Calories from Fat; Chol 65 mg; Sod 40 mg.

Dixie Sheldon, Coos Bay Area HFH, Coos Bay, OR

Chocolate Mousse

Yield: 12 servings

2 cups semisweet
  chocolate chips
1/2 cup hot water
6 egg yolks

1/4 cup sugar
1 cup whipping cream,
  whipped
1 teaspoon rum extract

■ Melt chocolate chips with hot water in double boiler, stirring constantly. Cool slightly. Beat egg yolks and sugar in mixer bowl until thick. Stir into chocolate mixture. Fold in whipped cream. Stir in rum flavoring. Spoon into serving bowl. Chill for several hours.
Approx Per Serving: Cal 259; Prot 3 g; Carbo 21 g; Fiber 1 g; T Fat 20 g; 66% Calories from Fat; Chol 134 mg; Sod 16 mg.

Cindy Owen, HFH of Wausau, Wausau, WI

Next-Best-Thing To Robert Redford

Yield: 15 servings

1 cup flour
1/2 cup margarine,
  softened
1 cup finely chopped
  pecans
8 ounces cream cheese,
  softened
12 ounces whipped
  topping
1 cup confectioners'
  sugar

1 4-ounce package
  vanilla instant
  pudding mix
1 4-ounce package
  chocolate instant
  pudding mix
3 cups milk
1 2-ounce chocolate
  candy bar, grated
1/4 cup finely chopped
  pecans

■ Pat mixture of flour, margarine and 1 cup pecans evenly into 9x13-inch baking pan. Bake at 350 degrees for 15 minutes or until light brown. Cool. Beat cream cheese, 1 cup whipped topping and confectioners' sugar in mixer bowl until light and fluffy. Spread over baked layer. Combine pudding mixes and milk in bowl, stirring until thickened. Spoon into prepared pan. Top with remaining whipped topping, candy bar and 1/4 cup pecans.
Approx Per Serving: Cal 412; Prot 5 g; Carbo 40 g; Fiber 1 g; T Fat 27 g; 57% Calories from Fat; Chol 24 mg; Sod 247 mg.

Kathleen C. Groner, Jackson County, HFH Eastern
Blue Springs, MO

Ice Cream Delight

Yield: 18 servings

80 butter crackers
1/4 cup butter
1/2 gallon vanilla ice
  cream, softened
1 cup milk

1 6-ounce package
  pistachio instant
  pudding mix
16 ounces whipped
  topping

■ Crush crackers. Mix with butter in bowl. Reserve 1/2 cup. Pat remaining crumbs into 9x13-inch dish. Combine ice cream, milk and instant pudding mix in bowl; mix well. Fold in whipped topping. Spread over crumb layer. Sprinkle with reserved crumbs. Chill for 2 hours.
Approx Per Serving: Cal 332; Prot 4 g; Carbo 39 g; Fiber <1 g; T Fat 20 g; 51% Calories from Fat; Chol 35 mg; Sod 282 mg.

Karen Lee Smith, Greater East Liverpool HFH
East Liverpool, OH

Fresh Orange Mousse

Yield: 6 servings

2 envelopes
  unflavored gelatin
¹/₄ cup water
¹/₄ cup superfine sugar
3 egg yolks

Grated rind of 1 orange
Juice of 3 oranges
3 egg whites
2 tablespoons sugar

- Mix gelatin and water in saucepan. Let stand for several minutes. Cook over low heat until gelatin dissolves, stirring constantly. Beat ¹/₄ cup sugar and egg yolks in bowl until thickened. Add orange rind; mix well. Whisk in gelatin and orange juice. Chill just until set, stirring occasionally. Beat egg whites with 2 tablespoons sugar in mixer bowl until stiff. Fold into chilled mixture. Chill until set.

  Approx Per Serving: Cal 116; Prot 5 g; Carbo 18 g; Fiber 1 g; T Fat 3 g; 22% Calories from Fat; Chol 106 mg; Sod 32 mg.

Andrea Natasha McKee, Trinity Presbyterian, Starkville, MS

Orange Charlotte

Yield: 12 servings

2 cups boiling orange
  juice
1 cup boiling water
1 3-ounce package
  orange gelatin
1 3-ounce package
  lemon gelatin

¹/₃ cup sugar
2 cups whipping
  cream, whipped
2 tablespoons sugar
¹/₄ cup grated coconut

- Mix boiling orange juice, boiling water, gelatin and ¹/₃ cup sugar in bowl. Let stand until cool and thickened. Fold in 1 cup whipping cream. Spoon into greased 4 to 6-cup mold. Chill until firm. Invert onto serving platter. Spread with mixture of 1 cup whipping cream and 2 tablespoons sugar. Sprinkle with coconut. Garnish with mint leaves.

  Approx Per Serving: Cal 243; Prot 2 g; Carbo 26 g; Fiber <1 g; T Fat 15 g; 55% Calories from Fat; Chol 54 mg; Sod 61 mg.

Elise V. Winter, HFH International Board of Directors
Jackson, MS

Pavlova

Yield: 8 servings

This is a traditional dessert from New Zealand.

2 cups sugar
4 egg whites
2 tablespoons boiling
  water

1 teaspoon vanilla
  extract
1 teaspoon vinegar

- Preheat oven to 325 degrees. Place baking sheet in oven to heat. Combine sugar, egg whites, boiling water, vanilla and vinegar in mixer bowl; mix well. Beat for 10 to 15 minutes or until egg whites are stiff. Shape into 8-inch circle 3 to 4 inches thick on baking parchment. Place baking parchment on heated baking sheet. Place in oven. Reduce oven temperature to 275 degrees. Bake for 1 hour. Turn off oven. Let stand in oven with door ajar until cool. Garnish with whipped cream, chocolate shavings and sliced kiwifruit.

  Approx Per Serving: Cal 202; Prot 2 g; Carbo 50 g; Fiber 0 g; T Fat 0 g; 0% Calories from Fat; Chol 0 mg; Sod 26 mg.

Fiona Eastwood, Homestead HFH, Homestead, FL

Easy Peach Cobbler

Yield: 6 servings

¹/₂ cup melted butter
1 cup flour
1 cup sugar

1 cup milk
1 16-ounce can sliced
  peaches

- Combine butter, flour, sugar, milk and undrained peaches in baking pan; mix well. Bake at 350 degrees for 40 minutes or until brown and bubbly.

  Approx Per Serving: Cal 421; Prot 4 g; Carbo 66 g; Fiber 1 g; T Fat 17 g; 35% Calories from Fat; Chol 47 mg; Sod 152 mg.

Laurie Potthoff, Black Hills Area HFH, Rapid City, SD

Peach Cobbler

Yield: 8 servings

1 cup flour
2 teaspoons baking
  powder
1/2 teaspoon salt
1/2 cup shortening
1/4 cup milk
4 cups sliced fresh
  peaches

1 1/3 cups sugar
1/4 cup flour
2 tablespoons lemon
  juice
2 tablespoons water
2 tablespoons butter

■ Sift 1 cup flour, baking powder and salt in bowl; mix
well. Cut in shortening until crumbly. Stir in milk.
Knead until dough is no longer sticky and is easily
handled. Roll into shape of baking dish on lightly
floured surface. Arrange peaches in greased baking
dish. Sprinkle with sifted mixture of sugar and 1/4 cup
flour. Sprinkle with lemon juice and water. Dot with
butter. Top with pastry; prick with fork. Bake at 400
degrees for 15 minutes. Reduce oven temperature to
350 degrees. Bake for 15 minutes.
Approx Per Serving: Cal 381; Prot 3 g; Carbo 58 g;
Fiber 2 g; T Fat 16 g; 37% Calories from Fat;
Chol 9 mg; Sod 245 mg.

Arthur Thompson, Stroud HFH, Stroud, OK

Peaches and Cream Dessert

Yield: 9 servings

3/4 cup flour
1 4-ounce package
  vanilla pudding and
  pie filling mix
1 teaspoon baking
  powder
1 egg, beaten
1/2 cup milk
3 tablespoons melted
  margarine

1 16-ounce can sliced
  peaches, drained,
  chopped
1/3 cup peach juice
1/2 cup sugar
8 ounces cream cheese,
  softened
1 tablespoon sugar
1/2 teaspoon cinnamon

■ Combine first 3 ingredients in bowl; mix well. Stir in
mixture of egg, milk and margarine. Spoon into
greased 8x8-inch baking pan. Top with peaches. Beat
juice, 1/2 cup sugar and cream cheese in mixer bowl
until light and fluffy. Spread over peaches. Sprinkle
with mixture of 1 tablespoon sugar and cinnamon.
Bake at 350 degrees for 45 minutes.
Approx Per Serving: Cal 293; Prot 4 g; Carbo 40 g;
Fiber 1 g; T Fat 14 g; 41% Calories from Fat;
Chol 53 mg; Sod 235 mg.

John Maciok, Northern Straits HFH, St. Ignace, MI

Frozen Peach Delight

Yield: 8 servings

1 21-ounce can peach
  pie filling
1 14-ounce can
  sweetened
  condensed milk
1 8-ounce can crushed
  pineapple, drained
1/4 cup lemon juice

1/4 teaspoon almond
  extract
1/2 cup whipping
  cream, whipped
1/3 cup maraschino
  cherries, cut into
  halves

■ Combine pie filling, condensed milk, pineapple,
lemon juice and almond flavoring in bowl; mix well.
Fold in whipped cream and cherries. Spoon into 5x9-
inch dish. Freeze until firm.
Approx Per Serving: Cal 309; Prot 5 g; Carbo 53 g;
Fiber 1 g; T Fat 10 g; 28% Calories from Fat;
Chol 37 mg; Sod 91 mg.

Jan Rozeboom, HFH of South Central Minnesota
Mankato, MN

Layered Dessert with Peaches

Yield: 12 servings

1 1/2 cups finely
  crushed vanilla
  wafers
3/4 cup butter, softened
3 cups confectioners'
  sugar
5 egg yolks
1 1/2 teaspoons grated
  lemon rind
1 1/2 tablespoons lemon
  juice

1 1/2 cups whipping
  cream
3 tablespoons
  confectioners' sugar
1 teaspoon vanilla
  extract
1 29-ounce can sliced
  peaches, drained
1/2 cup finely crushed
  vanilla wafers

■ Spread 1 1/2 cups vanilla wafer crumbs in greased
8x12-inch dish. Cream butter, 3 cups confectioners'
sugar and egg yolks in mixer bowl. Add lemon rind
and lemon juice; mix well. Spread in prepared pan.
Beat whipping cream and 3 tablespoons confectioners'
sugar in mixer bowl until stiff. Stir in vanilla. Reserve
1/2 cup sliced peaches. Chop remaining peaches. Fold
into whipped cream mixture. Spread in prepared pan.
Sprinkle with 1/2 cup vanilla wafer crumbs. Chill until
firm. Top with reserved sliced peaches.
Approx Per Serving: Cal 459; Prot 3 g; Carbo 53 g;
Fiber 1 g; T Fat 27 g; 52% Calories from Fat;
Chol 170 mg; Sod 170 mg.

Janet McSweeney, Greater Lawrence HFH, Andover, MA

Pineapple Surprise

Yield: 12 servings

1 16-ounce package
    vanilla wafers,
    crushed
1 cup butter, softened
3 cups confectioners'
    sugar

4 eggs
2 cups drained crushed
    pineapple
2 cups whipping cream
1/4 cup sugar

■ Reserve 1/4 of the vanilla wafer crumbs. Pat remaining crumbs into nonstick 9x13-inch dish. Beat butter and confectioners' sugar in mixer bowl. Add eggs 1 at a time, mixing well after each addition. Spread in prepared pan. Top with pineapple. Beat whipping cream in mixer bowl until soft peaks form. Add sugar, beating until stiff. Spread over pineapple. Top with remaining wafer crumbs. Chill for 24 hours.
Approx Per Serving: Cal 627; Prot 5 g; Carbo 68 g; Fiber 1 g; T Fat 39 g; 54% Calories from Fat; Chol 190 mg; Sod 309 mg.

Jean F. Frost, New Hampshire HFH, Gilford, NH

Fresh Fruit Pizza

Yield: 12 servings

1 package sugar cookie
    mix, prepared
8 ounces cream cheese,
    softened
8 ounces whipped
    topping
1 cup sliced
    strawberries
1/2 orange, cut into
    sections

1 banana, sliced
1 kiwifruit, sliced
1/2 cup blueberries
1/2 cup sugar
1 tablespoon cornstarch
1/2 cup orange juice
1/4 cup water
1 tablespoon lemon
    juice
Salt to taste

■ Line 10-inch pizza pan with cookie dough. Bake at 375 degrees for 10 minutes or until light brown. Remove to wire rack to cool. Combine cream cheese and whipped topping in bowl; mix well. Spread over baked layer. Arrange fruit in decorative pattern over cream cheese layer. Combine sugar, cornstarch, orange juice, water, lemon juice and salt in saucepan; mix well. Boil for 1 minute, stirring constantly. Spoon over fruit. Chill until set.
Approx Per Serving: Cal 369; Prot 4 g; Carbo 45 g; Fiber 2 g; T Fat 21 g; 49% Calories from Fat; Chol 42 mg; Sod 258 mg.

Eileen Peters, Maumee Valley HFH, Sylvania, OH

Philadelphia Sweets

Yield: 120 servings

2 cups semisweet
    chocolate chips
1 cup chopped walnuts
3/4 cup sweetened
    condensed milk
1 teaspoon vanilla
    extract

1/4 teaspoon salt
1 4-ounce container
    chocolate mint
    sprinkles

■ Melt chocolate chips in saucepan over low heat, stirring constantly. Stir in next 4 ingredients. Let stand for 5 minutes or until cool enough to handle. Shape into 1-inch balls. Coat with sprinkles. Place on waxed paper-lined tray. Chill for 2 hours or until firm. Store in refrigerator in covered container.
Approx Per Serving: Cal 31; Prot <1 g; Carbo 4 g; Fiber <1 g; T Fat 2 g; 51% Calories from Fat; Chol 1 mg; Sod 9 mg.

Lillian Polisar, HFH of Boca-Delray, Boca Raton, FL

Pralines

Yield: 36 servings

2 cups sugar
3/4 teaspoon baking
    soda
1 cup milk

2 to 3 cups pecan
    halves
1 1/2 tablespoons butter

■ Mix sugar and baking soda in 3-quart saucepan with wooden spoon. Stir in milk. Bring to a boil over medium heat, stirring occasionally. Reduce heat to low. Cook to 234 to 240 degrees on candy thermometer, soft-ball stage, stirring constantly. Remove from heat. Stir in pecans and butter. Beat until thick enough to drop from spoon. Drop by tablespoonfuls onto waxed paper. Add drops of hot water if mixture gets too thick.
Approx Per Serving: Cal 111; Prot 1 g; Carbo 13 g; Fiber 1 g; T Fat 7 g; 52% Calories from Fat; Chol 2 mg; Sod 24 mg.

Marney Gibbs, Staunton-Augusta HFH, Staunton, VA

Banana Pudding

Yield: 12 servings

2 cups sugar
1 cup flour
Salt to taste
1   14-ounce can
   sweetened
   condensed milk
4 egg yolks, beaten

2 cups water
1   16-ounce package
   vanilla wafers
7 bananas, sliced
4 egg whites
1 tablespoon sugar

■ Combine 2 cups sugar, flour and salt in saucepan; mix well. Stir in mixture of sweetened condensed milk and enough water to measure 2 cups, egg yolks and 2 cups water. Cook over medium heat until thickened, stirring constantly. Alternate layers of vanilla wafers, bananas and pudding mixture in ovenproof dish until all ingredients are used. Beat egg whites in mixer bowl until soft peaks form. Add 1 tablespoon sugar gradually, beating until stiff peaks form. Spread over pudding. Bake at 350 degrees until light brown.
Approx Per Serving: Cal 539; Prot 8 g; Carbo 103 g; Fiber 2 g; T Fat 12 g; 19% Calories from Fat; Chol 106 mg; Sod 205 mg.

Bobby Loveland, HFH of the Kokomo Community, Kokomo, IN

Kay's Citrus Pudding

Yield: 4 servings

2 bananas, sliced
4 oranges, cut into
   sections
2 grapefruits, cut into
   sections

1/2 cup sugar
1 cup water
1 tablespoon cornstarch
1 cup sugar

■ Combine bananas with orange and grapefruit sections in bowl; mix well. Sprinkle with 1/2 cup sugar. Let stand until sugar is absorbed. Drain fruit. Spoon into bowl. Combine water, cornstarch and 1 cup sugar in saucepan. Boil until thickened, stirring constantly. Pour over fruit. Chill, covered, overnight.
Approx Per Serving: Cal 507; Prot 4 g; Carbo 130 g; Fiber 8 g; T Fat 1 g; 1% Calories from Fat; Chol 0 mg; Sod 3 mg.

Mrs. Robert E. Mayes, HFH of Boca-Delray, Boynton, FL

Dirt Pudding

Yield: 10 servings

2 cups milk
1   4-ounce package
   chocolate instant
   pudding mix
8 ounces whipped
   topping, thawed

1   16-ounce package
   Oreo cookies,
   crushed

■ Beat milk and pudding mix in mixer bowl until smooth. Let stand for 5 minutes. Fold in whipped topping and 1/2 of the cookie crumbs. Place 1 tablespoon cookie crumbs in each of ten 10-inch plastic cups. Spoon pudding over cookies. Top with remaining crumbs. Chill for 1 hour. Garnish with gummy worms, chopped pecans or candy flowers.
Approx Per Serving: Cal 365; Prot 4 g; Carbo 51 g; Fiber 1 g; T Fat 17 g; 40% Calories from Fat; Chol 7 mg; Sod 316 mg.

Anita L. Sailor, HFH-Colville Valley Partners, Colville, WA

Golden Syrup Pudding

Yield: 8 servings

2 tablespoons Lyle's
   Golden Syrup
1/2 cup margarine,
   softened
1/2 cup sugar
2 eggs, beaten

1 1/2 cups sifted
   self-rising flour
Warm water
2 tablespoons Lyle's
   Golden Syrup

■ Pour 2 tablespoons syrup in bottom of 2-quart pudding mold. Cream margarine and sugar in mixer bowl until light and fluffy. Add eggs; mix well. Fold in flour and enough warm water to form soft dough. Spoon into prepared mold. Steam for 1 1/2 hours. Invert onto serving platter. Spoon 2 tablespoons syrup over pudding. Serve with Bird's Custard Sauce using directions on Golden Syrup bottle.
Approx Per Serving: Cal 283; Prot 4 g; Carbo 38 g; Fiber 1 g; T Fat 13 g; 41% Calories from Fat; Chol 53 mg; Sod 409 mg.

Shirley Reid, Burlington County HFH, Mt. Holly, NJ

Yield: 6 servings

Lemon Pudding

1 cup sugar
3 tablespoons flour
3 tablespoons butter,
  softened
1 cup milk

2 egg yolks, beaten
Grated rind and juice
  of 1 lemon
2 egg whites, stiffly
  beaten

■ Combine sugar, flour and butter in bowl; mix well. Stir in milk, egg yolks, lemon rind and lemon juice. Fold in egg whites. Spoon into buttered baking dish. Place dish in pan of hot water. Bake at 300 degrees for 1 hour or until edges pull from sides of pan.
Approx Per Serving: Cal 247; Prot 4 g; Carbo 39 g; Fiber <1 g; T Fat 9 g; 32% Calories from Fat; Chol 92 mg; Sod 86 mg.

Alberta Cunningham, HFH of Wausau, Wausau, WI

Yield: 18 servings

Pumpkin Dessert Squares

3 eggs, beaten
1 30-ounce can
   pumpkin
2/3 cup packed brown
   sugar
1/3 cup sugar
1/2 teaspoon cinnamon
1/2 teaspoon ginger

1 teaspoon salt
1 2-layer package
   yellow cake mix
1 cup chopped pecans
1/2 cup melted
   margarine
8 ounces whipped
   topping

■ Combine first 7 ingredients in bowl; mix well. Spoon into greased 9x13-inch baking pan. Sprinkle with cake mix. Top with pecans; drizzle with margarine. Bake at 350 degrees for 1 hour. Cut into squares. Serve with whipped topping.
Approx Per Serving: Cal 333; Prot 3 g; Carbo 45 g; Fiber 1 g; T Fat 16 g; 43% Calories from Fat; Chol 36 mg; Sod 374 mg.

Marge Prince, Newaygo HFH, Fremont, MI

Yield: 12 servings

Crumb-Topped Rhubarb

3 cups diced rhubarb
1 tablespoon flour
1/2 cup sugar
1 teaspoon cinnamon
1/8 teaspoon salt
6 tablespoons flour

1/2 cup packed brown
   sugar
1/2 cup quick-cooking
   oats
6 tablespoons butter,
   softened

■ Combine rhubarb, 1 tablespoon flour, sugar, cinnamon and salt in bowl; mix well. Spoon into greased 8x12-inch baking pan. Mix 6 tablespoons flour, brown sugar and oats in bowl. Cut in butter until crumbly. Sprinkle over rhubarb mixture. Bake at 350 degrees for 40 minutes or until brown.
Approx Per Serving: Cal 162; Prot 1 g; Carbo 26 g; Fiber 1 g; T Fat 6 g; 33% Calories from Fat; Chol 16 mg; Sod 77 mg.

Modell Hall, Stroud HFH, Stroud, OK

Yield: 12 servings

Rhubarb Charlotte

6 cups chopped rhubarb
1/2 cup sugar
1 cup water
1 6-ounce package
   strawberry gelatin
2 cups whipping
   cream, whipped
1 teaspoon vanilla
   extract

36 ladyfingers, split
1/4 cup sugar
1 1/2 tablespoons
   cornstarch
1 to 2 drops of red
   food coloring
1 cup sliced
   strawberries

■ Cook rhubarb, 1/2 cup sugar and water in saucepan until tender. Purée in blender. Reserve 1 cup mixture. Combine remaining rhubarb mixture and gelatin in bowl; mix well. Chill for 45 minutes or until slightly thickened. Fold in whipped cream and vanilla. Layer ladyfingers and rhubarb mixture in bowl until all ingredients are used, ending with rhubarb. Combine reserved rhubarb purée, 1/4 cup sugar, cornstarch and red food coloring in saucepan. Cook over medium heat until thickened, stirring constantly. Cool; spread over rhubarb. Top with strawberries. Chill until set.
Approx Per Serving: Cal 380; Prot 5 g; Carbo 53 g; Fiber 2 g; T Fat 17 g; 40% Calories from Fat; Chol 54 mg; Sod 86 mg.

Margaret Michaletz, Steele County HFH, Owatonna, MN

*F*or I [Jesus] was hungry and you gave me something to eat, I was thirsty and you gave me something to drink, I was a stranger and you invited me in, I needed clothes and you clothed me, I was sick and you looked after me, I was in prison and you came to vist me.

Matthew 25:35-36

Springtime Rhubarb Meringue
Yield: 16 servings

2/3 cup butter, softened
12/3 cups flour
3/4 cup sugar
6 egg yolks, beaten
2 cups sugar
1/2 teaspoon salt
6 tablespoons flour
1 cup half and half
6 cups chopped
  rhubarb

2 tablespoons
  cornstarch
1/4 cup cold water
1 cup boiling water
6 egg whites
3/4 cup sugar
2 teaspoons vanilla
  extract
Salt to taste

■ Mix butter, 12/3 cups flour and 3/4 cup sugar in bowl until crumbly. Pat into 9x13-inch baking pan. Bake at 350 degrees for 10 minutes. Combine next 6 ingredients; mix well. Spoon over baked layer. Bake for 45 minutes. Combine cornstarch and cold water in saucepan; mix well. Stir in boiling water. Cook over medium heat until thickened, stirring constantly. Cool. Beat egg whites in mixer bowl until soft peaks form. Add 3/4 cup sugar gradually, beating until stiff peaks form. Fold in vanilla and salt. Beat in cooled cornstarch mixture at low speed. Beat at high speed until well blended. Spread over baked layers. Bake for 10 to 12 minutes or until brown.
Approx Per Serving: Cal 357; Prot 5 g; Carbo 59 g; Fiber 2 g; T Fat 12 g; 29% Calories from Fat; Chol 106 mg; Sod 162 mg.

Elizabeth Cook, HFH of South Central Minnesota
Mankato, MN

Scandinavian Rice
Yield: 4 servings

2 cups milk
1/4 cup rice
1/4 teaspoon salt
2 teaspoons vanilla
  extract
1 envelope unflavored
  gelatin
1/3 cup cold water

2 tablespoons butter
1/4 cup sugar
2 cups whipped
  topping
1/3 cup slivered
  almonds
1/4 cup raspberry jam

■ Scald milk in saucepan. Add rice; mix well. Cook over low heat for 20 minutes. Blend in salt and vanilla. Stir in mixture of gelatin and cold water. Add butter and sugar; mix well. Let stand to cool. Fold in whipped topping and almonds. Top with jam.
Approx Per Serving: Cal 469; Prot 9 g; Carbo 53 g; Fiber 2 g; T Fat 25 g; 48% Calories from Fat; Chol 32 mg; Sod 248 mg.

Alice E. Shriver, Jefferson, IA

Ritz Cracker Dessert
Yield: 18 servings

60 Ritz crackers,
  crushed
1/2 cup melted butter
1/2 cup chopped
  walnuts
3 4-ounce packages
  vanilla instant
  pudding mix

2 cups milk
1/2 gallon vanilla ice
  cream, softened
8 ounces whipped
  topping
10 Ritz crackers,
  crushed

■ Combine 60 crushed crackers, butter and walnuts in bowl; mix well. Pat into nonstick 9x13-inch baking pan. Beat pudding mixes and milk in mixer bowl until thickened. Add ice cream; mix well. Spoon into prepared pan. Spread with whipped topping. Sprinkle with 10 crushed crackers. Chill until set.
Approx Per Serving: Cal 371; Prot 5 g; Carbo 45 g; Fiber 1 g; T Fat 22 g; 49% Calories from Fat; Chol 44 mg; Sod 353 mg.

Carrie Leffingwell, Ashland-Ironton Area HFH
South Webster, OH

Chocolate Sauce for Ice Cream
Yield: 8 servings

1/2 cup butter
1 ounce unsweetened
  chocolate
2 cups semisweet
  chocolate chips

1 teaspoon vanilla
  extract

■ Melt butter and unsweetened chocolate in double boiler. Add chocolate chips and vanilla; mix well. Cook until blended, stirring constantly. Store, covered, in refrigerator. Reheat in double boiler.
Approx Per Serving: Cal 335; Prot 2 g; Carbo 25 g; Fiber 2 g; T Fat 29 g; 70% Calories from Fat; Chol 31 mg; Sod 103 mg.

Carrie Stell, HFH of Grayson County, Denison, TX

Hot Fudge Sauce

Yield: 32 servings

1 cup butter
4¹/₂ cups confectioners'
    sugar
1 12-ounce can
    evaporated milk

4 ounces unsweetened
    chocolate

- Melt butter in double boiler. Add confectioners' sugar and evaporated milk, stirring until sugar dissolves. Add chocolate, stirring until melted. Cook over hot water for 30 minutes. Do not stir. Remove from heat. Beat until creamy. Store in refrigerator.

Approx Per Serving: Cal 148; Prot 1 g; Carbo 19 g; Fiber 1 g; T Fat 8 g; 49% Calories from Fat; Chol 19 mg; Sod 60 mg.

Jeanne Jensen, Fergus Falls Area HFH, Fergus Falls, MN

Strawberry Crunch

Yield: 10 servings

1 cup sifted flour
¹/₂ cup chopped pecans
    or walnuts
¹/₃ cup packed brown
    sugar
¹/₂ cup melted butter
2 egg whites

²/₃ cup sugar
1 10-ounce package
    frozen strawberries,
    thawed
1 cup whipping cream,
    whipped

- Spread mixture of first 4 ingredients in 9x13-inch baking pan. Bake at 350 degrees for 20 minutes, stirring occasionally. Reserve ¹/₃ of the crumb mixture. Pat remaining crumbs in pan. Mix egg whites, sugar and undrained strawberries in mixer bowl. Beat at high speed for 10 minutes or until stiff peaks form. Fold in whipped cream. Spoon over baked layer. Sprinkle with reserved crumb mixture. Freeze overnight. May substitute 2 cups sliced fresh strawberries for frozen strawberries. Add ¹/₃ cup sugar and 2 tablespoons lemon juice.

Approx Per Serving: Cal 343; Prot 3 g; Carbo 35 g; Fiber 1 g; T Fat 22 g; 57% Calories from Fat; Chol 57 mg; Sod 101 mg.

Lois Robbins, Odessa R-VII Area HFH, Odessa, MO
Anne Parker, George School Campus Chapter, Newtown, PA

Summer Cooler

Yield: 12 servings

3 cups sugar
3 cups water
Juice of 3 oranges

Juice of 3 lemons
3 bananas, mashed

- Bring sugar and water to a boil in saucepan, stirring until sugar dissolves. Let stand to cool. Stir in orange juice, lemon juice and bananas. Freeze until slushy. Beat with mixer. Freeze until set.

Approx Per Serving: Cal 231; Prot <1 g; Carbo 60 g; Fiber 1 g; T Fat <1 g; 1% Calories from Fat; Chol 0 mg; Sod 2 mg.

Kim Dodd, Warren County HFH, Clear Brook, VA

Sweet Dreams Crunch

Yield: 10 servings

1 21-ounce can cherry
    pie filling
Lemon juice to taste

1 2-layer package
    white cake mix
¹/₂ cup melted butter

- Spread pie filling in lightly greased 9x9-inch baking pan. Sprinkle with lemon juice. Beat cake mix and butter in mixer bowl until well mixed. Crumble over pie filling and juice mixture. Bake at 325 degrees for 1 hour or until golden brown. Cool in pan for 15 minutes before serving.

Approx Per Serving: Cal 357; Prot 3 g; Carbo 57 g; Fiber 1 g; T Fat 14 g; 34% Calories from Fat; Chol 25 mg; Sod 386 mg.

Lois Reed, Pemi-Valley Habitat, Wentworth, NH

Sweet Secret
Yield: 8 servings

1¹/₂ cups flour
1 cup sugar
¹/₂ teaspoon baking
　soda
¹/₂ teaspoon nutmeg
1 teaspoon cinnamon

¹/₂ teaspoon salt
1 cup canned pumpkin
1 cup oil
2 eggs, beaten
4 ounces sweetened
　chocolate, melted

■ Combine first 7 ingredients in bowl; mix well. Mix pumpkin, oil and eggs in bowl. Stir into dry ingredients. Spoon into greased 5x9-inch baking pan. Drizzle chocolate over top, allowing some to mix with batter. Bake at 350 degrees for 1 hour or until edges pull from sides of pan.
Approx Per Serving: Cal 525; Prot 5 g; Carbo 53 g; Fiber 2 g; T Fat 34 g; 56% Calories from Fat; Chol 56 mg; Sod 216 mg.

Kathy Cintula, Madison Tri-Area HFH, Madison, OH

Butter Pecan Ice Cream Torte
Yield: 12 servings

2¹/₂ cups graham
　cracker crumbs
6 tablespoons sugar
²/₃ cup butter, softened
4 cups butter pecan ice
　cream, softened
2 cups milk

2　4-ounce packages
　vanilla instant
　pudding mix
2 envelopes whipped
　topping mix
3 Heath candy bars,
　crushed

■ Combine first 3 ingredients in bowl; mix well. Pat into nonstick 9x13-inch baking pan. Bake at 350 degrees for 10 minutes. Beat ice cream, milk and pudding mixes in mixer bowl until blended. Spread over baked layer. Chill for 2 hours or until set. Prepare whipped topping mixes using package directions. Spread over chilled layer. Sprinkle with crushed candy bars.
Approx Per Serving: Cal 511; Prot 6 g; Carbo 63 g; Fiber 1 g; T Fat 27 g; 47% Calories from Fat; Chol 56 mg; Sod 462 mg.

Rosalie Duffton, Northern Straits HFH, St. Ignace, MI

Cherry Torte
Yield: 16 servings

1 cup melted margarine
2 cups flour
3 tablespoons sugar
1 envelope whipped
　topping mix
¹/₂ cup milk
1 teaspoon vanilla
　extract

8 ounces cream cheese,
　softened
1 cup confectioners'
　sugar
2　21-ounce cans
　cherry pie filling

■ Mix first 3 ingredients in bowl. Pat into nonstick 11x15-inch baking pan. Bake at 350 degrees for 12 minutes. Remove to wire rack to cool. Combine whipped topping mix, milk and vanilla in mixer bowl. Add cream cheese and confectioners' sugar; mix well. Spread on baked layer. Top with pie filling.
Approx Per Serving: Cal 340; Prot 4 g; Carbo 43 g; Fiber 1 g; T Fat 18 g; 47% Calories from Fat; Chol 18 mg; Sod 208 mg.

Jane Ann Bishop, HFH of Butler County, Valencia, PA

Pistachio Torte
Yield: 24 servings

1 cup flour
2 tablespoons
　confectioners' sugar
¹/₂ cup butter, softened
¹/₂ cup chopped
　walnuts
8 ounces cream cheese,
　softened
²/₃ cup confectioners'
　sugar

4 ounces whipped
　topping
2　4-ounce packages
　pistachio instant
　pudding mix
2¹/₂ cups milk
4 ounces whipped
　topping
¹/₄ cup finely chopped
　walnuts

■ Combine flour, 2 tablespoons confectioners' sugar, butter and ¹/₂ cup walnuts in mixer bowl. Beat to consistency of cookie dough. Pat into ungreased 9x13-inch baking pan. Bake at 375 degrees for 10 minutes. Combine cream cheese, ²/₃ cup confectioners' sugar and 4 ounces whipped topping in mixer bowl. Beat until smooth. Spread over cooled baked layer. Beat pudding mixes and milk in mixer bowl until smooth. Spread over cream cheese mixture. Top with 4 ounces whipped topping. Sprinkle with ¹/₄ cup walnuts. Chill until serving time.
Approx Per Serving: Cal 206; Prot 3 g; Carbo 21 g; Fiber <1 g; T Fat 13 g; 55% Calories from Fat; Chol 24 mg; Sod 137 mg.

Brian Kozlowski
Univ. of Wisconsin-Stevens Point Campus Chapter
Waukesha, WI

Berry Trifle

Yield: 10 servings

1   12-ounce pound
cake, cut into 1-inch
cubes
1/2 cup cream sherry
4 cups strawberries,
cut into quarters
2 tablespoons
confectioners' sugar
1 cup raspberries

1 cup blueberries
1 cup nonfat plain
yogurt
1/4 cup chopped mint
1/2 cup cream sherry
1/2 cup whipping
cream, whipped
Mint leaves

■ Line bottom of large glass bowl with cake. Drizzle with 1/2 cup sherry. Let stand for 30 minutes. Purée 2 cups strawberries and 1 tablespoon confectioners' sugar in blender. Pour over cake. Sprinkle with raspberries, blueberries, and 1 cup strawberries. Purée 1 cup strawberries, 1 tablespoon confectioners' sugar, yogurt, mint and 1/2 cup sherry in blender. Pour over berries. Chill, covered, for 4 to 6 hours. Top with whipped cream before serving. Top with mint leaves and garnish with additional berries.
Approx Per Serving: Cal 320; Prot 4 g; Carbo 40 g; Fiber 3 g; T Fat 11 g; 31% Calories from Fat; Chol 92 mg; Sod 152 mg.

Pat Bourque, Pemi-Valley Habitat, Warren, NH

Orange Cream Trifle

Yield: 12 servings

1   11-ounce can
mandarin oranges
2   4-ounce packages
vanilla instant
pudding mix
2 envelopes whipped
topping mix

4 cups milk
1 cup whipping cream
1 teaspoon almond
extract
2   3-ounce packages
ladyfingers, split
1/4 cup sugar

■ Drain mandarin oranges, reserving liquid. Place oranges in paper towel-lined dish. Chill in freezer. Combine pudding mixes, whipped topping mixes, milk, cream and almond flavoring in mixer bowl. Beat at low speed just until blended. Beat at medium-high speed for 5 minutes or until thickened. Line bottom and side of 2-quart bowl with 2/3 of the ladyfingers. Drizzle with 1/2 of the reserved liquid. Spoon half the pudding mixture into prepared bowl. Top with remaining ladyfingers. Drizzle with remaining liquid. Mound remaining pudding over top. Top with orange sections. Heat sugar in heavy skillet over high heat until sugar melts and turns medium brown, stirring constantly. Drizzle in thin strands over trifle.
Approx Per Serving: Cal 294; Prot 5 g; Carbo 42 g; Fiber 1 g; T Fat 13 g; 38% Calories from Fat; Chol 38 mg; Sod 181 mg.

Mrs. Art Dykhuis, Kalamazoo Valley HFH, Paw Paw, MI

Sherry Trifle

Yield: 10 servings

1   3-ounce package
ladyfingers, split
3 tablespoons
raspberry jam
3 egg yolks
2 teaspoons cornstarch
2 tablespoons
superfine sugar

2 cups milk
5 tablespoons sherry
2 bananas, sliced
1 cup whipping cream,
whipped

■ Spread ladyfingers with jam. Arrange in glass serving bowl. Beat egg yolks, cornstarch and sugar in mixer bowl until smooth. Bring milk to a boil in saucepan. Stir a small amount of hot milk into egg yolk mixture; stir egg yolk mixture into hot milk. Cook over medium heat until thickened, stirring constantly. Cool slightly. Drizzle sherry over ladyfingers. Arrange bananas over ladyfingers. Spoon custard over top. Chill until set. Spread with whipping cream. Garnish with glazed cherries, angelica and toasted almonds.
Approx Per Serving: Cal 219; Prot 4 g; Carbo 21 g; Fiber 1 g; T Fat 13 g; 54% Calories from Fat; Chol 103 mg; Sod 39 mg.

Gwynneth W. Lippincott, Burlington County HFH
Mount Holly, NJ

Habitat always moves on the shoulders of volunteers.

Tortoni
Yield: 6 servings

1 cup whipping cream
1/4 cup sugar
1 teaspoon vanilla
  extract
1/8 teaspoon almond
  extract
1/4 cup chopped
  almonds

1 egg white
1 tablespoon instant
  coffee
Salt to taste
2 tablespoons sugar
6 maraschino cherries

■ Beat whipping cream in mixer bowl until soft peaks form. Add 1/4 cup sugar, beating until stiff peaks form. Fold in flavorings and chopped almonds. Beat egg white, coffee powder and salt in mixer bowl until stiff. Stir in 2 tablespoons sugar. Fold into whipped cream mixture. Spoon into paper-lined muffin cups. Top with maraschino cherries. Freeze until firm. Place in refrigerator before serving. May store, covered, in freezer for several weeks.
Approx Per Serving: Cal 227; Prot 2 g; Carbo 17 g; Fiber 1 g; T Fat 18 g; 67% Calories from Fat; Chol 54 mg; Sod 25 mg.

Maggie Craig Chrisman, HFH International Board of Directors
Paradise Valley, AZ

Tortoni by Claudia
Yield: 24 servings

1/2 gallon vanilla ice
  cream, softened
56 vanilla wafers,
  finely crushed
1 cup slivered almonds
1 cup chopped
  maraschino cherries

2 to 4 drops of red
  food coloring
1 to 2 teaspoons
  almond extract
1 cup whipping cream,
  whipped
24 maraschino cherries

■ Combine ice cream, vanilla wafer crumbs, almonds, 1 cup maraschino cherries, food coloring and almond flavoring in bowl; mix well. Spoon into foil-lined muffin cups. Freeze until firm. Top with whipped cream and maraschino cherries.
Approx Per Serving: Cal 218; Prot 3 g; Carbo 23 g; Fiber 1 g; T Fat 13 g; 52% Calories from Fat; Chol 39 mg; Sod 78 mg.

Tina Swanson, Enid HFH, Enid, OK

Wasp Nest Cake
Yield: 12 servings

1 4-ounce package
  vanilla pudding and
  pie filling mix
2 cups milk
1 2-layer package
  yellow cake mix

2 cups butterscotch
  chips
1 cup chopped pecans

■ Combine pudding mix and milk in saucepan; mix well. Prepare pudding using package directions. Let stand to cool. Add cake mix; stirring until smooth. Spoon into greased 9x13-inch baking pan. Sprinkle with butterscotch chips and pecans. Bake at 350 degrees for 30 minutes.
Approx Per Serving: Cal 407; Prot 5 g; Carbo 60 g; Fiber 1 g; T Fat 17 g; 37% Calories from Fat; Chol 6 mg; Sod 365 mg.

Rita DeWitte, Hawkins HFH, Rogersville, TN

Racine Kringles
Yield: 6 servings

4 cups flour
1 teaspoon salt
1 tablespoon (heaping)
  sugar
1 cake yeast
1 cup butter
2 eggs, slightly beaten
1 cup milk

1/4 cup melted butter
3/4 cup raspberry jam
1 cup confectioners'
  sugar
1 tablespoon butter
1/2 teaspoon vanilla
  extract
2 tablespoons milk

■ Sift flour, salt and sugar in bowl; mix well. Add crumbled yeast. Cut in 1 cup butter until crumbly. Make well in center of mixture. Pour in mixture of eggs and milk; mix well. Chill, covered, overnight. Divide into 6 portions. Roll each portion into a very thin rectangle on lightly floured surface. Brush with 1/4 cup butter. Spread jam down center. Fold over to enclose filling; seal edges. Place on nonstick baking sheet. Bake at 350 degrees for 1 hour. Frost with mixture of confectioners' sugar, 1 tablespoon butter, vanilla and milk.
Approx Per Serving: Cal 910; Prot 13 g; Carbo 116 g; Fiber 3 g; T Fat 45 g; 44% Calories from Fat; Chol 186 mg; Sod 743 mg.

Marcella Langfeldt, HFH of Wausau, Pickerel, WI

CAKES
PIES – COOKIES

"For every house is built by someone, but God is the builder of everything."
Hebrews 3:4

Sunny Angel Food Cake

Yield: 12 servings

3/4 cup sugar
1/2 cup flour
6 egg whites, at room temperature
1/8 teaspoon salt
1/2 teaspoon cream of tartar
3/4 cup flour

1 teaspoon baking powder
6 egg yolks
3/4 cup sugar
1/8 teaspoon salt
1/4 cup boiling water
1 teaspoon vanilla extract

■ Sift 3/4 cup sugar and 1/2 cup flour together. Beat egg whites in mixer bowl until foamy. Add 1/8 teaspoon salt and cream of tartar. Beat until stiff peaks form. Fold in sifted dry ingredients gently. Spoon into ungreased 10-inch tube pan. Sift 3/4 cup flour and baking powder together. Beat egg yolks, 3/4 cup sugar and 1/8 teaspoon salt in bowl for 3 minutes. Add sifted dry ingredients and boiling water alternately, beating well after each addition. Stir in vanilla. Spoon over egg white layer in tube pan. Bake at 325 degrees for 45 minutes. Invert on funnel to cool completely. Loosen cake from side of pan. Invert onto cake plate. May frost with favorite icing.
Approx Per Serving: Cal 184; Prot 4 g; Carbo 35 g; Fiber <1 g; T Fat 3 g; 14% Calories from Fat; Chol 106 mg; Sod 102 mg.

Harriett Meckfessel, Highlands County HFH, Avon Park, FL

Apple Knobby Cake

Yield: 9 servings

1 cup sugar
3 tablespoons butter, softened
1 egg
3 cups chopped apples
3/4 cup chopped walnuts

1/2 teaspoon vanilla extract
1 cup flour
1 teaspoon baking soda
1/2 teaspoon nutmeg
1/2 teaspoon salt

■ Combine sugar, butter, egg, apples, walnuts, vanilla, flour, baking soda, nutmeg and salt in bowl in order listed, mixing well after each addition. Spoon into oiled 8x8-inch cake pan. Bake at 350 degrees for 40 to 45 minutes or until cake tests done.
Approx Per Serving: Cal 268; Prot 4 g; Carbo 41 g; Fiber 2 g; T Fat 11 g; 35% Calories from Fat; Chol 34 mg; Sod 251 mg.

Mildred Patenaude, HFH of Chico, Paradise, CA

Autumn Apple Cake

Yield: 24 servings

1 cup currants
3 cups flour
2 teaspoons baking soda
1 teaspoon salt
1 teaspoon cinnamon
1/2 teaspoon nutmeg
1 1/2 cups vegetable oil
1 cup sugar

1 cup packed dark brown sugar
4 eggs
1 teaspoon vanilla extract
3 cups thinly sliced peeled apples
1 cup chopped pecans

■ Soak currants in water to cover in small bowl for 1 hour; drain. Sift flour, baking soda, salt, cinnamon and nutmeg together. Beat oil, sugar and brown sugar in mixer bowl for 6 minutes. Add eggs 1 at a time, beating well. Add vanilla; mix well. Add sifted dry ingredients, beating constantly. Fold in currants, apples and pecans. Spoon into greased 9-inch tube pan. Bake at 350 degrees for 1 1/2 hours or until cake tests done. Cool in pan on wire rack.
Approx Per Serving: Cal 323; Prot 3 g; Carbo 39 g; Fiber 1 g; T Fat 18 g; 49% Calories from Fat; Chol 36 mg; Sod 175 mg.

David Pearson, Glens Falls Area HFH, Gansevoort, NY

Fresh Apple Cake

Yield: 12 servings

2 cups sugar
2 cups flour
2 teaspoons baking soda
2 teaspoons cinnamon
1 teaspoon salt
3 eggs, beaten

1 cup oil
2 teaspoons vanilla extract
4 cups shredded green apples
3/4 cup pecans

■ Combine sugar, flour, baking soda, cinnamon, salt, eggs, oil and vanilla in bowl; mix well. Stir in apples and pecans. Spoon into greased and floured 9x13-inch cake pan. Bake at 350 degrees for 40 to 45 minutes or until cake tests done.
Approx Per Serving: Cal 490; Prot 4 g; Carbo 65 g; Fiber 3 g; T Fat 25 g; 45% Calories from Fat; Chol 53 mg; Sod 334 mg.

Tina M. Valentine, Northwest Nebraska HFH, Chadron, NE

Country Apple Cake

Yield: 12 servings

1 2-layer package
   yellow cake mix
1/3 cup margarine,
   softened
1 egg
1/4 cup packed brown
   sugar
2 tablespoons
   cornstarch
1 cup water
1 tablespoon lemon
   juice

4 cups thinly sliced
   apples
1/2 cup packed brown
   sugar
1/2 cup chopped
   walnuts
1 teaspoon cinnamon
1 cup sour cream
1 egg
1 teaspoon vanilla
   extract

■ Combine cake mix, margarine and egg in mixer bowl. Mix at low speed until crumbly. Press into ungreased 9x13-inch cake pan. Mix 1/4 cup brown sugar and cornstarch in saucepan. Stir in water, lemon juice and and apples. Simmer for 5 minutes. Spread in prepared cake pan. Mix 1/2 cup brown sugar, walnuts and cinnamon in small bowl. Sprinkle over apple layer. Mix sour cream, egg and vanilla in bowl. Pour over layers. Bake at 350 degrees for 40 to 50 minutes or until brown. Serve warm or cooled. Store, covered, in refrigerator.
Approx Per Serving: Cal 405; Prot 4 g; Carbo 61 g; Fiber 1 g; T Fat 17 g; 37% Calories from Fat; Chol 44 mg; Sod 351 mg.

Shirley A. Watson, Battle Creek Area HFH, Bellevue, MI

English War Bride Apple Cake

Yield: 12 servings

1/2 cup butter, softened
1 cup sugar
2 eggs
1 3/4 cups flour
1 teaspoon baking
   powder
1/8 teaspoon salt

8 to 10 apples, peeled,
   cored, cut into
   quarters
1/2 cup butter
1 cup sugar
2 eggs
Cinnamon to taste

■ Cream 1/2 cup butter and 1 cup sugar in bowl. Add 2 eggs; mix well. Sift in flour, baking powder and salt; mix well. Spread in buttered springform pan. Arrange apples in a spiral over top. Bake at 350 degrees for 1 hour. Melt 1/2 cup butter in saucepan over low heat. Stir in 1 cup sugar, 2 eggs and cinnamon. Pour over cake. Reduce temperature to 325 degrees. Bake for 15 minutes longer.
Approx Per Serving: Cal 417; Prot 4 g; Carbo 63 g; Fiber 3 g; T Fat 18 g; 37% Calories from Fat; Chol 112 mg; Sod 203 mg.

Esther Mullavey, New Hampshire HFH, West Franklin, NH

Happy Apple Cake

Yield: 15 servings

Finishing the cabinets can be a joy.

2 cups flour
2 teaspoons baking
   soda
2 teaspoons cinnamon
1 teaspoon salt
2 eggs, well beaten
2 cups sugar
1 1/2 cups oil
3 cups chopped apples

3/4 cup chopped pecans
1 teaspoon vanilla
   extract
1 1/2 cups confectioners'
   sugar
6 ounces cream cheese,
   softened
1/8 teaspoon salt
1/4 cup chopped pecans

■ Sift flour, baking soda, cinnamon and 1 teaspoon salt together. Cream eggs and sugar in mixer bowl until light and fluffy. Add sifted dry ingredients, oil, apples, 3/4 cup pecans and vanilla; mix well. Pour into greased 9x12-inch cake pan. Bake at 350 degrees for 45 to 60 minutes or until cake tests done. Mix confectioners' sugar, cream cheese and 1/8 teaspoon salt in bowl until of spreading consistency. Stir in 1/4 cup pecans. Spread over cooled cake.
Approx Per Serving: Cal 520; Prot 4 g; Carbo 57 g; Fiber 2 g; T Fat 32 g; 54% Calories from Fat; Chol 41 mg; Sod 313 mg.

Lucille Slonaker, Highlands County HFH, Sebring, FL

Grandma Goss's Apple Cake

Yield: 12 servings

This recipe was brought from England in the mid 1800s.

1 1/2 cups flour
1 1/2 teaspoons baking powder
1/4 teaspoon salt
1 cup sugar
1/3 cup shortening
2 eggs
1/2 cup milk
1/2 teaspoon vanilla extract
2 Granny Smith apples, peeled, thinly sliced
Cinnamon to taste
Sugar to taste

■ Mix flour, baking powder and salt together. Cream 1 cup sugar and shortening in bowl until light and fluffy. Add eggs; mix well. Stir in dry ingredients, milk and vanilla in order listed, stirring until smooth after each addition. Spoon into 9x9-inch cake pan. Arrange apples slices in decorative manner on top of dough. Sprinkle with cinnamon and additional sugar. Bake at 375 degrees for 30 minutes. Turn off oven. Leave cake in oven for 10 minutes longer. Remove to wire rack to cool completely.

Approx Per Serving: Cal 204; Prot 3 g; Carbo 32 g; Fiber 1 g; T Fat 7 g; 31% Calories from Fat; Chol 37 mg; Sod 102 mg.

Mrs. Nathaniel P. Rutter, Homestead HFH, Naples, FL

Fresh Apple-Coconut Cake

Yield: 16 servings

3 eggs
2 cups sugar
1 1/4 cups oil
1/4 cup orange juice
1 teaspoon vanilla extract
3 cups flour
1/4 teaspoon salt
1 teaspoon baking soda
1 teaspoon cinnamon
1 cup chopped pecans
1 cup coconut
1 cup grated peeled tart apples
1/2 cup butter
1 cup sugar
1/2 teaspoon baking soda
1/2 cup buttermilk

■ Beat eggs until frothy. Add 2 cups sugar gradually, beating constantly. Add oil in a small steady stream, beating constantly. Add orange juice and vanilla; mix well. Sift flour, salt, 1 teaspoon baking soda and cinnamon together. Reserve 1/2 cup mixture. Add remaining flour mixture to beaten mixture; mix well. Toss reserved sifted dry ingredients with pecans and coconut. Fold into batter with apples. Spoon into greased and floured tube pan. Bake at 325 degrees for 1 1/2 hours. Melt 1/2 cup butter in saucepan over low heat. Add 1 cup sugar, 1/2 teaspoon baking soda and buttermilk. Bring to a boil. Spoon over hot cake. Pierce holes in top of cake with wooden pick.

Approx Per Serving: Cal 526; Prot 5 g; Carbo 60 g; Fiber 2 g; T Fat 31 g; 52% Calories from Fat; Chol 56 mg; Sod 182 mg.

Sadye H. Wier, Starkville HFH, Starkville, MS

Fresh Banana Cake

Yield: 18 servings

1 teaspoon baking soda
1 teaspoon water
3 tablespoons sour milk
1 tablespoon vinegar
1 1/2 cups sugar
1 2/3 cups flour
2/3 cup shortening
1 cup mashed bananas
1/2 teaspoon salt
1 teaspoon vanilla extract
2 egg whites, stiffly beaten
2 tablespoons butter
1 teaspoon vanilla extract
1/2 1-pound package confectioners' sugar
1/4 cup (or more) milk

■ Dissolve baking soda in water. Mix sour milk and vinegar in cup. Combine sugar, flour, shortening, bananas, salt, 1 teaspoon vanilla, baking soda mixture and vinegar mixture in bowl; mix well. Fold in egg whites. Pour into nonstick 9x13-inch cake pan. Bake at 350 degrees for 55 minutes. Melt butter in saucepan. Beat in 1 teaspoon vanilla, confectioners' sugar and milk until of spreading consistency. Spread over cooled cake.

Approx Per Serving: Cal 262; Prot 2 g; Carbo 44 g; Fiber 1 g; T Fat 9 g; 31% Calories from Fat; Chol 4 mg; Sod 125 mg.

Murl Cook, HFH of South Central Minnesota, Mankato, MN

Super Deluxe Cake

Yield: 15 servings

1 2-layer package
   yellow cake mix
1 20-ounce can
   crushed pineapple
1 cup sugar
1 4-ounce package
   vanilla instant
   pudding mix

1 cup coconut
8 ounces whipped
   topping
1/2 cup chopped pecans

■ Prepare and bake cake mix using package directions for 9x13-inch cake pan. Pierce cooled cake several times. Heat pineapple and sugar in saucepan until sugar is dissolved. Spoon over cake. Chill for 1 hour. Prepare pudding using package directions. Stir in coconut. Spread over pineapple. Cover with whipped topping. Sprinkle with pecans. Chill.

Approx Per Serving: Cal 475; Prot 5 g; Carbo 79 g; Fiber 1 g; T Fat 18 g; 34% Calories from Fat; Chol 5 mg; Sod 239 mg.

Joann Rubio, HFH of Wichita Falls, Wichita Falls, TX

"Better Than Kisses" Chocolate Cake

Yield: 20 servings

1 2-layer package
   yellow cake mix
1/2 cup water
3 eggs
1 cup sour cream
1/2 cup oil
4 ounces German's
   sweet chocolate,
   grated

1 cup chocolate chips
1 6-ounce package
   chocolate or vanilla
   instant pudding mix
1/4 cup confectioners'
   sugar

■ Combine cake mix, water, eggs, sour cream and oil in bowl; mix well. Stir in grated chocolate, chocolate chips and pudding mix. Pour into greased and floured bundt pan. Bake at 350 degrees for 45 minutes or until top is fairly firm. Cool in pan for 30 minutes. Invert onto serving plate. Sprinkle with confectioners' sugar.

Approx Per Serving: Cal 303; Prot 3 g; Carbo 40 g; Fiber <1 g; T Fat 16 g; 45% Calories from Fat; Chol 37 mg; Sod 232 mg.

Katherine E. Scales, Greenville County HFH, Greenville, SC

Black Magic Cake

Yield: 15 servings

1 3/4 cups flour
2 cups sugar
3/4 cup baking cocoa
2 teaspoons baking
   soda
1 teaspoon baking
   powder
1 teaspoon salt
2 eggs
1 cup buttermilk
1 cup brewed coffee

1/2 cup oil
1 teaspoon vanilla
   extract
2 1/2 cups confectioners'
   sugar
8 ounces cream cheese,
   softened
1/2 cup butter, softened
1 teaspoon vanilla
   extract

■ Combine first 6 ingredients in mixer bowl. Add eggs, buttermilk, coffee, oil and 1 teaspoon vanilla; mix well. Beat at medium speed for 2 minutes. Pour into nonstick 9x13-inch cake pan. Bake at 350 degrees for 35 to 40 minutes or until cake tests done. Combine confectioners' sugar, cream cheese and butter in bowl; beat well. Stir in 1 teaspoon vanilla. Spread over cooled cake.

Approx Per Serving: Cal 433; Prot 5 g; Carbo 61 g; Fiber 2 g; T Fat 21 g; 41% Calories from Fat; Chol 62 mg; Sod 399 mg.

Beverly Schroeder, Sheboygan County HFH, Kohler, WI

Self-Frosted Brown Sugar Cake

Yield: 9 servings

2 cups packed brown
   sugar
2 1/2 cups flour
1/2 cup butter, softened
1 egg, beaten
1 cup buttermilk

1 teaspoon baking soda
1/2 cup raisins
1/2 cup chopped
   walnuts
1 teaspoon vanilla
   extract

■ Combine brown sugar, flour and butter in mixer bowl; mix by hand. Remove and reserve 1 cup brown sugar mixture for frosting. Cream remaining mixture in mixer bowl until light and fluffy. Add egg, buttermilk and baking soda; beat well. Stir in raisins and walnuts. Beat in vanilla. Pour into buttered 9x9-inch pan. Spread with reserved mixture. Bake at 350 degrees for 40 minutes or until cake tests done.

Approx Per Serving: Cal 534; Prot 7 g; Carbo 95 g; Fiber 2 g; T Fat 16 g; 26% Calories from Fat; Chol 52 mg; Sod 243 mg.

Ruth L. Otto, HFH of South Central Minnesota
Mankato, MN

Blackberry Jam Cake
Yield: 16 servings

3 cups flour
1 teaspoon baking soda
1 teaspoon allspice
1 tablespoon cinnamon
1 cup butter, softened
2 cups sugar
4 eggs, beaten
1 cup buttermilk
1 cup seedless
   blackberry jam

1/4 cup orange juice
1 cup raisins
1 cup chopped pecans
1/2 cup margarine
1 cup packed brown
   sugar
1/4 cup milk
2 cups confectioners'
   sugar

■ Sift flour, baking soda, allspice and cinnamon together. Cream butter and sugar in mixer bowl until light and fluffy. Beat in eggs. Add flour mixture and buttermilk alternately to creamed mixture, beating well after each addition. Stir in jam and orange juice. Fold in raisins and pecans. Pour into greased and floured angel food cake pan. Bake at 350 degrees for 1½ hours. Cool in pan for several minutes. Invert onto serving plate. Melt margarine in saucepan over low heat. Add brown sugar. Cook for 2 minutes, stirring constantly. Add milk. Bring to a boil. Remove from heat; cool. Add confectioners' sugar gradually, beating until of spreading consistency. Spread frosting over cooled cake.

Approx Per Serving: Cal 588; Prot 6 g; Carbo 91 g; Fiber 2 g; T Fat 24 g; 36% Calories from Fat; Chol 85 mg; Sod 258 mg.

Louise Potts Gray, Ashland-Ironton Area HFH, Ashland, KY

Brown Mountain Cake
Yield: 12 servings

1 cup butter, softened
2 cups sugar
3 eggs
3 cups flour
1 cup buttermilk
1/2 cup warm water
3 tablespoons baking
   cocoa

1 teaspoon baking soda
1 teaspoon vanilla
   extract
1 cup butter
2 cups sugar
1 cup evaporated milk
1 teaspoon vanilla
   extract

■ Cream 1 cup butter and 2 cups sugar in mixer bowl until light and fluffy. Add eggs 1 at a time, beating well after each addition. Add flour and buttermilk alternately to creamed mixture, beating well after each addition. Mix water, baking cocoa and baking soda in bowl. Add to flour mixture; beat well. Stir in 1 teaspoon vanilla. Pour into 2 greased and floured 9-inch round cake pans. Bake at 350 degrees for 35 to 40 minutes or until layers test done. Cool in pans for 10 minutes. Remove to wire rack to cool completely. Melt 1 cup butter in saucepan over medium heat. Add 2 cups sugar and evaporated milk. Cook to soft-ball stage, stirring constantly. Remove from heat. Beat in vanilla. Let stand to cool. Beat until of spreading consistency. Spread between layers and over top and side of cake.

Approx Per Serving: Cal 701; Prot 7 g; Carbo 94 g; Fiber 1 g; T Fat 34 g; 43% Calories from Fat; Chol 143 mg; Sod 390 mg.

Nora R. Dawson, Peach Area HFH, Fort Valley, GA

Chocolate Lovers' Cake
Yield: 12 servings

3 cups flour
2 cups sugar
1/2 cup baking cocoa
1 teaspoon salt
2 teaspoons baking
   soda
2 teaspoons vinegar
2 cups cold water
2 teaspoons vanilla
   extract
2/3 cup oil
6 tablespoons butter,
   softened

2 ounces unsweetened
   chocolate, melted
1 1-pound package
   confectioners' sugar
2 tablespoons corn
   syrup
1 teaspoon vanilla
   extract
1/4 cup (or more) fresh
   or canned milk

■ Combine first 5 ingredients in bowl; mix well. Add vinegar, water, vanilla and oil; mix well. Pour into greased 9x13-inch glass baking dish. Bake at 350 degrees for 30 minutes. Cool in dish. Combine butter and chocolate in bowl; mix well. Add confectioners' sugar, corn syrup and vanilla; mix well. Beat in enough milk to make of spreading consistency. Spread over cooled cake.

Approx Per Serving: Cal 623; Prot 5 g; Carbo 108 g; Fiber 3 g; T Fat 22 g; 30% Calories from Fat; Chol 16 mg; Sod 369 mg.

Jack and Joanne Kemp, HFH International Board of Directors
Washington, D.C.

Filled Chocolate Bundt Cake

Yield: 16 servings

3 cups flour
3/4 cup baking cocoa
2 teaspoons baking
  soda
1/2 teaspoon salt
2 cups sugar
1 cup oil
2 eggs
1 cup buttermilk

1 cup hot coffee
8 ounces cream cheese,
  softened
1/4 cup sugar
1 egg
1 cup chocolate chips
1/2 cup coconut
1 teaspoon vanilla
  extract

■ Sift flour, baking cocoa, baking soda and salt together. Cream 2 cups sugar and oil in mixer bowl until light and fluffy. Add eggs and buttermilk; beat well. Add flour mixture and coffee alternately to creamed mixture, beating well after each addition. Combine cream cheese, 1/4 cup sugar, egg, chocolate chips, coconut and vanilla in bowl; mix well. Layer half the flour mixture, cream cheese mixture and remaining flour mixture in greased and floured bundt pan. Bake at 350 degrees for 1 hour and 10 minutes to 1 hour and 15 minutes or until cake tests done. Cool in pan for several minutes. Invert onto serving plate. May add 1/2 cup chopped nuts to batter.
Approx Per Serving: Cal 459; Prot 6 g; Carbo 56 g; Fiber 2 g; T Fat 25 g; 48% Calories from Fat; Chol 56 mg; Sod 244 mg.

Theresa Ruhl, Morgan County HFH, Wiggins, CO

Honey's Chocolate-Cherry Cake

Yield: 15 servings

This 1-egg cake, a favorite with everyone, came out of Depression times. It was made by a very dear aunt.

1 teaspoon baking soda
1 cup buttermilk
1 cup sugar
1/2 cup shortening
1 egg
1/8 teaspoon salt
1 teaspoon vanilla
  extract
2 ounces unsweetened
  chocolate, melted,
  cooled
1 1/2 cups sifted flour
1/4 cup maraschino
  cherry juice

1/2 cup chopped
  walnuts
7 maraschino cherries,
  cut into quarters
2 cups sugar
2 ounces unsweetened
  chocolate
1 cup milk
1/8 teaspoon (scant) salt
1 teaspoon vanilla
  extract
2 tablespoons butter
7 maraschino cherries,
  cut into quarters

■ Dissolve baking soda in buttermilk. Cream 1 cup sugar and shortening in mixer bowl until light and fluffy. Beat in egg. Add 1/8 teaspoon salt and 1 teaspoon vanilla; beat well. Stir in 2 ounces chocolate. Add flour, cherry juice and buttermilk alternately to creamed mixture, beating well after each addition. Stir in walnuts and cherries. Pour into greased and floured 9x13-inch cake pan. Bake at 350 degrees for 30 to 35 minutes or until cake tests done. Cool in pan. Combine remaining 2 cups sugar, remaining 2 ounces chocolate, milk and remaining 1/8 teaspoon salt in heavy 4-quart saucepan; mix well. Cook over medium-low heat to soft-ball stage, stirring constantly with wooden spoon. Remove from heat. Beat in remaining 1 teaspoon vanilla and butter. Add remaining cherries; beat until of spreading consistency. Cool slightly. Spread frosting over cake.
Approx Per Serving: Cal 362; Prot 4 g; Carbo 54 g; Fiber 2 g; T Fat 16 g; 38% Calories from Fat; Chol 21 mg; Sod 134 mg.

Carolynn Treu, HFH of Wausau, Wausau WI

Chocolate Upside-Down Cake

Yield: 9 servings

1 cup flour
1/2 teaspoon salt
3/4 cup sugar
2 teaspoons baking
  powder
1 tablespoon baking
  cocoa
1/2 cup milk
2 tablespoons melted
  butter

1 teaspoon vanilla
  extract
1/2 cup chopped pecans
1/2 cup sugar
1/2 cup packed brown
  sugar
3 tablespoons baking
  cocoa
1 cup water

■ Combine first 9 ingredients in bowl; mix well. Pour into ungreased 8x8-inch cake pan. Mix sugar, brown sugar, 3 tablespoons baking cocoa and water in bowl. Pour over batter in pan. Bake at 325 degrees for 45 minutes. Garnish with whipped cream.
Approx Per Serving: Cal 297; Prot 3 g; Carbo 56 g; Fiber 2 g; T Fat 8 g; 24% Calories from Fat; Chol 9 mg; Sod 227 mg.

Beverly Abbott, HFH of Wausau, Wausau, WI

Chocolate Cake with Marshmallow Icing   *Yield: 12 servings*

2 cups milk
4 ounces unsweetened
  chocolate
1/4 cup shortening
2 cups sugar
1/4 teaspoon salt
1 teaspoon vanilla
  extract
2 eggs
2 cups sifted cake flour

1 1/2 teaspoons baking
  soda
2 tablespoons water
2 egg whites
1 cup light corn syrup
8 large marshmallows,
  chopped
1 ounce unsweetened
  chocolate

- Cook milk and 4 ounces chocolate in saucepan until chocolate is melted, stirring frequently. Chill for several hours or overnight. Cream shortening, sugar, salt, vanilla and eggs in mixer bowl until light and fluffy. Add chocolate mixture; beat well. Add flour gradually, beating well after each addition. Dissolve baking soda in water. Stir into batter. Pour batter into 2 greased and floured 8-inch round cake pans. Bake at 350 degrees for 35 minutes or until layers test done. Cool in pans for several minutes. Remove to wire racks to cool completely. Combine egg whites and corn syrup in double boiler over hot water. Beat until thickened and fluffy. Add marshmallows. Cook until marshmallows are melted, beating constantly. Spread between layers and over top and side of cooled cake. Melt remaining 1 ounce chocolate. Drizzle over cake. Marbleize gently with knife.

Approx Per Serving: Cal 417; Prot 6 g; Carbo 75 g; Fiber 2 g; T Fat 13 g; 26% Calories from Fat; Chol 41 mg; Sod 202 mg.

Betty Nelson, Burlington County HFH, Mt. Laurel, NJ

Easy Chocolate Cake   *Yield: 15 servings*

1 teaspoon baking soda
1 cup strong black
  coffee
1 1/2 cups flour
1/2 cup baking cocoa
1/2 teaspoon salt

1/2 cup margarine,
  softened
1 cup sugar
2 eggs
1 teaspoon vanilla
  extract

- Dissolve baking soda in coffee. Mix flour, baking cocoa and salt in bowl. Add margarine, sugar, eggs, coffee mixture and vanilla; mix well. Pour into non-stick 9x13-inch cake pan. Bake at 375 degrees for 25 to 30 minutes or until cake tests done.

Approx Per Serving: Cal 169; Prot 3 g; Carbo 24 g; Fiber 1 g; T Fat 7 g; 38% Calories from Fat; Chol 28 mg; Sod 208 mg.

*Mrs. Dexter Haller, North Bradley Church of God
Coleman, MI*

Fudge Ribbon Cake   *Yield: 12 servings*

2 cups flour
2 cups sugar
1 teaspoon salt
1 teaspoon baking
  powder
1/2 teaspoon baking
  soda
1/2 cup butter, softened
1 1/3 cups milk
2 eggs
4 envelopes
  Choco-Bake
1 teaspoon vanilla
  extract
2 tablespoons butter,
  softened

8 ounces cream cheese,
  softened
1/4 cup sugar
1 tablespoon cornstarch
1 egg
2 tablespoons milk
1/2 teaspoon vanilla
  extract
1/4 cup milk
1/4 cup butter
1 cup milk chocolate
  chips
1 teaspoon vanilla
  extract
2 1/2 cups sifted
  confectioners' sugar

- Combine flour, 2 cups sugar, salt, baking powder and baking soda in mixer bowl. Add 1/2 cup butter and 1 cup milk. Beat at low speed for 1 1/2 minutes or until well blended. Add remaining 1/3 cup milk, 2 eggs, Choco-Bake and 1 teaspoon vanilla. Beat at low speed for 1 1/2 minutes. Spread half the batter in greased and floured 9x13-inch cake pan. Cream 2 tablespoons butter, cream cheese, 1/4 cup sugar and cornstarch in mixer bowl. Add egg, 2 tablespoons milk and 1/2 teaspoon vanilla. Beat at high speed until smooth and creamy. Spread over batter. Top with remaining batter. Bake at 350 degrees for 50 to 60 minutes or until cake tests done. Bring 1/4 cup milk and 1/4 cup butter to a boil in saucepan. Remove from heat. Stir in chocolate chips. Add vanilla and confectioners' sugar. Beat until of spreading consistency. Spread over cooled cake.

Approx Per Serving: Cal 626; Prot 8 g; Carbo 85 g; Fiber 2 g; T Fat 30 g; 42% Calories from Fat; Chol 115 mg; Sod 453 mg.

Joyce M. Hales, Venice Area HFH, Sarasota, FL

Cocoa Cake

Yield: 15 servings

2 cups flour
³/₄ cup baking cocoa
1¹/₄ teaspoons baking soda
¹/₂ teaspoon salt
³/₄ cup butter, softened
1³/₄ cups sugar
2 eggs
1 teaspoon vanilla extract
1¹/₃ cups water

■ Sift first 4 ingredients together. Cream butter and sugar in mixer bowl. Add eggs and vanilla; beat well. Add flour mixture and water alternately to creamed mixture, beating well after each addition. Pour into greased 9x13-inch cake pan. Bake at 350 degrees for 35 to 40 minutes or until cake tests done.
Approx Per Serving: Cal 254; Prot 3 g; Carbo 38 g; Fiber 2 g; T Fat 11 g; 37% Calories from Fat; Chol 53 mg; Sod 228 mg.

Anna Lenhardt, Deming HFH, Deming, NM

White Chocolate Cake

Yield: 15 servings

2¹/₂ cups flour
1¹/₂ teaspoons baking powder
¹/₂ teaspoon salt
¹/₃ pound white chocolate
¹/₂ cup water
1 cup margarine, softened
2 cups sugar
1 cup buttermilk
4 egg whites, softly beaten
1 cup chopped almonds
1 3-ounce can coconut
¹/₂ cup raspberry jam
8 ounces whipped topping

■ Sift flour, baking powder and salt together. Heat chocolate and water in saucepan until chocolate is melted. Cream margarine and sugar in mixer bowl. Add flour mixture, buttermilk and melted chocolate alternately to creamed mixture, beating well. Fold in egg whites. Stir in almonds and coconut. Pour into 3 greased and floured 9-inch round cake pans. Bake at 350 degrees for 30 minutes. Cool in pans for 10 minutes. Remove to wire rack to cool completely. Spread jam between layers. Spread top and side of cake with whipped topping. Chill until serving time.
Approx Per Serving: Cal 503; Prot 7 g; Carbo 64 g; Fiber 3 g; T Fat 26 g; 45% Calories from Fat; Chol 3 mg; Sod 293 mg.

Margo T. Borders, HFH of Metro Louisville, Louisville, KY

Chocolate Fudge Cake

Yield: 15 servings

3 cups flour
2 cups sugar
2 teaspoons baking soda
1 teaspoon salt
2 tablespoons vinegar
6 tablespoons baking cocoa
2 cups water
2 teaspoons vanilla extract
³/₄ cup canola oil

■ Sift first 4 ingredients together. Combine with vinegar, baking cocoa, water, vanilla and oil in mixer bowl. Beat well; batter will be very thin. Pour into greased and floured 9x13-inch cake pan. Bake at 325 degrees for 10 minutes. Increase oven temperature to 350 degrees. Bake for 30 minutes. Cool in pan. May spread with favorite chocolate frosting.
Approx Per Serving: Cal 296; Prot 3 g; Carbo 47 g; Fiber 1 g; T Fat 12 g; 34% Calories from Fat; Chol 0 mg; Sod 253 mg.

Bonnie Mandly, Cobb County HFH, Marietta, GA

Best-Ever and Easy Coconut Cake

Yield: 24 servings

1 2-layer package white cake mix
3 eggs
1 12-ounce can evaporated milk
8 ounces whipped topping
1 14-ounce package coconut

■ Prepare and bake cake mix using package directions for 9x 13-inch cake pan, substituting 3 eggs for 2. Pierce hot cake with fork. Pour evaporated milk over cake. Cool in pan. Mix whipped topping and half the coconut in bowl. Spread over cake. Sprinkle with remaining coconut. Chill until serving time.
Approx Per Serving: Cal 286; Prot 4 g; Carbo 38 g; Fiber 2 g; T Fat 14 g; 43% Calories from Fat; Chol 13 mg; Sod 167 mg.

Marie W. Yelton, Rutherford County HFH
Rutherfordton, NC

Fresh Coconut Cake

Yield: 16 servings

1 cup butter, softened
2 cups sugar
4 eggs
3 cups cake flour, sifted
1 tablespoon baking powder
1/2 teaspoon salt
1 cup milk
1 teaspoon almond extract

Milk from 1 coconut
2 cups sugar
1 large coconut, grated
1 teaspoon vanilla extract
1 teaspoon lemon juice
1/4 teaspoon salt
2 tablespoons (heaping) cornstarch
1/4 cup water

■ Cream butter and 2 cups sugar in mixer bowl. Beat in eggs 1 at a time. Sift flour, baking powder and 1/2 teaspoon salt together. Add to batter alternately with milk, mixing well after each addition. Stir in almond extract. Spoon into 3 greased and floured 9-inch cake pans. Bake at 350 degrees for 20 to 25 minutes or until layers test done. Cool. Brush a small amount of coconut milk over cake layers. Add enough water to remaining coconut milk to measure 2 1/2 cups. Combine with 2 cups sugar in saucepan. Bring to a rapid boil. Boil for 5 minutes. Add 2/3 of the grated coconut. Cook for 5 to 8 minutes. Stir in vanilla, lemon juice and 1/4 teaspoon salt. Blend cornstarch into 1/4 cup water. Add to saucepan. Cook for 2 minutes or until thickened, stirring constantly. Chill until firm. Spread between layers and over top of cake. Chill. Sprinkle with remaining coconut. Store cake in refrigerator.

Approx Per Serving: Cal 458; Prot 4 g; Carbo 71 g; Fiber 2 g; T Fat 19 g; 36% Calories from Fat; Chol 86 mg; Sod 302 mg.

Cecelia B. Magill, Mid-Hudson Valley HFH
Poughkeepsie, NY

Coconut Cream Cake

Yield: 15 servings

1 2-layer package yellow cake mix
1 4-ounce package vanilla instant pudding mix
1 1/3 cups water
4 eggs
1/4 cup oil
1 cup coconut
1 cup chopped pecans
8 ounces cream cheese, softened

2 tablespoons evaporated milk
2 tablespoons butter, softened
1/2 teaspoon vanilla extract
3 1/2 cups confectioners' sugar
1 cup coconut
1 tablespoon melted butter

■ Combine cake mix, pudding mix, water, eggs and oil in bowl; mix well. Stir in 1 cup coconut and pecans. Pour into 3 greased and floured 8-inch round cake pans. Bake at 350 degrees for 35 minutes. Combine cream cheese, evaporated milk, 2 tablespoons butter and vanilla in bowl. Beat in confectioners' sugar until of spreading consistency. Stir in coconut. Spread between layers and over top of cake; do not frost side of cake. Combine 1 cup coconut and 1 tablespoon butter in bowl. Spread on nonstick baking sheet. Toast until brown. Sprinkle over cake.

Approx Per Serving: Cal 503; Prot 5 g; Carbo 70 g; Fiber 2 g; T Fat 24 g; 41% Calories from Fat; Chol 78 mg; Sod 341 mg.

Cynthia Strzelecki, HFH of St. Joseph County, Notre Dame, IN

Great-Grandmother's Devil's Grub

Yield: 16 servings

1/4 cup butter, softened
1 cup sugar
1 egg, beaten
2 1-ounce squares unsweetened chocolate, melted
1/2 teaspoon vanilla extract
1 1/4 cups flour
1/2 teaspoon salt
1 cup sour milk or buttermilk

1/4 cup butter, softened
2 cups confectioners' sugar
1 or 2 tablespoons strong hot coffee
1/4 teaspoon vanilla extract
2 1-ounce squares unsweetened chocolate
1 tablespoon butter

■ Cream 1/4 cup butter and sugar in mixer bowl. Beat in egg, 2 squares melted chocolate and 1/2 teaspoon vanilla. Add flour and salt alternately with sour milk, mixing well after each addition. Spoon into lightly greased and floured tube pan. Bake at 350 degrees for 40 minutes or until cake tests done. Cool on wire rack. Cream 1/4 cup butter and confectioners' sugar in mixer bowl. Beat in coffee and 1/4 teaspoon vanilla. Spread over cake. Melt 2 squares chocolate with 1 tablespoon butter in saucepan; mix well. Drizzle over cake.

Approx Per Serving: Cal 249; Prot 3 g; Carbo 37 g; Fiber 1 g; T Fat 11 g; 38% Calories from Fat; Chol 33 mg; Sod 133 mg.

William R. Haas, Westchester County HFH, Ossining, NY

Pioneer Eggless Cake

Yield: 15 servings

2 cups sugar
1 cup coffee
1 cup water
1/2 cup shortening
1 cup raisins
2 cups flour
2 teaspoons baking
    powder

1 teaspoon baking soda
1 teaspoon cinnamon
1/4 teaspoon each
    allspice and ground
    cloves
1/2 teaspoon salt
1 cup applesauce
1 cup chopped walnuts

■ Combine sugar, coffee, water, shortening and raisins in saucepan. Simmer for 10 minutes; cool to room temperature. Mix flour, baking powder, baking soda, spices and salt in large bowl. Add raisin mixture, applesauce and walnuts; mix well. Spoon into greased and floured 9x13-inch cake pan. Bake at 350 degrees for 30 minutes. Cool on wire rack.

Approx Per Serving: Cal 322; Prot 3 g; Carbo 53 g; Fiber 2 g; T Fat 12 g; 32% Calories from Fat; Chol 0 mg; Sod 174 mg.

Margaret Ping, Mid-Yellowstone Valley, HFH, Billings, MT

Traditional Shaker Boiled Fruitcake

Yield: 12 servings

1 cup sugar
1 cup water
1/2 cup shortening
1 cup raisins
1 teaspoon cinnamon
1/2 teaspoon each
    nutmeg and ground
    cloves

1 egg
2 cups (scant) flour
1 teaspoon baking soda
Salt to taste
1/4 cup mixed candied
    fruit
1/4 cup chopped pecans

■ Combine first 7 ingredients in saucepan. Bring to a boil; reduce heat. Simmer for 20 minutes. Cool to room temperature. Combine with egg in large bowl; mix well. Add flour, baking soda, salt, fruit and pecans; mix well. Spoon into greased loaf pan. Bake at 350 degrees for 40 minutes or until cake tests done. Cool in pan for several minutes; remove to wire rack to cool completely.

Approx Per Serving: Cal 295; Prot 3 g; Carbo 48 g; Fiber 2 g; T Fat 11 g; 33% Calories from Fat; Chol 18 mg; Sod 77 mg.

Charles Cooper

Mother's Fruitcakes

Yield: 12 servings

This fruitcake is popular even with people who don't like fruitcake.

1 pound pitted dates
4 slices candied
    pineapple
4 ounces each red and
    green candied
    cherries
4 cups walnuts
1 cup flour

1 cup sugar
1 teaspoon baking
    powder
1/4 teaspoon salt
4 eggs, beaten
1 teaspoon vanilla
    extract

■ Chop dates, fruit and walnuts into small pieces; combine in bowl. Sift flour, sugar, baking powder and salt over fruit mixture; toss to coat well. Stir in eggs and vanilla. Spoon into 2 lightly greased 5x9-inch loaf pans. Bake at 250 degrees for 2 hours. Cool in pans for 30 minutes; remove to wire rack to cool completely. May substitute pecans for walnuts or rum extract for vanilla extract.

Approx Per Serving: Cal 580; Prot 10 g; Carbo 83 g; Fiber 6 g; T Fat 27 g; 40% Calories from Fat; Chol 71 mg; Sod 101 mg.

Maggie Moyers, Yuba/Sutter HFH, Yuba City, CA

Gingerbread

Yield: 9 servings

1/2 cup all-purpose
    flour
1 cup whole wheat
    flour
2 teaspoons baking
    powder

1 teaspoon ginger
1/2 cup butter
1/2 cup hot strong coffee
2 eggs
1/2 cup sugar
1/2 cup molasses

■ Mix all-purpose flour, whole wheat flour, baking powder and ginger in bowl. Melt butter in hot coffee in small bowl. Beat eggs in large bowl. Stir in sugar, molasses and coffee mixture. Add dry ingredients; mix well. Spoon into 8x8-inch glass dish. Microwave on High for 8 minutes, turning 1/4 turn every minute for first 5 minutes.

Approx Per Serving: Cal 260; Prot 4 g; Carbo 36 g; Fiber 2 g; T Fat 12 g; 40% Calories from Fat; Chol 75 mg; Sod 178 mg.

Jacqueline A. Johnson, HFH of Wausau, Merrill, WI

Microwave Black Forest Cake

Yield: 16 servings

1 2-layer package chocolate cake mix
1 21-ounce can cherry pie filling

3 eggs
1/2 to 3/4 can chocolate frosting

■ Combine cake mix, pie filling and eggs in mixer bowl; beat until well mixed. Spread frosting in microwave-safe bundt pan sprayed with nonstick cooking spray. Spoon batter into prepared pan. Microwave on High for 13 minutes. Let stand in pan for 5 minutes. Invert onto serving plate. May spread with additional frosting if desired. May use other flavors of cake mix, pie filling and frosting, such as spice cake mix with apple pie filling or lemon cake mix with lemon pie filling.
Approx Per Serving: Cal 266; Prot 3 g; Carbo 47 g; Fiber 1 g; T Fat 8 g; 27% Calories from Fat; Chol 40 mg; Sod 320 mg.

Christina Jackson, Grants Pass Area HFH, Grants Pass, OR

Milky Way Cake

Yield: 16 servings

6 Milky Way candy bars
1 cup butter, softened
2 cups sugar
4 eggs

3 cups flour
1/2 teaspoon baking soda
1 1/4 cups buttermilk

■ Melt candy bars with 1/2 cup butter in saucepan over low heat. Cream remaining 1/2 cup butter with sugar in mixer bowl. Beat in eggs. Add mixture of flour and baking soda alternately with buttermilk, mixing well after each addition. Fold in candy mixture. Spoon into greased and floured bundt pan. Bake at 325 degrees for 1 hour and 10 minutes. Cool in pan for several minutes; remove to wire rack to cool completely.
Approx Per Serving: Cal 408; Prot 6 g; Carbo 60 g; Fiber 1 g; T Fat 17 g; 36% Calories from Fat; Chol 90 mg; Sod 213 mg.

Elaine Austin, HFH of Wichita Falls, Wichita Falls, TX

Swedish Nut Cake

Yield: 15 servings

1 3/4 cups sugar
2 cups flour
2 teaspoons baking soda
2 eggs
1 10-ounce can crushed pineapple
1 teaspoon vanilla extract
1/2 cup chopped walnuts

1/2 cup margarine, softened
8 ounces cream cheese, softened
1 3/4 cups confectioners' sugar
1 teaspoon vanilla extract
1/2 cup chopped walnuts

■ Combine sugar, flour, baking soda, eggs, crushed pineapple, 1 teaspoon vanilla and 1/2 cup chopped walnuts in large bowl; mix well. Spoon into greased and floured 9x13-inch cake pan. Bake at 350 degrees for 40 to 45 minutes or until cake tests done. Cool on wire rack. Combine margarine, cream cheese, confectioners' sugar and 1 teaspoon vanilla in mixer bowl; beat until smooth. Spread over cake; sprinkle with 1/2 cup chopped walnuts.
Approx Per Serving: Cal 388; Prot 5 g; Carbo 56 g; Fiber 1 g; T Fat 17 g; 39% Calories from Fat; Chol 45 mg; Sod 237 mg.

Wilma Lawther, Morgan County HFH, Brush, CO

Pineapple Cake

Yield: 15 servings

2 cups flour
2 cups sugar
2 teaspoons baking soda
2 eggs
1 20-ounce can crushed pineapple

6 ounces cream cheese, softened
1/4 cup butter, softened
2 1/2 to 3 cups confectioners' sugar
1 teaspoon vanilla extract

■ Mix flour, sugar and baking soda in bowl. Add eggs and undrained pineapple; mix well. Spoon into greased 9x13-inch cake pan. Bake at 350 degrees for 35 to 40 minutes or until cake tests done. Beat cream cheese, butter, confectioners' sugar and vanilla in bowl until smooth. Spread on hot cake. Cool on wire rack.
Approx Per Serving: Cal 362; Prot 4 g; Carbo 71 g; Fiber 1 g; T Fat 8 g; 19% Calories from Fat; Chol 49 mg; Sod 180 mg.

Susan Osoinach, HFH of Wichita Falls, Wichita Falls, TX

Oatmeal Cake

Yield: 15 servings

1 cup quick-cooking
  oats
1¼ cups boiling water
½ cup shortening
1 cup sugar
1 cup packed brown
  sugar
2 eggs
1⅓ cups flour

1 teaspoon each
  baking soda,
  cinnamon and salt
¼ cup butter
¼ cup evaporated milk
¾ cup packed brown
  sugar
1 cup coconut
1 cup chopped pecans

■ Mix oats with boiling water in bowl; let stand for 20 minutes. Cream shortening, sugar and 1 cup brown sugar in mixer bowl until light and fluffy. Beat in eggs. Mix in oats. Sift in flour, baking soda, cinnamon and salt; mix well. Spoon into greased 9x13-inch cake pan. Bake at 350 degrees for 40 to 45 minutes or until cake tests done. Combine butter, evaporated milk and ¾ cup brown sugar in saucepan. Cook for 3 to 4 minutes, stirring to mix well. Stir in coconut and pecans. Spread over hot cake. Broil until bubbly.
Approx Per Serving: Cal 411; Prot 4 g; Carbo 60 g; Fiber 2 g; T Fat 18 g; 39% Calories from Fat; Chol 38 mg; Sod 252 mg.

Rosemary Reynolds, HFH of Wausau, Wausau, WI

Oatmeal-Chocolate Chip Cake

Yield: 15 servings

1¾ cups boiling water
1 cup oats
1 cup sugar
1 cup packed brown
  sugar
½ cup margarine
2 eggs
1¾ cups flour

1 teaspoon baking soda
1 teaspoon baking
  cocoa
½ teaspoon salt
2 cups chocolate chips
¾ cup chopped
  walnuts

■ Pour water over oats in bowl; let stand for 10 minutes. Add sugar, brown sugar and margarine, stirring until margarine melts. Beat in eggs. Sift in next 4 ingredients; mix well. Stir in half the chocolate chips. Spoon into greased and floured 9x13-inch cake pan; sprinkle with remaining chocolate chips and walnuts. Bake at 350 degrees for 40 minutes. Cool on wire rack.
Approx Per Serving: Cal 412; Prot 5 g; Carbo 60 g; Fiber 2 g; T Fat 19 g; 40% Calories from Fat; Chol 28 mg; Sod 219 mg.

Veronica M. Morgan, Butler County HFH, El Dorado, KS

Poppy Seed Cake

Yield: 16 servings

2 ounces poppy seed
1 cup butter, softened
1½ cups sugar
4 egg yolks
2 cups cake flour
½ teaspoon baking
  powder

1 teaspoon baking soda
1 cup sour cream
1 tablespoon vanilla
  extract
4 egg whites, stiffly
  beaten

■ Soak poppy seed in water in bowl for several minutes; drain. Combine butter, sugar and egg yolks in mixer bowl; beat until smooth. Add mixture of next 3 ingredients alternately with sour cream, mixing well after each addition. Beat in poppy seed and vanilla. Fold in egg whites. Spoon into ungreased tube or bundt pan. Bake at 350 degrees for 1 hour. Cool on wire rack. Garnish with confectioners' sugar.
Approx Per Serving: Cal 296; Prot 4 g; Carbo 31 g; Fiber 1 g; T Fat 18 g; 53% Calories from Fat; Chol 91 mg; Sod 182 mg.

Phyllis Schwede, HFH of Wausau, Wausau, WI

Butter Pound Cake

Yield: 15 servings

1 cup butter, softened
3 cups sugar
6 egg yolks
1 teaspoon each
  vanilla, almond and
  butter extract

3 cups flour
1 cup sour cream
¼ teaspoon baking
  soda
6 egg whites, stiffly
  beaten

■ Cream butter and sugar in mixer bowl. Beat in egg yolks 1 at a time. Beat in flavorings. Add flour alternately with mixture of sour cream and baking soda, beginning and ending with flour and mixing well. Fold in egg whites. Spoon into floured tube pan. Bake at 300 degrees for 1½ hours. Cool on wire rack.
Approx Per Serving: Cal 418; Prot 6 g; Carbo 59 g; Fiber 1 g; T Fat 18 g; 44% Calories from Fat; Chol 125 mg; Sod 149 mg.

*Linda Dorough, First Presbyterian Church
Mount Pleasant HFH, Mt. Pleasant, TX*

Brown Sugar Pound Cake

Yield: 16 servings

1 cup shortening
1/2 cup butter, softened
1 cup sugar
1 1-pound package
   light brown sugar
5 eggs
3 cups flour

1/2 teaspoon baking
   powder
1 cup finely chopped
   pecans
1 cup milk
1 teaspoon vanilla
   extract

■ Cream first 4 ingredients in mixer bowl. Beat in eggs 1 at a time. Mix flour and baking powder together. Toss pecans with a small amount of mixture. Add remaining flour mixture to batter alternately with milk, mixing well. Stir in vanilla and pecans. Spoon into greased and floured tube pan. Bake at 325 degrees for 1 1/2 hours. Cool in pan for several minutes; remove to wire rack to cool completely.

Approx Per Serving: Cal 487; Prot 5 g; Carbo 60 g; Fiber 1 g; T Fat 26 g; 47% Calories from Fat; Chol 84 mg; Sod 100 mg.

Susan Shuman, Dublin/Laurens County HFH, Dublin, OH

Coconut Pound Cake

Yield: 16 servings

1 cup margarine,
   softened
3/4 cup shortening
3 cups sugar
5 eggs
3 cups flour

1 cup milk
1 teaspoon each
   vanilla, almond and
   butter extract
1 7-ounce can flaked
   coconut

■ Cream first 3 ingredients in mixer bowl until light and fluffy. Beat in eggs. Add flour alternately with milk, mixing well after each addition. Beat in flavorings. Fold in coconut. Spoon into greased and floured 10-inch tube pan. Bake at 300 degrees for 1 1/2 hours or until cake tests done. Cool in pan for 20 minutes; remove to wire rack to cool completely.

Approx Per Serving: Cal 505; Prot 5 g; Carbo 61 g; Fiber 2 g; T Fat 27 g; 48% Calories from Fat; Chol 69 mg; Sod 166 mg.

Jane A. Clark, Farmville, VA

Coconut-Pecan Pound Cake

Yield: 16 servings

1/2 cup shortening
1 cup margarine,
   softened
3 cups sugar
6 eggs
3 cups cake flour, sifted
1/4 teaspoon salt
1 cup milk
1/2 teaspoon each
   almond and vanilla
   extract

1 3-ounce can coconut
1/4 cup margarine,
   softened
8 ounces cream cheese
1 1-pound package
   confectioners' sugar
1 tablespoon butter
   extract
1/2 cup chopped
   pecans, toasted

■ Cream first 3 ingredients in mixer bowl. Beat in eggs 1 at a time. Add mixture of flour and salt alternately with milk, mixing well. Beat in flavorings and coconut. Spoon into greased and floured tube pan. Bake at 325 degrees for 1 hour and 25 minutes or until cake tests done. Cool in pan for several minutes; remove to wire rack to cool completely. Combine 1/4 cup margarine, cream cheese and confectioners' sugar in mixer bowl; beat until smooth. Add butter extract; mix well. Spread over cake; sprinkle with pecans.

Approx Per Serving: Cal 671; Prot 6 g; Carbo 92 g; Fiber 1 g; T Fat 33 g; 43% Calories from Fat; Chol 97 mg; Sod 277 mg.

Jo Butler, First Presbyterian Church
Mount Pleasant HFH, Mt. Pleasant, TX

Cream Cheese Pound Cake

Yield: 16 servings

1 1/2 cups margarine,
   softened
8 ounces cream cheese,
   softened
3 cups sugar

2 teaspoons vanilla
   extract
6 eggs, at room
   temperature
3 cups flour

■ Cream first 4 ingredients in mixer bowl until light and fluffy. Add eggs and flour 1/3 at a time, mixing well after each addition. Spoon into greased and floured 10-inch tube pan. Bake at 325 degrees for 1 1/2 hours. Cool on wire rack.

Approx Per Serving: Cal 462; Prot 6 g; Carbo 56 g; Fiber 1 g; T Fat 24 g; 47% Calories from Fat; Chol 95 mg; Sod 270 mg.

Sandra M. Hartley, Cartersville-Bartow County HFH
Cartersville, GA

Pineapple Pound Cake

Yield: 16 servings

1/2 cup shortening
1 cup margarine, softened
2 3/4 cups sugar
6 eggs
3 cups flour
1 teaspoon baking powder
1 teaspoon vanilla extract

1/4 cup milk
3/4 cup crushed pineapple
1/4 cup melted margarine
1 cup crushed pineapple
1 1/2 cups confectioners' sugar

- Cream shortening, 1 cup margarine and sugar in mixer bowl. Beat in eggs 1 at a time. Add mixture of flour and baking powder alternately with vanilla and milk, mixing well. Stir in 3/4 cup undrained pineapple. Spoon into greased and floured tube pan. Place in cold oven. Set oven temperature at 325 degrees. Bake cake for 1 1/4 hours. Cool in pan for several minutes; remove to wire rack to cool completely. Mix 1/4 cup melted margarine, 1 cup pineapple and 1 1/2 cups confectioners' sugar in bowl. Spread over cake.

Approx Per Serving: Cal 499; Prot 5 g; Carbo 69 g; Fiber 1 g; T Fat 23 g; 41% Calories from Fat; Chol 80 mg; Sod 217 mg.

Annie Dell Kennard, Starkville HFH, Starkville, MS

Sour Cream Pound Cake

Yield: 16 servings

1 cup margarine, softened
6 eggs
3 cups sugar
3 cups minus 3 tablespoons flour, sifted

1/4 teaspoon baking soda
1 cup sour cream
2 teaspoons vanilla extract

- Combine margarine, eggs and sugar in mixer bowl; beat until smooth. Add flour; beat for 2 minutes. Sprinkle baking soda over batter. Add sour cream and vanilla; beat for 2 minutes. Spoon into greased and floured tube pan. Bake at 325 degrees for 1 1/2 hours. Cool in pan for several minutes; remove to wire rack to cool completely.

Approx Per Serving: Cal 387; Prot 5 g; Carbo 55 g; Fiber 1 g; T Fat 17 g; 38% Calories from Fat; Chol 86 mg; Sod 182 mg.

Mary Wright, HFH of Abilene, Abilene, TX

Yogurt Pound Cake

Yield: 16 servings

1 cup margarine, softened
2 3/4 cups sugar
6 eggs
3 cups sifted flour
1/4 teaspoon baking soda

1/2 teaspoon salt
1 cup plain yogurt
1/2 teaspoon each lemon, orange and vanilla extract

- Cream margarine and sugar in mixer bowl. Beat in eggs 1 at a time. Sift flour, baking soda and salt together. Add to creamed mixture alternately with yogurt, mixing well. Beat in flavorings. Spoon into greased and floured 10-inch tube or bundt pan. Bake at 350 degrees for 1 1/2 hours. Cool in pan for 15 minutes; remove to wire rack to cool completely. Frost as desired or garnish with confectioners' sugar.

Approx Per Serving: Cal 351; Prot 5 g; Carbo 52 g; Fiber 1 g; T Fat 14 g; 36% Calories from Fat; Chol 82 mg; Sod 247 mg.

Sylvia Hafey, Fall River, MA

Apple and Pecan Pudding Cake

Yield: 9 servings

2 eggs
1 cup sugar
3/4 cup flour
1 teaspoon baking powder
1/2 teaspoon cinnamon

1/4 teaspoon nutmeg
1 teaspoon vanilla extract
1 1/2 cups chopped apples
3/4 cup chopped pecans

- Beat eggs in mixer bowl. Add sugar; beat until thick. Sift in flour, baking powder, cinnamon and nutmeg; mix well. Stir in vanilla, apples and pecans. Spoon into greased and floured 8x8-inch cake pan. Bake at 350 degrees for 40 to 50 minutes or until cake tests done. Serve cake with whipped topping, vanilla or lemon sauce.

Approx Per Serving: Cal 220; Prot 3 g; Carbo 35 g; Fiber 1 g; T Fat 8 g; 32% Calories from Fat; Chol 47 mg; Sod 53 mg.

Meg Klein, Washington County HFH, Marietta, OH

Spicy Apple Pudding Cake

Yield: 9 servings

1 egg
1 cup sugar
¼ cup oil
3 large apples, grated or finely chopped
1 teaspoon vanilla extract
1 cup flour
1 teaspoon baking soda

1 teaspoon cinnamon
¼ teaspoon nutmeg or allspice
2 tablespoons sugar
2 tablespoons water
2 tablespoons margarine
1 cup (about) confectioners' sugar

■ Beat egg in mixer bowl. Add 1 cup sugar and oil; beat until smooth. Stir in apples and vanilla. Stir in next 4 ingredients. Spoon into greased 8x8-inch cake pan. Bake at 350 degrees for 45 minutes. Combine 2 tablespoons sugar, water and margarine in saucepan. Cook until sugar dissolves. Stir in enough confectioners' sugar to make glaze. Spread over hot cake.
Approx Per Serving: Cal 307; Prot 2 g; Carbo 55 g; Fiber 1 g; T Fat 9 g; 27% Calories from Fat; Chol 24 mg; Sod 130 mg.

Gladys M. Bradley, Crawford County HFH, Milltown, IN

Lemon Pudding Cake

Yield: 9 servings

4 egg yolks
½ cup lemon juice
1 tablespoon melted butter
1 teaspoon grated lemon rind

1½ cups sugar
½ cup sifted flour
½ teaspoon salt
1½ cups milk
4 egg whites, stiffly beaten

■ Beat first 4 ingredients in mixer bowl until thick. Add mixture of sugar, flour and salt to batter alternately with milk, mixing well. Fold in egg whites. Spoon into greased 8x8-inch baking pan; set in larger pan of hot water. Bake at 350 degrees for 45 minutes or until brown.
Approx Per Serving: Cal 226; Prot 5 g; Carbo 41 g; Fiber <1 g; T Fat 5 g; 20% Calories from Fat; Chol 104 mg; Sod 173 mg.

Alice Berger, Burlington County HFH, Columbus, NJ

Red Velvet Cake

Yield: 16 servings

2 eggs, beaten
1½ cups sugar
1½ cups oil
1 teaspoon vinegar
3 cups cake flour
1 teaspoon baking soda
1 cup buttermilk
1 teaspoon vanilla extract

1 small bottle of red food coloring
½ cup butter
8 ounces cream cheese
1 1-pound package confectioners' sugar
1 cup chopped pecans
1 teaspoon vanilla extract

■ Combine first 4 ingredients. Add sifted mixture of flour and baking soda alternately with buttermilk, mixing well. Beat in 1 teaspoon vanilla and food coloring. Spoon into greased and floured 10-inch tube pan. Bake at 350 degrees for 45 minutes. Cool in pan for several minutes; remove to wire rack to cool completely. Melt butter and cream cheese in saucepan over low heat. Add confectioners' sugar; mix well. Stir in pecans and 1 teaspoon vanilla. Spread over cake.
Approx Per Serving: Cal 624; Prot 4 g; Carbo 71 g; Fiber 1 g; T Fat 37 g; 53% Calories from Fat; Chol 58 mg; Sod 168 mg.

Sarah M. Harris, Peach Area HFH, Fort Valley, GA

Red Devil's Food Cake

Yield: 15 servings

½ cup butter, softened
1½ cups sugar
2 eggs
¼ cup baking cocoa
2 tablespoons hot coffee
1 teaspoon red food coloring
2 cups sifted flour
1 teaspoon baking soda

1 teaspoon salt
1 cup sour milk
1 teaspoon vanilla extract
2 cups sugar
½ cup milk
½ cup butter
1 teaspoon vanilla extract

■ Cream ½ cup butter and 1½ cups sugar in mixer bowl. Beat in eggs. Combine next 3 ingredients in bowl. Add to creamed mixture; mix well. Add sifted mixture of flour, baking soda and salt alternately with sour milk, mixing well. Beat in 1 teaspoon vanilla. Spoon into greased and floured 9x13-inch cake pan. Bake at 350 degrees for 45 minutes. Cool on wire rack. Boil 2 cups sugar, ½ cup milk and ½ cup butter in saucepan for 1 minute; place saucepan in pan of cold water. Beat boiled mixture until of spreading consistency. Beat in 1 teaspoon vanilla. Spread over cake.
Approx Per Serving: Cal 373; Prot 4 g; Carbo 60 g; Fiber 1 g; T Fat 14 g; 33% Calories from Fat; Chol 65 mg; Sod 321 mg.

Wanda Marmaduke, Knox County HFH, Oaktown, IN

Rhubarb Cake

Yield: 15 servings

2 cups packed brown sugar
2 eggs
2 cups flour
1 teaspoon baking soda
1 cup milk
1/2 cup margarine

1 teaspoon vanilla extract
2 cups chopped rhubarb
1 cup packed brown sugar
1/2 cup chopped pecans
1 teaspoon cinnamon

■ Combine first 7 ingredients in bowl; stir until smooth. Stir in rhubarb. Spoon into greased and floured 9x13-inch cake pan. Mix 1 cup brown sugar, pecans and cinnamon in small bowl. Sprinkle over cake batter. Bake at 350 degrees for 40 minutes.
Approx Per Serving: Cal 370; Prot 4 g; Carbo 68 g; Fiber 1 g; T Fat 10 g; 24% Calories from Fat; Chol 31 mg; Sod 167 mg.

Jane Emge, Southwest Iowa HFH, Shenandoah, IA

Mother Elliott's Rhubarb Shortcake

Yield: 12 servings

3 to 4 cups chopped rhubarb
3 tablespoons butter, softened
3/4 cup sugar
1/2 cup milk
1 cup flour

1 teaspoon baking powder
1/4 teaspoon salt
1 cup sugar
1 tablespoon cornstarch
1/4 teaspoon salt
1 cup boiling water

■ Spread rhubarb in buttered 8x12-inch cake pan. Cream butter and 3/4 cup sugar in mixer bowl. Stir in milk. Sift in next 3 ingredients; mix well. Spoon into prepared cake pan. Mix 1 cup sugar, cornstarch and 1/4 teaspoon salt in small bowl. Sprinkle over batter. Pour water over top. Bake at 375 degrees for 1 hour.
Approx Per Serving: Cal 193; Prot 2 g; Carbo 40 g; Fiber 1 g; T Fat 3 g; 15% Calories from Fat; Chol 9 mg; Sod 147 mg.

Harriet L. Elliott, Southwest Iowa HFH, Farragut, IA

Italian Ricotta Cake

Yield: 16 servings

1 2-layer white or yellow cake mix
2 cups ricotta cheese
Grated rind of 1 large orange
1/2 cup coarsely chopped chocolate
2 tablespoons Triple Sec

2 tablespoons Crème de Cacao
1/8 teaspoon salt
1 or 2 tablespoons confectioners' sugar
12 ounces whipped topping

■ Prepare and bake cake mix using package directions for two 8 or 9-inch layers. Cool. Split layers. Spread mixture of next 7 ingredients between cake layers. Frost with whipped topping. Store in refrigerator.
Approx Per Serving: Cal 392; Prot 7 g; Carbo 50 g; Fiber <1 g; T Fat 18 g; 42% Calories from Fat; Chol 16 mg; Sod 208 mg.

Dottie Popavero, Mid-Hudson Valley HFH, Poughkeepsie, NY

Sausage-Coffee Cake

Yield: 8 servings

1 pound pork sausage
1 1/2 cups sugar
1 1/2 cups brown sugar
2 eggs
3 cups sifted flour
1 teaspoon baking powder

1 teaspoon each pumpkin pie spice and ginger
1 teaspoon baking soda
1 cup cold strong coffee
1 cup raisins, plumped
1 cup chopped pecans

■ Combine sausage, sugar and brown sugar in bowl; mix well. Add eggs; beat until well mixed. Sift next 4 ingredients together. Add to beaten mixture alternately with mixture of baking soda and coffee. Fold in raisins and pecans. Spoon into greased and floured small bundt pan. Bake at 350 degrees for 1 1/2 hours or until cake tests done. Cool in pan for 15 minutes.
Approx Per Serving: Cal 774; Prot 13 g; Carbo 140 g; Fiber 3 g; T Fat 20 g; 23% Calories from Fat; Chol 75 mg; Sod 533 mg.

Mary Carol Sloan, Cartersville-Bartow County HFH Cartersville, GA

This college student enjoys contributing her time and labor.

Sausage Cake

Yield: 16 servings

1 cup raisins
1 pound sausage
2 cups packed brown
  sugar
3 cups flour
2 teaspoons baking
  powder

1 teaspoon each
  baking soda,
  cinnamon and
  nutmeg
1 cup chopped pecans

■ Plump raisins in water to cover in saucepan. Drain, reserving 1 cup cooking liquid. Combine next 7 ingredients, raisins and reserved raisin cooking water in bowl; mix well. Stir in pecans. Spoon into greased and floured cake pan. Bake at 350 degrees for 1 hour or until cake tests done.
Approx Per Serving: Cal 344; Prot 6 g; Carbo 61 g; Fiber 2 g; T Fat 9 g; 24% Calories from Fat; Chol 11 mg; Sod 282 mg.

Lorin Halsey, HFH of the Kokomo Community, Kokomo, IN

Watergate Bundt Cake

Yield: 16 servings

This recipe has lots of "undercover" stuff in it.

1 2-layer package
   yellow or white cake
   mix
3 eggs
1/2 cup oil
2 4-ounce packages
   pistachio instant
   pudding mix

11/4 cups lemon-lime
   soda
1 envelope whipped
   topping mix
11/4 cups milk

■ Combine cake mix, eggs, oil, 1 package pudding mix and soda in mixer bowl; beat for 4 to 5 minutes. Spoon into greased and floured bundt or tube pan. Bake at 350 degrees for 40 to 50 minutes or until cake tests done. Cool in pan for 30 minutes; remove to serving plate. Combine remaining package pudding mix with whipped topping mix and milk in mixer bowl; beat at high speed for 5 minutes or until thick. Chill. Spread onto cake or spoon onto servings as desired.
Approx Per Serving: Cal 279; Prot 3 g; Carbo 41 g; Fiber <1 g; T Fat 12 g; 37% Calories from Fat; Chol 43 mg; Sod 291 mg.

Mary Warren, Maricopa HFH, Sun City, AZ

Watergate Cake

Yield: 15 servings

1 2-layer package
   white cake mix
3/4 cup oil
3 eggs
1 cup lemon-lime soda,
   at room temperature
1/2 cup coconut
1/2 cup chopped pecans
1 teaspoon coconut
   extract

2 4-ounce packages
   pistachio instant
   pudding mix
2 envelopes whipped
   topping mix
1 cup milk, chilled
1 teaspoon vanilla
   extract

■ Combine cake mix, oil, eggs, soda, coconut, pecans, coconut extract and 1 package pudding mix in mixer bowl; mix well. Spoon into greased and floured 9x13-inch cake pan. Bake using package directions. Cool on wire rack. Combine remaining package pudding mix, whipped topping mix, milk and vanilla in bowl; mix using directions on whipped topping envelope. Spread over cake. Store in refrigerator.
Approx Per Serving: Cal 372; Prot 4 g; Carbo 45 g; Fiber 1 g; T Fat 20 g; 48% Calories from Fat; Chol 45 mg; Sod 295 mg.

Sherri Ritter, Okeechobee HFH, Okeechobee, FL

Zucchini-Choco-Mocha Bundt Cake

Yield: 16 servings

1 2-layer package
   chocolate cake mix
4 eggs, beaten
3/4 cup corn oil
1 4-ounce package
   chocolate instant
   pudding mix
2 teaspoons instant
   coffee granules

1 teaspoon vanilla
   extract
2 cups grated zucchini
1/4 cup baking cocoa
1/4 cup butter, softened
2 tablespoons hot water
1 cup (about)
   confectioners' sugar

■ Combine first 6 ingredients in mixer bowl. Stir in zucchini; beat for 3 to 4 minutes. Spoon into greased and floured bundt pan. Bake at 350 degrees for 45 minutes. Cool in pan for 10 minutes; remove to wire rack to cool completely. Combine baking cocoa, butter and hot water in bowl. Add enough confectioners' sugar to make of glaze consistency. Drizzle over cake.
Approx Per Serving: Cal 322; Prot 4 g; Carbo 39 g; Fiber 1 g; T Fat 19 g; 50% Calories from Fat; Chol 61 mg; Sod 329 mg.

Shirley A. Wiemers, Sugar Creek HFH, Bella Vista, AR

Grandma Bell's Cupcake Secret

Yield: 12 servings

2 cups melted vanilla
  or favorite ice cream
2 cups flour
1 teaspoon baking soda

1 teaspoon baking
  powder
2 tablespoons (about)
  milk

- Combine melted ice cream, flour, baking soda and baking powder in bowl; whisk until smooth, adding milk if needed for desired consistency. Spoon into greased muffin cups, filling ½ to ⅔ full. Bake at 350 degrees for 14 to 20 minutes or until cupcakes test done. Remove to wire rack to cool.

Approx Per Serving: Cal 123; Prot 3 g; Carbo 21 g; Fiber 1 g; T Fat 3 g; 20% Calories from Fat; Chol 10 mg; Sod 117 mg.

Bill Bell, HFH Delaware County, PA, Drexel Hill, PA

Black Bottom Cupcakes

Yield: 18 servings

8 ounces cream cheese,
  softened
1 egg
⅓ cup sugar
⅛ teaspoon salt
1 cup chocolate chips
1½ cups flour
1 cup sugar
¼ cup baking cocoa

1 teaspoon baking soda
½ teaspoon salt
1 cup water
⅓ cup oil
1 tablespoon vinegar
1 teaspoon vanilla
  extract
1 cup chopped walnuts
2 tablespoons sugar

- Combine cream cheese, egg, ⅓ cup sugar and ⅛ teaspoon salt together in bowl; beat until smooth. Stir in chocolate chips. Sift flour, 1 cup sugar, baking cocoa, baking soda and ½ teaspoon salt together in large bowl. Add water, oil, vinegar and vanilla; mix well. Spoon chocolate mixture into 18 greased muffin cups. Spoon cream cheese mixture over batter. Sprinkle with chopped walnuts and 2 tablespoons sugar. Bake at 350 degrees for 30 to 35 minutes or until cupcakes test done. Cool on wire rack. Store in refrigerator.

Approx Per Serving: Cal 278; Prot 4 g; Carbo 32 g; Fiber 1 g; T Fat 17 g; 51% Calories from Fat; Chol 26 mg; Sod 164 mg.

*Idelle Walton, HFH of South Central Minnesota
Madison Lake, MN*

Brown Sugar Frosting

Yield: 16 servings

2 cups packed brown
  sugar

½ cup shortening
½ cup milk

- Boil all ingredients in saucepan for 2 minutes, stirring constantly; remove from heat. Stir for 5 minutes or until thickened.

Approx Per Serving: Cal 189; Prot <1 g; Carbo 34 g; Fiber 0 g; T Fat 7 g; 31% Calories from Fat; Chol 1 mg; Sod 18 mg.

Diane Lynn Lurie, HFH of Oshkosh, Oshkosh, WI

Fruit Fluff Frosting

Yield: 16 servings

1 cup sugar
1 egg white

1 cup fresh or frozen
  raspberries

- Beat sugar, egg white and raspberries in bowl at high speed until stiff peaks form. My use to frost angel food cake and serve immediately.

Approx Per Serving: Cal 53; Prot <1 g; Carbo 13 g; Fiber <1 g; T Fat <1 g; 1% Calories from Fat; Chol 0 mg; Sod 3 mg.

Donna Hoff, Chemung County HFH, Pine City, NY

Volunteers and
homeowners at work; the
appetites will show up
sooner or later.

Deluxe Apple Pie

Yield: 6 servings

1 recipe 2-crust pie
  pastry
6 medium apples,
  sliced
1 tablespoon cornstarch
1 teaspoon cinnamon
1/4 teaspoon salt
3 tablespoons sugar
3 tablespoons melted
  butter

1/3 cup dark corn syrup
1/4 cup packed brown
  sugar
2 tablespoons flour
3 tablespoons dark
  corn syrup
2 tablespoons butter
1/4 cup chopped
  walnuts

■ Line 9-inch pie plate with half the pie pastry. Spread apples in prepared pie plate. Mix cornstarch, cinnamon, salt, sugar, melted butter and 1/3 cup corn syrup in bowl. Pour over apples. Top with remaining pastry, sealing edge and cutting vents. Bake at 425 degrees for 45 minutes. Combine brown sugar, flour, 3 tablespoons corn syrup, remaining butter and walnuts in bowl; mix well. Spread over pie. Bake for 10 minutes longer.
Approx Per Serving: Cal 635; Prot 5 g; Carbo 89 g; Fiber 4 g; T Fat 31 g; 43% Calories from Fat; Chol 26 mg; Sod 563 mg.

Betty Whittum, Oregon Trail HFH, Hermiston, OR

Open-Faced Sour Cream-Apple Pie

Yield: 6 servings

2 large tart apples,
  peeled
1 cup sour cream
3/4 cup sugar
2 tablespoons flour
1/4 teaspoon salt
1 teaspoon vanilla
  extract

1 egg
1 unbaked 8-inch pie
  shell
1/2 cup packed brown
  sugar
1/3 cup flour
1/4 cup butter, softened

■ Cut apples into 1/4-inch slices; cut slices into thirds. Combine sour cream, sugar, 2 tablespoons flour, salt, vanilla and egg in mixer bowl; beat until sugar dissolves. Stir in apples. Spoon into pie shell. Bake at 400 degrees for 25 minutes. Combine brown sugar, 1/3 cup flour and butter in small bowl. Stir with fork until crumbly. Sprinkle mixture over hot pie. Bake for 20 minutes longer or until topping is golden brown.
Approx Per Serving: Cal 537; Prot 5 g; Carbo 74 g; Fiber 2 g; T Fat 26 g; 42% Calories from Fat; Chol 73 mg; Sod 359 mg.

Nellie R. Awmiller, Morgan County HFH, Fort Morgan, CO

Banana Cream Pie

Yield: 6 servings

1 6-ounce package
  banana cream
  pudding and pie
  filling mix
1 baked 9-inch pie
  shell

3/4 4-ounce package
  banana cream
  instant pudding mix
1/2 cup milk
16 ounces whipped
  topping

■ Cook pudding and pie filling mix using package directions. Let stand for 2 hours or until cool. Spoon into pie shell. Mix 3/4 package instant pudding mix with 1/2 cup milk in large bowl. Stir in whipped topping. Spread over pie. Chill until serving time.
Approx Per Serving: Cal 601; Prot 7 g; Carbo 70 g; Fiber 1 g; T Fat 34 g; 50% Calories from Fat; Chol 18 mg; Sod 484 mg.

Rosalie Duffton, Northern Straits HFH, St. Ignace, MI

Fresh Blueberry Pie

Yield: 6 servings

This pie must be eaten the day it is made because the crust gets soggy. But that's usually not a problem because it's the best blueberry pie you'll ever eat!

1 cup sugar
3 tablespoons
  cornstarch
1 cup water
1/2 cup blueberries,
  puréed
1 tablespoon butter

1 baked 9-inch pie
  shell
1/2 teaspoon cinnamon
4 cups blueberries
Grated lemon peel to
  taste

■ Mix sugar and cornstarch in saucepan. Stir in water. Cook over medium heat until thickened, stirring constantly. Add puréed blueberries and butter, stirring until butter melts. Fill pie shell with 4 cups blueberries; top with lemon peel. Pour sauce over top. Chill for 2 hours.
Approx Per Serving: Cal 371; Prot 3 g; Carbo 65 g; Fiber 4 g; T Fat 12 g; 29% Calories from Fat; Chol 5 mg; Sod 207 mg.

Eleanor Spencer, Pemi-Valley Habitat, Plymouth, NH

George Washington Pie

Yield: 12 servings

1½ cups graham
  cracker crumbs
½ cup sugar
¼ cup butter, softened
2 eggs
1 cup sugar

8 ounces cream cheese,
  softened
1 21-ounce can
  blueberry pie filling
8 ounces whipped
  topping

■ Combine graham cracker crumbs, ½ cup sugar and butter in bowl; mix well. Reserve ½ cup mixture for topping. Press remaining mixture into bottom of 9x13-inch baking pan. Beat eggs, 1 cup sugar and cream cheese in mixer bowl. Spread over crumb layer. Bake at 350 degrees for 15 minutes or until light brown. Let stand until cool. Spread with pie filling. Top with whipped topping. Sprinkle with reserved crumb mixture. Chill until serving time. May substitute cherry or apple pie filling for blueberry.
Approx Per Serving: Cal 381; Prot 4 g; Carbo 54 g; Fiber 1 g; T Fat 18 g; 41% Calories from Fat; Chol 67 mg; Sod 212 mg.

Diana Peterson, Northern Straits HFH, St. Ignace, MI

Red Ribbon Cherry Pie

Yield: 8 servings

2 cups flour
1 teaspoon salt
⅔ cup shortening
¼ cup ice water
½ cup cherry juice
3 tablespoons
  cornstarch

1⅓ cups sugar
⅛ teaspoon salt
¼ teaspoon red food
  coloring
2½ cups drained sour
  cherries
1 tablespoon butter

■ Combine flour and 1 teaspoon salt in bowl. Cut in shortening until crumbly. Add water gradually, mixing with fork until mixture forms ball. Divide into 2 portions. Roll on floured surface. Fit half the pastry into 9-inch deep-dish pie plate. Combine cherry juice, cornstarch, sugar, ⅛ teaspoon salt and food coloring in 4-quart saucepan. Cook over medium heat until thickened, stirring constantly. Stir in cherries gently. Spoon into prepared pie plate. Dot with butter. Top with remaining pastry, sealing edge. Bake at 450 degrees for 10 minutes. Reduce temperature to 350 degrees. Bake for 30 minutes longer.
Approx Per Serving: Cal 427; Prot 4 g; Carbo 62 g; Fiber 2 g; T Fat 20 g; 40% Calories from Fat; Chol 4 mg; Sod 313 mg.

Georgia L. Hultquist, Morgan County HFH
Fort Morgan, CO

Cherry Pie

Yield: 6 servings

2 cups flour
½ teaspoon salt
¼ cup milk
½ cup vegetable oil
2 16-ounce cans water
  pack cherries,
  drained
1⅓ cups sugar

3 tablespoons Minute
  tapioca
¼ teaspoon almond
  extract
2 tablespoons
  margarine
1 tablespoon
  cinnamon sugar

■ Mix flour and salt in bowl. Pour milk into oil; do not stir. Add milk mixture to flour in steady steam, moving flour mixture away from sides with fork; do not stir. Pat half the dough between waxed paper. Roll flat. Peel off top layer of waxed paper, replacing it with another piece. Remove bottom layer of waxed paper. Press into 9-inch pie plate. Repeat with remaining dough, reserving it for top. Mix cherries, sugar, tapioca and almond extract in bowl. Spoon into prepared pie plate. Dot with margarine. Remove waxed paper from reserved dough. Place over filling, pressing to seal edge. Sprinkle pie with cinnamon sugar. Bake at 350 degrees for 40 to 50 minutes or until golden brown.
Approx Per Serving: Cal 630; Prot 6 g; Carbo 103 g; Fiber 2 g; T Fat 23 g; 32% Calories from Fat; Chol 12 mg; Sod 220 mg.

Renae and Gary Redenbacher, Scotts Valley, CA
Orville Redenbacher's Popping Corn

*H*abitat is the perfect ministry for me. *Caring people who care not only that a house is built but that a community is built. Giving respect and an opportunity to worthy people. A chance to praise God amongst all different denominations. A catharsis in swinging my hammer and no government paperwork!*

Gary Redenbacher, Habitat volunteer

Coconut Cream Pie

Yield: 6 servings

2/3 cup sugar
1/4 cup cornstarch
1/4 teaspoon salt
3 cups milk
4 egg yolks
1/4 cup margarine
2 teaspoons vanilla
extract

1   3-ounce can coconut
1 baked 9-inch pie
shell
1 cup whipping cream
2 tablespoons
confectioners' sugar

■ Combine sugar, cornstarch and salt in 3-quart sauce-pan. Stir in milk. Cook over medium heat until thickened, stirring constantly. Boil for 1 minute longer. Beat egg yolks slightly in small bowl. Stir a small amount of hot mixture into yolks; stir yolks into hot mixture. Reduce heat to low. Cook for 2 minutes or until thick, stirring constantly. Remove from heat. Add margarine and vanilla, stirring until margarine melts. Reserve 1/3 cup coconut. Stir remaining coconut into mixture. Cool. Spread in pie shell; cover with plastic wrap. Chill until set. Toast reserved coconut in saucepan over medium heat. Beat whipping cream with confectioners' sugar in bowl until stiff peaks form. Spread over pie. Top with toasted coconut.
Approx Per Serving: Cal 649; Prot 9 g; Carbo 55 g; Fiber 2 g; T Fat 45 g; 61% Calories from Fat; Chol 213 mg; Sod 436 mg.

Janet Dye, HFH International, Americus, GA

Velvety Custard Pie

Yield: 6 servings

4 eggs, slightly beaten
1/2 cup sugar
1/4 teaspoon salt
1 teaspoon vanilla
extract

2 1/2 cups hot scalded
milk
1 unbaked 9-inch pie
shell
Nutmeg to taste

■ Stir first 4 ingredients together in bowl. Stir in hot milk gradually. Pour into pie shell. Sprinkle with nutmeg. Bake at 475 degrees for 5 minutes. Reduce temperature to 425 degrees. Bake for 10 minutes or until knife inserted halfway between center and edge comes our clean. Cool on rack.
Approx Per Serving: Cal 329; Prot 9 g; Carbo 35 g; Fiber 1 g; T Fat 17 g; 47% Calories from Fat; Chol 156 mg; Sod 361 mg.

Nell Penton Thomas, Starkville HFH, Starkville, MS

Mom's Fudge Pie

Yield: 8 servings

1 cup butter, softened
2 cups sugar
1 1/2 teaspoons vanilla
extract
1 ounce unsweetened
chocolate, melted

4 eggs
1 cup flour
1/2 cup baking cocoa
1 unbaked 10-inch pie
shell

■ Cream butter and sugar in bowl until light and fluffy. Beat in vanilla, melted chocolate and eggs. Add flour and baking cocoa; mix well. Pour into pie shell. Bake at 375 degrees for 25 minutes.
Approx Per Serving: Cal 649; Prot 8 g; Carbo 77 g; Fiber 3 g; T Fat 37 g; 50% Calories from Fat; Chol 169 mg; Sod 384 mg.

Susan Fuller, Southwest Iowa HFH, Shenandoah, IA

Lemon Meringue Pie

Yield: 6 servings

1 1/2 cups sugar
3 tablespoons
cornstarch
1/4 cup lemon juice
1 teaspoon grated
lemon rind
3 eggs, separated

1 1/4 cups boiling water
1 baked 9-inch pie
shell
6 tablespoons sugar
2 drops of lemon
extract

■ Combine first 4 ingredients in saucepan. Beat egg yolks. Add to lemon mixture. Stir in boiling water gradually. Cook over medium heat until thickened, stirring constantly. Pour into pie shell. Beat egg whites until soft peaks form. Add remaining sugar and lemon flavoring gradually, beating constantly until stiff peaks form. Spread over pie, sealing to edge. Bake at 425 degrees for 4 to 5 minutes or until golden brown.
Approx Per Serving: Cal 447; Prot 5 g; Carbo 80 g; Fiber 1 g; T Fat 13 g; 25% Calories from Fat; Chol 106 mg; Sod 219 mg.

Charlotte Reed, Talbot County HFH, St. Michaels, MD

Loquat Pie

Yield: 6 servings

35 fresh loquats, peeled
1/2 cup sugar
3 tablespoons cornstarch
3/4 cup orange juice
1/4 cup water
3 tablespoons margarine
1 recipe 2-crust pie pastry

■ Cut loquats into halves, discarding seed. Place loquats in bowl. Sprinkle with 1/4 cup sugar. Set aside. Combine remaining 1/4 cup sugar with cornstarch in saucepan. Stir in orange juice and water gradually. Cook over medium heat until thickened, stirring constantly. Stir in loquats and margarine. Cool slightly. Spoon into pastry-lined 8-inch pie plate. Top with remaining pastry; seal edge and cut vents. Bake at 400 degrees for 15 minutes. Reduce temperature to 350 degrees. Bake for 30 minutes. Cool on wire rack.
Approx Per Serving: Cal 306; Prot 2 g; Carbo 42 g; Fiber 1 g; T Fat 15 g; 43% Calories from Fat; Chol 0 mg; Sod 231 mg.

Betty Wheeler, Space Coast HFH, Titusville, FL

Maple-Walnut Pie

Yield: 6 servings

4 eggs, slightly beaten
3/4 cup packed light brown sugar
1 cup maple syrup
1/2 teaspoon salt
1/3 cup milk
1 cup walnut pieces
1 unbaked 9-inch pie shell

■ Preheat oven to 425 degrees. Combine eggs, brown sugar, maple syrup, salt and milk in bowl; mix well. Stir in walnuts. Pour into pie shell. Reduce oven temperature to 350 degrees. Bake for 45 to 50 minutes or until knife inserted near center comes out clean.
Approx Per Serving: Cal 601; Prot 9 g; Carbo 85 g; Fiber 2 g; T Fat 27 g; 39% Calories from Fat; Chol 144 mg; Sod 438 mg.

Corabelle Ammel, Upper Valley HFH
White River Junction, VT

Peach Glaze Pie Helen

Yield: 6 servings

This is easy, cool and refreshing when peaches are at their juicy flavorful best. If you can't get great peaches— wait. Use 4 cups sliced peaches or enough to fill a pie shell without overfilling.

1 1/4 cups flour
1 teaspoon salt
1/2 cup vegetable oil
2 tablespoons milk
1 1/2 tablespoons sugar
1 peach, peeled, crushed
Water
3 tablespoons cornstarch
1 cup sugar
1 unbaked 9-inch pie shell
4 cups peeled peaches, sliced

■ Mix flour, salt, oil, milk and 1 1/2 tablespoons sugar in bowl. Pat over bottom and up side of 9-inch pie plate. Bake at 350 degrees for 15 to 20 minutes. Cool on wire rack. Place crushed peach in measuring cup. Add enough water to measure 1 cup. Mix cornstarch and sugar in saucepan. Stir in crushed peach mixture. Cook over medium heat until thickened and clear, stirring constantly. Spoon some of the mixture into pie shell. Fill with sliced peaches. Pour remaining sauce over top. Chill completely.
Approx Per Serving: Cal 618; Prot 6 g; Carbo 87 g; Fiber 4 g; T Fat 29 g; 41% Calories from Fat; Chol 1 mg; Sod 543 mg.

Gretchen Reynolds, HFH of Evansville, Evansville, IN

Kissa's Easy Pecan Pie

Yield: 6 servings

3 eggs
1/4 cup melted butter
2 cups packed dark brown sugar
1/4 cup milk
1 teaspoon vanilla extract
1 cup pecans
1 unbaked 9-inch pie shell

■ Beat eggs, butter, brown sugar, milk and vanilla in mixer bowl. Stir in pecans. Pour into pie shell. Bake at 325 degrees for 50 minutes. Cool on wire rack.
Approx Per Serving: Cal 737; Prot 7 g; Carbo 106 g; Fiber 2 g; T Fat 34 g; 41% Calories from Fat; Chol 129 mg; Sod 327 mg.

Kelly Moran, Northern Straits HFH, St. Ignace, MI

Pecan Pie

Yield: 6 servings

3 eggs
³/₄ cup sugar
2 tablespoons melted butter
1 teaspoon vanilla extract
³/₄ cup light corn syrup
Salt to taste
1 cup chopped pecans
1 unbaked 9-inch pie shell

▪ Stir eggs and sugar together in bowl. Stir in butter, vanilla, corn syrup, salt and pecans. Pour into pie shell. Bake at 450 degrees for 10 minutes. Reduce temperature to 350 degrees. Bake for 25 minutes or until set in the center.
Approx Per Serving: Cal 566; Prot 6 g; Carbo 73 g; Fiber 2 g; T Fat 30 g; 46% Calories from Fat; Chol 117 mg; Sod 269 mg.

Carrie Holloway, Rapides HFH, Pineville, LA

Pumpkin Crunch Pie

Yield: 6 servings

³/₄ cup sugar
¹/₈ teaspoon salt
1 teaspoon pumpkin pie spice
2 tablespoons flour
¹/₄ teaspoon baking soda
1 cup pumpkin
1 egg
2 tablespoons melted margarine
1¹/₄ to 1¹/₂ cups milk
1 unbaked 9-inch pie shell
2 tablespoons brown sugar
1 tablespoon butter, softened
3 tablespoons flaked coconut
¹/₄ cup chopped pecans

▪ Mix first 5 ingredients. Mix pumpkin and egg in bowl. Add dry ingredients; mix well. Stir in margarine and milk. Pour into pie shell. Mix brown sugar, butter, coconut and pecans in small bowl. Sprinkle evenly over top. Bake at 400 degrees for 10 minutes. Reduce temperature to 350 degrees. Bake until knife inserted near center comes out clean.
Approx Per Serving: Cal 432; Prot 6 g; Carbo 53 g; Fiber 2 g; T Fat 23 g; 47% Calories from Fat; Chol 49 mg; Sod 365 mg.

Lori DeBok, First Presbyterian Church, Jefferson, IA

Edna Holm's Rhubarb Pie

Yield: 6 servings

My grandfather married my grandmother after she served him this pie.

3 cups (heaping) chopped rhubarb
1 cup sugar
3 tablespoons flour
¹/₄ teaspoon salt
3 egg yolks, beaten
1 tablespoon melted butter
1 unbaked 9-inch pie shell

▪ Scald rhubarb; drain. Combine with next 5 ingredients in bowl. Pour into pie shell. Bake at 350 degrees for 45 minutes. May top with meringue.
Approx Per Serving: Cal 354; Prot 4 g; Carbo 52 g; Fiber 2 g; T Fat 15 g; 37% Calories from Fat; Chol 112 mg; Sod 296 mg.

Debby Rake, Southwest Iowa HFH, Shenandoah, IA

Rhubarb Cream Pie

Yield: 8 servings

1¹/₂ cups flour
¹/₂ teaspoon salt
¹/₂ cup shortening
4 to 5 tablespoons cold water
4 cups chopped rhubarb
2 egg yolks
1 egg
1 cup sugar
Nutmeg to taste
2 tablespoons flour
3 tablespoons water
2 egg whites, at room temperature
3 tablespoons sugar

▪ Sift flour and salt together. Cut in shortening until crumbly. Add cold water 1 teaspoon at a time, mixing with fork until mixture forms ball. Roll dough on lightly floured surface. Fit into 10-inch pie plate. Fill with rhubarb. Beat egg yolks and egg in bowl. Add 1 cup sugar, nutmeg, flour and water; mix well. Pour over rhubarb. Bake at 350 degrees for 1 hour or until set. Beat egg whites until soft peaks form. Add remaining sugar gradually, beating until stiff peaks form. Spread over pie, sealing to edge. Bake for 15 minutes longer.
Approx Per Serving: Cal 363; Prot 6 g; Carbo 52 g; Fiber 2 g; T Fat 15 g; 38% Calories from Fat; Chol 80 mg; Sod 160 mg.

Reva Swanson, Newaygo HFH, Newaygo, MI

Amish Sugar Cream Pie

Yield: 10 servings

3/4 cup sugar
1/8 teaspoon salt
2 1/2 cups half and half
1/4 cup packed brown
  sugar
1/4 cup cornstarch

1/2 cup butter
1 teaspoon vanilla
  extract
1 lightly baked 9-inch
  pie shell
1/8 teaspoon cinnamon

■ Combine sugar, salt and half and half in saucepan. Bring to a boil, stirring constantly. Combine brown sugar and cornstarch in another saucepan. Whisk in hot half and half mixture. Add butter. Cook over medium heat for 5 minutes or until thickened, whisking constantly. Simmer for 1 minute. Stir in vanilla. Pour into pie shell. Sprinkle with cinnamon. Bake at 325 degrees for 20 minutes or until golden brown on top. Cool on wire rack.
Approx Per Serving: Cal 345; Prot 3 g; Carbo 35 g; Fiber <1 g; T Fat 22 g; 57% Calories from Fat; Chol 47 mg; Sod 242 mg.

Mae Brooks, Hawkins HFH, Rogersville, TN

Meringue Pie Crust

Yield: 6 servings

3 egg whites, at room
  temperature
1 cup sugar
1/4 teaspoon vanilla
  extract

3/4 cup crushed saltine
  crackers
1/2 cup chopped pecans
1/4 teaspoon cinnamon

■ Beat egg whites until frothy. Add sugar gradually, beating constantly until stiff peaks form. Add vanilla; mix well. Fold in remaining ingredients gently. Spread over bottom and side of well greased pie plate. Bake at 350 degrees for 30 minutes. Cool.
Approx Per Serving: Cal 246; Prot 3 g; Carbo 43 g; Fiber 1 g; T Fat 8 g; 27% Calories from Fat; Chol 4 mg; Sod 162 mg.

Alice Proctor, Mount Pleasant HFH, Mount Pleasant, TX

Never-Fail Pie Crusts

Yield: 12 servings

2 1/2 cups flour
1/8 teaspoon salt
3/4 cup shortening

1/4 cup butter
6 to 8 tablespoons milk

■ Sift flour and salt into mixing bowl. Cut in shortening and butter until crumbly. Add milk 1 tablespoon at a time, mixing with fork. Divide into 2 portions. Roll 1/8 inch thick on lightly floured surface.
Approx Per Serving: Cal 248; Prot 3 g; Carbo 20 g; Fiber 1 g; T Fat 17 g; 62% Calories from Fat; Chol 12 mg; Sod 59 mg.

J. Bernice Leichtman, Black Hills Area HFH, Rapid City, SD

No-Fail Easy Pie Crust

Yield: 12 servings

6 tablespoons
  shortening
6 tablespoons
  margarine

1 1/3 teaspoons salt
1/4 cup cold water
2 cups flour

■ Beat first 4 ingredients in bowl until creamy. Stir in flour. Roll into 2 circles on floured waxed paper.
Approx Per Serving: Cal 179; Prot 2 g; Carbo 16 g; Fiber 1 g; T Fat 12 g; 60% Calories from Fat; Chol 0 mg; Sod 272 mg.

Lois DeCourcey, Grants Pass Area HFH, Grants Pass, OR

Finished in one week! The 1992 Jimmy Carter Work Project in Washington, D.C. at the completion of ten houses.

Apple Pie Bars

Yield: 24 servings

6 apples, peeled, sliced
1½ cups sugar
⅛ teaspoon salt
1 teaspoon cinnamon
2 egg yolks
11 tablespoons (about) milk
2½ cups flour
1 teaspoon sugar

1 cup shortening
2 egg whites, stiffly beaten
2 cups confectioners' sugar
1 tablespoon butter, softened
1 teaspoon vanilla extract

■ Mix first 4 ingredients in bowl; set aside. Place egg yolks in 1-cup measure. Add enough milk to measure ⅔ cup. Mix with flour, 1 teaspoon sugar and shortening in large bowl. Divide dough into halves. Roll on floured surface into 10x15-inch rectangle. Layer pastry, apple mixture and remaining pastry in non-stick 10x15-inch baking pan. Brush with egg whites. Bake at 400 degrees for 20 to 25 minutes or until brown. Combine confectioners' sugar, butter and vanilla in bowl. Stir in enough water to make of glaze consistency. Drizzle over top. Cool. Cut into bars.
Approx Per Serving: Cal 244; Prot 2 g; Carbo 38 g; Fiber 1 g; T Fat 10 g; 36% Calories from Fat; Chol 20 mg; Sod 24 mg.

Gayle Nieman, Fergus Falls Area HFH, Rothsay, MN

Angel Cookies

Yield: 60 servings

1 cup packed brown sugar
1 cup sugar
4 cups flour
2 cups shortening
2 teaspoons cream of tartar

2 teaspoons baking soda
¼ teaspoon salt
1 teaspoon vanilla extract
2 eggs

■ Combine all ingredients in bowl; mix well. Shape into small balls. Place on greased cookie sheet. Bake at 350 degrees for 20 minutes. Cool on wire rack.
Approx Per Serving: Cal 123; Prot 1 g; Carbo 14 g; Fiber <1 g; T Fat 7 g; 51% Calories from Fat; Chol 7 mg; Sod 41 mg.

Betty Yearous, Morgan County HFH, Ft. Morgan, CO

Apricot Bars

Yield: 32 servings

⅔ cup dried apricots
⅓ cup sifted flour
½ teaspoon baking powder
¼ teaspoon salt
½ cup margarine, softened
¼ cup sugar
1 cup sifted flour

1 cup packed brown sugar
2 eggs, beaten
½ teaspoon vanilla extract
½ cup chopped walnuts
8 teaspoons (or more) confectioners' sugar

■ Combine apricots with water to cover in saucepan. Boil for 10 minutes; drain. Sift ⅓ cup flour, baking powder and salt together. Mix margarine, sugar and 1 cup flour in bowl until crumbly. Press into greased 8x8-inch baking pan. Bake at 350 degrees for 25 minutes. Beat brown sugar into eggs at low speed in mixer bowl. Add flour mixture and vanilla; mix well. Stir in walnuts and apricots. Spread over baked layer. Bake at 350 degrees for 30 minutes or until layer tests done; dessert will be browned. Cool in pan. Invert onto wire rack. Place crust side down on cutting board. Cut into bars. Roll in confectioners' sugar.
Approx Per Serving: Cal 108; Prot 1 g; Carbo 17 g; Fiber <1 g; T Fat 4 g; 36% Calories from Fat; Chol 13 mg; Sod 64 mg.

Richard Farrell, Firelands HFH, Sandusky, OH

Banana Jumbos

Yield: 42 servings

3 cups flour
1½ teaspoons baking soda
½ teaspoon salt
1 cup butter-flavored shortening
1 cup sugar

2 eggs
1 cup mashed ripe bananas
½ cup buttermilk
1 teaspoon vanilla extract

■ Sift flour, baking soda and salt together. Combine shortening, sugar and eggs in bowl; mix well. Stir in bananas, buttermilk and vanilla. Stir in flour mixture. Chill for 1 hour. Drop by rounded tablespoonfuls 2 inches apart onto lightly greased cookie sheet. Bake at 375 degrees for 10 minutes or until brown.
Approx Per Serving: Cal 104; Prot 1 g; Carbo 13 g; Fiber <1 g; T Fat 5 g; 45% Calories from Fat; Chol 10 mg; Sod 61 mg.

Mary Albright, Ringle, WI

Applesauce Brownies

Yield: 15 servings

2 cups flour
2 tablespoons baking cocoa
1¹/₂ teaspoons baking soda
¹/₂ teaspoon salt
¹/₂ teaspoon cinnamon
³/₄ cup sugar
³/₄ cup packed brown sugar
¹/₂ cup margarine, softened
2 eggs
1³/₄ cups applesauce
1 teaspoon vanilla extract
2 tablespoons sugar
¹/₂ cup chopped pecans
1 cup chocolate chips

■ Sift flour, baking cocoa, baking soda, salt and cinnamon together. Cream ³/₄ cup sugar, brown sugar and margarine in mixer bowl until light and fluffy. Beat in eggs. Add flour mixture and applesauce alternately to creamed mixture, beating well after each addition. Stir in vanilla. Spoon into nonstick 9x13-inch baking pan. Mix 2 tablespoons sugar, chopped pecans and chocolate chips in bowl. Sprinkle mixture over dough. Bake at 350 degrees for 30 minutes or until wooden pick inserted in center comes out clean. Cool. Cut into squares.
Approx Per Serving: Cal 330; Prot 4 g; Carbo 51 g; Fiber 2 g; T Fat 14 g; 36% Calories from Fat; Chol 28 mg; Sod 243 mg.

Marie Vallette, Black Hills Area HFH, Rapid City, SD

Best-Ever Brownies

Yield: 12 servings

¹/₂ cup margarine
2 ounces unsweetened chocolate
2 eggs
1 teaspoon vanilla extract
1¹/₄ cups sugar
³/₄ cup plus 2 tablespoons flour
¹/₂ to 1 cup chopped pecans

■ Melt margarine and chocolate in saucepan. Cool to room temperature. Beat eggs and vanilla in bowl. Add sugar gradually, beating until pale yellow. Stir in chocolate mixture. Add flour gradually, beating well after each addition. Stir in pecans. Spread in well greased 9x9-inch baking pan. Bake at 350 degrees for 20 to 25 minutes or until brownies test done. Cool. Cut into squares. May spread cooled brownies with favorite thin chocolate frosting if desired.
Approx Per Serving: Cal 285; Prot 3 g; Carbo 31 g; Fiber 2 g; T Fat 18 g; 54% Calories from Fat; Chol 36 mg; Sod 102 mg.

Elaine Rich, Highlands County HFH, Sebring, FL

Best-Friend Brownies

Yield: 28 servings

4 ounces melted unsweetened chocolate
²/₃ cup melted shortening
4 eggs
2 cups sugar
1¹/₂ cups flour
1 teaspoon baking powder
1 teaspoon salt

■ Mix melted chocolate and shortening in bowl. Stir in eggs and sugar. Add flour, baking powder and salt; mix well. Pour into greased and floured 9x13-inch baking pan. Bake at 350 degrees for 30 minutes. Cool. Cut into squares.
Approx Per Serving: Cal 155; Prot 2 g; Carbo 21 g; Fiber 1 g; T Fat 8 g; 44% Calories from Fat; Chol 30 mg; Sod 98 mg.

Jeni Hiett Umble, Orange County HFH, Irvine, CA

Betsy's Brownies

Yield: 9 servings

¹/₂ cup melted butter
2 ounces melted chocolate
1 cup sugar
¹/₂ cup sifted flour
1 teaspoon baking powder
1 teaspoon vanilla
¹/₂ cup chopped walnuts
2 eggs

■ Combine butter, chocolate, sugar, flour, baking powder and vanilla in bowl; mix well. Stir in walnuts and eggs. Spread in greased 9x9-inch baking pan. Bake at 350 degrees for 30 minutes. Cool. Cut into squares. May double recipe and bake in 9x13-inch pan.
Approx Per Serving: Cal 292; Prot 4 g; Carbo 30 g; Fiber 2 g; T Fat 19 g; 56% Calories from Fat; Chol 75 mg; Sod 139 mg.

Elizabeth J. Wagner, Barry County HFH, Middleville, MI

Brownies to Die For!
Yield: 36 servings

4 ounces melted
  unsweetened
  chocolate
1 cup melted butter
2¼ cups sugar
4 eggs, slightly beaten
1 cup flour
2 teaspoons vanilla
  extract
½ teaspoon salt
1½ cups chopped
  pecans

3 cups confectioners'
  sugar
¼ cup butter, softened
1 teaspoon vanilla
  extract
3 ounces cream cheese,
  softened
¼ cup (or more) milk
4 ounces semisweet
  chocolate
¼ cup butter, softened

■ Combine first 4 ingredients in bowl; mix well. Stir in flour, 2 teaspoons vanilla, salt and pecans. Pour into greased 9x13-inch baking pan. Bake at 325 degrees for 25 minutes or until brownies test done. Combine confectioners' sugar, ¼ cup butter, 1 teaspoon vanilla and cream cheese in bowl; mix well. Stir in enough milk to make of spreading consistency. Spread over cooled brownies. Let stand to set completely. Mix semisweet chocolate and ¼ cup butter in bowl. Spread over top. Cool. Cut into squares.
Approx Per Serving: Cal 250; Prot 3 g; Carbo 28 g; Fiber 1 g; T Fat 16 g; 54% Calories from Fat; Chol 47 mg; Sod 110 mg.

Charlotte Flanders, Arkansas Valley HFH, Ft. Smith, AR

Delicious Chocolate Chip Brownies
Yield: 20 servings

1 cup chocolate chips
1 cup sugar
½ cup unsweetened
  applesauce
2 tablespoons
  margarine
3 egg whites
1¼ cups flour

¼ teaspoon baking
  soda
¼ teaspoon salt
1 teaspoon vanilla
  extract
1 cup chocolate chips
⅓ cup chopped
  walnuts

■ Combine first 4 ingredients in glass bowl. Microwave on High for 2 minutes or until chocolate and margarine are melted. Stir until blended. Stir in egg whites. Add flour, baking soda, salt and vanilla; mix well. Stir in remaining 1 cup chocolate chips and walnuts. Spread in greased 8x11-inch glass baking dish. Bake at 350 degrees for 30 minutes or just until set. Cool completely. Cut into squares.
Approx Per Serving: Cal 181; Prot 2 g; Carbo 27 g; Fiber 1 g; T Fat 9 g; 40% Calories from Fat; Chol 0 mg; Sod 61 mg.

Margaret Haglund, Concordia College Chapter
Moorhead, MN

Light Chocolate Brownies
Yield: 16 servings

6 tablespoons light
  corn oil spread
1 cup sugar
½ cup baking cocoa
1 teaspoon vanilla
  extract
½ cup frozen egg
  substitute, thawed

½ cup flour
¼ cup chopped
  walnuts
¼ cup (or more)
  confectioners' sugar

■ Melt corn oil spread in saucepan over medium heat. Add sugar. Cook until sugar is dissolved, stirring constantly. Remove from heat. Stir in baking cocoa and vanilla. Add egg substitute; mix well. Stir in flour and walnuts. Pour into 8x8-inch baking pan coated with nonstick cooking spray. Bake at 350 degrees for 25 minutes or until edges begin to pull away from pan. Cool in pan on wire rack. Sprinkle with confectioners' sugar. Cut into squares.
Approx Per Serving: Cal 119; Prot 2 g; Carbo 19 g; Fiber 1 g; T Fat 5 g; 33% Calories from Fat; Chol <1 mg; Sod 67 mg.

Ruth Wood, Rogue Valley HFH, Medford, OR

Swedish Brownies
Yield: 16 servings

1 cup margarine, melted
2 cups sugar
1½ cups sifted flour
2 teaspoons vanilla
  extract

¼ cup baking cocoa
1 cup chopped pecans
3 eggs

■ Combine first 6 ingredients in bowl. Beat in eggs. Pour into nonstick 9x9-inch baking pan. Bake at 375 degrees for 25 to 30 minutes or until top springs back when lightly touched. Cool. Cut into squares.
Approx Per Serving: Cal 305; Prot 3 g; Carbo 35 g; Fiber 1 g; T Fat 18 g; 51% Calories from Fat; Chol 40 mg; Sod 148 mg.

Therese Schneider, Grants Pass Area HFH, Grants Pass, OR

Mint Brownies

Yield: 50 servings

1 cup sugar
1/2 cup margarine,
  softened
4 eggs
1 16-ounce can
  chocolate syrup
1 cup flour
1/2 teaspoon baking
  powder
1/2 cup margarine,
  softened

2 cups confectioners'
  sugar
2 tablespoons milk
1 teaspoon peppermint
  extract
Green food coloring
1/2 cup margarine
1 cup chocolate chips

■ Combine sugar, 1/2 cup margarine, eggs, chocolate syrup, flour and baking powder in bowl; mix well. Pour into greased cake roll pan. Bake at 350 degrees for 20 minutes. Chill for 20 minutes or until cooled. Mix 1/2 cup margarine, confectioners' sugar, milk, peppermint extract and food coloring in bowl. Spread over baked layer. Chill for 20 minutes or until cooled. Melt 1/2 cup margarine and chocolate chips in saucepan. Pour over peppermint layer. Chill in refrigerator. Cut into squares.

Approx Per Serving: Cal 136; Prot 1 g; Carbo 18 g; Fiber <1 g; T Fat 7 g; 46% Calories from Fat; Chol 17 mg; Sod 81 mg.

Marsha Fitzgerald, HFH of Wausau, Rothschild, WI

Peanut Butter Brownies

Yield: 16 servings

2/3 cup flour
1 teaspoon baking
  powder
1/4 teaspoon salt
1/2 cup chunky peanut
  butter
1/4 cup margarine,
  softened

1 cup packed brown
  sugar
1 teaspoon vanilla
  extract
2 eggs

■ Sift flour, baking powder and salt together. Cream peanut butter and margarine in mixer bowl until light and fluffy. Add brown sugar and vanilla; beat well. Beat in eggs. Add sifted dry ingredients; beat well. Spread in greased 8x8-inch baking pan. Bake at 350 degrees for 25 to 30 minutes or until top looks dry and wooden pick inserted in center comes out clean. Cool in pan on wire rack. Cut into 2-inch squares.

Approx Per Serving: Cal 166; Prot 3 g; Carbo 22 g; Fiber <1 g; T Fat 8 g; 40% Calories from Fat; Chol 27 mg; Sod 143 mg.

*Barbara S. Keller, Americus-Sumter County HFH
Americus, GA*

Pecan Brownies

Yield: 15 servings

1 cup margarine,
  softened
8 tablespoons baking
  cocoa
4 eggs
2 cups sugar

1 1/2 cups flour
1 teaspoon baking
  powder
1 cup chopped pecans
2 teaspoons vanilla
  extract

■ Heat margarine and baking cocoa in saucepan over medium heat until margarine is melted and baking cocoa is dissolved, stirring constantly. Beat eggs in bowl until fluffy. Add sugar and cocoa mixture; mix well. Stir in flour and baking powder. Add pecans and vanilla; beat well. Pour into greased and floured 9x13-inch baking pan. Bake at 350 degrees for 30 minutes. Cool in pan. Cut into squares.

Approx Per Serving: Cal 339; Prot 4 g; Carbo 39 g; Fiber 2 g; T Fat 20 g; 50% Calories from Fat; Chol 57 mg; Sod 185 mg.

Nancy Trusty, Atlanta HFH, Atlanta, GA

White Brownies

Yield: 12 servings

1 1-pound package
  brown sugar
2 cups self-rising flour
1/2 cup butter, softened

2 eggs
1 teaspoon vanilla
  extract

■ Combine all ingredients in bowl; mix well. Spoon into nonstick 9x12-inch baking pan. Bake at 350 degrees for 15 to 20 minutes or until brownies rise and fall. Cut into squares. Serve warm. May add 1 cup chopped nuts to batter.

Approx Per Serving: Cal 295; Prot 3 g; Carbo 52 g; Fiber 1 g; T Fat 9 g; 26% Calories from Fat; Chol 56 mg; Sod 317 mg.

Elaine D. Smith, Highlands County HFH, Avon Park, FL

Zucchini Brownies

Yield: 15 servings

2 cups flour, sifted
1 teaspoon salt
1½ teaspoons baking soda
2 cups grated peeled zucchini

1¼ cups sugar
½ cup oil
2 teaspoons vanilla extract
½ cup baking cocoa

■ Sift flour, salt and baking soda together. Combine zucchini, sugar, oil and vanilla in mixer bowl; mix well. Add flour mixture; beat well. Stir in baking cocoa. Pour into greased and floured 9x13-inch baking pan. Bake at 350 degrees for 40 minutes or until brownies test done. Cool. Cut into squares. May spread with favorite frosting or dust with confectioners' sugar. May use 1½ recipes for 9x13-inch pan to achieve more cake-like brownies.

Approx Per Serving: Cal 197; Prot 3 g; Carbo 31 g; Fiber 2 g; T Fat 8 g; 35% Calories from Fat; Chol 0 mg; Sod 226 mg.

Nancy Purchase, Starkville HFH, Starkville, MS

Buckaroons

Yield: 72 servings

2 cups sifted flour
1 teaspoon baking soda
½ teaspoon baking powder
½ teaspoon salt
1 cup butter-flavored shortening
1 cup sugar
1 cup lightly packed brown sugar

2 eggs
1 teaspoon vanilla extract
2 cups rolled oats
1 cup chocolate chips
½ cup chopped pecans or peanuts

■ Sift flour, baking soda, baking powder and salt together. Cream shortening, sugar and brown sugar in mixer bowl until light and fluffy. Add eggs and vanilla. Beat for 1 minute. Add flour mixture gradually, beating well after each addition. Stir in oats, chocolate chips and pecans; dough will be stiff. Drop by teaspoonfuls onto ungreased cookie sheet. Bake at 350 degrees for 12 to 15 minutes or until lightly browned. May substitute 1 cup butterscotch chips for chocolate chips and ½ cup raisins for pecans.

Approx Per Serving: Cal 90; Prot 1 g; Carbo 12 g; Fiber <1 g; T Fat 5 g; 44% Calories from Fat; Chol 6 mg; Sod 33 mg.

Sybil Wolf, Morgan County HFH, Fort Morgan, CO

Butter Cookies

Yield: 36 servings

3 cups flour
½ teaspoon baking powder
⅛ teaspoon salt
½ cup butter, softened

½ cup shortening
¾ cup sugar
1 egg, beaten
2 teaspoons vanilla extract

■ Sift flour, baking powder and salt together. Cream butter, shortening and sugar in mixer bowl until light and fluffy. Add egg and vanilla; beat well. Add flour mixture gradually, beating well after each addition. Roll out dough on pastry cloth. Cut or press into desired shapes. Place on nonstick cookie sheet. Bake at 375 degrees for 8 to 10 minutes or until lightly browned. Cool on wire rack.

Approx Per Serving: Cal 104; Prot 1 g; Carbo 12 g; Fiber <1 g; T Fat 6 g; 49% Calories from Fat; Chol 13 mg; Sod 36 mg.

Patricia Arledge-Brenko, Kiski Valley HFH, Pittsburgh, PA

Butterscotch Bars

Yield: 12 servings

1 cup butterscotch chips
2 tablespoons peanut butter

3 cups cornflakes

■ Melt butterscotch chips in saucepan. Stir in peanut butter. Pour over cornflakes in bowl; mix well. Press into 8x8-inch dish. Let stand until set but still warm. Cut into bars.

Approx Per Serving: Cal 87; Prot 2 g; Carbo 11 g; Fiber <1 g; T Fat 4 g; 41% Calories from Fat; Chol 0 mg; Sod 92 mg.

Julie Richter, Sheboygan County HFH, Sheboygan, WI

Old-Fashioned Butter Cookies

Yield: 48 servings

1 pound butter,
  softened
1 cup sugar

4 cups sifted flour
1 cup unsifted flour

- Cream butter and sugar in mixer bowl until light and fluffy. Add sifted flour; mix well. Knead on breadboard with unsifted flour. Press onto nonstick cookie sheet. Prick with fork. Bake at 325 degrees for 20 minutes or until cookies are lightly tinged with brown. Cool slightly on cookie sheet. Cut into 1x3-inch slices. Do not substitute margarine for butter in this recipe.
  Approx Per Serving: Cal 128; Prot 1 g; Carbo 13 g; Fiber <1 g; T Fat 8 g; 54% Calories from Fat; Chol 21 mg; Sod 65 mg.

Eleanor Krueschke, Mesilla Valley HFH, Las Cruces, NM

Chewy Bars

Yield: 12 servings

2 tablespoons butter
5½ tablespoons flour
⅛ teaspoon baking
  soda
2 eggs

1 cup packed brown
  sugar
1 cup chopped walnuts
1 teaspoon vanilla
  extract

- Melt butter in 8x8-inch baking pan. Sift flour and baking soda together. Beat eggs in mixer bowl. Stir in brown sugar. Add flour mixture, walnuts and vanilla; mix well. Pour over melted butter. Bake at 350 degrees for 25 to 30 minutes or until done. Cool in pan. Cut into bars. May sprinkle with confectioners' sugar.
  Approx Per Serving: Cal 193; Prot 3 g; Carbo 27 g; Fiber 1 g; T Fat 9 g; 41% Calories from Fat; Chol 41 mg; Sod 47 mg.

Patricia Lemieux, Pinellas HFH, St. Petersburg, FL

Banana-Chocolate Chip Cookies

Yield: 60 servings

⅓ cup butter, softened
½ cup sugar
1 egg
½ teaspoon salt
½ teaspoon baking
  soda
1 teaspoon baking
  powder

½ teaspoon vanilla
  extract
½ cup mashed bananas
1 cup flour
1 cup chocolate chips

- Combine all ingredients in bowl; mix well. Drop by spoonfuls onto nonstick cookie sheet. Bake at 350 degrees for 10 to 12 minutes or until brown. Cool on wire rack.
  Approx Per Serving: Cal 41; Prot <1 g; Carbo 5 g; Fiber <1 g; T Fat 2 g; 46% Calories from Fat; Chol 6 mg; Sod 40 mg.

Gina Zerr, Fergus Falls Area HFH, Fargo, ND

Chocolate Pizza

Yield: 40 servings

16 ounces almond bark
2 cups semisweet
  chocolate chips
2 cups miniature
  marshmallows
1 cup crisp rice cereal

1 cup peanuts
1 6-ounce jar red
  maraschino cherries
3 tablespoons green
  maraschino cherries
1 teaspoon oil

- Reserve 2 ounces almond bark for topping. Combine remaining almond bark with chocolate chips in glass bowl. Microwave on High for 2 minutes. Microwave for 1 to 2 minutes longer or until smooth, stirring every 30 seconds. Stir in marshmallows, cereal and peanuts. Spoon into greased 12-inch pizza pan. Top with red and green maraschino cherries. Place reserved almond bark and oil in small glass bowl. Microwave on High for 2 minutes or until smooth, stirring every 15 seconds. Drizzle over pizza. Chill until firm. Store at room temperature.
  Approx Per Serving: Cal 143; Prot 3 g; Carbo 16 g; Fiber 1 g; T Fat 9 g; 52% Calories from Fat; Chol 2 mg; Sod 22 mg.

Kristina Jakubec, Lorain County HFH, Lorain, OH

The bricks have fallen down, but we will rebuild with dressed stone; the fig trees have been felled, but we will replace them with cedars.

Isaiah 9:10

Chocolate Chip Cookies

Yield: 24 servings

2 cups sifted flour
1 teaspoon baking soda
1/2 teaspoon salt
3/4 cup butter, softened
1 cup packed brown
  sugar
1/4 cup sugar

1 egg
1 1/2 teaspoons vanilla
  extract
1 cup chocolate chips
1/2 to 3/4 cup chopped
  pecans

■ Sift flour, baking soda and salt together. Cream butter, brown sugar and sugar in mixer bowl until light and fluffy. Add egg and vanilla; beat well. Add flour mixture gradually, beating well after each addition. Stir in chocolate chips and pecans. Drop by spoonfuls onto greased cookie sheet. Bake at 375 degrees for 10 to 12 minutes or until browned. Cool on wire rack.

Approx Per Serving: Cal 200; Prot 2 g; Carbo 25 g; Fiber 1 g; T Fat 11 g; 48% Calories from Fat; Chol 24 mg; Sod 136 mg.

Tom Edgell, Greater East Liverpool HFH, East Liverpool, OH

Chocolate Chip-Oatmeal Cookies

Yield: 36 servings

1 cup margarine,
  softened
3/4 cup packed brown
  sugar
3/4 cup sugar
2 eggs
1 3/4 cups flour
1 teaspoon baking soda

1 teaspoon baking
  powder
2 cups rolled oats
1 teaspoon vanilla
  extract
1 cup chocolate chips
1 cup chopped pecans

■ Combine first 9 ingredients in bowl; mix well. Stir in chocolate chips and pecans. Chill thoroughly. Drop dough by spoonfuls onto nonstick cookie sheet. Bake at 400 degrees until light brown. Cool on wire rack.

Approx Per Serving: Cal 173; Prot 2 g; Carbo 21 g; Fiber 1 g; T Fat 10 g; 49% Calories from Fat; Chol 12 mg; Sod 99 mg.

Charles L. and Grace Rogers, Highlands County HFH
Sebring, FL

Low-Fat Chocolate Chip Cookies

Yield: 60 servings

3 cups flour
1 1/2 teaspoons baking
  soda
1 teaspoon salt
1 1/4 cups brown sugar
1/2 cup sugar
1/2 cup margarine,
  softened

1 teaspoon vanilla
  extract
2 egg whites
1/3 cup water
2 cups semisweet
  chocolate chips

■ Sift flour, baking soda and salt together. Cream brown sugar, sugar, margarine and vanilla in mixer bowl until light and fluffy. Beat in egg whites. Add flour mixture and water alternately to creamed mixture, beating well after each addition. Stir in chocolate chips. Drop by teaspoonfuls onto lightly greased cookie sheet. Bake at 350 degrees for 10 to 12 minutes or until lightly browned. Cool slightly. Remove to wire rack to cool completely.

Approx Per Serving: Cal 89; Prot 1 g; Carbo 14 g; Fiber <1 g; T Fat 4 g; 35% Calories from Fat; Chol 0 mg; Sod 79 mg.

Kim Miknis, Americus-Sumter County HFH, Americus, GA

Chocolate Chunk Breakers

Yield: 24 servings

1/2 cup shortening
1/3 cup margarine,
  softened
1 cup packed brown
  sugar
1/4 cup sugar
1 1/4 teaspoons molasses
2 eggs
1 teaspoon vanilla
  extract

2 cups flour
1/2 teaspoon salt
1/2 teaspoon baking
  soda
1 1/2 cups semisweet
  chocolate chunks
3/4 cup pecan pieces

■ Cream shortening, margarine, brown sugar, sugar and molasses in mixer bowl until light and fluffy. Add eggs and vanilla; beat well. Add flour, salt and baking soda; mix well. Stir in chocolate and pecans. Drop by spoonfuls onto lightly greased cookie sheet. Bake at 375 degrees for 8 to 10 minutes or until light brown. Cool on wire rack.

Approx Per Serving: Cal 232; Prot 2 g; Carbo 28 g; Fiber 1 g; T Fat 14 g; 50% Calories from Fat; Chol 18 mg; Sod 104 mg.

Kent Workman, Michigan State University Campus Chapter
East Lansing, MI

Christmas Cookie Cutouts

Yield: 96 servings

4 cups (or more) flour
2 teaspoons baking
  powder
1 teaspoon baking soda
1/8 teaspoon salt
1/8 teaspoon nutmeg

1 cup butter, softened
1 cup lard
2 cups sugar
3 tablespoons apple
  cider vinegar
4 eggs

■ Sift flour, baking powder, baking soda, salt and nutmeg together. Cream butter and lard in mixer bowl until light and fluffy. Add sugar; beat well. Stir in vinegar and eggs. Add flour mixture gradually, beating well after each addition. Chill for several minutes. Roll on floured surface. Cut with cookie cutters. Place on nonstick cookie sheet. Bake at 400 degrees for 8 minutes or until brown. Cool on wire rack.
Approx Per Serving: Cal 75; Prot 1 g; Carbo 8 g; Fiber <1 g; T Fat 4 g; 52% Calories from Fat; Chol 16 mg; Sod 33 mg.

Sue I. Bartenstein, Sheboygan County HFH, Waldo, WI

Cowboy Cookies

Yield: 48 servings

1 cup sugar
1¼ cups packed light
  brown sugar
1 cup shortening
2 eggs
1 teaspoon vanilla
  extract
2 cups sifted flour

1 teaspoon baking soda
1/2 teaspoon salt
1/2 teaspoon baking
  powder
2 cups quick-cooking
  oats
1 cup semisweet
  chocolate chips

■ Combine all ingredients in bowl in order given, mixing by hand after each addition. Shape into 1-inch balls. Place on greased cookie sheet. Bake at 350 degrees for 15 minutes or until light brown. Cool on wire rack.
Approx Per Serving: Cal 132; Prot 1 g; Carbo 19 g; Fiber 1 g; T Fat 6 g; 40% Calories from Fat; Chol 9 mg; Sod 50 mg.

Su S. Rowles, HFH in Crawford County, Crestline, OH

Egg Yolk Cookies

Yield: 108 servings

1 cup butter, softened
1½ cups sugar
6 egg yolks, lightly
  beaten
2¼ cups flour
1 teaspoon baking soda

1 teaspoon cream of
  tartar
1 teaspoon vanilla
  extract
1/2 cup (or more) sugar

■ Combine butter, 1½ cups sugar, egg yolks, flour, baking soda, cream of tartar and vanilla in bowl; mix well. Shape into 3/4-inch balls. Roll in remaining sugar. Place 3 inches apart on greased cookie sheet. Bake at 350 degrees for 10 minutes or until brown. Cool on wire rack. Watch carefully while baking; these cookies brown quickly.
Approx Per Serving: Cal 42; Prot <1 g; Carbo 6 g; Fiber <1 g; T Fat 2 g; 43% Calories from Fat; Chol 16 mg; Sod 23 mg.

Ella May Green, Morgan County HFH, Fort Morgan, CO

Ginger Cookies

Yield: 96 servings

8 cups flour
8 teaspoons baking
  soda
2 teaspoons cloves
2 teaspoons to 1
  tablespoon ginger
4 teaspoons cinnamon

2 teaspoons salt
3 cups margarine,
  softened
4 cups sugar
1 cup dark molasses
4 eggs
1/2 cup (or more) sugar

■ Sift flour, baking soda, cloves, ginger, cinnamon and salt together. Combine margarine, sugar, molasses and eggs in bowl; mix well. Add flour mixture gradually, mixing well after each addition. Shape into 1-inch balls. Roll in remaining sugar. Place on greased cookie sheet. Bake at 350 degrees for 8 to 10 minutes or until light brown. Cool on wire rack.
Approx Per Serving: Cal 135; Prot 1 g; Carbo 19 g; Fiber <1 g; T Fat 6 g; 40% Calories from Fat; Chol 9 mg; Sod 186 mg.

Carmelle Keith, Grants Pass HFH, Grants Pass, OR

Old-Fashioned Gingersnaps

Yield: 36 servings

3 to 3½ cups flour
2 teaspoons cinnamon
2 teaspoons ginger
1 teaspoon salt
4 teaspoons baking soda
¾ teaspoon ground cloves
2 cups sugar
1½ cups shortening
2 eggs
½ cup molasses
¼ cup (or more) sugar

■ Mix flour, cinnamon, ginger, salt, baking soda and cloves together. Cream sugar and shortening in mixer bowl until light and fluffy. Add eggs and molasses; beat well. Add flour mixture gradually, beating well after each addition. Chill overnight. Shape into 1-inch balls. Roll in remaining sugar. Place on nonstick cookie sheet. Bake at 375 degrees for 12 to 15 minutes or until cookies begin to flatten. Cool on wire rack.
Approx Per Serving: Cal 182; Prot 2 g; Carbo 24 g; Fiber <1 g; T Fat 9 g; 44% Calories from Fat; Chol 12 mg; Sod 111 mg.

George Schutts, HFH of Green County, Monroe, WI

Granola Cookies

Yield: 54 servings

1 cup sugar
½ cup oil
⅓ cup honey
2 eggs
¼ cup water
2 cups flour
1¾ cups quick-cooking oats
1 teaspoon baking soda
1 teaspoon salt
1 teaspoon cinnamon
½ cup chopped dried apricots
½ cup raisins
½ cup chopped pecans
½ cup chocolate chips
½ cup flaked coconut

■ Mix sugar, oil, honey, eggs and water in bowl. Add flour, oats, baking soda, salt and cinnamon; mix well. Add apricots, raisins, pecans, chocolate chips and coconut; mix well. Drop by teaspoonfuls 2 inches apart onto greased cookie sheet. Bake at 350 degrees for 8 minutes or until almost no indentation remains when lightly touched. Cool on wire rack.
Approx Per Serving: Cal 97; Prot 1 g; Carbo 15 g; Fiber 1 g; T Fat 4 g; 36% Calories from Fat; Chol 8 mg; Sod 58 mg.

Eleanor Kleman, Prince George's County HFH
Upper Marlboro, MD

Honey Bars

Yield: 40 servings

1 cup sugar
1 egg
¼ cup honey
¾ cup oil
2 cups self-rising flour
1 teaspoon cinnamon
½ cup chopped pecans
2 tablespoons melted margarine
1 cup confectioners' sugar
2 tablespoons water
1 teaspoon vanilla extract

■ Mix sugar, egg, honey and oil in bowl. Add flour, cinnamon and pecans; mix well. Spread in cake roll pan. Bake at 375 degrees for 18 minutes. Mix margarine, confectioners' sugar, water and vanilla in bowl. Spread over warm dessert. Cut into bars.
Approx Per Serving: Cal 112; Prot 1 g; Carbo 15 g; Fiber <1 g; T Fat 6 g; 46% Calories from Fat; Chol 5 mg; Sod 76 mg.

Alice H. Spurgeon, Rapides HFH, Pineville, LA

Layered Bars

Yield: 15 servings

¾ cup sugar
½ cup packed brown sugar
1 cup graham cracker crumbs
¼ cup milk
½ cup margarine
1 16-ounce package club crackers
⅔ cup crunchy peanut butter
½ cup chocolate chips
½ cup butterscotch chips

■ Combine sugar, brown sugar, graham cracker crumbs, milk and margarine in saucepan. Cook for 5 minutes, stirring frequently. Layer half the club crackers, cooked mixture and remaining crackers in 9x13-inch dish. Melt peanut butter, chocolate chips and butterscotch chips in saucepan. Pour over layers. Let stand to cool. Cut into bars.
Approx Per Serving: Cal 409; Prot 6 g; Carbo 53 g; Fiber 1 g; T Fat 22 g; 46% Calories from Fat; Chol 1 mg; Sod 511 mg.

Ina Davidson, Hawkins HFH, Rogersville, TN

Lemon Bars

Yield: 48 servings

1 cup margarine
2 cups flour
1/2 cup confectioners' sugar
Grated rind of 1 lemon
1/2 cup lemon juice
2 cups sugar

1/4 cup flour
4 eggs, well beaten
1/2 teaspoon baking powder
1/4 cup confectioners' sugar

■ Mix margarine, 2 cups flour and 1/2 cup confectioners' sugar in bowl. Pat into nonstick 9x13-inch baking pan. Bake at 325 degrees for 20 minutes. Combine lemon rind, lemon juice, sugar, 1/4 cup flour, eggs and baking powder in bowl; mix well. Pour over warm crust. Bake for 30 minutes. Sprinkle with 1/4 cup confectioners' sugar. Cut into bars.
Approx Per Serving: Cal 102; Prot 1 g; Carbo 15 g; Fiber <1 g; T Fat 4 g; 38% Calories from Fat; Chol 18 mg; Sod 54 mg.

Barbara Tilly, Chelan and Douglas Co. HFH, Wenatchee WA

Lumberjacks

Yield: 48 servings

4 cups flour
1 teaspoon baking soda
1 teaspoon salt
1 teaspoon ginger
2 teaspoons cinnamon

1 cup sugar
1 cup shortening
1 cup molasses
2 eggs
1/4 cup (or more) sugar

■ Sift flour, baking soda, salt, ginger and cinnamon together. Cream 1 cup sugar and shortening in mixer bowl until light and fluffy. Stir in molasses and eggs. Add sifted flour mixture; mix well. Shape into small balls. Roll in remaining sugar. Place on greased cookie sheet. Bake at 350 degrees for 12 to 15 minutes or until light brown. Cool on cookie sheet for several minutes. Remove to wire rack to cool completely.
Approx Per Serving: Cal 113; Prot 1 g; Carbo 17 g; Fiber <1 g; T Fat 5 g; 36% Calories from Fat; Chol 9 mg; Sod 66 mg.

Kathy Hollis

Molasses Squares

Yield: 36 servings

3 cups flour
1 teaspoon each nutmeg, allspice, cinnamon and salt
1 1/2 cups sugar

1 cup shortening
1/2 cup molasses
3 eggs
1 teaspoon baking soda
1/4 cup hot water

■ Sift first 5 ingredients together. Mix sugar, shortening, molasses and eggs in bowl. Add flour mixture; mix well. Dissolve baking soda in hot water. Beat into dough. Spread in nonstick 11x15-inch pan. Bake at 350 degrees until browned. Cut into squares; drizzle with favorite confectioners' sugar glaze.
Approx Per Serving: Cal 136; Prot 2 g; Carbo 19 g; Fiber <1 g; T Fat 6 g; 41% Calories from Fat; Chol 18 mg; Sod 89 mg.

Lois Remillard, Oregon Trail HFH, Hermiston, OR

Carol's Nighty Nights

Yield: 24 servings

2 egg whites
2/3 cup sugar
1/2 teaspoon vanilla extract

1 cup chocolate chips
1 cup finely chopped walnuts or pecans

■ Preheat oven to 350 degrees. Line cookie sheet with foil, shiny side down. Beat egg whites in mixer bowl until stiff peaks form. Add sugar and vanilla gradually, beating constantly until stiff peaks form again. Fold in chocolate chips and walnuts. Drop by spoonfuls onto prepared cookie sheet. Place in oven. Turn off oven immediately. Let stand for 8 hours without opening oven door.
Approx Per Serving: Cal 91; Prot 1 g; Carbo 11 g; Fiber 1 g; T Fat 6 g; 52% Calories from Fat; Chol 0 mg; Sod 6 mg.

Carol I. McCord, Eastern Jackson County HFH
Stewartsville, MO

Chocolate Chip-Oatmeal Cookies
Yield: 48 servings

1 cup sifted flour
1/2 teaspoon baking
 soda
1/2 teaspoon salt
1/2 cup sugar
1/2 cup packed brown
 sugar
1/2 cup shortening

1/2 teaspoon vanilla
 extract
1 egg
1 tablespoon water
1 cup rolled oats
1 cup chocolate chips
1/2 cup chopped
 walnuts

■ Sift flour, baking soda and salt together. Mix sugar, brown sugar, shortening and vanilla in bowl. Stir in egg and water. Add sifted flour mixture; mix well. Stir in oats, chocolate chips and chopped walnuts. Drop by spoonfuls onto nonstick cookie sheet. Bake at 350 degrees for 10 to 12 minutes or until browned. Cool on cookie sheet for several minutes. Remove to wire rack to cool completely.
Approx Per Serving: Cal 80; Prot 1 g; Carbo 10 g; Fiber <1 g; T Fat 4 g; 47% Calories from Fat; Chol 4 mg; Sod 34 mg.

Judy Ryerse, Northern Straits HFH, St. Ignace, MI

Oatmeal Cookies with Nuts
Yield: 60 servings

1 cup margarine,
 softened
1 1/4 cups firmly packed
 brown sugar
1/2 cup sugar
2 eggs
2 teaspoons vanilla
 extract

2 tablespoons milk
1 3/4 cups flour
1 teaspoon baking soda
1/2 teaspoon salt
2 1/2 cups rolled oats
1 cup coarsely chopped
 pecans

■ Beat margarine, brown sugar and sugar in mixer bowl until creamy. Add eggs, vanilla and milk; beat well. Add flour, baking soda and salt; mix well. Stir in oats and pecans. Drop by rounded tablespoonfuls onto ungreased cookie sheet. Bake at 375 degrees for 9 to 10 minutes for chewy cookies or for 12 to 13 minutes for crisp cookies. Cool on cookie sheet for 1 minute. Remove to wire rack to cool completely.
Approx Per Serving: Cal 97; Prot 1 g; Carbo 13 g; Fiber 1 g; T Fat 5 g; 44% Calories from Fat; Chol 7 mg; Sod 72 mg.

Mary Frank Johnson, Americus-Sumter County HFH
Americus, GA

Oatmeal-Raisin Cookies
Yield: 48 servings

1 1/2 cups flour
1/2 teaspoon baking
 soda
1/2 teaspoon salt
2 teaspoons cinnamon
2 teaspoons nutmeg
2 teaspoons allspice
1 cup sugar

1 cup margarine,
 softened
2 eggs
1 teaspoon vanilla
 extract
3 cups rolled oats
1 cup raisins
1 cup chopped pecans

■ Sift flour, baking soda, salt, cinnamon, nutmeg and allspice together. Cream sugar and margarine in mixer bowl until light and fluffy. Stir in eggs and vanilla. Add flour mixture gradually, beating well. Stir in oats, raisins and pecans. Drop by teaspoonfuls onto greased cookie sheet. Bake at 350 degrees for 12 to 14 minutes or until brown. Cool on wire rack.
Approx Per Serving: Cal 114; Prot 2 g; Carbo 14 g; Fiber 1 g; T Fat 6 g; 47% Calories from Fat; Chol 9 mg; Sod 79 mg.

Peggy Vasbinder, Americus-Sumter County HFH
Americus, GA

Reduced-Calorie Oatmeal-Raisin Cookies
Yield: 30 servings

1 1/4 cups rolled oats
3/4 cup flour
1/2 teaspoon cinnamon
1/2 teaspoon baking
 powder
1/4 teaspoon salt
1/2 cup reduced-calorie
 margarine, softened

1/4 cup packed dark
 brown sugar
5 envelopes artificial
 sweetener
2 egg whites
1 teaspoon vanilla
 extract
1/3 cup chopped raisins

■ Sift first 5 ingredients together. Cream margarine, brown sugar and sweetener in mixer bowl until light and fluffy. Beat in egg whites and vanilla. Add flour mixture gradually, beating well. Stir in raisins. Drop by heaping teaspoonfuls onto cookie sheet coated with nonstick cooking spray. Bake at 375 degrees for 8 minutes or until brown. Cool on wire rack.
Approx Per Serving: Cal 55; Prot 1 g; Carbo 9 g; Fiber 1 g; T Fat 2 g; 28% Calories from Fat; Chol 0 mg; Sod 65 mg.

Shirley Collichio, Orleans County HFH, Albion, NY

Baby Harold's Party Cookies

Yield: 24 servings

2 egg yolks
1/2 cup packed brown
  sugar
1/2 teaspoon salt
2 cups flour
1 cup butter-flavored
  shortening

2 egg whites, stiffly
  beaten
1 cup finely ground
  pecans
1/2 cup confectioners'
  sugar
2 tablespoons water

■ Combine egg yolks, brown sugar, salt, flour and shortening in bowl; mix well. Shape into 1-inch balls. Dip into beaten egg whites. Roll in pecans. Place on nonstick cookie sheet. Bake at 375 degrees for 5 minutes. Make indentation in each ball with back of spoon. Reduce oven temperature to 300 degrees. Bake for 15 minutes or until browned. Cool on cookie sheet for several minutes. Remove to wire rack to cool completely. Mix confectioners' sugar and water in bowl until of spreading consistency. Spread over cookies.
Approx Per Serving: Cal 211; Prot 2 g; Carbo 18 g; Fiber 1 g; T Fat 15 g; 63% Calories from Fat; Chol 18 mg; Sod 52 mg.

Susan Schaut, HFH of Oshkosh, Oshkosh, WI

Peanut Butter-Chocolate Bars

Yield: 75 servings

1/2 9-ounce package
  chocolate wafer
  cookies
1/2 cup salted peanuts
1/4 cup margarine,
  softened
1 1/4 cups graham
  cracker crumbs
1 cup confectioners'
  sugar

3/4 cup creamy peanut
  butter
1 teaspoon vanilla
  extract
1/4 cup margarine,
  softened
1/4 cup chopped salted
  peanuts
1/2 cup miniature
  chocolate chips

■ Pulverize cookies and 1/2 cup peanuts in blender. Mix with 1/4 cup margarine in bowl. Press into 7x11-inch dish. Chill until set. Combine graham cracker crumbs, confectioners' sugar, peanut butter, vanilla and 1/4 cup margarine in bowl; mix well. Knead by hand until smooth. Pat over chilled crust. Sprinkle with 1/4 cup peanuts and chocolate chips. Cover with plastic wrap. Press peanuts and chocolate chips firmly into peanut butter layer. Chill, covered, for 3 hours or longer. Cut into 1-inch bars.
Approx Per Serving: Cal 62; Prot 1 g; Carbo 6 g; Fiber <1 g; T Fat 4 g; 56% Calories from Fat; Chol 0 mg; Sod 54 mg.

Kathy Jakubec, Lorain County HFH, Lorain, OH

Peanut Butter-Marshmallow Bars

Yield: 48 servings

1 2-layer package
  yellow cake mix
1/2 cup margarine
1 egg
3 cups miniature
  marshmallows
2/3 cup corn syrup

1/4 cup margarine
2 teaspoons vanilla
  extract
2 cups peanut butter
  chips
2 cups crisp rice cereal
2 cups salted peanuts

■ Mix cake mix, 1/2 cup margarine and egg in bowl until crumbly. Press into ungreased 9x13-inch baking pan. Bake at 350 degrees for 12 to 15 minutes or until browned. Sprinkle with marshmallows. Bake for 1 to 2 minutes longer or until marshmallows are warm. Combine corn syrup, 1/4 cup margarine, vanilla and peanut butter chips. Cook until margarine and chips are melted, stirring constantly. Remove from heat. Stir in cereal and peanuts. Spoon over marshmallows. Spread to cover. Cool. Cut into bars.
Approx Per Serving: Cal 174; Prot 4 g; Carbo 21 g; Fiber 1 g; T Fat 9 g; 45% Calories from Fat; Chol 4 mg; Sod 164 mg.

Sara Kisseberth, Bluffton College Campus Chapter
Arlington, OH

Habitat for Humanity works in partnership with God and people everywhere, from all walks of life, to develop communities with God's people in need by building and renovating houses so that there are decent houses in decent communities in which people can live and grow into all that God intended.

Peanut Butter Things

Yield: 48 servings

1/2 cup margarine, softened
1/2 cup sugar
1/2 cup packed brown sugar
1 egg
1/3 cup peanut butter
1/2 teaspoon baking soda
1/4 teaspoon salt

1/2 teaspoon vanilla extract
1 cup flour
1 cup rolled oats
1 cup chocolate chips
1/2 cup confectioners' sugar
1/3 cup peanut butter

■ Cream margarine, sugar and brown sugar in mixer bowl. Add next 5 ingredients; mix well. Stir in flour and oats. Spread in greased 9x13-inch baking pan. Bake at 350 degrees for 20 minutes. Sprinkle with chocolate chips. Let stand for 5 minutes. Spread chocolate evenly over all. Mix confectioners' sugar and 1/3 cup peanut butter in bowl until crumbly. Sprinkle over chocolate. Cool in pan. Cut into bars.
Approx Per Serving: Cal 97; Prot 2 g; Carbo 12 g; Fiber 1 g; T Fat 5 g; 46% Calories from Fat; Chol 4 mg; Sod 60 mg.

Martha M. Davis, HFH of Metro Louisville, Louisville, KY

Salted Peanut Cookies

Yield: 84 servings

1 cup sugar
1 cup packed brown sugar
1 cup shortening
2 eggs
1 cup cornflakes
1 cup rolled oats
1 cup salted peanuts

2 cups flour
1 teaspoon baking powder
1 teaspoon baking soda
1/2 teaspoon salt
1 teaspoon vanilla extract

■ Mix sugar, brown sugar and shortening in bowl. Beat in eggs. Stir in cornflakes, oats and peanuts. Add flour, baking powder, baking soda and salt; mix well. Stir in vanilla. Drop by teaspoonfuls onto ungreased cookie sheet. Bake at 350 degrees for 10 to 12 minutes or until browned. Cool for several minutes on cookie sheet. Remove to wire rack to cool completely.
Approx Per Serving: Cal 71; Prot 1 g; Carbo 9 g; Fiber <1 g; T Fat 4 g; 44% Calories from Fat; Chol 5 mg; Sod 40 mg.

Marilyn Spaulding, Newaygo HFH, Newaygo, MI

Blue Ribbon Pineapple Drop Cookies

Yield: 60 servings

2 cups sifted flour
1 teaspoon baking powder
1 teaspoon baking soda
1 teaspoon salt
1/2 cup shortening
1 cup sugar

1 egg
1/2 teaspoon vanilla extract
1/2 cup crushed pineapple, drained
1 1/4 teaspoons nutmeg
5 tablespoons sugar

■ Sift first 4 ingredients together. Cream shortening and 1 cup sugar in mixer bowl until light and fluffy. Beat in egg and vanilla. Stir in pineapple. Add flour mixture gradually, mixing well after each addition. Drop by teaspoonfuls onto greased cookie sheet. Mix nutmeg and 5 tablespoons sugar. Sprinkle over cookies. Bake at 350 degrees for 10 to 12 minutes or until browned. Cool on cookie sheet for several minutes. Remove to wire rack to cool completely.
Approx Per Serving: Cal 48; Prot 1 g; Carbo 8 g; Fiber <1 g; T Fat 2 g; 34% Calories from Fat; Chol 4 mg; Sod 56 mg.

Mary Robinson, Trout Lake, MI

Polynesian Bars

Yield: 24 servings

3/4 cup whole wheat flour
3/4 cup unbleached flour
1 1/2 cups rolled oats
3/4 cup margarine, softened
1/2 cup coconut

1/2 cup chopped pecans
4 cups chopped dates
2 cups crushed pineapple
3/4 cup water
1 teaspoon vanilla extract

■ Combine flours, oats, margarine, coconut and pecans in bowl; mix until crumbly. Press half of mixture into greased 9x13-inch baking pan. Combine dates, pineapple with juice, water and vanilla in saucepan. Cook over medium heat until thickened, stirring frequently. Spread over shell to edges of pan. Pat remaining crumb mixture over filling. Bake at 350 degrees for 30 minutes. Cool in pan. Cut into bars.
Approx Per Serving: Cal 217; Prot 3 g; Carbo 36 g; Fiber 4 g; T Fat 8 g; 33% Calories from Fat; Chol 0 mg; Sod 69 mg.

Jeanne Lound Schaller, Midland County HFH, Midland, MI

Poor Man Cookie Bars

Yield: 36 servings

1 cup raisins
1¹/₂ cups water
¹/₂ cup margarine
1 egg, slightly beaten
1 teaspoon vanilla
  extract

2 cups flour
1 teaspoon baking soda
1 cup sugar
¹/₄ teaspoon salt
1 cup chopped pecans

- Bring raisins and water to a boil in saucepan. Add margarine; mix well. Beat in egg and vanilla. Let stand to cool. Mix flour, baking soda, sugar, salt and chopped pecans in bowl; mix well. Stir in raisin mixture. Pour into greased 10x15-inch baking pan. Bake at 350 degrees for 20 minutes or until browned. Cool in pan. Cut into bars.

Approx Per Serving: Cal 107; Prot 1 g; Carbo 15 g; Fiber 1 g; T Fat 5 g; 41% Calories from Fat; Chol 6 mg; Sod 70 mg.

Florence M. Richardson, Starkville HFH, Starkville, MS

Lovin' Dough's Potato Chip Cookies

Yield: 60 servings

1 pound butter,
  softened
1 cup sugar
3¹/₂ cups flour
1 cup crushed potato
  chips

¹/₂ cup chopped pecans
5 tablespoons (or
  more) confectioners'
  sugar

- Cream butter and sugar in mixer bowl until light and fluffy. Beat in flour and potato chips. Stir in pecans. Drop by heaping teaspoonfuls onto nonstick cookie sheet. Bake at 350 degrees for 10 minutes or until lightly browned around edges. Cool for several minutes on cookie sheet. Sprinkle with confectioners' sugar. Remove to wire rack to cool completely. Do not substitute margarine for butter in this recipe.

Approx Per Serving: Cal 107; Prot 1 g; Carbo 10 g; Fiber <1 g; T Fat 7 g; 59% Calories from Fat; Chol 17 mg; Sod 56 mg.

Hilda Kemp, Highlands County HFH, Sebring, FL

Ranger Cookies

Yield: 24 servings

1 cup flour
¹/₄ teaspoon baking
  powder
¹/₂ teaspoon baking soda
¹/₂ teaspoon salt
²/₃ cup shortening
1 cup packed brown
  sugar

1 egg, well beaten
1 teaspoon vanilla
  extract
³/₄ cup rolled oats
¹/₂ cup chopped
  walnuts
¹/₂ cup chopped dates
1 cup cornflakes

- Sift flour, baking powder, baking soda and salt together twice. Cream shortening and brown sugar in mixer bowl until light and fluffy. Beat in egg and vanilla. Add flour mixture gradually, beating well after each addition. Add oats, chopped walnuts and chopped dates; mix well. Stir in cornflakes. Drop by spoonfuls onto ungreased cookie sheet. Bake at 375 degrees for 10 to 12 minutes or until browned. Cool on cookie sheet for several minutes. Remove to wire rack to cool completely.

Approx Per Serving: Cal 155; Prot 2 g; Carbo 21 g; Fiber 1 g; T Fat 8 g; 44% Calories from Fat; Chol 9 mg; Sod 85 mg.

Velma D. Scarlett, Hamilton Area HFH, Hamilton, NY

In New York City, a formerly neglected building is reclaimed as a home for 19 families—a real reason to celebrate.

Chocolate-Dipped Shortbread Cookies

Yield: 54 servings

2 cups flour
1 cup butter, softened
1/2 cup sifted
    confectioners' sugar
1 teaspoon vanilla
    extract
1 cup semisweet
    chocolate chips

1 tablespoon
    shortening
1 cup semisweet
    chocolate chips
3/4 cup finely chopped
    pecans

■ Combine flour, butter, confectioners' sugar and vanilla in bowl; mix well. Stir in 1 cup chocolate chips. Drop by rounded teaspoonfuls onto ungreased cookie sheet. Shape into 2-inch logs or press into circles using glass dipped in flour. Bake at 350 degrees for 10 to 12 minutes or until brown. Cool completely. Melt shortening and 1 cup chocolate chips in double boiler over 1 cup hot water. Remove from heat. Dip 1 end of each cookie into chocolate mixture. Roll dipped end in pecans. Chill for 1 hour or until firm.

Approx Per Serving: Cal 96; Prot 1 g; Carbo 8 g; Fiber <1 g; T Fat 7 g; 63% Calories from Fat; Chol 9 mg; Sod 30 mg.

Elena Viti

Spice Cookies

Yield: 52 servings

1 cup butter
1 cup shortening
1 1/2 cups sugar
1 1/2 cups brown sugar
3 eggs, beaten
4 to 4 1/2 cups flour
1 cup ground walnuts

1 tablespoon cinnamon
1 teaspoon allspice
1 teaspoon cloves
1 teaspoon nutmeg
1 teaspoon baking soda
2 teaspoons baking
    powder

■ Cream butter, shortening, sugar and brown sugar in mixer bowl until light and fluffy. Add eggs, beating well. Stir in flour, ground walnuts, cinnamon, allspice, cloves, nutmeg, baking soda and baking powder until soft dough forms. Shape into 1 1/2-inch rolls on waxed paper, rolling up to enclose dough. Chill in refrigerator overnight. Slice 1/4 to 1/2 inch thick; arrange on cookie sheet. Bake at 375 degrees for 12 to 15 minutes or until light brown. Cool on wire rack.

Approx Per Serving: Cal 181; Prot 2 g; Carbo 21 g; Fiber 1 g; T Fat 10 g; 50% Calories from Fat; Chol 22 mg; Sod 66 mg.

June Dettaan, Lakeshore HFH, Holland, MI

Never-Fail Sugar Cookies

Yield: 36 servings

1 cup margarine,
    softened
1 cup sugar
2 eggs, beaten
4 teaspoons milk
2 teaspoons baking
    powder
1 teaspoon baking soda

1 teaspoon vanilla
    extract
3 cups flour
1/4 teaspoon salt
1 egg yolk
1/4 teaspoon water
Food colorings

■ Cream margarine and sugar in mixer bowl until light and fluffy. Beat in eggs and milk. Add baking powder, baking soda, vanilla, flour and salt, stirring well. Chill until firm. Roll out and cut into desired shapes; place on cookie sheet. Mix egg yolk with water; divide into 4 equal portions. Add different food coloring to each portion. Paint cookies with pastry brush. Bake at 350 degrees for 10 minutes or until light brown. Cool on wire rack.

Approx Per Serving: Cal 111; Prot 2 g; Carbo 14 g; Fiber <1 g; T Fat 6 g; 46% Calories from Fat; Chol 18 mg; Sod 120 mg.

Betty Hoerter, HFH of Wausau, Wausau, WI

But he has always given evidence of his existence by the good things he does . . . .

Acts 14:17

Quick Crisp Sugar Cookies

Yield: 30 servings

2¼ cups sifted flour
½ teaspoon baking
  soda
1 teaspoon baking
  powder
½ teaspoon salt

½ cup shortening
1 cup sugar
2 eggs
1 teaspoon vanilla
  extract
1 tablespoon milk

- Sift flour, baking soda, baking powder and salt together in large mixer bowl. Add shortening, sugar, eggs, vanilla and milk. Beat at low speed for 3 minutes, scraping side of bowl while beating. Shape into log; wrap in waxed paper. Chill for 2 hours. Roll out to ⅛-inch thickness. Cut into desired shapes with cookie cutter dipped in sugar. Place on nonstick cookie sheet. Bake at 425 degrees for 10 minutes or until golden brown. Cool on wire rack.

Approx Per Serving: Cal 93; Prot 1 g; Carbo 13 g; Fiber <1 g; T Fat 4 g; 37% Calories from Fat; Chol 14 mg; Sod 65 mg.

Corrine Van Shelton, HFH of South Central Minnesota
Mankato, MN

Thunder Butte Bars

Yield: 24 servings

1 cup margarine,
  softened
2 cups sugar
4 eggs, beaten
1 teaspoon vanilla
  extract
¼ teaspoon coconut
  extract
1½ cups flour
1½ cups chopped
  pecans

1½ cups flaked coconut
1 7-ounce jar
  marshmallow cream
2 cups confectioners'
  sugar
¼ cup evaporated milk
1 teaspoon vanilla
  extract
¼ cup butter, softened
2 tablespoons baking
  cocoa

- Cream 1 cup margarine, sugar, eggs, 1 teaspoon vanilla and coconut extract in mixer bowl until light and fluffy. Add flour, chopped pecans and flaked coconut, stirring well. Spread over lightly greased jelly roll pan. Bake at 350 degrees for 25 minutes. Spread marshmallow cream over top; cool. Mix confectioners' sugar, evaporated milk, 1 teaspoon vanilla, ¼ cup butter and baking cocoa in bowl. Spread over marshmallow layer. Cut into bars.

Approx Per Serving: Cal 331; Prot 3 g; Carbo 43 g; Fiber 1 g; T Fat 17 g; 46% Calories from Fat; Chol 41 mg; Sod 126 mg.

Darcy Frank, Moorhead State University Campus Chapter
Blaine, MN

English Toffee Squares

Yield: 16 servings

1 cup melted butter
1 cup sugar
2 cups sifted flour
1 egg yolk
1 teaspoon vanilla
  extract

1 egg white, lightly
  beaten
2 cups finely chopped
  walnuts

- Combine first 5 ingredients in bowl; mix well. Spread in greased 9x13-inch pan. Cover with beaten egg white; sprinkle with walnuts. Bake at 350 degrees for 20 minutes or until light brown. Allow to cool before removing from pan. Cut into squares.

Approx Per Serving: Cal 303; Prot 4 g; Carbo 26 g; Fiber 1 g; T Fat 21 g; 61% Calories from Fat; Chol 44 mg; Sod 102 mg.

Ruth M. Fox, HFH-Lima Area, Lima, OH

Vanilla Cookies

Yield: 24 servings

½ cup butter, softened
6 tablespoons sugar
6 tablespoons brown
  sugar
1 egg
½ teaspoon baking
  soda

1½ cups flour
1 teaspoon water
6 ounces white
  chocolate chunks
½ teaspoon vanilla
  extract

- Cream butter, sugar and brown sugar in mixer bowl. Beat in egg. Add baking soda, flour and water; mix well. Fold in white chocolate chunks and vanilla. Drop by spoonfuls onto cookie sheet. Bake at 375 degrees for 8 to 10 minutes or until light brown. Cool on wire rack.

Approx Per Serving: Cal 127; Prot 2 g; Carbo 16 g; Fiber <1 g; T Fat 6 g; 44% Calories from Fat; Chol 21 mg; Sod 60 mg.

Michael Schlecht, Furman University Campus Chapter
Roswell, GA

Church Windows

Yield: 36 servings

2 cups semisweet
  chocolate chips
1/2 cup butter
1 10-ounce package
  multi-colored
  miniature
  marshmallows

1 cup finely chopped
  pecans
1/2 to 1 cup flaked
  coconut

■ Melt chocolate chips and butter in saucepan over low heat. Let stand until cool. Stir in marshmallows, pecans and coconut. Shape into two 1 1/2 to 2-inch thick rolls. Chill completely. Cut into slices to serve.
Approx Per Serving: Cal 127; Prot 1 g; Carbo 13 g; Fiber 1 g; T Fat 9 g; 58% Calories from Fat; Chol 7 mg; Sod 30 mg.

Cristy Cobb, Erskine College Campus Chapter, Sumter, SC

Foolproof Dark Chocolate Fudge

Yield: 24 servings

3 cups semisweet
  chocolate chips
1 14-ounce can
  sweetened
  condensed milk

1/8 teaspoon salt
1/2 to 1 cup chopped
  walnuts
1 1/2 teaspoons vanilla
  extract

■ Combine chocolate chips, condensed milk and salt in saucepan. Cook over low heat until chocolate chips melt, stirring constantly. Stir in walnuts and vanilla. Spread evenly in 9x9-inch waxed paper-lined dish. Chill for 2 hours. Cut into squares.
Approx Per Serving: Cal 193; Prot 3 g; Carbo 22 g; Fiber 1 g; T Fat 12 g; 52% Calories from Fat; Chol 6 mg; Sod 36 mg.

Karen Borges

Cream Cheese Fudge

Yield: 45 servings

This recipe won second-place prize at Lorain County Fair.

2 cups confectioners'
  sugar
4 ounces cream cheese,
  softened
2 ounces unsweetened
  chocolate, melted

1 tablespoon milk
1 teaspoon vanilla
  extract

■ Grease 5x9-inch pan; line with waxed paper. Cream confectioners' sugar and cream cheese in mixer bowl. Beat in chocolate, milk and vanilla. Spread in prepared pan. Chill for 8 hours. Cut into squares.
Approx Per Serving: Cal 37; Prot <1 g; Carbo 6 g; Fiber <1 g; T Fat 2 g; 37% Calories from Fat; Chol 3 mg; Sod 8 mg.

Kara Jakubec, Lorain County HFH, Lorain, OH

Toffee Bars

Yield: 36 servings

1 cup butter, softened
1 cup packed brown
  sugar
1 egg
1 teaspoon vanilla
  extract

2 cups flour
1 1/2 cups chocolate
  chips
1 cup chopped pecans

■ Cream butter in mixer bowl. Add brown sugar, egg, vanilla and flour in mixer bowl in order listed, mixing well after each addition. Spread in ungreased 10x15-inch baking pan. Bake at 350 degrees for 12 to 15 minutes. Sprinkle with chocolate chips. Bake for 30 seconds longer or until chocolate chips melt. Spread chocolate chips; sprinkle with pecans. Cool completely. Cut into bars.
Approx Per Serving: Cal 159; Prot 2 g; Carbo 17 g; Fiber 1 g; T Fat 10 g; 55% Calories from Fat; Chol 20 mg; Sod 50 mg.

Elaine Larson, HFH of South Central Minnesota
Mankato, MN

*M*ay the God who gives endurance and encouragement give you a spirit of unity among yourselves as you follow Christ Jesus, so that with one heart and mouth you may glorify the God and Father of our Lord Jesus Christ.

Romans 15:5-6

INDEX

"My people will live in peaceful dwelling places, in secure homes, in undisturbed places of rest."

Isaiah 32:18

Index

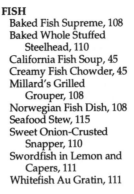

Order Form

To order additional copies of this cookbook, please contact your local Habitat for Humanity affiliate or campus chapter.

If the cookbook is not available locally, you may order copies from Habitat for Humanity International. To order the cookbook or other *Partners in the Kitchen* items, or to receive any of the complimentary materials listed below, return this completed form to the address below. If you prefer, order by phone or fax (number below). Note that applicable taxes are included in all pricing.

◻   *Partners in the Kitchen* cookbook(s), #1410   Qty. _____ x $ 9.95@ =_____
          (6 or more: $7.95@)

◻   *Partners* apron(s). BBQ-style, in teal, #1749   Qty. _____ x $11.95@ =_____

◻   *Partners* recipe box(s), handcrafted, #1814   Qty. _____ x $12.95@ =_____

◻   *Partners in the Kitchen* Package(s), #1745
      includes 1@ of the above   Qty. _____ x $29.95@ =_____

◻   Postage and Handling (see chart below) $_____

                                 Total Amount $_____

◻   Please send more information about the ministry of Habitat for Humanity.

◻   Please send me a complimentary subscription to *Habitat World*, the bi-monthly newspaper about Habitat for Humanity's work around the world.

Name _____

Address _____

City_____State _____ Zip_____

Method of Payment:

◻ Check   ◻ Money Order (no cash)   ◻ Visa   ◻ MC

Visa/MC number _____ Expires _____

Phone (_____)_____
        area code

Signature_____

Postage and Handling (USA only):

Order Total:	Charges:
$10.00 or less	$ 2.00
$10.00–$19.99	$ 2.75
$20.00–$49.99	$ 5.00
$50.00–$99.99	$ 7.00
$100.00 or more	$11.00

Mail order form and payment to:
Habitat for Humanity International
121 Habitat St.
Americus, GA 31709-3498
Ph: (912) 924-6935, ext. 304
Fax: (912) 924-6541